American history and how, in some cases, those few came by their own concepts. For it is certain that, though historians have from time to time considered themselves "scientists," there is much in our history that has been preserved, or ignored, by the writers of it because of human limitations. Also, adds Mr. Kraus, it is imperative that the reader of any history should understand the historian; he should know his bias, his resources, and his blind spots, which every historian has, no matter how good or how well known.

For the teacher, student, or lay reader of American history, there is no other single volume anywhere which will direct, stimulate, and enlarge the appreciation and perspective of American historical writing in the fashion of *The Writing of American History*.

The Writing of American History

The WRITING *of* AMERICAN HISTORY

by Michael Kraus

UNIVERSITY OF OKLAHOMA PRESS
Norman

BY MICHAEL KRAUS

The Writing of American History (Norman, 1953)
The Atlantic Civilization: Eighteenth Century Origins (Ithaca, 1949)
(Co-author), *William Hickling Prescott* (New York, 1943)
A History of American History (New York, 1937)
Intercolonial Aspects of American Culture
on the Eve of the Revolution (New York, 1928)

Library of Congress Catalog Card Number: 53-8815

Publishing Division of the University
First Edition, December, 1953
Second Printing, by offset, November, 1960
Third Printing, September, 1963
Manufactured in the U.S.A.

To My Alma Mater

THE CITY COLLEGE

New York

Preface

STUDIES in American historiography were relatively few until recently. At various times in the past brief summaries had appeared in such leading periodicals as *The Monthly Anthology* and the *North American Review*. (George Bancroft wrote an article in the latter in 1838.) On later occasions critical essays on historians were printed in Henry B. Dawson's *Historical Magazine*. Moses Coit Tyler included historians in his study of American literature. It was not, however, until J. Franklin Jameson published his sketch of American historical writing in 1891 that any satisfactory treatment of the subject appeared. Jameson's short study stopped before reaching the developments that occurred in the 1880's, after which time some of our most important contributions were made. John Spencer Bassett also turned his attention to the subject, publishing in 1917 *The Middle Group of American Historians,* which dealt mainly with Sparks, Bancroft, and the archivist Peter Force. Professor Arthur M. Schlesinger, in his stimulating *New Viewpoints in American History* (1922), discussed some contributions of contemporary scholars in rewriting our history. But no survey of the whole field of American historical writing was available until my volume, *A History of American History,* appeared in 1937. Later, that same year, *The Marcus W. Jernegan Essays in American Historiography,* William T. Hutchinson, editor, was published. Since then the number of studies in this field has rapidly increased, and gives every promise of continued growth.

This book, though based on my original work, has been rewritten and expanded to carry the study to date. Since the materials are so voluminous and it was necessary to be selective, I have given scant attention to specialized histories—military, naval, constitutional, diplomatic, and religious—in order to concentrate on the writings that deal with American history in a comprehensive manner. Obviously, it was impossible to include in a single volume all works worthy of consideration; arbitrary choices had to be made, but I hope writings of fundamental importance have not been overlooked.

I wish to thank my colleague, Professor Oscar Zeichner, for reading a portion of the manuscript and making valuable suggestions. To my wife, Vera Edelstadt, I express gratitude for her aid.

MICHAEL KRAUS

New York City
October 6, 1953

Contents

	Preface	vii
I	Introduction THE NORSE VOYAGES . . DISCOVERING THE NEW WORLD . . RICHARD HAKLUYT	3
II	The First Settlements JOHN SMITH . . EDWARD WINSLOW . . WILLIAM WOOD . . WILLIAM BRADFORD . . JOHN WINTHROP . . EDWARD JOHNSON . . NATHANIEL MORTON . . WILLIAM HUBBARD . . INCREASE MATHER . . HISTORIES OF THE INDIAN WARS . . COTTON MATHER	14
III	The Era of Colonialism ROBERT BEVERLEY . . JOHN OLDMIXON . . JOHN LAWSON . . WILLIAM BYRD . . CADWALLADER COLDEN . . DANIEL NEAL . . THOMAS PRINCE . . JOHN CALLENDER . . WILLIAM STITH . . WILLIAM SMITH . . SAMUEL SMITH . . WILLIAM DOUGLASS	38
IV	The Growing National Spirit: 1750–1800 THOMAS HUTCHINSON . . ROBERT PROUD . . ALEXANDER HEWAT . . GEORGE CHALMERS . . WILLIAM GORDON . . DAVID RAMSAY . . JEREMY BELKNAP . . GEORGE MINOT . . HANNAH ADAMS . . MERCY OTIS WARREN . . JOHN DALY BURK . . BENJAMIN TRUMBULL . . JEDIDIAH MORSE . . JOHN MARSHALL . . PARSON WEEMS	57
V	Gathering the Records—Awaiting the National Historian GATHERING THE RECORDS . . ABIEL HOLMES . . TIMOTHY PITKIN . . THREE EUROPEAN HISTORIANS OF AMERICA	89
VI	Patriots, Romantics—and Hildreth JARED SPARKS . . GEORGE BANCROFT . . JOHN GORHAM PALFREY . . RICHARD HILDRETH . . THE SOUTHERN VIEWPOINT . . GEORGE TUCKER . . CHARLES E. A. GAYARRÉ . . BIOGRAPHY . . WASHINGTON IRVING . . THOMAS HART BENTON	108

VII Francis Parkman 145

VIII The Rise of the "Scientific School" 157

STUDY OF THE ERA OF DISCOVERY AND EXPLORATION . . IMPETUS TO HISTORY FROM THE CIVIL WAR AND THE CENTENNIAL, 1876 . . BIBLIOGRAPHY AND SPECIALIZED HISTORY . . HISTORY TEACHING IN THE COLLEGES

IX Henry Adams 177

X The Nationalist School 190

HERMANN VON HOLST . . JAMES SCHOULER . . JOHN W. BURGESS . . JAMES FORD RHODES . . JOHN FISKE . . WOODROW WILSON . . TWO HISTORIANS OF THE PEOPLE: MCMASTER AND OBERHOLTZER . . JUSTIN WINSOR . . THE AMERICAN NATION . . EDWARD CHANNING

XI The Imperial School of Colonial History 242

MOSES COIT TYLER . . GEORGE OTTO TREVELYAN . . JOHN A. DOYLE . . HERBERT LEVI OSGOOD . . GEORGE LOUIS BEER . . CHARLES MC-LEAN ANDREWS . . NEW LIGHT ON THE NAVIGATION ACTS: LAW-RENCE A. HARPER AND OLIVER M. DICKERSON . . CLARENCE WAL-WORTH ALVORD . . LAWRENCE HENRY GIPSON

XII The Frontier and Sectional Historians 271

THE WEST: HUBERT HOWE BANCROFT, REUBEN GOLD THWAITES, THEODORE ROOSEVELT, FREDERICK JACKSON TURNER, HERBERT EUGENE BOLTON; OTHER HISTORIANS OF THE WEST . . NEW ENG-LAND: CHARLES FRANCIS ADAMS, JAMES TRUSLOW ADAMS, SAMUEL ELIOT MORISON . . THE SOUTH: PHILIP ALEXANDER BRUCE, ALEX-ANDER BROWN, EDWARD MCCRADY, WILLIAM ARCHIBALD DUN-NING, ULRICH BONNELL PHILLIPS, WILLIAM E. DODD, THE CIVIL WAR AND RECONSTRUCTION

XIII Biography 315

ALBERT J. BEVERIDGE . . ALLAN NEVINS . . DOUGLAS SOUTHALL FREEMAN

XIV Contemporary Trends 345

ECONOMIC HISTORY . . A HISTORY OF AMERICAN LIFE . . VERNON L. PARRINGTON . . CHARLES AUSTIN BEARD . . CONCLUSION

Index 377

The Writing of American History

I

Introduction

THE WRITING of American history began before there were any Americans; it began in Europe long before John Smith wrote his first chronicle of events in the Jamestown colony. This historical writing depicted the exploration and settlement of a world that had outgrown its European limitations, and it envisioned limitless fields to conquer. Sometimes it had the blustering quality of the successful Elizabethan adventurer, sometimes the pathos of quest defeated. Not until William Bradford wrote the *History of Plimoth Plantation* do we have a full-bodied narrative reciting the pleasures and pains of a transplanted people. To the end of the seventeenth century American historians were European emigrants or the sons of emigrants, and were so near to the days of colonial foundation that they could not easily take the backward glance of the historian without also taking the forward view of the prophet. To them God had let His countenance shine upon the New World, and for decades to come historians continued to wonder at the marvel of divine intercession in the affairs of America.

With the appearance of Cotton Mather's work we have American history by an American. Mather himself was one of the first to use the word "American." His contemporary, Robert Beverley, the Virginian, was also a historian with a definite native stamp. This period of our historiography was almost exclusively regional in scope, and continued so down to the Revolution. Only a very few writers took a comprehensive view of all the colonies, and they were not provincial born. Some work of genuine merit, even when measured by later standards, was produced in this colonial period. Such writers as Thomas Prince, Thomas Hutchinson, and William Stith developed a method of historical research that was of great significance in establishing a scholarly tradition.

The War of Independence pervaded much of American historical writing in the last quarter of the eighteenth century and the first six decades of the nineteenth. Although the great struggle took shape as a glorious epic in the minds of citizens of the young Republic, its poetry was not evident in the many prosaic treatments accorded it. Provincialism was still the hallmark of most historians; the histories of colonies had become the histories of states. Some individuals, however, such as Abiel Holmes and Timothy Pitkin, were now taking the whole of the American nation for their theme. Jared Sparks contributed the largest addition to the growing library of Revolutionary literature, but it was left for George Bancroft to transcend all other names in the popular imagination. Bancroft, like his contemporaries Prescott and Motley, belonged to the school of romantic historiography that flourished in America and Europe in the mid-nineteenth century. Bancroft's history, in its anxiety to celebrate the virtues of democracy, shed an unreal halo over early America, attributing to it ideals of which the colonists were unconscious. But Bancroft, a spokesman for Jackson, was not alone in allowing a political bias to guide his pen. It should be remembered that the struggles between the Federalists and the anti-Federalists—Hamiltonians and Jeffersonians—were reflected for generations in the books of their ideological descendants.

After the 1870's American historical writing ceased to consider itself a branch of literature, and claimed the exalted position given to those subjects called "scientific." The influence of Ranke became paramount, and the German seminar was transplanted to the University of Michigan, Harvard, and Johns Hopkins. As yet the teaching of history and the writing of history were, in the main, distinct crafts. Skilled amateurs with a broad humanistic culture continued to contribute the larger part of our historical narratives, as they had done before the Civil War. Within a short time this was no longer true. There were only eleven professors of history in the United States in 1880. Within two decades, however, their number had greatly increased and they wrote history as well as taught it. The year 1884 was the *annus mirabilis,* marking the birth of the American Historical Association and the copyright of the first volume of Justin Winsor's *Narrative and Critical History of America,* the open-sesame to American historical materials. In this period, too, the dazzling generalizations of Comte and Buckle on the unfolding of civilization stirred imaginative Americans to seek clues to their own country's development. Darwin and Spencer stimulated the intellectual world in all its phases, and American historical scholars quickly seized on so fruitful an insight as the theory of evolution.

A swarm of specialists now scoured the field and in limited surveys charted their small portions of American history. Some were courageous enough (and sufficiently long lived) to take extended periods of our history, covering the whole of American territory. The strong bias of earlier writing was moderated and the content of the volumes changed. The glamour of war and the intricacies of politics shared space with, or were even shunted aside by, details of institutional developments. Americans, like their European colleagues, turned to the history of civilization (*Kulturgeschichte*), and in McMaster's *History of the People of the United States,* whose first volume appeared in 1883, we have the real precursor of the social-history school in America. The vastness of collected materials soon made it almost impossible for a single individual to cover the whole of American history, and comprehensiveness could be achieved only by co-operative enterprise.

It is an old adage that we should study the past to understand the present. But we should also study the present to understand why contemporary historians interpret the past as they do. Our conception of the past has been molded by our historians whose personal tastes have chosen particular episodes around which to fashion their stories. Actually events do not live because of their occurrence; they live because writers have re-created them. Deeds themselves are short lived, and the memory of them depends upon the skill of the narrator. Paul Revere's ride, for example, was quickly vanishing from the records in the first half of the nineteenth century when Longfellow snatched it from approaching oblivion and gave it a dramatic place in our history. The writer of prose was quick to catch the impulse communicated by the poet, and Revere now rides on in spirited passages in our narratives. We may well consider the personalities as well as the works of those who have written our history, for it is often through our knowledge of the historian that we can understand the history he has written.

THE NORSE VOYAGES

In medieval lore there was mention of a lost continent in the West and of islands in the Atlantic that had disappeared beneath the sea, but the earliest authentic references to voyages of Europeans to America were found in the Icelandic sagas. Two sagas have come down to us which had as their main theme the voyages to Vinland, but elsewhere in Icelandic literature were references to Vinland and its surroundings. The two sagas were the *Saga of Eric the Red,* considered the more dependable source for the Norse voyages, and the "Flatey Book," or the *Vinland History of the Flat Island Book (Flateyjarbók).* These works, as written down, were later than Adam of Bremen's *Description of the Northerly Lands* (*ca.* 1070). Adam, a writer on ecclesiastical history, had lived for a while at the court of the Danish king where he learned about Vinland, its grapevines and its wheatfields.[1] Adam of Bremen's manuscript was the first to use the name Vinland; the king of Denmark, Svend Estridson, "spoke of an island in that ocean discovered by many, which is called Vinland, for the reason that vines grow wild there, which yields the best of wine."

The voyage of Leif, son of Eric, from Norway, and the discoveries that he made in the year 1000 were told in the *Saga of Eric the Red*: "Leif put to sea when his ship was ready for the voyage. For a long time he was tossed about upon the ocean, and came upon lands of which he had previously had no knowledge. There were self-sown wheat fields and vines growing there. There were also those trees there which are called mansur [maple] and of all these they took specimens. Some of the timbers were so large that they were used in building. . . ." The Norse leader "was called Leif the Lucky ever after." The *Flat Island Book* said of the return: "A cargo sufficient for the ship was cut and when the spring came, they made their ship ready, and sailed away; and from its products Leif gave the land a name, and called it Wineland."[2]

In the Eric saga we are told that "there began to be much talk at Brattahlid [Greenland] to the effect that Wineland the Good should be explored, for, it was said, that country must be possessed of many goodly qualities. And so it came to pass, that Karlsefni and Snorri fitted out their ship, for the purpose of going in search of that country." This was in the spring of 1003. More of the narrative centered around the personality and accomplishments of Thorfinn Karlsefni than around Eric and his children, and hence the saga has sometimes been called after the

[1] Matthias Thórdarson, *The Vinland Voyages* (trans. by Thorstina Jackson Walters, New York, 1930), 56, 57, n. 64.

[2] *The Northmen, Columbus and Cabot,* J. F. Jameson (ed.), *Original Narratives of Early American History* (New York, 1906), 25, 26, 53.

name of Thorfinn. In all, 160 men and women sailed southwestward. The Norsemen saw many wild beasts and a heavily wooded region which they called "Markland" (forest land).

These voyagers had arrived with livestock prepared for a permanent settlement, and "they remained there that winter. No snow came there, and all of their livestock lived by grazing." The Norse engaged in trade with the natives, whom they called "Skrellings," exchanging bits of red cloth for furs. "It so happened, that a bull, which belonged to Karlsefni and his people, ran out from the woods, bellowing loudly. This so terrified the Skrellings, that they sped out to their canoes, and then rowed away to the southward along the coast." When they came back, they were in a belligerent mood and a battle followed. "It now seemed clear to Karlsefni and his people, that although the country thereabouts was attractive, their life would be one of constant dread and turmoil by reason of the [hostility of the] inhabitants of the country, so they forthwith prepared to leave, and determined to return to their own country."

Historians differ as to whether it was New England or farther north where Leif Ericson and Thorfinn Karlsefni landed. The number of people who went with Thorfinn and their comparatively elaborate preparation indicated that they were planning to stay. Apparently the hostility of the natives was too much of a handicap. The unexpected bellowing of a Norse bull, it has been amusingly suggested, delayed the settlement of America for five hundred years.[3]

DISCOVERING THE NEW WORLD

The Norse sagas contained the earliest historical narratives of settlement in America. They remained in manuscript for hundreds of years; in fact Columbus' story was in print before that of the Norsemen. Between the sagas and the narratives of later centuries there was scarcely any continuity. Not until the works of Spanish historians appeared did a chain of narration begin which linked up with our own day. Memories of adventure were still fresh when narrators wrote of the discovery and

[3] G. M. Gathorne-Hardy, *The Norse Discoverers of America: The Wineland Sagas* (Oxford, 1920), Part II; Edward Reman, *The Norse Discoveries and Explorations in America* (New York, 1949); F. J. Pohl, *The Lost Discovery: Uncovering the Track of the Vikings in America* (New York, 1952), says Vinland was on Cape Cod.

settlement of new lands, and their publications contained subject matter of unending novelty.

It was fortunate for American history that printing had already been developed when Columbus announced his discovery. Knowledge of earlier discoveries had been limited to a handful of scholars, who had access to the few manuscript records. Now the printed accounts informed numerous readers of the voyages made in the great era of exploration. Peter Martyr and Hakluyt knew they were privileged observers at the birth of the Atlantic community, and with great care they recorded the New World beginnings.

Peter Martyr was living in Spain, employed in the diplomatic service, when Columbus made known his discovery. From the first, Martyr was alive to its meaning. To a friend, Count John Borromeo, in Milan, he wrote on October 20, 1494, "I have begun to write a work concerning this great discovery. If I am suffered to live I shall omit nothing worthy of being recorded. . . . At all events I shall supply the learned world, in undertaking the history of great things, with a vast sea of new material."[4]

The letters that Martyr wrote to his friends about the discoveries were at length elaborated into the chapters that formed his history, *De Orbe Novo*. Portions of it were published from time to time, but not until 1530 did the history appear in its complete form. In addition to the information he received at first hand from the discoverers themselves, Martyr had access to official documents which enabled him to fill out important details in his narrative. His inclusion of fantastic items was no reflection on Martyr's worth as a historian, because for centuries after his death almost anything was believed of this "western hemisphere"—a phrase he originated.[5]

Of great significance in the historiography of the New World was the work of Bartolomé de las Casas, Apostle of the Indies. Early in the sixteenth century, 1502, Las Casas went to Española (Haiti) where he performed a valuable missionary service to the Indians. Devastatingly critical of Spanish cruelties to the natives, his *Short Relation of the Destruction of the Indies* was a highly colored disclosure of the brutalities that accompanied European expansion. Incidentally, Las Casas' booklet,

[4] J. B. Thacher, *Christopher Columbus* (3 vols., New York, 1903–1904), I, 62–63.

[5] F. A. MacNutt, *De Orbe Novo: The Eight Decades of Peter Martyr D'Anghera* (New York, 1912).

reprinted frequently elsewhere in Europe, served as efficient propaganda against the Spaniards.

The work that associated Las Casas more directly with historians of America was the *Historia General de las Indias,* begun in 1527 while he was still resident in Española. The book, which he finished many years later, remained in manuscript form for over three centuries, but many scholars made use of it before its publication. Despite the exaggerations and diffuseness that marked much of Las Casas' work, his history has continued to have great value for the student. Personally acquainted with many of the early discoverers, he had in his possession Columbus' papers and other documents which have since disappeared.[6] These made of his work a storehouse where subsequent historians found the materials for their books. His long association with the New World made him better qualified to write its story than any other contemporary. He lived to complete the narrative only to 1520, but many students agree with Samuel E. Morison's estimate of Las Casas' work, that it was "a great and noble history . . . the one book on the history of America that I should wish to preserve if all others were destroyed."

Antonio de Herrera was one of those who saw the work of Las Casas in manuscript. He made generous use of it, omitting the criticisms directed by Las Casas at colonists and explorers, in his *Historia General de los Hechos de los Castellanos en las Islas y Tierra Firme del Mar Océano* (1601–15). The *General History of the Indies,* as it is known, included the story of the discovery to the year 1554. In his position as historiographer to the Indies there were available to Herrera innumerable sources of information (many of which have since been lost), and thus his work took on a comprehensiveness that gave it great importance. It opened with the opinions of ancient peoples on the world outside of Europe and then proceeded to give the reasons why Columbus thought of finding a new world. A very large part of the work was on the discoveries and activities of the conquistadors; there was little on life in the New World, administration, or similar matters. This deficiency was to a degree compensated for by a short *Descripción de las Indias Occidentales,* which was published at the same time as the *General History.*

At the time Las Casas was writing his history, another work was in progress under the authorship of Gonzalo Fernández de Oviedo y

[6] F. A. MacNutt, *Bartolomé de las Casas* (New York, 1909); Lewis Hanke, *Bartolomé de las Casas* (The Hague, 1951), Chap. II.

Valdés. As a young page at court, Oviedo had seen the reception accorded Columbus on his triumphant return in 1493, and his later career was largely associated with the New World. He was named chief chronicler of the Indies in 1532, and three years later a part of his *Historia General y Natural de las Indias Occidentales* was published. Complete publication awaited action by the Spanish Royal Academy of History in 1851, which issued it in four volumes with a biography and critical notes.

Oviedo wrote on the flora and fauna of the West Indies and the natural resources of the continent, but a large proportion of political history was also included. In general he went about his task with good judgment, but his materials appeared rather to have mastered him. There was a lack of proportion in the narration of events that sometimes made it difficult to follow him with interest. His learning was encyclopedic: "nothing was hidden to his penetrating view," observed his biographer and editor.[7] Washington Irving, however, thought that Oviedo was less to be depended upon for the history of Columbus' voyages than for those of lesser note.[8] Like other early works, Oviedo's was more valuable to the writers of later narratives as a body of material than as a finished product in itself.

Other historians celebrated more particularly the achievements of the better-known conquerors. The conquest of Mexico by Cortés was recorded by Francisco López de Gómara in his *Chronicle of New Spain.* Gómara also wrote a *History of the Indies,* which was concerned chiefly with Columbus and the Peruvian conquest. An old companion in arms with Cortés, Bernal Díaz del Castillo, sought to correct Gómara's inaccuracies. His work, *A True History of the Conquest of New Spain,* marked with a vigorous personal flavor, was issued in 1632, in three volumes. Pizarro's adventure was chronicled at his order by Francisco de Xérez in the *True Narrative of the Conquest of Peru* in 1534, and at a later date, 1605, de Soto's story was published in Garcilaso's *History of Florida.*

Translations of Spanish works soon informed the rest of Europe of the stirring events across the seas, and within a short time collections of voyages were made so that the reader had easier access to these reports. The most famous of these collections in the sixteenth century was the

[7] See 1851–55 ed., p. lxxxiii.

[8] Washington Irving, *The History of the Life and Voyages of Christopher Columbus,* (3 vols., New York, 1850), III, 429.

work of the Italian, Giovanni Battista Ramusio, perhaps the greatest geographer of his day. He devoted a volume in his series, *Delle Navigazioni e Viaggi,* to American voyages. Ramusio's publication, said Henry Harrisse, an expert on the literature of discovery, opened a new era in the literary history of voyages and navigation. The Italian geographer was the first man of mature judgment and wide scholarship to edit the narratives of the early voyages. The link between Ramusio and the English students of the history of discovery was direct and immediate.[9]

RICHARD HAKLUYT

English interest in overseas expansion, both practical and literary, quickly mounted after a slow start. One of the significant aspects of culture in Elizabethan England was the emphasis on geography and history, and the demand for historical literature was so great that summaries and condensations of larger works were published for the popular taste. The greatness of England and the spread of her power overseas were celebrated in numerous histories written in Tudor and Stuart days. The English bourgeoisie experienced a very rapid development in the sixteenth century, and to the need for broader economic opportunities perceived by a rising capitalist class was joined a swelling national confidence in England's imperial destiny.

Richard Eden was the first Englishman of importance to acquaint his countrymen with the new worlds in the East and West. In 1553 he published his *Treatise of the New India,* a translation of some material from Sebastian Muenster's *Cosmography.* A more elaborate work of Eden's appeared two years later, *The Decades of the Newe Worlde.* This was a translation of part of Martyr's work, Oviedo's, and López de Gómara's, as well as of other historians. Eden's work made available for the first time in England a considerable body of information on overseas territories, and it acquainted the English with the most important historians of New World discoveries. "With this book," said a modern student, "England woke to the new day."[10] Eden himself advocated that a

[9] H. Harrisse, *Bibliotheca Americana Vetustissima* (New York, 1866), 457. See also F. T. McCann, *English Discovery of America to 1585* (New York, 1952), for the origins of the "New World" concept in England.

[10] G. B. Parks, *Richard Hakluyt and the English Voyages* (New York, 1928), 23; McCann, *English Discovery,* Chap. VII; Elizabeth Baer, in *Essays Honoring Lawrence C. Wroth* (Portland, Maine, 1951), emphasizes the influence of Martyr on Eden.

British colony be established in America. Some years after Eden's publication, Thomas Hariot, an Oxford professor and adviser to Raleigh, wrote from personal experience *A briefe and true report of the New found land of Virginia* (1588). Hariot's informative work, illustrated by John White, a fellow-member of the North Carolina colony, was translated into several languages, and for many decades thereafter it fixed in the minds of its readers a romantic image of the New World.

More important than all others in awakening Englishmen to the significance of overseas empire was Richard Hakluyt. The expansion of England was greatly stimulated by his publications. Perhaps no historian again wielded so much power over a nation's destiny until the nineteenth century, when German writers helped create Bismarck's empire.

Hakluyt was the adviser of Gilbert and Raleigh, and the history of his career is largely "the intellectual history of the beginnings of the British Empire."[11] When he was thirty years of age, in 1582, Hakluyt published his *Divers Voyages touching the discovery of America. . . .* Two years later Raleigh chose him to present his case to the Queen, which he did in a paper called *The Discourse on the Western Planting.* Hakluyt had already become in fact an organizer of geographical publishing, and his enthusiasm resulted in the issuance of a number of publications with which his name was not openly associated.

The work which established Hakluyt's fame was *The principall Navigations, Voiages and Discoveries of the English nation,* published in 1589, and usually called *The English Voyages.* Hakluyt had gradually evolved a plan to include in one large volume the whole record of English maritime activity from Arthur's day to the Armada. The bulk of the book, however, was on English enterprise in the sixteenth century. With the exception of the medieval travel reports, his narratives were based on eyewitness accounts. As interesting as many of the narratives he printed was his own story of a two-hundred-mile trip he made to consult the last survivor of an early voyage to Newfoundland. This book earned for Hakluyt a place with the Italian compiler Ramusio, whose own work had inspired the Englishman's collection.

Between 1598 and 1600, Hakluyt's last great publication appeared. It was an enlargement of the *Voyages* with the title *The Principal Navigations, Voyages, Traffics, and Discoveries of the English Nation,* in

[11] Parks, *Richard Hakluyt,* 2.

three volumes. The greatly increased body of matter in Hakluyt's masterpiece, especially on the regions westward, was a reflection of the expansion of English maritime activity in the decade between 1589 and 1598. The Englishman, who in 1575 had access to a few scattered books of travel in his native tongue, by 1600 had a full library which made him a sharer in spirit of English imperial enterprise. For the most part Hakluyt did not include the records of the organizations at home; rather, his volumes recorded the movements of English traders and discoverers overseas.

The Principal Navigations was unquestionably one of the most important works of the century, and it was the British historian Froude who called it the "prose epic of the modern English nation." But Hakluyt was more than the historian of English expansion. The settlement of England's first colony in America owed much to his energy, and he was listed among the directors of the Virginia Company. Because he focused England's interest on the lands overseas, his place is high among her empire builders.

On the death of Hakluyt a large mass of his manuscripts passed into the hands of a fellow clergyman, Samuel Purchas, who seized the opportunity to carry on the work of the illustrious editor. In 1625 Purchas continued the collection of his predecessor in a five-volume work published with the title *Hakluytus Posthumus or Purchas his Pilgrimes.* To Hakluyt's papers as a nucleus Purchas added records of universal travel as well as of the latest English voyages. Unlike Hakluyt, who was not only a historian but also a participant in the process of English expansion, Purchas was essentially an antiquarian, with little understanding of the chronicles he compiled. Nevertheless, his work, along with that of his master, was of inestimable service to later historians. In the nineteenth century the distinguished historian, Jared Sparks, remarked that to Purchas and Hakluyt his generation was "still indebted as were our ancestors two hundred years ago, for almost all the knowledge which we possess respecting the early discoveries in America."[12]

[12] *North American Review*, Vol. XXIX (October, 1829), 432. See, in addition to Parks' biography of Hakluyt, the spirited essay by Professor Walter Raleigh in his *Early English Voyages* (Glasgow, 1910); also Boies Penrose, *Travel and Discovery in the Renaissance*, 1420–1620 (Cambridge, Mass., 1952), Chap. 17.

II

The First Settlements

THE MEN—John Smith, William Bradford, and John Winthrop—who led the colonists in establishing the first settlements wrote their own story. The new settlers brought with them the strong Elizabethan tradition that emphasized historical writing. As pioneers in a new land, however, they were less concerned with past events than with history in the making, and their chronicles have the flavor of freshness that comes from first discovery. Hidden away in a corner of the universe, as so many of the early settlers felt themselves to be, they were often apologetic for detailing events that were big with meaning for them but which they felt would be thought trivial by the world outside. Cotton Mather once expressed this thought in his characteristic manner: "If a war between us and a handful of Indians do appear no more than a Batrachomyomachie [battle of frogs and mice] to the world abroad, yet unto us at home it hath been considerable enough to make a history."[1]

The Argonauts were conscious of the importance of their work for posterity, and they were fearful lest the record vanish. Their children's children must know of the dangers met and overcome in settling a new world in order that they might be proud of their forbears and draw courage from their courage. There was need to render unto God a statement of actions done in His name and to thank Him for beneficent guidance. The task of the historian was not to entertain the reader, but to discover his people's place in God's plan for the universe. To the Puritan all history displayed divine wisdom, and the past had been merely the prologue to the settlement of New England.

The monastic chroniclers of medieval Europe had their successors in New England's long line of minister historians. That strain, however, was weak in Southern historical writing, for the religious element

[1] Cotton Mather, *Magnalia Christi Americana* (2 vols., Hartford, 1855), II, 581.

was of less significance in the settlement of the South. Virginia's historians had closer ties with Hakluyt, who savored more freely this mundane world.

JOHN SMITH

John Smith was of the breed of Elizabethan adventurers whose exploits have been preserved by Hakluyt, and though he was a captain in pursuit of gain, so glamorous an air of adventure surrounded his chase that he seemed rather a contemporary of Don Quixote than a man of business. Smith served in an executive capacity in the young Virginia colony, but his strong temper soon drew him into bitter controversy over the management of Jamestown. After leaving Virginia, Captain Smith was employed by the Plymouth Company, for whom he rendered distinguished services. From 1615 to his death, in 1631, Smith lived in England, turning his restless hand to the composition of several works of literature.

His strictly historical works were two: *A True Relation* . . . and a more extensive book, *The Generall Historie of Virginia, New-England and the Summer Isles.* The other works of Smith were of a descriptive character and, though not historical writings, they were of importance as historical material.

A True Relation, a brief tract, was written hurriedly in the Virginia wilderness in May, 1608, a year after the founding of the colony. In a racy, virile style Smith told of his personal experiences (the pronoun "I" was prominent in his writings), and the small space devoted to the events in Jamestown was colored with his strong bias against some fellow-members on the council. With simple clarity he spoke of the uncertainties of settlement, of the dwindling food supply and how it was replenished: "Our provision being now within twentie dayes spent, the Indians brought us great store both of Corne and bread ready made; and also there came such aboundance of Fowles into the Rivers, as greatly refreshed our weake estates, whereuppon many of our weake men were presently able to goe abroad. As yet we had no houses to cover us, our Tents were rotten and our Cabbins worse then nought; our best commoditie was Yron which we made into little chissels. The president and Captaine Martins sicknes constrayned me to be Cape Marchant, and yet to spare no paines in making houses for the company; who notwithstanding our misery, little ceased their mallice, grudging and muttering."

Smith's encounters with the Indians filled most of his pages, and though he was sometimes worsted, it was only great odds that overcame him; he was always a match for his opponents if there were not too many of them. He closed his *True Relation* on a note of optimism: "We now remaining being in good health, all our men wel contented, free from mutinies, in love one with another and as we hope in a continual peace with the Indians: where we doubt not . . . in after times to see our Nation to enjoy a Country, not onely exceeding pleasant for habitation, but also a very profitable for comerce in general."

In 1612, at Oxford, another publication under Smith's name was issued. It was *A Map of Virginia: with a Description of the Countrey . . . whereunto is annexed the proceedings of those Colonies. . . .* Smith wrote the "Description" while his friends combined to write the "proceedings." The men who had been opposed to Captain Smith in the colony received short shrift in the narrative.

Virginia, said Smith, was a country "that may have the prerogative over the most pleasant places of Europe, Asia, Africa, or America, for large and pleasant navigable rivers: heaven and earth never agreed better to frame a place for mans habitation . . . were it fully manured and inhabited by industrious people." After pointing out England's dependence on other countries for various commodities, Smith struck a true mercantilist note in his plea for the colonization of Virginia: "Here is a place a nurse for souldiers, a practise for marriners, a trade for marchants, a reward for the good, and that which is most of all a businesse (most acceptable to God) to bring such poore infidels to the true knowledge of God and his holy Gospell." This description of the new colony revealed Smith as a careful observer of nature, topography, and Indian customs, although like others he ignored the difficulties of settlement.

While the *Generall Historie,* published in 1624, exhibited many of the animosities that characterized the *True Relation,* it earned Smith a place among American historians; only a small portion of the former, however, was written by him. The work was divided into six books, of which the fourth is the most interesting to the student of American historical writing.

Smith gave a graphic description of the "starving time," when the settlers were reduced to eating roots, nuts, berries, some even resorting to cannibalism. Here Smith told, rather simply, the story of his rescue by Pocahontas, which most students largely discredit, although Charles

M. Andrews expressed faith in its likelihood. "After some six weeks fatting amongst those Salvage Courtiers, at the minute of my execution, she hazarded the beating out of her own braines to save mine; and not onely that, but so prevailed with her father, that I was safely conducted to Jamestowne." (Smith embroidered this incident in various retellings.) The introduction of Negro slavery, so momentous for later America, was mentioned casually under date of 1619: "About the last of August came in a dutch man of warre that sold us twenty Negars." A number of pages vividly described the terrible Indian massacre of 1622 which reduced the twelve hundred settlers of the colony by over three hundred.

As a kind of valedictory Smith penned these parting lines at the close of the fourth book: "Thus far I have travelled in this Wildernesse of Virginia, not being ignorant for all my paines this discourse will be wrested, tossed and turned as many waies as there is leaves. . . . But here I must leave all to the triall of time, both my selfe, Virginia's preparations, proceedings and good events: praying to that great God the protector of all goodnesse to send them as good successe as the goodnesse of the action and Country deserveth, and my heart desireth."

It is the conclusion of Virginia's most recent and best-informed historian that Smith's works have much reliable information and that the captain was a man of real courage. A careful study of the sources now available has in the main substantiated Smith's judgment of conditions in the colony and the maladministration of the Virginia Company. The trial of time, to which Smith appealed, has left him high among those who have deserved well of posterity.[2]

EDWARD WINSLOW

Somewhat similar in spirit and purpose to the *True Relation* from Virginia was the small production from New England known as *Mourt's Relation*. There was a continuing demand at home for publications on the lands new found beyond the horizon, and leaders among the first settlers wrote their unfading narratives for eager English eyes. *Mourt's Relation,* or *Journal of the English Plantations Settled at Plimouth,* was first printed in 1622, in London. William Bradford and Edward Winslow were the authors of this slim volume, which recorded the daily

[2] W. F. Craven, *Dissolution of the Virginia Company* (New York, 1932), 5. See J. M. Morse, "John Smith and his Critics," *Journal of Southern History,* Vol. I (May, 1935), 123–37.

happenings of the first year in the newly planted colony. Winslow served as governor of Plymouth, but his most valuable work was done in England as agent for the Bay Colony. Mourt (George Morton) was a fellow Pilgrim in London who published the manuscript (against the will of Winslow) because he thought "it not a misse to make them [the journals] more generall." Written by participants in the events described, *Mourt's Relation* was of the highest authority.

It referred to the famous Mayflower Compact in these words: "It was thought good there shoud be an association and agreement, that we should combine together in one body, and to submit to such government and governours, as we shoud by common consent agree to make and choose." The sense of wonder, the contact with phenomena of nature new to him, and the caution of man in unusual surroundings were vividly present in Winslow's *Journal.* With much delight the writer chronicled the recognition and discovery of familiar and unfamiliar trees "and the best water that ever we drunke." Punctuating this narrative of the infant colony were the shots of muskets and the war whoops of unfriendly Indians.

When the time came for a more permanent habitation, said the *Journal,* "we tooke notice how many Families they were, willing all single men that had no wives to joyne with some Familie, as they thought fit, that so we might build fewer houses, which was done . . . so Lots were cast where every man should lie [build his house] which was done, and staked out." Treaties and alliances with Indian neighbors were important steps in securing the safety of the colony. "Wee have found the Indians very faithfull in their Covenant of Peace with us . . . we often goe to them and they come to us," said the *Journal.* Far friendlier to the Indian was this narrative of the original settlers than the work of Cotton Mather eighty years removed.[3]

WILLIAM WOOD

Although Smith and Winslow wrote descriptions of the Indians and their environment, it was their history of white settlement which mainly holds our attention. Other writers, however, had far less interest in history than in arousing enthusiasm among prospective settlers or in furnishing vicarious adventure to the fireside reader. They were anxious

[3] Winslow was also the author of *Good News from New England* (1624), a continuation of *Mourt's Relation.*

to bring to the attention of Europeans a knowledge of conditions to be encountered in the New World, the novelties of nature, and, the most fascinating novelty of all, the Indians. An interesting example of this type of literature was *New Englands Prospect,* which appeared in London in 1634. William Wood, its author, had been in America for four years. His small book answered questions that many prospective emigrants were asking.

The book was divided into two parts: The first treated of the topography of the region, the climate, the fauna and flora, and "what provision is to be made for a Journey at Sea, and what to carry with us for our use at hand." The second was a study of the Indians and their customs. In the section on Indians, "Of their Kings government, and Subjects obedience," Wood struck a note that was to interest the critics of royalty in Europe: "For though hee [the king] hath no Kingly Robes, to make him glorious in the view of his Subjects, nor dayly Guardes to secure his person, or Court-like attendance, nor sumptuous Pallaces, yet doe they yeeld all submissive subjection to him, accounting him their Soveraigne." Wood was thinking of conditions in England when he wrote of the Indians' punishment for thieving: "For theft, as they have nothing to steale worth the life of a man, therefore they have no law to execute for trivialls; a Subject being precious in the eye of his Prince, where men are so scarce."

Wood's book was a sprightly composition. Within a few years it went through several editions; its compactness and logical organization must have appealed to the inquiring voyager. Unlike many other writers, who painted the colony all dark or all bright, depending on their prejudices, Wood included a few pages "Of the evills, and such things as are hurtful in the Plantation." Wolves were mentioned as a danger, and particular attention was called to the rattlesnake. The "Musketoe" was acknowledged to be a nuisance, although Wood said he had been troubled "as much with them or some like them, in the Fen country of England." He observed that many of the early difficulties of the settler were due to his own negligence: "The root of their want sprung up in England; for many hundreds hearing of the plenty of the Country, were so much their owne foes and Countries hindrance, as to come without provision; which made things both deare and scant." Wood assured the voyager of freedom from want and a comfortable home, if he carried provisions enough for a year and a half, and if he were industrious.

America was a Utopia that could be won by the man willing to work, "for all New England must be workers in some kinde," wrote Wood, in a spirit peculiarly American. "So little is the poverty of the Country," he continued, "that I am perswaded if many in England which are constrained to begge their bread were there, they would live better than many doe here, that have money to buy it."

WILLIAM BRADFORD

The most important of the founders' narratives was that by William Bradford. He knew the history of the Pilgrims at first hand; he had been among the earlier fugitives to Holland, and he was the foremost figure in Plymouth Colony. The history of Bradford's manuscript was itself of unusual interest. After various wanderings it found a home in the palace of the Bishop of London. The Bishop presented it in 1896 to Massachusetts, whose leading historical society published it in 1912, in an authoritative form under the direction of Worthington C. Ford. (Earlier editions had appeared before that date.)

Bradford's *History of Plimoth Plantation* was used in manuscript by later historians for over two hundred years before it was printed. It remains today the prime source for the story of the colony from the time the Mayflower sailed, and even a little earlier, down to 1646. Thomas Prince, Hubbard, Cotton Mather, and Hutchinson all used Bradford's work when writing their own histories. It not only has permanent value for American history, but it also possesses singular charm as literature.[4] The writing was unpretentious and earnest, as befit a Pilgrim. The rhythm of its language paid musical tribute to the memory of the deceased William Brewster: "He had this blesing added by the Lord to all the rest, to dye in his bed, in peace, amongst the mids of his friends, who mourned & wepte over him and ministered what help & comforte they could unto him, and he againe recomforted them whilst he could."

Bradford's narrative revealed as clearly as words might the ideal Pilgrim, who, though not a learned man, was a thoughtful one with a rare degree of intelligence. Under his title Bradford began: "And first

[4] E. F. Bradford, "Conscious Art in Bradford's *History of Plimoth Plantation*," *New England Quarterly*, Vol. I (April, 1928), 133–57. For a modern text of Bradford's history see S. E. Morison, *Of Plymouth Plantation, 1620–1647* (New York, 1952); for an enjoyable biography, Bradford Smith, *Bradford of Plymouth* (Philadelphia, 1951).

of the occasion and indusments ther unto; the which that I may truly unfould, I must begine at the very roote & rise of the same. The which I shall endevor to manefest in a plaine stile, with singular regard unto the simple trueth in all things." Like his contemporaries Bradford was certain that it was God's intercession that kept Plymouth Colony alive, although he was grateful, too, for the aid offered by the natives Squanto and Samoset.

The forthright character of the historian and his unaffected simplicity shone in contrast to the frequent pomp and splendor of John Smith's self-created circumstance. There was vividness also in his writing, as his description of a storm attested: "It blew downe many hundered thousands of trees, turning up the stronger by the roots, and breaking the hiegher pine trees of in the midle, and ye tall yonge oaks & walnut trees of good biggnes were wound like a withe, very strang and fearfull to behould." Amidst the seventeenth-century atmosphere of bitter theological wrangling it was refreshing to read Bradford's tender judgment on Roger Williams: "But he is to be pitied, and prayed for, and so I shall leave the matter, and desire the Lord to shew him his errors, and reduse him into the way of truth, and give him a setled judgment and constancie in the same. . . ."

Bradford could write with anger, too, when he related the behavior of Thomas Morton of "Meriemounte," who was "lord of misrule." Morton and his rollicking companions "set up a May-pole, drinking and dancing aboute it many days togeather, inviting the Indean women, for their consorts, dancing and frisking togither, (like so many fairies, or furies rather) and worse practises." Apart from his critical attitude toward the personal behavior of Morton, Bradford was incensed at him because of his traffic in arms with the Indians. "O the horriblenes of this vilaine!" exclaimed the historian, "how many both Dutch & English have been latly slaine by those Indeans, thus furnished." He went on to appeal to "princes & parlements . . . to prevente this mischeefe" before the Indians might overthrow the white settlements.

Bradford had cause to fear the collapse of his colony which had been born in great travail. He clearly recalled the early days of the settlement in the Dutch provinces and enumerated the reasons why the Pilgrims became dissatisfied with conditions in Holland. They had intended moving "not out of any newfangledness," he carefully explained, "but for sundrie weightie & solid reasons." Among other motives was the desire for a home where the struggle of life would be less hard: "As necessitie was a taskmaster over them, so they were forced to be such . . . to their dearest children; the which as it did not a little wound the tender harts of many a loving father & mother, so it produced likewise sundrie sad & sorowful effects. For many of their children, having lernde to bear ye yoake in their youth, and willing to bear parte of their parents burden, were, oftentimes, so oppressed with their hevie labours, that though their minds were free and willing, yet their bodies bowed under the weight of the same, and became decreped in their early youth; the vigor of nature consumed in the very budd as it were."

The place that held greatest promise for his small group, said Bradford, "was some of those vast & unpeopled countries of America, which are fruitfull & fitt for habitation" and which was "devoyd of all civill inhabitants." Objections had been raised against removal to the New World, where famine would be their portion, disease their companion, and the Indian their enemy. To these and further objections, the brave answer was made, "that all great & honourable actions are accompanied with great difficulties, and must be both enterprised and overcome with answerable courages. It was granted the dangers were great, but not desperate; the difficulties were many, but not invincible."

Then followed delays while plans were made for the voyage. Bradford explained why he wrote at length about the preliminaries: "I have bene the larger in these things that their children may see with what difficulties their fathers wrastled in going throug these things in their first beginnings. . . ."

Finally they got under way, and "after longe beating at sea they fell with that land which is called Cape Cod; the which being made & certainly knowne to be it, they were not a litle joyfull." After some deliberation the ship was turned southward "to finde some place aboute Hudsons river for their habitation. But after they had sailed that course aboute halfe the day, they fell amongst deangerous shoulds and roring breakers, and they were so farr intangled ther with as they conceived them selves in great danger, & the wind shrieking upon them withall, they resolved to bear up againe for the Cape [Cod] and thought themselves hapy to gett out of those dangers before night overtooke them, as by Gods providence they did. And the next day they gott into the Cape-harbor wher they ridd in saftie."

From ocean storms they had been delivered only to face a hostile wilderness in late fall. The last days of November and the early days of December were spent in searching out a hospitable location, and "the 25 day [of December] begane to erecte the first house for comone use to receive them and their goods." Thus ended the first book of Bradford's *Plimoth Plantation*. "The rest of this History," he wrote, "I shall, for brevitis sake, handle by way of annalls, noteing only the heads of principall things."

The tragedy of the first winter Bradford revealed in all its horror, but he remembered also the courage that it called forth. "Ther dyed sometimes 2. or 3. of a day" during those cruel months; "that of 100. & odd persons scarce 50 remained." And of these on various occasions, only six or seven were sufficiently strong to be about and attend to the needs of the other survivors. The surprise of meeting with the Indians Samoset and Squanto, who could speak English and who were willing to help them gather the fruits of the new land, lighted up the gloom of the dark first winter.

Difficulties continued to beset the Pilgrims. Under date of 1622, Bradford wrote: "Now the wellecome time of harvest approached, in which all had their hungrie bellies filled." But the harvest was insufficient, and "also much was stolne both by night & day, before it became scarce eatable & much more afterward." Soon after, Bradford wrote, "God fedd them out of the sea for the most part," and thus early the cod became sacred in Massachusetts. An infrequent note of humor was struck in Bradford's answer to objections by prospective emigrants that mosquitoes were an annoyance; "They are too delicate and unfitte to begine new plantations and colonies, that cannot enduer the biting of a muskeeto; we would wish such to keepe at home till at least they be muskeeto proofe."

Slowly prospering despite hardships, the colony sent for another pastor, Charles Chansey, to assist John Reinor. Bradford then mentioned a minor controversy that ensued which illustrated the influence of environment upon religion: "Ther fell out some differance about baptising he [Chansey] holding it ought only to be by diping, and putting the whole body under water, and that sprinkling was unlawfull. The church yeelded that immersion, or dipping, was lawfull, but in this could countrie not so conveniente."

Bradford's work, in manuscript and in print, has been most effective in gaining for the Pilgrims and their settlement the distinctive place they hold in the history of America and in the folklore of her people. One of the finest legacies of the Plymouth settlement was the story told by Bradford, and his words have enriched the spirit of America. A grateful posterity endowed the Pilgrims with a wealth of virtue and accomplishment, but the myths that were created about them are less interesting than the facts of their history.

JOHN WINTHROP

It was fortunate for historical students that the dominant figures in Virginia and Plymouth wrote their narratives of the early settlement. Since a third leader, John Winthrop, added his record of the transplantation of Englishmen to Massachusetts Bay, the student of history has at his hand the story of the first settlements by those best equipped to tell it. All three had good judgment and sufficient literary skill to re-create for the reader the life of their day which, but for their efforts, might have gone unrecorded.

John Winthrop, lord of the manor of Groton, was one of the most important creators of the Bay Colony which he served as governor and deputy-governor for nineteen years. With far more than the limited resources at the command of the Plymouth Colony, the Puritan group initiated one of the greatest mass migrations of modern times. A good part of the record of the early years of that settlement was preserved in Winthrop's *Journal,* known also as *The History of New England from 1630 to 1649*. It has long been recognized as the most valuable chronicle of the Bay Colony. Though not published in its entirety until the nineteenth century, New England historians had used it while still in manuscript.

The disconnected annals that are Winthrop's *Journal* are less interesting than is Bradford's history, whose greater unity and narrative charm made it a more distinguished performance. In justice to Winthrop it should be noted that his writing was done in the press of a very active life, more so than was Bradford's, and it is suggested that his *Journal* was to be the basis of a more carefully written account.

The work began on board the *Arbella,* "Riding at the Cowes, near the Isle of Wight," on Easter Monday, 1630. The day before, Winthrop had written to his wife: "We are preparinge (by Gods assistance) to sett sayle in the morninge . . . and now (my sweet soule) I must once againe take my last farewell of thee in old England. It goeth verye neere to my heart to leave thee. . . ." After a stormy voyage, the Puritans finally made port, and after a monotonous fare on board ship, they were glad to go ashore and gather "a store of fine strawberries." The frequent references to the entrance and departure of ships, some with needed corn from Virginia, others with passengers from England, the transfer of livestock to the new community, the toll that wolves levied on the cattle —all these were part of the narrative of the beginnings of settlement. Sometimes there appeared items of greater moment, as when Winthrop remarked, under date of 1632, that "this government was . . . in the nature of a parliament." The process of expansion was briefly referred to in March, 1633: "The governor's son, John Winthrop, went with twelve more, to begin a plantation at Agawam, after called Ipswich."

Under date of 1635 the annalist wrote: "The deputies having conceived great danger to our state, in regard that our magistrates, for want of positive laws, in many cases, might proceed according to their discretions, it was agreed that some men should be appointed to frame a body of grounds of law, in resemblance to a Magna Charta, which . . . should be received for fundamental laws." Along with information of a political character, Winthrop wrote about the costs of cattle, corn, and wages paid to workmen. "The scarcity of workmen had caused them to raise their wages to an excessive rate," he said in 1633, and because this resulted in increased prices of commodities, "sometimes double to that they cost in England," the court ordered that carpenters, masons, and the like should get only two shillings per day, and laborers eighteen pence. No commodity was to cost more than four pence in the shilling above what it would sell for in England.

Roger Williams and Anne Hutchinson often appeared in the pages of Winthrop, who was more lenient in his judgments upon them than were many of his contemporaries. Mrs. Hutchinson was "a woman of a ready wit and bold spirit," who had "brought over with her two dangerous [theological] errors." In justification of his own share in the controversy, Winthrop wrote that "he saw, that those brethren, etc. were so divided from the rest of the country in their judgment and practice, as it could not stand with the public peace, and they should continue amongst us. So, by the example of Lot in Abraham's family, and after Hagar and Ishmael, he saw they must be sent away."

Despite serious rifts the colony continued to grow. "There came over this summer [1638] twenty ships, and at least three thousand persons, so as they were forced to look out new plantations. One was begun at Merrimack, and another four or five miles above Concord, and another at Winicowett." Winthrop made plain the constitutional problems that the youthful settlement had to meet: "The people," he wrote in 1639, "had long desired a body of laws, and thought their condition very unsafe, while so much power rested in the discretion of magistrates"; the "Body of Liberties" was the result of this agitation.

Events in far-off England had serious economic effects in the colony during the early 1640's and caused important changes in the distribution of population. "The sudden fall of land and cattle, and the scarcity of foreign commodities, and money, etc., with the thin access of people from England, put many into an unsettled frame of spirit, so as they concluded there would be no subsisting here, and accordingly they began to hasten away, some to the West Indies, others to the Dutch, at Long Island, etc. . . . and others back for England." Winthrop was very much concerned over this departure of many settlers.

In the same year, 1642, he noticed the first commencement in an English American college: "Nine bachelors commenced at Cambridge; they were young men of good hope. . . ." Three years later Winthrop wrote that "by agreement of the commissioners [of the New England Confederation] . . . every family in each colony gave one peck of corn or twelve pence to the college at Cambridge."

In 1646 an occasion arose, said Winthrop, to consider "in what relation we stood to the state of England." The remarks that followed are of great interest to the student of American political theory who would understand some of the ideas that appear so prominently in the eighteenth-century Revolutionary era. Although owing "allegiance and subjection" to the mother country, some New Englanders maintained they "might be still independent in respect of government, as Normandy, Gascoyne, etc. were, though they had dependence upon the crown of France, and the kings of England did homage, etc., yet in point of government they were not dependent upon France." The *Journal* ended in the early days of 1649, the year of Winthrop's death, with an entry characteristically referring to the "righteous hand of God" raised against a man for profaning the Sabbath.

Winthrop's work sometimes reads like a newspaper which features sensational news rather than routine affairs: fires, shipwrecks, and sex scandals. On the other hand there was much which told of the creation of a society that built itself homes, schools, ships, and taverns. Scattered through it were the details, which when grouped together, told of the construction of a social organization more enduring than houses or ships or taverns. In the *Journal,* too, are the materials to help us judge the author, wise beyond most of his colleagues, the aristocratic servant of his people. There can be only agreement with William Hubbard, another historian of Massachusetts, who wrote of Winthrop: "A worthy gentleman, who had done good in Israel, having spent not only his whole estate . . . but his bodily strength and life, in the service of the country; not sparing, but always as the burning torch, spending. . . ."

EDWARD JOHNSON

Edward Johnson came over to New England in 1630 with Winthrop, but shortly after returned to England. In 1636, however, he came back to America to stay. He was the leading figure in the founding of Woburn, and down to his death in 1672 remained one of the important personalities in his town. He was town clerk and surveyor and served in the General Court of Massachusetts. In this legislative body he met representatives of other towns whose information, added to his own intimate knowledge, enabled him to reconstruct a large part of the history of the colony.

The Wonder-Working Providence of Sion's Savior in New England was Johnson's contribution to historical writing. The volume was printed under another title and without the author's name, in London in 1654, but the work has become known by the quaint title which savors so much of the seventeenth-century Johnsonian mind. "The author," wrote his descendant and editor, J. Franklin Jameson, "was convinced . . . that there had been set up in New England an ecclesiastical and civil polity more closely according with the Word of God than any other which the world had seen, and that the Lord had manifested His approval by doing marvelous things in the wilderness for these His chosen people."[5] Throughout, Johnson spoke the language described by French wit as the *patois de Canaan.*

Johnson's was the first published history of Massachusetts, but it does not rank with the works of Bradford and Winthrop. *The Wonder-Working Providence,* as it is called, is difficult reading. It is burdened

[5] *Johnson's Wonder-Working Providence,* J. F. Jameson (ed.), *Original Narratives* (New York, 1910), 10.

by frequent rhetorical and poetic flights, is poorly arranged and contains many errors. It has little of the gentleness of Bradford or the culture and comparative tolerance of Winthrop. Johnson wrote history from the standpoint of the rank and file, thoroughly orthodox and intensely partisan. Against the detractors of New England, like Merrymount Morton, Johnson spoke the language of a crusader.

The volume was divided into numerous short chapters; Book I, Chapter XIII, gave the financial cost of migration, or as Johnson put it, "of the charges expended by this poore People, to injoy Christ in his purity of his Ordinances." "The money is all Christs," added Johnson, "and certainly hee will take it well that his have so disposed of it to his advantage." As one might expect from so orthodox a character, Johnson's words were bitter against Anne Hutchinson.

The Puritan was a militant Christian, and the references to the "Souldiers of Christ in New England" were plentiful; their slaughter of the Pequot Indians was cruelly depicted. In Book II, Chapter XXII, was the classic description "of the manner of planting Towns and Churches in N. E.," with particular emphasis upon Johnson's own town of Woburn. After describing how the officials laid out the town and distributed the land, Johnson went on "to declare how this people proceeded in religious matters . . . it being as unnatural for a right N. E. man to live without an able Ministery, as for a Smith to work his iron without a fire." Johnson's work, it should be mentioned, also had interesting material for Massachusetts economic and social history.

At the conclusion of his first book Johnson had written: "Yet let them [critics of New England] also know the Souldiers of Christ in N. E. are not of such a pusillanimous Spirit, but . . . resolved . . . to keepe the government our God hath given us, and for witnesse hee hath so done, let this History manifest." This history manifested the tenaciousness of the Puritan will and indicated, as one critic observed, that Johnson "handled the pen as he did the sword and the broad axe—to accomplish something with it." Unlike Winthrop and Bradford, who were themselves leading actors on the political stage and wrote with authority on the whole development of their respective colonies, Johnson emphasized the routine life of the community. In *The Wonder-Working Providence* the virtues as well as the limitations of the middle-class Puritan mind were laid bare. The Puritan had great courage and daring, but to dissent his hostility was unrelenting.

NATHANIEL MORTON

Nathaniel Morton, nephew of William Bradford, had unusual opportunities to write a history; in addition to his kinship with the leader of the Plymouth Colony he was himself a member of the official family by reason of long tenure as clerk of the colony court. He was one of Plymouth's most important men and was reputed to know more of the colony's history than anyone else.

The short title of Morton's history, issued in 1669, was *New England's Memorial.* His audience was larger than might be supposed, for the reading of history for recreation was general among the literate public. New Englanders had a strong civic sense, and many of them were people with comparatively rich intellectual backgrounds. The proportion of university men to the whole population was very high; the ministers in particular made every sacrifice to send their sons to Harvard. Almost all of New England's literary output before 1700—tracts, pamphlets, verse, and histories—were by the Harvard-trained clergy. Because of them a continuous tradition of intellectual vitality was maintained.

Two ministers, John Higginson and Thomas Thacher, sponsored Morton's volume, pointing out that a history was much needed. They hoped that it would stimulate similar compositions in other colonies, and that ultimately a comprehensive history of New England would be written.

Morton acknowledged that most of his material came from his uncle, Bradford, but other sources of information, including Winslow's *Journal,* were also available to him. His history was a chronology which took the record of Pilgrim annals through 1668. Up to 1646 the work was almost entirely an abridgment of Bradford's unpublished manuscript, and this part of Morton's volume was therefore extremely valuable. The remainder of the book was largely concerned with elections, the deaths of prominent individuals, and the blights of nature on man, animals, and crops. With the publication of Bradford's own manuscript in the nineteenth century, Morton's work became relatively valueless, but for a long time his volume and Johnson's had been New England's standard histories. Fortunately Morton did more than *write* history; his care in preserving historical materials was long remembered. In the nineteenth century a grateful student said, "Had it not been for [Morton's] attention to manuscripts . . . the present generation would have very imperfect accounts of what was done . . . in New Plymouth in New England, when they were only in the womb of their existence."[6]

WILLIAM HUBBARD

William Hubbard was graduated with Harvard's first class in 1642, and later served as president of his alma mater. He was also active in politics, opposing the Andros government on the issue of tax collections. In 1677, while others were likewise at work on histories of the Indian wars, Hubbard published a *Narrative of the Troubles with the Indians in New England.* He wrote another, more important work, *A General History of New England from the Discovery to MDCLXXX,* which remained unpublished until 1815, though it was frequently used in manuscript.

The government of Massachusetts, in 1682, supported Hubbard with a grant of fifty pounds toward the completion of his history, and later scholars thought the money well spent. Ezra Stiles, noted president of Yale in the eighteenth century, classed the works of Hubbard, Bradford, and Winthrop as "the three most considerable accounts of the first settlement of New England." Much of Hubbard's history was in the form of annals like Winthrop's *Journal;* in fact there was little of importance added, in the period before 1650, to the material he found in Winthrop and Bradford. His view of the founding of Massachusetts Bay was different, however, from that of Winthrop. It is worth noting, too, that Hubbard's work was more secular than the histories written by his contemporaries.

Although Hubbard was supposed to write a chronicle of some sixty years of New England's history, the major portion was devoted to the first half of the period, on which his authorities were more complete. He hurried over the following three decades to 1680. His short last chapter was a description of New Netherland, plagiarized from Daniel Denton's sketch of the colony. The region had recently been added to British possessions, and Hubbard ended his history with the remark, "a true description of the country about New York was thought necessary to be published . . . for the encouragement of any that may have a mind to move themselves thither." Though prized by students in the eighteenth century, Hubbard's history was neglected by later writers.

[6] *The Monthly Anthology,* Vol. VII (1809), 64.

However, in recent works by Morison and Andrews, Hubbard has been somewhat re-established in esteem.[7]

INCREASE MATHER

Increase Mather, who has been called the foremost Puritan, belonged to one of New England's first families. He took a very active part in the life of Massachusetts as an official and as a minister, as well as president of Harvard. In 1676 he wrote the *Brief History of the War with the Indians* (King Philip's War), a day-by-day chronicle of the events reported orally and by letters when the news was fresh. Mather had an eye for the dramatic, and his narrative vividly pictured the struggle. In this volume Mather wrote: "I earnestly wish that some effectual Course may be taken (before it be too late) that a first *History of New England* be written and published to the World. That is a thing that hath been often spoken of but was never done to this day, and yet the longer it is deferred, the more difficulty will there be in effecting of it." (Mather apparently had no high opinion of the works of Johnson and Morton). It was reserved for his son Cotton to make the attempt twenty years later.

In 1677 Increase Mather published his *Relation of the Troubles . . . in New England. . . .* In this volume Mather again revealed his capacity to narrate the picturesque and significant, but it has been pointed out that important materials reflecting unfavorably on Massachusetts were omitted. As a moral lesson Mather took occasion to draw a distinction between those who, he said, had come to America for reasons of trade "and worldly interests, by whom the Indians have been scandalized," and other settlers who had come because of religious motives. The traders, said Mather, "have been attended with blasting ruining Providences," while the others "have been signally owned by the Lord Jesus, for the like hath been rarely known in the World, that a Plantation should be raised out of nothing." To which the nineteenth-century editor of Mather, S. G. Drake, answered: "That any Settlement was, or could have been made independent of Trade is preposterous."[8]

In composing his history of King Philip's War, Mather was conscious of a rivalry with other New England historians, particularly Hubbard.

[7] Hubbard's history was printed in the Mass. Hist. Soc. *Collections,* 2nd ser., Vols. V–VI (1848).

[8] S. G. Drake, *Early History of New England . . .* (Boston, 1864), 238.

But Mather was never one to doubt his own intellectual superiority. He felt that his own work was superior to that of Hubbard's, whose book, said one contemporary, had more mistakes than truths.[9] However, Mather's outlook was generally broad enough to welcome other workers in a common cause—the composition of New England's history. He corresponded with them on the subject, and Nathaniel Morton wrote to Mather asking him "to sett on foot and put forward a Generall History of New England." By communicating to his son Cotton a desire to write history, the father may be said to have put well forward the project of a history of New England.

HISTORIES OF THE INDIAN WARS

Hubbard and the Mathers, father and son, were not the only historians of the Indian wars. The struggles between the whites and natives were of absorbing interest; the narrow escapes from Indian capture and the sudden raids on lonely farms were the very essence of chilling narrative. Few writers, however, were able to capture the drama of forest conflict.

Although several contemporaries left accounts of the Pequot War, Captain John Mason wrote the one best known. His *History of the Pequot War* (1677) was a callous account of the struggle.[10] The exploits of another noted Indian-fighter, Colonel Benjamin Church, one of the best soldiers New England produced, were commemorated in the volume by his son Thomas, *Entertaining Passages Relating to Philip's War . . .* (1716). Full of the nervous tension of Indian warfare, it remained a great favorite with readers long after its original publication. Stories of cruelty and heroism similarly filled the pages of Samuel Penhallow's *History of the Wars of New England with the Eastern Indians 1703–1725,* which was published in the year of the author's death, 1726. Penhallow, who was chief justice of New Hampshire, belonged in the tradition of Bradford, Winthrop, and Morton—community leaders who wrote the history of their times.

Daniel Gookin also wrote of the Indians, but his was a gentler spirit that sought to understand them and promote a friendlier relation between them and the whites. With the exception of John Eliot he was perhaps the most distinguished friend the Indians had. He wrote two

[9] K. B. Murdock, *Increase Mather* (Cambridge, Mass., 1925), 110–11.

[10] Charles Orr (ed.), *History of the Pequot War* (Cleveland, 1897), contains four contemporary accounts.

books; one, *Historical Collections of the Indians in New England,* remained unpublished until 1792, and the other, *An Historical Account of the . . . Christian Indians,* was also published long after it was written (1836). In the second book Gookin sought to protect from the fury of the whites the Christian Indians who had not joined with King Philip. Gookin's position was of course opposed to popular opinion, and his protests were disregarded.

Similar in theme but different in narrative construction were the hair-raising accounts of men and women captured by the Indians and later restored to white civilization. Their stories, generally referred to as "Indian captivities," have held enthralled generations of readers who first marveled at the tale of Mrs. Mary Rowlandson captured during King Philip's War. "Now away we must go with those Barbarous Creatures, with our bodies wounded and bleeding, and our hearts no less than our bodies. . . . Oh the roaring, and singing, and dancing, and yelling of those black creatures in the night, which made the place a lively resemblance of hell. . . . All was gone, my Husband gone . . . my Children gone, my Relations and Friends gone. . . . There remained nothing to me but one poor wounded Babe." This and other narratives of captivity were published again and again for an awed but unsated audience. Americans today, who know Indians only as museum pieces, are still thrilled by these old "captivities."

COTTON MATHER

Cotton Mather was colonial New England's "literary behemoth." A bibliography of over four hundred titles justifies the description. A rich intellectual heritage had helped to endow him with a capacious memory that filed away references in all fields of knowledge which, appropriately and inappropriately, his pedantic mind would later parade across the pages of his numerous works. Mather had vast erudition; on his death in 1728 an obituary said of him: "He was perhaps the principal ornament of this Country, the greatest scholar that ever was bred in it."

The influence of his father's historical interests served to spur on a pen that needed no urging; about 1693 the son determined to write a general church history of New England. It was finished four years later, sent to London to be published, and, after many delays that caused heartaches in the Mather household, appeared in 1702. In his diary, on October 30 of that year Cotton Mather wrote, "Yesterday I first saw my Church-

History since the Publication of it."[11] It was called *Magnalia Christi Americana; or the Ecclesiastical History of New England.*

In his General Introduction the author said: "I write the Wonders of the Christian Religion, flying from the deprivations of Europe, to the American Strand; and . . . report the wonderful displays of His infinite Power, Wisdom, Goodness, and Faithfulness, wherewith His Divine Providence hath irradiated an Indian Wilderness." "Of all History it must be confessed," said Mather, "that the palm is to be given unto Church History, wherein the dignity, the suavity, and the utility of the subject is transcendent." He wrote that he had endeavored, "with all good conscience, to decline this writing meerly for a party," but he asked that readers be lenient toward historians who were not expected to be infallible in everything.

The story of the Plymouth colonists, whom Mather called "Plymoutheans," was a well-written, straightforward account which evidently gained much from an acquaintance with Bradford's manuscript. New England was settled solely to plant the Gospel, said Mather. "About an hundred and ninety-eight ships were employed in passing the perils of the seas, in the accomplishment of this renowned settlement [of New England] whereof, by the way, but one miscarried in those perils. . . . The God of Heaven served as it were a summons upon the spirits of his people in the English nation; stirring up the spirits of thousands . . . with a most unanimous inclination to leave all the pleasant accommodations of their native country, and go over a terrible ocean, into a more terrible desert, for the pure enjoyment of all his ordinances."

The historian agreed with his father, Increase Mather, that "of all historical narratives, those which give a faithful account of the lives of eminent saints, must needs be the most edifying." There was a note of beauty in the reference to John Eliot, the apostle to the Indians. "He was one who lived in heaven while he was on earth," said Mather, "and there is no more than pure justice in our endeavours that he should live on earth after he is in heaven. He that will write of Eliot, must write of charity, or say nothing."

Mather, however, had not Eliot's humanity for the Indians. He revealed, rather, the usual contempt of the settler who thought the natives were uselessly cluttering up the land. "These abject creatures live in a

[11] "The Diary of Cotton Mather," Mass. Hist. Soc. *Collections,* 7th ser., Vol. VII, Part I (1911), 445.

country full of mines; we have already made entrance upon our iron," he noted. "Our shiftless Indians were never owners of so much as a knife till we come among them; their name for an English man was a knife-man. They live in a country full of the best ship-timber under heaven; but never saw a ship till some came from Europe hither." European settlers were therefore justified in taking over so fair a portion of God's territory from infidels who knew not how to use it.

When Mather came to write of his college, he maintained that Harvard promoted a more critical intelligence than schools in England. Harvard, he said, did not show "such a veneration for Aristotle as is express'd at Queen's Colledge in Oxford; where they read Aristotle on their knees, and those who take degrees are sworn to defend his philosophy." He was very proud of his college, among whose names "it will be found that, besides a supply of ministers for our churches from this happy seminary, we have hence had a supply of magistrates, as well as physicians, and other gentlemen, to serve the commonwealth with their capacities." "Europe, as well as America," he declared, "has from this learned seminary been enriched with some worthy men."

In his "Remarkable Providences" (the sixth book), Mather attempted to carry out a plan proposed by his father years before. His "Church History is [now] become able to entertain the world with a collection of remarkable providences that have occurr'd among the inhabitants of New England. . . . Having received sufficient attestations, I shall now invite the reader to consider them." They included unusual rescues from disaster at sea or from hostile Indians, as well as stories of criminals who paid for their capital crimes. It is partly because of his chapter, "Relating the Wonders of the Invisible World," that Mather's reputation has severely suffered. But in this he indicated that he, an erudite man, was not above the superstitions of his day, in which he was joined by others in America and Europe who were perhaps equally learned. "Molestations from evil spirits," he asserted, "have so abounded in this country, that I question whether any one town has been free from sad examples of them."

In his account of the Salem witchcraft episode, Mather mentioned that the "increasing number and quality of the persons accus'd" of witchcraft amazed the officials. "And at last it was evidently seen that there must be a stop put, or the generation of the children of God would fall under that condemnation. Henceforth, therefore, the juries generally acquitted such as were tried, fearing they had gone too far," and Governor Phips reprieved the condemned. Mather added that "it was thought safer to under-do, especially in matters capital, where what is once compleated cannot be retrieved." His conscience was somewhat soothed by noting "the like mistakes in other places [England and France] so that New England is not the only place circumvented by the 'wiles of the wicked and wily serpent' in this kind."

The last book in the *Magnalia* was concerned with the "Wars of the Lord" against heretics and Indians. Mather was comparatively lenient toward Roger Williams, whom "many judicious persons judged . . . to have had the 'root of the matter' in him, during the long winter of [his] retirement." "There was always a good correspondence held between him and many worthy and pious people in the colony from whence he had been banish'd." Mather was not so gentle toward Anne Hutchinson, "the prime seducer of the whole faction which now began to threaten the country."

The Quakers were the object of his bitter invective: "I know not whether the sect which hath appeared in our days under the name of Quakers be not upon many accounts the worst of hereticks, but this I know, they have been the most venomous of all to the churches of America." However, he distinguished between "the old Foxian Quakerism . . . the grossest collection of blasphemies and confusions that ever was heard of," and "the new turn that such ingenious men as Mr. Penn have given to it," so that it had "become quite a new thing." Mather argued that no magistrate should "take the life of an offender solely for the crime of heresy," but the state must nevertheless protect itself against sedition.

Mather's work ended on a doleful note: "It must, after all, be confessed, that we have had one enemy more pernicious to us than all the rest, and that is 'our own backsliding heart,' which has plunged the whole country into so wonderful a degeneracy, that I have sometimes been discouraged from writing the church-history of the country. . . . God knows what will be the End."

Mather's *Magnalia,* one of the most influential books in American historiography, has been variously appraised. Barrett Wendell, in his biography, *The Puritan Priest,* rated it among the great works of English literature in the seventeenth century, while bitter critics of Puritanism have execrated it. Morison, who made considerable use of it in his

Builders of the Bay Colony, indicated that he had a higher opinion of it than have most historians. Despite Mather's pedantry and inaccuracy and the fact that he "was not above *suppressio veri,*" said Morison, he "does succeed in giving a living picture of the persons he writes about, and he was near enough to the first generation to catch the spirit and flavor of the times."[12]

Mather chose his style to suit his theme; it could be simple and direct, as in his *Essays to do Good,* or, as in the *Magnalia,* it could be heavily laden with classical allusions and rhetorical fancies. His history has no form and seems to have been literally thrown together. "All the time I have had for my Church-History," Mather said, "hath been . . . chiefly, that which I might have taken else for less profitable recreations; and it hath all been done by snatches." Jumbled together with much new material, were reprints of many of his earlier writings, and the history was of such bulk as to make it the largest work which had been produced in the British colonies.

In another of his works, *Manuductio ad Ministerium,* 1726, Mather laid down a plan for a scholar's preparation for the ministry. History was to "be read with constant reflection upon God's power as revealed in past events"; but in studying history the reader was always to "believe with Discretion." On another occasion, when referring to Indian folklore, Mather had written: "There is very little in any Tradition of our Savages, to be rely'd upon." It is a pity that the skepticism he showed toward the tales of "red devils" was absent when he wrote of the devilish spirits in white man's society.

[12] See also interesting remarks on Mather in *North American Review,* Vol. VI (January, 1818), 255–72.

III

The Era of Colonialism

IN THE EIGHTEENTH CENTURY American historians continued to speak of colonial beginnings in awesome wonderment, grateful for divine guidance. But most of the later colonial historians, with their strong secular approach, tended to locate the causes of events in a mundane and not in a supernatural plane. Ministers, it is true, continued to write history, but even in New England they no longer monopolized the field. The secularization of life in the Western world included America in its sweep. European letters deeply influenced colonial life, which went through profound changes in its economic and intellectual phases during the half-century following King Philip's War.[1] Doctors, lawyers, merchants, and planters became historians, and their broad interests were reflected in the volumes they wrote. A critical temper was clearly evident in much of their work, and a skepticism characteristic of later scholarship was revealed in their volumes. The best of these historians, though greatly handicapped in gathering materials, turned out narratives which compared favorably with those of English contemporaries.

From annals of conflicts with nature and malignant spirits, writers turned to narratives of conflicts with governors and imperial administrators; the Indian, however, still played a dominant part in the lives of the colonists and therefore merited the space given him in histories. Historians wrote with a consciousness of Anglo-French rivalry for interior America, and their volumes strengthened imperial sentiment. With the passing of a century a society had emerged fairly well stabilized, proud of its past, and confident of the future. Historians were conscious of the

[1] C. K. Shipton, "Provincial Literary Leaven," *New England Quarterly,* Vol. IX (June, 1936).

necessity to correct English misconceptions of America, and their writing revealed a nascent pride in the evolution of a distinctive colonial society diverging from that of the homeland.

ROBERT BEVERLEY

Robert Beverley was the type of Virginia aristocrat who easily combined politics and literature. Like many other Virginians, Beverley spent much time in England; in fact, it was while he was abroad that he determined to write the history of his colony. The publisher of Oldmixon's *British Empire in America* had asked Beverley to read the portion of the manuscript on Virginia and the many mistakes he found therein prompted him to write his own version. "It would take a Book larger than his own to expose [Oldmixon's] errors," said Beverley in disgust. The Virginian added that he had undertaken the task because his province had "been so misrepresented to the common People of England."

The *History of Virginia* appeared in 1705 and in an enlarged edition in 1722.[2] The purely historical narrative was of less general interest than were other parts of the *History*. Beverley's feelings toward the colonial governors, most of whom he disliked, were rather obvious. His dependence on John Smith was well advised, for his interpretation of the dissolution of the Virginia Company was nearer the truth than were the narratives of many later historians. Beverley's material on the Indians must have proved very interesting to contemporary readers, who learned from the pictures and accompanying explanatory remarks a great deal about Indian care of children, their homes, dress, and social organization. The historian supplied ammunition for critics of society who, in their idealization of aborigines, made of them "noble savages." "They claim no Property in Lands," said Beverley, "but they are in Common to a whole Nation. . . . They seem as possessing nothing, and yet enjoying all Things . . . without toiling and perplexing their Minds for Riches."

The historian painted a picture of his colony that would attract the prospective emigrant who had been frightened by exaggerations of burdensome work. Slaves, he said, were "not worked near so hard nor so many Hours in a Day as the Husbandmen, and Day-Labourers in Eng-

[2] I have used the second edition; this revised edition lacks many of the sharp comments on politics contained in the original; see L. B. Wright's edition of Beverley's *The History and Present State of Virginia* (Chapel Hill, 1947).

land." Pride in his colonial home, coupled with a promoter's zeal, led Beverley to say: "This may in Truth be term'd the best poor Man's Country in the World. But as they have no body that is poor to beggary, so they have few that are rich; their Estates being regulated by the Merchants in England, who it seems know best what is Profit enough for them in the Sale of their Tobacco, and other Trade." (This resentment of Virginia planters against their London factors was to grow with increasing strength in the next sixty years.) Even Paradise had no more to offer than Virginia, whose climate must indeed be a "happy" one, "since it is very near the same Latitude with the Land of Promise."

Beverley's writing was fresh, his comments often shrewd, and his appreciation of nature exceptional. His style had a noticeably lighter touch than most of contemporary New England historical literature, which often appears labored by contrast.

JOHN OLDMIXON

John Oldmixon's history was familiar to American writers, who usually quoted it only to condemn it as had Beverley. Oldmixon was as much a pamphleteer as he was a historian, and in common with other pamphleteers he knew no restraint when speaking of his political opponents.

In 1708 he published a two-volume work, *The British Empire in America. . . .* The first volume dealt with the continental colonies, the second with the West Indies. Oldmixon had never been in America and he admitted the probability of inaccuracies in his history.

His main interest in writing the narrative was to emphasize the value of the colonies for the mother country; thus his function was that of a pamphleteer doing an expanded job. While his work was held in disrepute by Americans, who frequently had access to the original authorities from whom Oldmixon drew, the latter's history was better than his critics asserted. It is especially important in at least one respect: it serves to remind the student that the English, when referring to the colonies, usually thought of the West Indies and the continental group together and as something of a unit. American historians, concentrating their attention on the continental colonies, forgot that more comprehensive point of view and thus largely missed the proper perspective of colonial history. Not until the twentieth century, particularly in the work of Charles M. Andrews, did American writers recapture that perspective.

JOHN LAWSON

The year after Oldmixon's history appeared, John Lawson, "Gent. Surveyor General of North Carolina," published *A New Voyage to Carolina* (1709). An account of a one-thousand-mile journey among the Indians was included in the volume. Lawson, who had gone to America in 1700, was slain by the Indians twelve years later, when they began to suspect him of designs upon their lands.

In his preface Lawson wrote, " 'Tis a great Misfortune, that most of our Travellers, who go to . . . America are Persons . . . of a very slender Education, who being hir'd by the Merchants to trade amongst the Indians . . . are yet, at their Return, uncapable of giving any reasonable Account" of their experiences. Lawson thought the French were superior in this regard.

The book was dedicated to the proprietors of Carolina, and it was to be expected that the advantages of settlement in this region would be glowingly pictured for prospective emigrants. After a description of edible products, Lawson wrote on "the Present State of Carolina," whose inhabitants, he said, "thro' the Richness of the Soil, live an easy and pleasant Life." They are, he added, "a straight, clean-limb'd People; the Children being seldom or never troubl'd with Rickets, or those other Distempers, that the Europeans are visited withal." Like the Indians, the whites had no bodily deformities. Women, who had been sterile elsewhere, "have remov'd to Carolina, and become joyful Mothers." Half the book was a detailed examination of Indian customs—not an unusual division of space in works on America in the eighteenth century. European interest in Indians was insatiable, and Lawson gave the public what it wanted. So well, too, did he perform his task of giving a natural history of the colony that, long after, ethnologists and historians continued to use his work, sometimes without acknowledgment.

WILLIAM BYRD

William Byrd II, author of the sprightly *History of the Dividing Line betwixt Virginia and North Carolina,* belonged to one of Virginia's leading families who ruled a princely domain. A large part of his life was spent in England, as a student in his younger years and as a colonial politician in later life. Although he enjoyed London's coffeehouses where he was much at home with the local wits, he had a great love for his native province and his hospitable Westover mansion. There he indulged his taste for letters among his four thousand volumes, the largest library in the colonies. He was a member of the Royal Society, a rare honor for a colonial.

Not until Byrd was nearly sixty did he attempt any comprehensive literary work; then during the next twelve years, to his death in 1744, he wrote the *Progress to the Mines, Journey to the Land of Eden,* and the two "Dividing Line" histories. Byrd, along with some other individuals, was appointed to settle the long-standing boundary controversy between the two provinces, and his "Dividing Line" histories were the narrative of his experiences on this survey in 1728. These histories were not published till long afterward; the second, known as *The Secret History of the Line* (and which was the more dependable of the two) did not appear until the twentieth century. Generally speaking, the *History of the Dividing Line* was a fairly faithful picture of the frontier, but by its selection of incidents the reader was left with misconceptions regarding life in North Carolina.

In his narrative Byrd included a short introduction on colonial history, a description of plant and wild life in the surveyed region, and Indian and pioneer society. Byrd had no illusions about the original Jamestown colony. It consisted, he said, of "about an Hundred men, most of them Reprobates of good Familys; . . . like true Englishmen, they built a Church that cost no more than Fifty Pounds, and a Tavern that cost Five hundred."

The North Carolinians, said Byrd, were an easygoing lot, paying tribute neither to God nor to Caesar; "they are not troubled with any Religious Fumes, and have the least Superstition of any People living. They do not know Sunday from any other day. . . . But they keep so many Sabbaths every week, that their disregard of the Seventh Day has no manner of cruelty in it, either to Servants or Cattle." There was no place in the world, said Byrd, "where the Inhabitants live with less Labour than in N. Carolina. It approaches nearer to the Description of Lubberland than any other, by the great felicity of the Climate, the easiness of raising Provisions, and the Slothfulness of the People." Where the survey began "dwelt a Marooner, that Modestly call'd himself a Hermit, tho' he forfeited that Name by Suffering a wanton Female to cohabit with Him. . . . as for raiment, he depended mostly upon his length of Beard, and She upon her Length of Hair."

The man who added extensively to the Byrd family acreage (over 150,000 acres to an already large holding) could also think more generally in imperial terms: "Our country has now been inhabited more than 130 years by the English, and still we hardly know any thing of the Appallachian Mountains . . . Whereas the French, who are later comers, have rang'd from Quebec Southward as far as the Mouth of the Mississippi . . . and to the West almost as far as California, which is either way above 2000 miles." The French knew the resources of the country because they had traversed it on foot. "So long as Woodsmen continue to range on Horseback," said this lover of the forest, "we shall be strangers to our own Country, and a few or no valuable Discoveries will ever be made."

Byrd was fond of the frontier, though he was not so careful a student of the psychology of the frontiersman as was a writer of the next generation, Crèvecoeur, author of the *Letters from an American Farmer*. The Virginia historian was a broad-minded, cultured aristocrat, the most brilliant forerunner of the imaginative group from the Old Dominion that dominated American life in the Revolutionary era.[3]

CADWALLADER COLDEN

Indians were more than mere biological novelties to the colonists. They were aids to commerce and threats to peace. They were determining factors in the diplomatic game played by the English and French for a continent. As political makeweights and as subjects of scientific inquiry, Indians attracted the attention of the versatile Cadwallader Colden. Like William Byrd, Colden had something of that imperial vision so lacking in many other officials in the colonies as well as in the mother country.

Colden was one of New York's most illustrious citizens. In his public life, during many years in office, he made his impress on colonial policy; in his life as a doctor, student, and writer his achievements merited him high rank. The end of his life coincided with the passing of English rule in 1776, a rule he had done so much to uphold during his career as lieutenant-governor.

Colden wrote *The History of the Five Indian Nations* . . . largely because he wished to convince the public in America and England of the importance of the Iroquois to the colony as a bulwark against the French

[3] J. S. Bassett (ed.), *Writings of Wm. Byrd of Westover* (New York, 1901); R. C. Beatty, *William Byrd of Westover* (Boston, 1932).

and as a means of holding the West. He was anxious also to draw attention to the fur trade. And lastly he wished to preserve the materials relating to Indian life. This first New York history was published in 1727 by William Bradford, the colony's pioneer printer, and it was later reprinted in England.

An English correspondent, Peter Collinson, the intellectual godfather to many Americans, urged Colden to continue with his work, saying that dependable books on the colonies were much in demand in London. He suggested, however, the omission of any material that might prove helpful to the French, "who are Ever on the Watch." Colden acceded to the request and, under great difficulties, worked on the continuation of the history, carrying the narrative down to the end of the seventeenth century.

Colden denounced the whites for degrading the Iroquois. If the vicious practices of the English continued to be "winked at," he said, the Five Nations would "joyn with every Enemy that can give them the hopes of Plunder." Colden justified an English interpretation of the history of the Iroquois because up to the time of his publication the French alone had written on this subject. His many references to the military adventures of small groups were excused on the ground that the Indian art of war was so expressed; Indian oratory was frequently quoted as proof of native genius. The author included lengthy accounts of treaties, believing them to be of great interest to contemporary readers.

With a regard for authenticity that was characteristic of other historians of his own day, Colden remarked: "He that first writes the History of matters which are not generally known ought to avoid as much as possible, to make the Evidence of the Truth depend entirely on his own Veracity and Judgment; For this reason I have often related several Transactions in the Words of the Registers. When this is once done, he that shall write afterwards need not act with so much Caution." The New Yorker disparaged insubstantial work: "Histories wrote with all the Delicacy of a fine Romance, are like French dishes, more agreeable to the Pallat than the Stomach, and less wholsom than more common and courser Dyet."

The historian introduced his subject with a short sketch of Indian government, and then went on to discuss the relations of the Five Nations with the English colonies. He blamed the Jesuits for alienating the Iroquois, though he could not refrain from lauding the bravery of the missionaries who lived among the Indians "at War with their Nation." Colden's observations on Indian character are still worth reading. His work was well known in his own day, for it was one of the few books in English that gave significant details about the history and institutions of the natives who occupied so strategic a place in the life of the colonists.[4]

Colden left in manuscript a continuation of his history which was not published until the twentieth century. It revealed again his preoccupation with the need to win the Iroquois to the English side. He also left a history of New York during the administrations of Governor Cosby and Lieutenant-Governor Clark, which included a section on Zenger's trial. The author, whose friend James Alexander was one of Zenger's counsel, was friendly to the printer charged with libel.[5]

Colden was always rather sensitive to criticism, but he held it a man's duty to his country to "patiently submit to Scoffs & Jests & revilings when he thinks he cannot avoid them by being usefull." He hoped that in writing his history he had been "in some degree usefull" to his country; "If it be so," he said, "I shall truely gain my end without any further view." The testimony of his contemporaries and of later generations is that Colden did indeed write a "usefull" book.

DANIEL NEAL

Daniel Neal was a dissenting minister in England who was very much interested in the life of New England. He corresponded with colonists who, in the pursuit of their own historical interests, made frequent reference to the contributions of their colleague in the mother country. Harvard recognized his work with the highest honor it could grant—the M.A. degree.

Neal's *History of New England . . . to . . . 1700* was published in two volumes in 1720. The New World was praised as a "Retreat for oppressed Protestants in all Parts of the World"; their sufferings in the Old World were pointed up to exhibit the advantages of the New. Neal's sources were the familiar names—Winslow, Morton, Wood, Increase Mather, Hubbard, and especially Cotton Mather. Neal asserted

[4] L. C. Wroth, *An American Bookshelf, 1755* (Philadelphia, 1934), 92. See article on Colden's history in *The Historical Magazine,* Vol. IX (January, 1865), 9–13, probably written by the editor, J. G. Shea.

[5] "Cadwallader Colden Papers," New York Hist. Soc. *Collections,* Vol. IX (1935), 283–355, 359–434.

that he wrote with "Freedom and Impartiality, tho' I can't help declaring myself sometimes on the Side of Liberty, and an Enemy to Oppression in all its Forms and Colours."

The early chapters were on the discovery of America, with a description of native civilization and a narrative of the Puritans in the Old World. Neal thought very highly of the clergy who went to New England. Though not all learned, they had a better share of learning "than most of their neighboring Clergy at that Time." The historian wrote profusely on missionary activities among the Indians, using materials composed by John Eliot. He also devoted much space to the Quakers, and his treatment was in the nature of an apologia for New England's attitude toward this sect. He was himself, however, opposed to depriving a man of his civil rights because of his religious doctrines; such deprivation should be visited only on the disturbers of the public peace. Writing a half-century after the events he described, Neal was pleased that New England's attitude had changed toward the Quakers.

The second volume, which continued the account after 1661, devoted many of its pages to the wars with the Indians, especially King Philip's War. The activities of Sir William Phips were chronicled at length, and so, of course, was the witchcraft episode. On these incidents and characters in New England's history Neal had fuller authorities than he had had for the early period, but in the main he transcribed much of what he found in Cotton Mather. He was hostile to the Mathers in his treatment of the witchcraft hysteria. "All the Confessions that were made, seem to me," said Neal, "either the effects of a distemper'd Brain, or extorted from Persons to save their Lives."

Neal was one of several writers who weighed the possibility of a revolt against the mother country. He thought it remote, believing New England disinclined to revolution. For, he maintained, in order to live, New England must trade with Europe; "so that if we could suppose them to rebel against England," they would only fall into the hands of another power "who would protect them no longer than he could sell them to advantage." Because it was New England's interest to remain subject to England, she was likely to do so, concluded Neal.

Another large-scale undertaking by Neal was a four-volume history of the Puritans (1732–38); this work had little material on the Puritans of New England, and most of that was interwoven with the history of their coreligionists in England. Although Neal's history of New England was harshly criticized by Thomas Hutchinson and others as scarcely more than an adaptation of Mather's *Magnalia,* it continued to be quoted by historians for many years. It contained the "medulla" of the *Magnalia,* said one writer, but it was superior in style, "with such sentiments and observations as Mather had not language to describe nor a head and heart to conceive."[6]

THOMAS PRINCE

Neal was an observer living in the homeland who recorded New England's history with sympathy. Better known and more valuable in the establishment of a continuous historical tradition was the work of a native New Englander, Thomas Prince. Prince, one of the many eighteenth-century historians from Massachusetts, was born in 1687. After study at Harvard he entered upon a pastorate in the South Church, Boston, which he held to his death in 1758. He had traveled widely abroad, and conscientious study fitted him for a career of distinction. He enjoyed an intercolonial reputation as one of the leading scholars in America.

Prince's interest in history was aroused at an early date. When he was but a freshman, he began collecting books for his "New England library." After naming the authors whose acquaintance he had made while still young—Morton, Johnson, Hubbard, the two Mathers (his friend Cotton Mather was a stimulus to historical writing)—Prince confessed: "I longed to see all things disposed in the order of time wherein they happened, together with the rise and progress of the several towns, churches, counties, colonies, and provinces throughout this country. . . . In my foreign travels, I found the want of a regular history of this country everywhere complained of." While in England, Prince had gathered books on our early history, and he thought that on his return, in 1717, he would have sufficient leisure to "attempt a brief account of facts at least in the form of annals." But the cares of his pastorate allowed him time only to collect materials and not to digest them.

In 1736 Prince brought out the first volume of his *Chronological History of New England*. He spoke of the large mass of manuscripts at his disposal, and his work, he said, was in part an effort to preserve valuable materials, some of which had already been destroyed by fire. Prince wrote that Bradford's grandson, Major John Bradford, had given him permis-

[6] *The Monthly Anthology,* Vol. VII (1809), 346–52, 414–21.

sion to use the Plymouth history "& take out of it what [he] thought proper for [his] New England chronology." The inveterate collector added the old Bradford manuscript to his own library, where it remained until the time of the Revolution.

Prince's standard of scholarship was unusually high, guided as it was by a healthy skepticism. "I would not take the least iota upon trust; if possible, I examined the original authors I could meet with. . . . I cite my vouchers to every passage; and I have done my utmost . . . to find out the truth, and . . . relate it in the clearest order." After paying his critical respects to writers who protest their own impartiality, Prince stated his credo: "I own I am on the side of pure Christianity; as also of civil and religious liberty, and this for the low as well as high, for the laity as well as the clergy, I am for leaving everyone to the freedom of worshipping according to the light of his conscience. . . . And I hope my inclination to these great principles will not bias me to a misrecital of facts, but rather to state them as I really find them for the public benefit."

Like the medieval historians Prince felt it necessary to start his work with man's beginning, from Adam, "Year one, first month, sixth day." His chronology went on to the birth of Christ, then to Columbus' discovery, the Introduction closing with the "discovery of New England by Captain Gosnold." After this very lengthy introduction Prince began with the chronology of New England. His history, which appeared in one volume, stopped with the events of 1630; the annals for the following three years, which were to be part of a second volume, were published separately, long after the first volume was issued; and publication then ceased. Nowhere in the American colonies of that period was there a demand for so detailed a history. In a letter referring to Prince's work, John Callender, a contemporary historian in Rhode Island, expressed sorrow that the *Chronology* was so ill received; "I look on it as an honor to the country, as well as to the author," he wrote, adding prophetically, "and doubt not but posterity will do him justice."[7]

With but few exceptions Prince adhered to his intention to give the unadorned facts. Some notable events, such as the discovery of America, drew from him unexpected comment: "We are now to turn our eyes to the west, and see a new world appearing in the Atlantic Ocean to the great surprise and entertainment of the other." The settlement of

[7] Rhode Island Hist. Soc. *Collections,* Vol. IV (1838), 178.

New England moved him to speak a more vibrant language than a dry chronology ordinarily uttered: "Divers attempts are made to settle this rough and northern country; first by the French . . . and then by the English, and both from mere secular views. But . . . a train of crosses accompany these designs of both nations . . . till a pious people of England, not there allowed to worship their Maker according to his institutions only . . . are spirited to attempt the settlement. . . . So there were just one hundred and one who sailed from Plymouth in England . . . their native and pleasant land, and encountered all the toils and hazards of the tumultuous ocean, in search of some uncultivated region in North Virginia, where they might quietly enjoy their religious liberties, and transmit them to posterity."

For the most part Prince's work was aridly factual. And yet it was the orderly arrangement of those facts and the tests to which he submitted them before their inclusion in his catalog that have given Prince his reputation as an American pioneer in scientific historical writing. The volume marked an improvement in research over previously published histories, but the best of Prince's contemporaries were equally scholarly. Probably as important as any inheritance we possess from him is the extremely valuable collection of Americana he spent so many years in gathering and which, though sadly diminished, rests now in the Boston Public Library.

The prophecy of Prince's contemporary that posterity would do him honor was abundantly fulfilled, and a long list of historians later paid their tributes to him. His *Chronology* inspired similar attempts and, as late as 1791, a keen student of history, John Pintard of New York, when compiling an American chronology, wrote to Jeremy Belknap, "I shall do pretty well as long as Prince holds out. But shall be at a loss after I part with him." Many historians, it might be added, clung to Prince to avoid getting lost.[8]

JOHN CALLENDER

Historians of New England, for the most part, confined their narratives to Massachusetts. In time, however, other New England colonies found their chroniclers. Among them was the author of a history of Rhode

[8] Mass. Hist. Soc. *Collections,* 6th ser., Vol. IV (1891), 489–91; see W. H. Whitmore, "Life and Labors of Thomas Prince," *North American Review,* Vol. XCI (October, 1860), 354–75.

Island, John Callender. Callender was a Baptist clergyman in Newport, Rhode Island, where a rich intellectual environment was conducive to his fruitful avocation—collecting historical materials. Some of these documents, it is interesting to note, were used more than a half-century later by Isaac Backus in his history of the Baptists. Callender contributed to historians more than the raw materials; his own composition, which was likewise useful to later writers, was *An Historical Discourse on the Civil and Religious Affairs of . . . Rhode Island* (1739).

In the spirit of his contemporaries, Callender said that he had sought to prevent mistakes by carefully reviewing "the publick Records, and my other Materials." Like others before and after him, he apologized for the portions that "will be tho't too minute or personal by Strangers." Callender asked that a group of individuals be formed to collect documents and private papers before they were all dispersed.

The historian's kindly outlook was more that of the rationalist spirit of the eighteenth century than of any narrow sectarianism. For example, in speaking of the religious differences among the Puritans that prompted the settlement of Rhode Island, he wrote: "In Reality the true Grounds of Liberty of Conscience, were not then known, or embraced by any Sect or Party of Christians; all Parties seemed to think, that as they only were in the Possession of the Truth, so they alone had a Right to restrain and crush all other Opinions." Nearly a quarter of Callender's small book was taken up with the religious disputes that led to the colony's founding. Belonging to a persecuted sect, libeled by other historians of New England, it was natural for Callender to justify the ways of the Baptists, but he went beyond a mere partisan plea: "It must be a mean, contracted way of thinking," he wrote, "to confine the Favour of God . . . to one Set of speculative Opinions, or any particular external Forms of Worship."

Too much of Callender's *Discourse* was a sermon in praise of liberty of conscience, and too little was connected with the history of the colony. True, it reads much easier than many similar writings of this period, but his own statement appears sufficiently descriptive: "I confess the Account I have been able to collect is very lame and imperfect." But it was the most important survey of the colony's history for more than one hundred years.[9]

[9] Callender's Discourse was reprinted in the Rhode Island Hist. Soc. *Collections,* Vol. IV (1838), 57–270.

WILLIAM STITH

When Prince was writing his history of New England, another minister was writing with equal care the story of Virginia. William Stith, who had been educated at Oxford, was rector of the parish of Henrico and a governor of William and Mary College. In 1747 he published *The History of the First Discovery and Settlement of Virginia*. Like his contemporaries, Stith was afraid that historical materials then available might be lost if not immediately used.

He began his history in a rather sophisticated tone: "Every Country," he wrote, "hath it's Fables concerning it's Original, which give great Scope to light and fanciful Historians, but are usually passed over with a slight Mention by the solid and judicious. The late Discovery of America, in historical and well-known Times, might, one would think, have exempted it from this common Fate of Nations. Yet . . . even this new World hath been endowed with it's Fabulous Age." He expressed "Contempt and Aversion for all such learned Trumpery" and wrote that he would apply himself "to give a plain and exact History of our Country, ever regarding Truth as the first requisite and principal Virtue in an Historian, and relating nothing without a sufficient Warrant and Authority."[10]

Stith's narrative reached only to 1624, and much of it was taken up with a detailed treatment of squabbles within the London Company. But he clung to his procedure doggedly, saying that "as these publick Papers contain the most authentic Reason and Account of things, and as they are the surest and most indubitable Materials, for an Historian to proceed upon, I shall not be turned from my Course, by the accidental Dislike of some Readers."

The earlier part of Stith's *History* was mainly based upon John Smith; for the latter part the "Records" of the London Company (made available through William Byrd's assistance) were the important source. Stith characterized Smith as an honest and reliable writer for the events with which he was connected in America, but considered him somewhat confused. As for the quarrels between the company and the king, Stith's sympathies lay with the former.

Although he wrote with the consciousness of America's growing

[10] A useful index to Stith's history was published by M. P. Robinson in Virginia State Library *Bulletin*, Vol. V, No. 1 (1912).

strength and challenged English historians to take account of her history, his narrative was temperate and written with unusual regard for scholarly standards. His errors of interpretation, which favored the company, were the result of too great faith in the court records, which were partisan in character, presenting as they did the point of view of Sir Edwin Sandys. But in behalf of Stith it should be added that since his day most historians who have also taken these records at their face value have misunderstood much of Virginia's early history.

Stith had promised that he would continue his work, but he never went on with it. It is supposed that so detailed a narrative was not to the taste of Virginia gentry, and this lack of support discouraged him. In point of scholarship Stith's contribution ranks with the very best produced in the colonial period and has long been one of the standard works in early Virginia history.[11]

WILLIAM SMITH

The most distinguished historical studies at this time were being produced in New England and Virginia, but able historians were also at work in the middle colonies. Their volumes incorporated valuable descriptions of contemporary society and reflected the bitter controversies that marked political developments in these provinces. William Smith, the historian of New York, was born there in 1728. His father was a person of prominence, holding several high offices in the province. The son was educated at Yale and then returned to his native city to study law. Very shortly he gained a large practice, becoming a leading member of the bar, and entered actively into politics.[12] Named a member of the council at the time when revolutionary discussions were alienating friends of long standing, Smith drew up a plan of colonial union that he hoped would prevent dismemberment of the British Empire. The historian became more conservative as the radical temper of the colonists increased, and when the war broke out Smith became a loyalist. He left for England when the British troops evacuated New York, and remained abroad until his appointment as chief justice of Canada in 1786. He held this post until his death in 1793.

[11] A valuable bibliographical essay on Stith's history is in *The Southern Literary Messenger,* Vol. XXXVII (September, 1863), 554.

[12] Smith and William Livingston published a digest of the laws of New York in two volumes (1752, 1762).

Because of the stigma of Toryism, Smith's history was long in disrepute, but it scarcely deserved such a fate. *The History . . . of New York* (1757) closed with the year 1732; a continuation to 1762 was later added. Smith was reluctant to write on the period following 1732 because his father, during those years, had been engaged in bitter controversy with the governor. The history of those times, he said, "will be better received from a more disinterested pen. . . . Besides, a writer who exposed the conduct of the living will inevitably meet with their fury and resentment. The prudent historian of his own times will always be a coward, and never give fire till death protects him from the malice and stroke of his enemy."

Although Smith did not write with a disinterested pen, he managed to avoid extremes. He was one of the leading dissenters in the colony, engaging in a number of serious religious controversies, and it was hardly possible for him to avoid partisanship. Because of favored family associations the historian knew many of the actors in the later part of his story. His writing, though good, did not escape that moralizing which was then characteristic of most historians. He often wrote with an editorial pen that asked support for a cause in which he was interested. Some sentences he neatly turned, as when writing of missionary activities among the Iroquois he remarked: "The French priests boast indeed of their converts, but they have made more proselytes to politics than religion."

The larger portion of Smith's work dealt with the eighteenth century. He had no direct acquaintance with the Dutch documents and understood little of the early history of the colony. Though he told a strictly political story, he added considerable descriptive material on geography, trade, religion, politics, and the law. To the modern reader these pages are probably the most interesting, particularly the references to the laws and courts of which Smith had direct knowledge. His education and wealth prompted him to write from the standpoint of an aristocrat, but he did supply some interesting information about the life of the poorer classes. He was proud of the place of his birth: "With respect to riches, there is not so great an inequality amongst us as is common in Boston, and some other places." He could also see the flaws in his colony: "Our schools are in the lowest order—the instructors want instruction; and, through a long shameful neglect of all the arts and sciences, our common speech is extremely corrupt, and the evidences of a bad taste, both as to thought and language, are visible in all proceedings, public and private. . . . In matters of religion we are not so intelligent, in general, as the inhabitants of the New England colonies; but both in this respect and morals, we certainly have the advantage of the southern provinces."

Throughout Smith's work appeared his sensitiveness against real and fancied Episcopal oppression, abetted by the government. The historian, provincial born, disliked many of the governors sent over from England, though he was partial to William Burnet. Smith's history was scorned by Cadwallader Colden, who thought it unfit "to pass for a chronicle of the Province of New York." Later generations, removed from eighteenth-century partisan strife, have, however, found much to praise in this story of old New York.[13]

SAMUEL SMITH

Samuel Smith, a contemporary of the like-named New Yorker, was the author of *The History of the Colony . . . of New Jersey. . . .* It appeared in 1765 under the imprint of James Parker, one of the most famous of colonial printers; it was found sufficiently serviceable to be issued in a second edition more than a century later (1877). Smith came of a Quaker merchant family and held several important public offices.

The writer said he was anxious to present the "plain state of facts" of New Jersey's history, because so little had "appeared abroad of what the settlers here have been doing." Unlike Prince, who went back to Adam for a beginning to his history of New England, Smith went no farther back than Columbus for his account of New Jersey. Nearly half of his book described the events of the seventeenth century. Interesting materials on immigration were included, along with the text of many documents not easily accessible to the eighteenth-century reader and which today are the joy of the genealogist.

In the pages on Lord Cornbury's administration Smith wrote as a patriotic colonial: "Tho things were carried to arbitrary lengths," he said; "there was not wanting in the province, men of discernment to see and lament the unhappy situation of their country, and of spirit to oppose its greatest enemies." Excessive space was given to the conflicts between colonials and Governor Cornbury, with whom many people

[13] See Colden's letters on Smith's history, 1759–60, New York Hist. Soc. *Collections,* Vol. VIII (1868), 181–235.

found it easy to quarrel. The historian's favorable judgment on Governor Hunter was tempered by the reflection that he "had a ready art at procuring money, few loved it more."

Like other historians Smith gave much attention to Indian customs and to the relations between the red men and the whites. His observations on the Indians were free from rancor; his Quaker background led him rather to emphasize their peaceful qualities.

There was nothing exciting about Smith's narrative, and it must be admitted that he adhered strictly to his intention to present his facts plainly. There was less of his own writing in his book than that of the authors of various public and private papers whom he quoted at great length. When describing the political state of the province in 1765, he said that "harmony reigns in a considerable degree in all branches of the legislature; the public business is consequently dispatched with ease, and at small expence." One gathers that these words were an index to Samuel Smith's character; he disliked any disturbance and expended little of himself emotionally.

WILLIAM DOUGLASS

Historians in this period were mainly concerned with their respective colonies, but they were aware of a broader field of historical inquiry. The dawning realization of unity among the colonies was already apparent. At least one colonial historian viewed the provinces as a whole, and although his work was inadequate, it was indicative of the American mind in transition. William Douglass was by profession a physician, in Boston, but his varied interests included the writing of a history whose fame was enhanced when Adam Smith referred to it in his *Wealth of Nations.*

Summary, Historical and Political . . . of the British Settlements in North America was the title of the publication brought out by Douglass in separate releases, beginning in 1747. Two volumes were ultimately bound together and issued before he died in 1752. He began with a short survey of ancient and modern colonization, and then went on to the settlement of North America, including Canada. The materials on the colonies outside of New England, however, were comparatively scanty.

In view of the strong animosities that lent acid to his pen, one is not impressed by his protestations of fairness: "I have no personal disregard or malice," he said, "and do write of the present times as if these things had been transacted a hundred years since." Such protestations, however, will deceive no reader, for the partisanship of Douglass was so obvious that it hardly offends today. The offenses of Douglass against historical scholarship and composition were many. Apart from his temperamental frailty, his work was badly organized, and seemed more like a mass of pungent, ill-digested notes than a finished history.

Douglass had written that, because of the dryness "of descriptions and bare relations . . . a little seasoning is used." The flavor of his contentious personality was more than enough "seasoning" for this historical potpourri. The digressions in which he indulged often took him far afield. In his closing chapter on Virginia he injected an irrelevant discussion of smallpox, and elsewhere he also included digressions on medicine. In the many footnotes that weighed down his pages, Douglass found an additional vent for his prejudices. He denied the necessity of studying original sources in the preparation of his history: "This is a laborious affair, being obliged to consult manuscript records." He sneered at New England historians, whom he considered "beyond all excuse, intolerably erroneous."

Despite the mass of misinformation that Douglass supplied, his volumes did possess value. A section, "Loose proposals towards regulating the British colonies," contained interesting material on imperial organization. His work included far more economic and social history than did the books of his contemporaries, and his strong dislike of anything tending toward inflation pleased later economists. For the most part, however, posterity was less impressed by Douglass' history than were his contemporaries, especially in Great Britain. The *Monthly Review,* in England, praised it highly, saying it contained a "fuller and more circumstantial account of North America, than is anywhere else to be met with."[14]

[14] *The Monthly Review* (October, 1755), quoted in Wroth, *An American Bookshelf, 1775,* 88–89. An important work, reflecting an imperial point of view, was Edmund Burke's *An Account of the European Settlements in America* (2 vols., London, 1757); within twenty years, six editions appeared. For colonial historians, see also Jarvis M. Morse, *American Beginnings* (Washington, 1952).

IV

The Growing National Spirit: 1750-1800

THE GROWING self-consciousness of Americans in the era of the Revolution fostered the study and writing of history, and was itself nurtured by historical narratives. Many histories of provinces and states appeared; now historians more frequently transcended local boundaries. The argument that state histories would "lay a good foundation for some future compiler in writing a general history of the country" encouraged Jeremy Belknap to write his history of New Hampshire.[1]

Ezra Stiles, president of Yale, was particularly conscious of America's strides toward maturity. Over a period of many years he corresponded with individuals in diverse places for his projected *Ecclesiastical History of New England & British America.* According to his own report, an Englishman offered to secure five thousand subscriptions for his history.[2] In an exchange of letters with Hutchinson, Stiles said that a European could not "do justice to the history of the American provinces." He was glad that Hutchinson (who was then writing a history of Massachusetts) was of New England descent, and urged him to broaden his narrative to include all four New England colonies in his survey: "You would thus write a complete history of an intire people."[3] Stiles said that his own plan was to write on "British American History"; at first he would write the history of New England "as of one intire emigration, people

[1] Letter from A. Wibird to Belknap, April 14, 1779, Mass. Hist. Soc. *Collections,* 6th ser., Vol. IV (1891), 139.

[2] Stiles, *Diary,* February 11, 1770.

[3] *New England Historical and Genealogical Register,* Vol. XXVI (1872), 159-64, 230-33, especially May 7, 1764.

and settlement, to deduce it through the civil, military, commercial, moral and ecclesiastical changes and revolutions to the late . . . war" (Seven Years' War). Although Stiles' work was never published, he left to his son-in-law, Abiel Holmes, many volumes of manuscripts which were of service in preparing the latter's *American Annals*.[4]

Other historians, notably the Baptist Isaac Backus, ranged over all the colonies in search of materials. His three-volume work, *A History of New England with Particular Reference to the . . . Baptists* (1777–96), supported his reputation as one of the leading champions of religious liberty in America. In accord with the best scholarship of his time, he sought out documentary sources and "names his principal vouchers on purpose to have his performance thoroughly examined." He objected to most of the existing histories as biased, particularly in their treatment of minority religious groups. When he reached the Revolution in his narrative, Backus broadened his work to include a discussion of the war, but on the whole it remained an ecclesiastical history.[5]

Shortly after the middle of the century, newspapers, magazines, and almanacs began to reflect a rising interest in history. One writer solicited subscriptions, through the newspapers, for a proposed work on the colonies.[6] Nathaniel Ames included in his almanac (1756) "An Account of the Several Provinces in North America," which was copied and expanded by a New York almanac. Another editor, Samuel Nevill, ran a history of North America in his *New American Magazine*. To prepare a large body of citizens for active participation in politics, Ames recommended the study of geography and history, adding the true note of nationalism, "it is proper to begin with the history of your own nation."[7]

A friendly Englishman, Dr. John Fothergill, in encouraging study of America, hoped one of her historians would describe her contemporary civilization, and he suggested that a fresh description be made every twenty years. "If the history of the actions of men in civil life are of any use to posterity," he wrote, "what advantages might not be gained by thus taking time by the forelock?"[8] Magazines devoted hundreds of

[4] The manuscript of Stiles' "History" is in the Yale University Library.

[5] Alvah Hovey, *A Memoir of . . . the Rev. Isaac Backus* (Boston, 1858).

[6] New York *Post-Boy*, May 5, 1755.

[7] S. Briggs, *The Essays . . . of Nathaniel Ames, Father and Son . . . from Their Almanacks* (Cleveland, 1891), 269–70, 381–83.

[8] Fothergill, Portfolio 38 (86), September 10, 1766, Friends House, London.

pages to general and national history, and in the 1780's there was a special interest in ancient history which, it was hoped, would furnish guidance to the young Republic.[9]

The Revolution was, of course, a strong impetus to historical writing. A "History of the Late War in America," a serial copied from the *Annual Register* (London), was run in *The Worcester Magazine* (1786–88). *The Columbian Magazine,* in 1789, also levied on the *Annual Register* for a historical digest of the war. *The Boston Magazine* (1783) seemed to specialize in history; indeed, some of its original backers helped organize the Massachusetts Historical Society a few years later. *The American Magazine,* edited by that strong nationalist Noah Webster, awakened interest and lively discussion in American history. Belknap published a series of biographical articles in *The Columbian Magazine* (1788) under the title of "The American Plutarch." Belknap's close friend Ebenezer Hazard, who had long been gathering materials, published his *Historical Collections* (2 vols., 1792–94), in order, as he said, to "lay the Foundation of a good American History." Belknap told Hazard that people wanted to know why he did not write history instead of publishing sources; a "regular history of the United States would be a more popular and profitable work than such a collection," but warned that "it would cost you years of labor."[10] Belknap and Hazard were part of a circle that assisted one another in historical pursuits; other members included William Gordon, David Ramsay, and Jedidiah Morse.[11]

In the warm glow of an exuberant independence, plans were formulated in the 1780's for national education, and, naturally, history was assigned a special place. "Above all," wrote Benjamin Rush, who was prominent in this movement, "let our youth be instructed in the history of the ancient republics, and the progress of liberty and tyranny in the different states of Europe." The young student was also to familiarize himself with American history, in particular the years just ended. Webster believed that the principal schoolbook in the country should be a manual of American history.

Every phase of American life felt the impact of eighteenth-century

[9] Cf. L. N. Richardson, *A History of Early American Magazines 1741–1789* (New York, 1931).

[10] Mass. Hist. Soc. *Collections,* 5th ser., Vol. III (1877), 258; May 16, 1791.

[11] Mass. Hist. Soc. *Collections,* 6th ser., Vol. IV (1891), 151; September 13, 1779; also Hazard MSS in Library of Congress.

rationalism which pervaded analyses of all aspects of society. Nathaniel Chipman urged a more careful investigation of the laws determining national development. Earlier historians, he maintained, had been too largely concerned with "battles and sieges only, the intrigues of statesmen, and the revolution of empires." For a deeper understanding of civilization, Chipman urged the study of the "history of man in society," and of "the development of the human mind."[12] Still another contemporary writer, Samuel H. Smith, speaking in the accents of the *philosophes,* stressed the educative value of history in liberating man from "fanaticism and superstition"; history would also teach the student to look upon war as the instrument "of vice and folly." A knowledge of the causes of mankind's progress or retrogression, said Smith, would enable man to view his own society more intelligently.[13] The New York lawyer and historian, William Smith, had long before urged the reading of history for prospective members of the bar. He understood also that history was distinguished from chronology and required the student to "take a larger scope."[14]

European observers were interested in the Revolution and sought information from leading Americans. To the Abbé de Mably, John Adams communicated his thoughts on the writing of America's Revolutionary history. After stating that "it is yet too soon to undertake a complete history of that great event," and that no one had the necessary materials for writing it, Adams explained that a writer should divide the history of America into several periods; the first was to 1761, when the disputes began; the second to 1775, fourteen years of "a war of the quill"; thence to 1778, when the "war was exclusively between Great Britain and the United States"; and finally the last period to the peace. "The whole of a long life, to begin at the age of twenty years," said Adams, "will be necessary to assemble from all nations, and from all parts of the world in which they are deposited, the documents proper to form a complete history of the American Revolution, because it is indeed the history of mankind during that epoch. The histories of France, Spain, Holland, England, and the neutral powers, must be united with that of America." Adams suggested a study of four New

[12] A. O. Hansen, *Liberalism and American Education in the Eighteenth Century* (New York, 1926), 56–57, 99.

[13] *Ibid.,* 153.

[14] William Smith's *Common Place Book,* New York Public Library.

England institutions—the towns, congregations, schools, and militia—to learn how the Revolutionary spirit was fostered.[15]

With peace came the histories of the war, and it was from the *Annual Register* (published under auspices friendly to America) that historians secured their material. Such was their debt to this English publication, that Orin G. Libby, writing on "Some Pseudo-Histories of the American Revolution," referred to seven works that plagiarized from this same source.[16] There were historians, however, whose work was original; among them Benjamin Trumbull, who reflected the sentiment of his contemporaries: "After the revolutionary war," he said, "it was the desire of many pious men, that the remarkable deliverances, which the United States of America had experienced might be fully exhibited to the public, as a tribute of praise to their Great Deliverer, and for the instruction of posterity." Such writing would bring the people of the country "into a more general acquaintance with each other," he said, "awaken their mutual sympathies, promote their union and general welfare."[17]

The phrases of Trumbull indicated that historians were still tracing the finger of God in history and that the past was to be studied for a guide to social behavior. With respect to the latter point, Trumbull and all the proponents of national education were in accord with one of the greatest historians of their century—Voltaire. The latter, like his fellows of the Enlightenment, looked upon the study of history as a training valuable in creating a virtuous citizenry. The historian was to describe the progress of society to his own day, presumably the highest goal yet achieved, and he was to suggest as well the lines of future conduct. Voltaire's writings were widely read overseas. That alert Boston clergyman Jonathan Mayhew wrote to Harvard's benefactor, Thomas Hollis, in thanks for the gift of Voltaire's *Philosophy of History* and the *Philosophical Dictionary*. He disagreed with their religious ideas, but added: "I cannot but think, these, as compositions, to be very fine performances. I have read them with delight, as containing much useful learning . . . & written throughout in a most spirited, entertaining & masterly way; so that I would not be long without them for twice their value."[18]

[15] *Works of John Adams* (10 vols., Boston, 1850–56), V, 491–96.

[16] Wisconsin Academy of Sciences, Arts and Letters, *Transactions,* Vol. XIII (1901), 419.

[17] *A General History of the United States of America* (Boston, 1810), preface.

[18] Bancroft *Transcripts,* January 7, 1766, New York Public Library.

Where earlier historians had seen the working of God's will, later writers saw the working of natural laws and were disinclined to observe providential interference in history. But throughout the nineteenth century and to our own day, despite the development of "scientific" history, there was a strong tendency to make history a lay sermon instructing the reader to enlightened social conduct. Although the lessons in modern histories may be somewhat different and their didactic quality less obvious than those of colonial histories, in spirit they are less widely separated than may superficially appear.

THOMAS HUTCHINSON

It is a significant fact that some of the most valuable histories of the Revolutionary era were written by men who became loyalists—Hutchinson, Hewat, Proud, and Chalmers. The tone of their works was conservative, and their concern was generally to justify the established order. Fate placed them on the defeated side, but the loss of men such as these historians had an adverse effect on the intellectual life of the young republic for a whole generation.

Thomas Hutchinson, historian, was but one aspect of a personality that devoted itself to a long life of public service which was cut off by the war of independence. Hutchinson's forebears had been prominent in Massachusetts from its early days. As a young man he was interested in politics, and in 1737 he entered the legislature, where he became an expert on public finance. During his long career he held the offices of chief justice, lieutenant-governor, and governor, gaining with each step the increasing confidence of a larger number of voters. The British government, too, had learned to place a similar confidence in Hutchinson. It was his fate to attempt the part of moderator between two antagonists who had passed beyond the stage of reasoning. Radical Americans would not listen to his words of loyalism; British ministers scorned his provincial advice.

Hutchinson left Massachusetts in 1774, never to return, although his spirit, spent in futility in London, sought anchorage in his native home. "I am not able to subdue a natural attachment to the very soil and air, as well as to the people of New England," he wrote in his exile. In these last bitter years of frustration, the historian found solace in the completion of his history. In his diary for October, 1778, he wrote: "I finished the revisal of my History, to the end of my Administration, and laid it by." The last volume remained in manuscript for fifty years before it was published in London, in 1828.

Even as a boy Hutchinson favored the study of history. From New England chronicles he went on to histories of Great Britain. "The history of Great Britain and of its dominions," he said, "was of all others the most delightful to me; and a thorough knowledge of the nature and constitution of the supreme and of the subordinate governments thereof, I considered as what would be peculiarly beneficial to me in the line of life upon which I was entering." Hutchinson was chiefly interested in institutional history, and his favored position made it possible to gather a great many manuscripts relating to New England. In the true spirit of the historian he explained that men were interested in the past because of the need to prolong their lives "to the utmost length."

In the last days of 1764 appeared the first volume of *The History of the Colony of Massachusetts Bay,* which brought the story to 1691. Following his political narrative, Hutchinson included chapters on religion, the laws, Indians, and the geographical conditions of settlement. He could on occasion be critical of his native province, as he was in recording the persecution of the Quakers. In a reflective passage the historian wrote that "after forty years, the greatest part of our first emigrants had finished their pilgrimage, and were arrived at the place of their everlasting abode. Some of them lamented their being born too soon to see New England in its most flourishing state. This will be the case," Hutchinson prophesied, "with their posterity for many generations to come." On the proud note that history could offer no parallel to the speed of American material development, Hutchinson closed.

The welcome reception accorded this volume stimulated Hutchinson to continue his history, and he had made considerable progress on it, carrying his story to 1730, when the political storm broke. In the summer of 1765, Stamp Act rioters broke into Lieutenant-Governor Hutchinson's home and scattered his possessions in the muddy streets. "But the loss to be most lamented," wrote a contemporary observer, "is that there was in one room, kept for that purpose, a large and valuable collection of manuscripts and original papers which he had been gathering all his lifetime. . . . As these related to the history and policy of the country, from the time of its settlement to the present, and was the only collection of its kind, the loss to the public is great and irretrievable." With the help of a friend, Hutchinson managed to recover the manuscript of the second volume of his *History,* which had been tossed about with other papers, and it bears to this day the mud stains of Boston's riotous streets of 1765. After bringing the story of the province down to 1750, he published it in 1767.[19]

The calm and moderate tone of the first volume was also characteristic of the second, despite the savage events that marked its progress. With much dignity, Hutchinson wrote in the preface to Volume II: "We shall never all be of one mind in our political principles." The author rarely permitted his personal feelings to intrude, believing it the historian's function to tell a disinterested story. A good account of the witchcraft episode was in these pages, and Hutchinson's words were sharp when he wrote: "In all ages of the world superstitious credulity has produced greater cruelty than is practised among the Hottentots, or other nations, whose belief of a deity is called in question." Like many another rationalist, Hutchinson, though liberal in intellectual matters, was conservative in politics: "In a well constituted government it is of importance to the people that the share even of the popular part of the constitution should not be unduly raised to the suppression of the monarchical or aristocratical parts." This volume contained a long narrative of the controversy between the advocates of paper money and the defenders of "hard money," among whom was numbered Hutchinson himself.

The third and last volume covered the period 1750–74, during which the author was very active in Revolutionary controversies. Even in this final volume, finished amid alien surroundings, though Hutchinson wrote about events that burned deep in his soul, no bitterness was revealed; for example, there was a very straightforward account of the Stamp Act riots. In the sadness of exile he knew the costs of civil war, and he wrote movingly of its evils. The judicial temper of Hutchinson's mind remained unruffled; his portraits of some political adversaries, though unflattering, were largely true. A few months before the first volume had come off the press, Hutchinson told Stiles that he might write a book on his own period, and remarked not ill-naturedly, "I threaten Mr. Otis sometimes that I will be revenged of him after I am dead."

Although Hutchinson was sincere in his aim to write the truth, being mortal he failed at various points. Despite his great industry, his public

[19] L. S. Mayo, Amer. Antiq. Soc. *Proceedings* (October, 1931); Hutchinson's second volume benefited from friendly criticisms of the first.

life exacted so much of his energy that he had not sufficient time to examine many pamphlets, newspapers, and legislative documents that might have served as corrective to some of his judgments. As a stylist, too, he was deficient, and he knew it. He once explained that his work was unpolished because the constant calls of public business never gave him time "to write two sheets at a sitting."[20] He confessed that he had "no talent at painting, or describing characters," adding that "it requires great delicacy." Perhaps the historian was too modest, for his literary skill increased the more he wrote, though he never spoke the language touched with magic. The writing had the vigor of the author's personality, and in his character portraits, Hutchinson often wrote very well. In fact, the modern reader usually finds these personal sketches the most interesting portions of the *History*. As the number of his pages lengthened, the note of political conservatism strengthened—a natural consequence of the stand the author took in the Revolutionary controversies.

Hutchinson's book was the first general history of that province which produced so many historians. One authority, William F. Poole, said that Hutchinson's three-volume *History* and his one-volume *Collection of Original Papers relative to the History . . . of Massachusetts Bay* (1769) were "the four most precious books" relating to that period of American history. The severest modern critic of Hutchinson, A. C. Goodell, charged that the historian did not make the best use of the materials at his command. The basis of his work, the legislative journals of governor and council, was inadequate, said Goodell, who further criticized Hutchinson for omitting a survey of the advance of civilization in New England in the eighteenth century.[21] While this criticism is, in some respects, justifiable, Hutchinson's work nevertheless ranks above all other colonial historians. His organization of materials and his historical sense were far beyond most of his contemporaries. His analysis of the Revolutionary controversy showed greater objectivity and was nearer the truth than that of any succeeding historian for almost a century.[22]

[20] J. K. Hosmer, *Life of Hutchinson* (Boston, 1896), 85–86.

[21] *American Historical Review*, Vol. II (October, 1896), 163–70.

[22] L. S. Mayo (ed.), Hutchinson's *The History of the Colony and Province of Massachusetts Bay* (3 vols., Cambridge, Mass., 1936).

ROBERT PROUD

Hutchinson was not the only historian whose work, written during the war years, awaited quieter days for publication. Robert Proud's *History of Pennsylvania* (2 vols., 1797–98), was written between 1776 and 1780, "but the great change in this country, which ensued," prevented publication at that time. In the spirit of Thomas Prince he answered for the authenticity of his materials. In the view of Proud, who was a loyalist, Pennsylvania's golden age lay in the past, before the Revolutionary years had tarnished its glory.

Proud was in his early thirties when he landed in Philadelphia from England in 1759. In his new home he became an instructor in a school conducted by fellow Quakers, where he remained until the outbreak of the Revolution. His loyalist associations during the war soured him against his rebellious neighbors. During the war he wrote to his brother in England that he "lived in a very private and retired Way, even like a Person dead amidst the Confusions, and conversing more with my Books than with Persons."[23]

Proud's history opened with a long introduction containing the memoirs of William Penn and an account of the rise of the Quakers. The historian described Penn's effort to obtain the grant, including in his narrative complete versions of important documents and letters. In the manner of other contemporary histories, Proud's writing was often a mere thread connecting pages of documents. The second volume continued from the year 1709 to 1771, but after 1725 the narrative was very thin and the selections from documents much fewer. Proud concluded the history proper with some characteristic remarks: "Thus far appears the manner of the rise, colonization, increase and happy establishment of the flourishing province of Pennsylvania, which . . . from a wilderness, became as a fruitful field. . . . But all things have their time. And both kingdoms and empires, as well as smaller states, and particular persons, must die."

Although the historical narrative was inadequate for the later years of the colony's history, the hundred pages or more that described the province in the ten years following 1760 offered some compensation. The historian of Pennsylvania took great pride in the number of hu-

[23] See Proud's letters in *Pennsylvania Magazine of History and Biography,* Vol. XXXIV (1910), 62–73.

mane institutions in his province. With justice, Proud made much of the religious toleration that prevailed in Pennsylvania. As did other historians of the time, he included many details on the Indians, but his critical sense was much sharper than that of most writers on the subject.

In a lengthy appendix the historian gathered documents that he could not fit into the text. At a time when these papers were scattered in various places, if in print at all, Proud's diligence in grouping them together was of real value. A fellow-Pennsylvanian over a hundred years ago correctly appraised Proud's history: "It is exactly that stately old fashioned article that its author himself was."[24]

ALEXANDER HEWAT

Historians of the South in the colonial period were few compared with their contemporaries in the North. Apart from Virginia, they were very rare and continued to be so for many years. During the Revolutionary era, however, when the English were eager for information on all parts of the empire, there began to appear historical material on the lesser-known colonies. In 1779 a two-volume work was published in London by Alexander Hewat, *An Historical Account of ... South Carolina and Georgia;* the major portion of the history dealt with South Carolina. Hewat had migrated from Scotland to Charleston, where, as a Presbyterian minister, he was in a position to learn much of the character of American society. Although he sided with the loyalists when the war broke out, and returned to Britain, his friendly relations with some of his neighbors in Charleston were maintained to the end of his life.

Hewat modestly referred to his work as "only a rough draught" intended to acquaint England with the commercial possibilities of the Southern colonies. Like others writing on Southern history, he could not resist a criticism of New England: "We may challenge the annals of any nation," he said, "to produce a code of laws more intolerant than that of the first settlers in New England."

The first volume ended with the change from the proprietary form of government in South Carolina to a royal province in 1728. A good deal of social history, as well as some natural history, was interspersed in this political narrative, but it was rarely related to the theme of politics. Hewat spoke of a new era in the government of South Carolina

[24] See biographical sketch of Proud by C. W. Thomson, Hist. Soc. of Penn., *Memoirs,* Vol. I (1826), 391–408.

when it became a royal province—an era of freedom, security, and happiness. He presented a good firsthand description of life in South Carolina —manners, the state of learning among the people, and the like. The narrative was brought down to the outbreak of the Revolution, and, although Hewat promised to write further on the subject, he published nothing more. In naming the causes for the disputes with the mother country, he made some interesting observations on the development of the colonial consciousness of power and the gradual rise in disaffection toward the mother country among the second and third generations of colonists.

Hewat's book was the first history of South Carolina and as such deserves the praise any pioneering work merits. David Ramsay, a contemporary historian, in recommending it to Belknap, said it was unsafe on the background of the war because of the author's Tory sentiments, but on other matters, "you may rely on his accounts."[25] Historians, including Bancroft, years afterward turned to the pages of Hewat for material not readily available elsewhere.

GEORGE CHALMERS

George Chalmers was one of the ablest historians in eighteenth-century America. In the early years of the troublous 1760's he had gone from Edinburgh to Maryland, where he practiced law. When the war of independence broke out, he sailed for London, where he was appointed to an important government post. There his official connection gave him access to state papers which he used intelligently in discussing many historical problems.

Chalmers believed that an examination of the development of the relations between England and the colonies would show that the constitutional position maintained by the rebellious Americans was wrong. With this thesis in mind, he published his *Political Annals of the Present United Colonies . . .* (1780), which narrated their history to the revolution of 1689. He observed that, although much attention had been given to the history of Great Britain and Ireland, neglect had too often been the portion of "that considerable part of the empire, the British colonies."

Chalmers said that he was issuing his volume because he thought "that it might at this time possibly do some good." His sources included

[25] Mass. Hist. Soc. *Collections,* 6th ser., Vol. IV (1891), 568–69; March 13, 1794.

the acts of assemblies, the printed collections of state papers, and the journals of the Board of Trade and Plantations—materials which contained items generally unfamiliar to other historians. "He hath always cited minutely the various authorities on which he relied," wrote Chalmers in the third person, "partly in order to authenticate his own assertions, but more to enable succeeding writers . . . to pursue his track with greater ease to themselves and advantage to the world."

Chalmers' examination of the legal status of the colonies left him critical of their demands. He was especially hostile to New England, and in general, to the whole North. "In the colonists of the south, we see a just regard to their liberties as Englishmen, and to the laws of the state; but in the proceedings of those of the north, we behold their characteristic principles breaking out; and their expressions of 'dependence upon England, and relationship to it,' were at that time what they have always been, mere words. For the essence of subordination is obedience." A marked characteristic of New England, said Chalmers, was "that she has at all times found delight amid scenes of turbulence."

At the close of his volume the author described the privileges emigrants really could claim as subjects of the crown in 1689: "The various plantations formed no more than the dependencies of a great kingdom which directed their affairs. And they enjoyed no portion of sovereignty." But the colonists, Chalmers added, "enjoyed perfect freedom" though their legislatures were restrained. Colonists were not inferior to Englishmen because both were equally subject to the king; "Colonial legislatures were only subordinate because they were neither co-ordinate nor supreme." Where the colonies invoked doctrines of natural rights to establish their claims, Chalmers traced the historical development of the colonies to prove those claims unwarranted.

Chalmers later brought out another work, his *Introduction to the History of the Revolt of the American Colonies,* in which he intended to prove that from an early date the colonists had aimed at independence, and secondly, that the British government had exhibited tragic negligence in permitting the provincial assemblies to increase their authority. Although he failed to substantiate his first thesis, he was successful in proving the second. The correspondence of governors and other crown officers in the colonies formed the basis for much of Chalmers' work. Obviously this meant that only the British official point of view was presented. "Yet we are enabled to ascertain from these volumes, better than from any others," wrote the editor of the Boston edition (1845), "the kind of intelligence which the ministers received from their agents in America, and to arrive at a clearer understanding of the grounds of their public acts."

Chalmers continued to show the same partiality to the Southern colonies that he had exhibited in the *Political Annals*. "The original Virginians," he wrote, "transmitted habits of respect for the constitution of England, which long engaged their obedience to her rules. . . . The enthusiasts, who planted New England derided the authority of their native land . . . and forming systems on congenial principles, they acted during sixty years rather as the allies than subjects of the state." Chalmers further charged that the "contagion" of the New England spirit of independence even before the end of the seventeenth century "soon overspread the southern colonies."

Although the books of Chalmers were thought to be unfair by many Americans, they were of value in stimulating them to a fresh study of their own history. His work, said one, "has ever been quoted by American writers with entire confidence and respect. . . . Judging from the free use which has constantly been made of [the *Political Annals*] . . . we may justly regard it as holding an important place in our historical literature." The fault of Chalmers was the fault of many of the most eminent Englishmen of his day in their attitude toward the colonies. He placed too great an emphasis on the legalistic approach to the problems that confronted the mother country and her rebellious provinces. In his later life the historian was reported as saying that the mother country should have yielded to expediency and not insisted on her legal rights in her relations with the colonies.[26] For many years American historians, even when they disagreed with details in Chalmers' work, looked to it as a standard by which to gauge the merit of their own achievements.

WILLIAM GORDON

Historians who lived in the Revolutionary era, even when writing on earlier periods, reflected the heightened pulse of the public. The nearer the writers approached the Revolution, the greater the acceleration of

[26] H. B. Adams, *Life and Writings of Jared Sparks* (2 vols., Boston, 1893), II, 383–84; see G. A. Cockroft, *The Public Life of George Chalmers* (New York, 1939), 57–63.

the pulse beat, although some authors maintained a fairly even temper in the course of writing their narratives. These historians were familiar with many of the events and personalities they described; thus their volumes were credited with veracity. But in the case of at least two, Gordon and Ramsay, that confidence seems to have been misplaced. For a hundred years William Gordon received respectful attention from students of American history because of the contribution he was supposed to have made to its records. And then an inquisitive scholar discovered it was all a mistake, that Gordon's history was not his own.

Gordon, who had come to America from England in 1770, was an ardent participant in colonial politics, although many American leaders were scarcely friendly to him. John Adams, for one, wrote in 1775: "I fear his indiscreet prate will do harm. . . . He is an eternal talker and somewhat vain, and not accurate nor judicious." Gordon appreciated the significance of current events, and he determined to collect information from the leading actors in America. He wrote to Adams, asking for assistance, mentioning that others, including Washington, had given him access to papers: "I am collecting materials for an history of the rise, progress, and successful issue of the American revolution."

When the war was over, Gordon thought that it would be safer to write his history in England, at which distance his intended impartial remarks on the colonies would prove less dangerous to his person. To Horatio Gates he wrote in 1782: "Should Great Britain mend its constitution by the shock it has rec'd . . . life liberty and character will be safer there than on this side the Atlantic; and an Historian may use the impartial pen there with less danger than here."[27] Unfortunately for Gordon, he found that England also objected to an impartial history. John Adams, then in London as American representative, described what had happened to Gordon's history. "His object was profit. He was told that his book would not sell if printed according to his manuscript. It was accordingly thrown into a new form of letters between a gentleman in England and one in America . . . the style and spirit was altered and accomodated more to the British taste and feelings. . . . Had the original manuscript been printed the work would have appeared very differently."

In February, 1789, Gordon wrote to Washington that he was send-

[27] "Letters of William Gordon," Mass. Hist. Soc. *Proceedings,* Vol. LXIII (1931), 309–613.

ing him the four volumes of his history, which had been published toward the close of the previous year; its title was *The History of the Rise, Progress and Establishment of the Independence of the United States of America. . . .* In his letter to Washington, Gordon revealed his standard of scholarship: "I apprehended it to be often necessary to introduce sentiments and information, while I suppressed the names of the writers from whose letters they were taken, and at times inserted them as though they were originally my own."

A modern student, Orin G. Libby, showed that Gordon inserted far more than he admitted.[28] Gordon's history copied the *Annual Register* "wholesale," said Libby, so that it is "one of the most complete plagiarisms on record." Nearly all the material available to him in America had been collected to no purpose—the *Annual Register* was evidently a more convenient source. Gordon was also heavily indebted to Ramsay's *History of the Revolution in South Carolina.* Ramsay had been kind enough to send Gordon his manuscript, but the latter was sufficiently unkind to use it frequently with no acknowledgment. The volumes of Gordon, once prized by Edward Channing as "the most valuable history of the Revolution from a British pen," have now been entirely rejected as a source for this period.

DAVID RAMSAY

For more than a century the work of David Ramsay, physician and distinguished political figure in South Carolina, had been looked upon with favor as historical literature of a high order. But he suffered the same deflation of a well-established reputation that William Gordon did.

Ramsay published *The History of the Revolution of South Carolina* in 1785, and four years later he brought out *The History of the American Revolution.* Both works were republished in Europe, the second appearing in several English editions and in translations on the Continent. He said that he had been collecting materials for years while he was a member of Congress and had "access to all the official papers of the United States." "Every letter written to Congress by General Washington," he said, "was carefully perused and its contents noted."

Despite Ramsay's opportunities for gathering materials, his claims

[28] O. G. Libby, "A critical examination of Gordon's *History of the American Revolution,*" American Historical Association *Annual Report* for the year 1899, Vol. I (1900), 365–83.

will no longer impress the reader. Libby, who had done a similar disservice for Gordon, proved beyond question that Ramsay plagiarized many of his pages from that fertile source of many histories—the *Annual Register*. Instead of utilizing the documents that were near at hand, Ramsay copied them as they were printed in the *Register*. He and Gordon, in many cases, had copied identical passages from the *Register*. Ramsay's account of events in the South, where he was presumably on familiar ground, also showed plagiarisms from the same periodical. Gordon and Ramsay changed indirect discourse to direct discourse in using the *Register*. "Each copied from the other," concluded Libby, "and the fault was shared mutually." The fault might also have been shared by publishers who wanted to profit from public interest in the American Revolution and encouraged the hasty preparation of books to meet the demand.

JEREMY BELKNAP

Jeremy Belknap belongs in the very front rank of historians who wrote in the Revolutionary period. So close in spirit to the modern historian was his approach that his work has been of lasting value. He was born in Boston in 1744 and received his education at Harvard. When he was twenty-two years of age, he was ministering to the religious needs of the community of Dover, New Hampshire, remaining there until 1786. After difficulties with his congregation he accepted a call to Boston the next year, and from then to the end of his life Belknap was satisfied with an arrangement that left him time for his literary activities.

Belknap had from his youth been interested in history, which his teacher, Thomas Prince, had strongly fostered. He was still a college student when he indicated his awareness of the high standards demanded of historians: "There are required so many qualifications and accomplishments in an Historian, and so much care and niceness in writing an history that some have reckoned it one of the most difficult labors human nature is capable of."[29]

In New Hampshire he gathered written and oral records, accepting hearsay with proper caution. To his correspondent, Ebenezer Hazard, he wrote of hunting in "garrets and ratholes of old houses" for private papers when not one paper in a hundred "would repay him for the

[29] J. S. Bassett, *The Middle Group of American Historians* (New York, 1917), 28.

trouble."[30] During the feverish days before military hostilities began, Belknap had stirred up enthusiasm for the patriot cause, and in the pages of his history describing the Revolution his feeling was too strong to be bound by the canons of impartiality.

In 1784, the first volume of Belknap's *History of New Hampshire* was published; it was, said the author, the first comprehensive narrative of that state. From the height of a rationalist's stand Belknap looked back scornfully to Puritan intolerance and seventeenth-century superstition. Speaking of King Philip's War, he said: "Our gravest historians have recorded many omens, predictions, and other alarming circumstances during this and the Pequot war, which in a more philosophical and less credulous age would not be worthy of notice." To his good friend Hazard, he once uttered the wish that they could be together to laugh at Mather's *Wonders of the Invisible World*.[31]

Undismayed by a discouraging public reception, Belknap went on with his history and brought out a second volume in 1791, followed by a third the next year. When, on the appearance of the first volume, Hazard urged him to hurry along the second, Belknap replied that it would take a few years. The first took him, "off and on, nine or ten years," he said, and then he added: "I know that it might be run through in a much shorter time by a Grub Street Gazetteer, who would take everything on trust and had materials ready prepared."[32]

In writing his second volume (1715–90), Belknap took issue with Chalmers' description of the people of New Hampshire, and on other matters, also, he differed with that well-known authority. A very interesting sentence near the close of this volume illustrated Belknap's perspicacity. "By the funding of the Continental debt, and the assumption of the debts of the individual states, into one general mass," he said, "a foundation is laid for the support of public credit; by which means the American revolution appears to be completed."

The last volume had a geographical description of the state, its natural history, the condition of its society, its manners, laws, and government. The list of subscribers indicated that many of the leading citizens of the country had begun to show an interest in Belknap's work. The

[30] Mass. Hist. Soc. *Collections,* 5th ser., Vol. II (1877), 293–98; January 13, 1784.

[31] Mass. Hist. Soc. *Collections,* 5th ser., Vol. III (1877), 198; October 22, 1789.

[32] Bassett, *The Middle Group of American Historians,* 40–41.

many technical difficulties in publishing the history made it impossible to produce as finished a product as Belknap would have wished; for example, it missed the benefit that his proofreading might have given it.[33] But qualified critics knew the virtues of his work. Tocqueville, in the 1830's, said that Belknap had "more general ideas and more strength of thought, than are to be met with in other historians, even to the present day."

While working on his history Belknap broached the idea of collecting the lives of noted Americans in an "American Biographical Dictionary."[34] Hazard and he worked on the project together, but for many years it lagged. Finally, in 1794, the first volume of the *American Biography* was published, and in 1798, the second. Considering the time and the limited materials available, the whole was a very creditable performance. Before Belknap's death, collections for a third volume had been begun, and to complete it, Hazard proposed a co-operative work, each contributor writing one life.[35]

From the fertile minds of Belknap and Hazard came fruitful ideas, sometimes a century in advance of their day. It was a long time before historians adopted the view Hazard expressed in a letter to Belknap: "British emissaries," he said, "have diligently propagated an idea that the Colonies were disaffected to the royal government, and thirsted after independence; and I think it a duty incumbent on every American historian to use his endeavours to wipe off so unjust an aspersion."[36] On the eve of the Revolution, Hazard had suggested to Jefferson that American state papers should be collected and published. Jefferson responded favorably, observing how much it would ease the path of "any historical genius which may happen to arise."

Belknap was chiefly responsible for the formation of the Massachusetts Historical Society; he was its leading member in its early years.[37] The long and valuable series of the Society's publications date from

[33] L. S. Mayo, "Jeremy Belknap and Ebenezer Hazard, 1782–1784," *New England Quarterly,* Vol. II (April, 1929), 183–98.

[34] J. B. Marcou, *Life of Jeremy Belknap,* 214; letters of May 12, 1779.

[35] Mass. Hist. Soc. *Collections,* 5th ser., Vol. III (1877); October 28, 1803.

[36] Mass. Hist. Soc. *Collections,* 5th ser., Vol. II (1877), 119–26; March 20, 1782; April 10, 1782.

[37] Mass. Hist. Soc. *Collections,* 5th ser., Vol. III (1877), 157, 165, 244–45; 6th ser., Vol. IV (1891), 446–48; August 26, 1788.

1792, when the first volume of its *Collections* was published, largely through Belknap's efforts.

Belknap's work as a historian was of the first importance, but perhaps of equal significance was the enthusiasm for historical study that he evoked in others. He was the first, said William Cullen Bryant, "to make American history attractive."[38] The death of so illustrious a scholar was a deep blow to New England. Writing to an American correspondent, Christoph D. Ebeling, the noted German historian of America, who knew Belknap's worth, said: "He died, alas, too early for your literature and history."[39] The small circle of people devoted to history with whom he gathered in the 1790's widened steadily in the following years, and the standards of Belknap's scholarship were a guide to excellence.

GEORGE MINOT

Historical writing has always been an instrument of party warfare, and its function in ideological conflicts was clearly recognized by Americans. Federalists were heirs to loyalist conservatism; Jeffersonians established a democratic tradition. George Minot and John Marshall were strong Federalists; Mrs. Mercy Warren, of Massachusetts, and John Daly Burk, historian of Virginia, belonged to the school of Jefferson.

George Minot was one of the earliest historians to fashion a Federalist view of American history. Unlike some students who sought political guidance from ancient history, Minot drew a lesson from the events of his own day to stress the value of strong government. Shays' Rebellion had caused shivers to run up and down the spines of conservatives, and Minot shared their anxiety. His volume, *The History of the Insurrections in the year 1786* . . . (1788), giving only the Federalist side of the controversy, failed to explain why the debt-burdened farmers flouted authority.

Minot belonged to the Boston group which recalled with mingled feelings the history that Hutchinson had left unfinished when he departed for England in 1774. Although the portrait of Hutchinson was maliciously etched in the mind of Mercy Otis Warren by her acid recollections, other historians felt no strong enmity against the governor

[38] S. A. Eliot, "Jeremy Belknap," Mass. Hist. Soc. *Proceedings,* Vol. LXVI (1942), 102–103.

[39] W. C. Lane, "Letters of Christoph D. Ebeling," Amer. Antiq. Soc. *Proceedings,* Vol. XXXV, Part 2 (October, 1925), 306; letter to Rev. Wm. Bentley, September 16, 1798.

who had died an exile in London. Rather there seemed to be disappointment that the history of Massachusetts, begun by Hutchinson, remained incomplete. Minot set himself the task of picking up the narrative where Hutchinson had left off in his second volume. In 1798 the former published his *Continuation of the History of . . . Massachusetts Bay,* which covered the eight years after 1748. Minot was at work on a second volume when he died in 1802, and it was brought out, unfinished, the next year. It ended with the Stamp Act riots of 1765, which elicited the condemnation of the historian who had treated in similar fashion Daniel Shays; the mob that destroyed Hutchinson's home was referred to as a "triumphant demonocracy."

Minot, who had had a thorough legal training and held a judicial position, gave a good account of the constitutional questions at issue between Massachusetts and England. His sources were few, but among them were the manuscripts of Jasper Mauduit, the colony's agent in England. Hutchinson, it will be remembered, did add a third volume to his own history, and with its publication in 1828, Minot's work was entirely eclipsed. His volume on Shays' Rebellion, however, was widely used and helped perpetuate the conservative interpretation of those troubled times.

HANNAH ADAMS

In the Revolutionary era proposals were made by various writers for histories of all the New England states and even for the whole United States. Benjamin Rush, for example, asked Belknap to write the history of the establishment of the federal government.[40] There was, however, more talk than action. A volume that attempted to fill the need for an inclusive survey was *A Summary History of New England . . .* (1799) by Hannah Adams. Miss Adams, a distant cousin of John Adams, was reputed to be the first American women to earn her livelihood by writing. "It was poverty,"she said, "that first induced me to become an author, or rather a compiler."[41] Her life spanned the period of the Revolution and the first thirty years of the nineteenth century. Toward the end of her life her friends (and there were many among the literati) settled an annuity upon her, and the timid, absent-minded old lady spent her last years poring over ancient tomes in the Boston Athenaeum.

[40] Mass. Hist. Soc., *Collections,* 6th ser., Vol. IV (1891), 473; January 5, 1791.
[41] *A Memoir of Miss Hannah Adams, Written by Herself* (1832), 22.

Miss Adams followed the procedure of other contemporary historians—she compiled her book on New England from the few volumes of history that had been written up to that time. She also quoted from Ezra Stiles' manuscript lectures on ecclesiastical history, which supplied much of her material on the state of learning in New England. In keeping with the spirit of her day, Miss Adams was critical of the intolerance of the early settlers. When her narrative approached the Revolution she mentioned the opposition that had been aroused by the proposed establishment of the Anglican episcopacy. Almost half of her volume was on the Revolution, and she drew much from Ramsay and Gordon, who were then considered the leading historians of the war. From the pages of Minot, the historian extracted a Federalist interpretation of Shays' Rebellion, and in Morse's *Geography* Miss Adams found the materials for her section on literature. An abridgment of the *Summary History* for the use of school children was published in 1807; this, too, was accorded a friendly welcome in New England. While Miss Adams' history was inadequate, there were few alternatives to her work at the beginning of the nineteenth century.

MERCY OTIS WARREN

A lady with an illustrious name, Mercy Otis Warren, set down her record of the Revolutionary era, her relationship with many of its leading figures having given her a special insight into the events of these years. The sister of James Otis and the wife of James Warren, she shared their intensely patriotic view of the struggle. It was in the home of Thomas Hutchinson, bought by the Warrens, that she wrote much of the history that singled out the exiled governor for her bitter scorn. In 1805 Mrs. Warren brought out her three-volume *History of the . . . American Revolution. . . .* Although published more than a score of years after the treaty of peace, Mrs. Warren said that she had been collecting materials "many years antecedent to any history since published"; it is probable that much of her work was written contemporaneously with the events described.

During the Revolution, Abigail Adams, wife of John Adams, had written to Mrs. Warren that "many very memorable events which ought to be handed down to posterity will be buried in oblivion merely for want of a proper hand to record them." Adams gave Mrs. Warren first-hand information regarding his negotiations with the Dutch; and a few years later another noted figure in Massachusetts politics, Benjamin Lincoln, offered the use of his papers to the historian.[42]

After some introductory remarks, Mrs. Warren began her history with the Stamp Act, and quickly the family bias toward Hutchinson became apparent. In the eyes of the historian, the governor was "dark, intriguing, insinuating, haughty and ambitious, while the extreme of avarice marked each feature of his character"; Machiavelli, she indicated, was his teacher. Most of Mrs. Warren's work dealt with military hostilities, and she broadened her study of the years of strife to include references to discontent in Ireland and domestic politics in England, which she attempted to relate to the American Revolution. The widening of the area of conflict, in Mediterranean and West Indian waters, was reflected in the enlarged scope of Mrs. Warren's history. In thus making her work more comprehensive, she was in accord with John Adams, who held that to write on the American Revolution one must write the history of mankind during that period. After her description of the war, said the author, her mind was "now at leisure for more general observations on the subsequent consequences, without confining it to time or place." The remarks that followed on the later history of the United States were practically valueless as historical writing. As honest John Adams bluntly wrote to Mrs. Warren: "After the termination of the Revolutionary war your subject was completed."[43]

A long correspondence with Mrs. Warren, initiated by Adams who felt himself aspersed by the historian, made a valuable addition to the work because of the inclusion of many interesting items on our diplomatic history. The Warren leaning to Jeffersonianism was a cause of friction with Adams, although friendly relations between the families were maintained to the end. Adams remarked ungallantly that history was "not the Province of the Ladies." "It is my opinion," he said, "that your History has been written to the taste of the nineteenth century, and accommodated to gratify the passions, prejudices, and feelings of the party who are now predominant."[44] To which she replied by saying that her history had been under consideration long before the nineteenth century and had received encouragement from Adams himself. Mrs.

[42] "Warren-Adams Letters," Mass. Hist. Soc. *Collections,* Vol. LXXII (1917); August 14, 1777; Vol. LXXIII (1925); October 24, 1782, March 25, 1790.

[43] Mass. Hist. Soc. *Collections,* 5th ser., Vol. IV (1878), 432; August 8, 1807.

[44] *Ibid.,* 463, 489–90.

Warren's writing was often diffuse, and her rhetorical passages were typical patriotic orations. To read her history is to get a vivid glimpse of the thoughts and feelings of many Revolutionary leaders.

JOHN DALY BURK

The spirit of Jefferson that hovered over Mrs. Warren's history completely suffused Burk's history of the Old Dominion. John Daly Burk was one of many Irish political refugees who came to America at the end of the eighteenth century. From New York he eventually found his way to Virginia, where, under Jefferson's encouragement, he turned to writing a history of his adopted state. (Burk was also a well-known dramatist.) The first three volumes of his *History of Virginia* . . . were published in 1804 and 1805, but he did not live to complete it. He was killed in a duel in 1808, and the fourth volume, the last published, was completed by two other writers, Skelton Jones and Louis Girardin. Ill fate dogged this work, for Jones had only just begun the last volume when he, too, was killed in a duel. Girardin wrote most of it, with Jefferson watching closely, suggesting content and interpretation.[45]

Burk dedicated his history to Jefferson, who permitted him the use of his library. The author referred briefly to his predecessors in the field: Smith was a "faithful guide" as far as he went, which was only twenty years; Beverley was a "mere annalist of petty incidents" and an "apologist of power." In addition to these authorities Burk claimed to have used the minutes of the London Company and the proceedings of the Virginia legislature; Byrd's manuscripts were also open to him.[46]

The first volume, to 1624, was very full, but the next, which covered almost a century, began to run thin. To "preserve unity and compactness," said Burk, he left out details of revenue and finance, the organization of courts of justice, and the condition of arts and manners. Despite his disparagement of Beverley, Burk freely used his work. The third volume, which brought the narrative to the outbreak of the Revolution, presented opportunities for the full display of the author's rhetoric; with this volume, however, he did something to raise Virginia's history out of its local setting to a place in relationship with the whole colonial

[45] E. Philips, "Louis Hue Girardin and Nicholas Gouin Dufief," Johns Hopkins University *Studies in Romance Literatures and Languages* (extra Vol. III, 1926).

[46] C. Campbell (ed.), *Some Materials to serve for a brief memoir of John Daly Burk* . . . (Albany, 1868), 33.

world. The last volume, on the war, ended with 1781. Although Burk spoke of his acquaintance with valuable sources, he made scarcely any use of the many records readily available. In general, Virginians have not been favorably impressed with his work.[47]

BENJAMIN TRUMBULL

Among the historians of the late eighteenth and early nineteenth centuries who labored to preserve the memorials of an earlier day, none worked harder than Benjamin Trumbull. Practically all his life was associated with his native province, Connecticut, whose history he narrated. For sixty years before his death in 1820 he had been pastor of the North Haven Congregational Church. Although his historical publications did not appear until late in life, Trumbull had been collecting materials over a period of many years.

In 1801 he published *A Century Sermon, or Sketches of the History of the Eighteenth Century. . . .* This was "a sketch of the works of God in the century past," he said, "and especially His dispensations towards America, the United States, New England, and this town" (North Haven). The publication was in the nature of a preliminary survey for Trumbull's larger work on the United States.

That comprehensive work appeared in 1810, *A General History of the United States of America . . . to 1792.* Three volumes were promised. The first took the narrative to the year 1765, but the other two were never published. Trumbull's materials were given to Jedidiah Morse, who was busy on his own historical projects. Trumbull spoke of his work as a thank-offering for divine aid granted to America in the Revolutionary years; his history, he hoped, would promote a national feeling. His difficulties in research were multiplied, he said, because of the interconnection of colonial and British history, "which rendered a constant study of the history of [England] as well as of America necessary to authenticate and elucidate the work." Following a familiar convention he gave much space to Indian civilization. And again, in the usual manner, the beginnings of white settlements were heavily stressed, but the period 1700–50 was hastily skimmed over. The wars from 1748 to 1763 were strongly emphasized, but Trumbull's volume was not badly proportioned, measured by the standards of his day.

The work for which Trumbull is best known is *A Complete His-*

[47] *Virginia Historical Register,* Vol. I (1848), 48.

tory of Connecticut . . . (Vol. I, 1797; 2 vol. edition, 1818). His history had been planned before the Revolution, but the war postponed publication for many years. "As this is the first history of the colony," said Trumbull, "the compiler judged it expedient to make it more full and particular, than otherwise might have been necessary or proper." He wished to assist future historians and was anxious that nothing of importance should be lost. He gave his sources, following a soundly established precedent when he wrote, "very little has been taken upon tradition." Remembering the experiences of Hazard and Belknap, we can well believe Trumbull's statement that "the labor of collecting materials . . . has been almost incredible."

In accordance with his promise Trumbull gave a very detailed and plainly written text. It contained religious, economic, and social history, with much valuable material on the growth of various towns, including even regions outside Connecticut borders. Trumbull thought that New England was settled "purely for the purposes of Religion"; he believed also that New England's treatment of the Indians after the Pequot War was very unfair. He was encyclopedic in his inclusiveness; he "got Connecticut by heart before he began writing its history," said Bancroft. "He could tell the name, birthplace, and career of every minister that had preached a good sermon, and every militiaman that had done a notable thing. Not a savage was overcome, not a backslider censured by the church, but he knew it all."[48] Not only did he know it all, but he felt the necessity to *tell* all, and the details were spun out to tedious length. He was Connecticut's first historian and proudly treasured her facts, observing conscientiously the New England injunction, "Despise not the day of small things."

JEDIDIAH MORSE

Trumbull's younger contemporary, Jedidiah Morse, grew up in the Revolutionary era when the self-consciousness of Americans sought expression in every field. He was born in 1761, attended Yale, became a member of the Society for the Propagation of the Gospel, and took a leading part in the Unitarian controversy that rocked New England. He is better remembered, however, as geographer and historian.

It was when he was teaching in New Haven, in 1783, that Morse became seriously interested in geography. Guthrie's *English Geography*

[48] *North American Review,* Vol. XLVI (April, 1838), 477–79.

was then generally used in American schools, but its materials on America were very thin. The next year Morse put his lectures into a book, *Geography made Easy,* which was the first on the subject published in America. He was constantly gathering information from wide sources, and on his travels he noted additional materials to be included in an enlarged edition of his geography. Belknap told him that "to be a true geographer it is necessary to be a Traveller"; he urged Morse to see things for himself and not get information from authors at second hand.[49]

In March, 1789, Morse's *American Geography* was published; in addition to the geographical material, there was much straight history. Some of his friends thought Morse should have restricted the geography to America exclusively, but he designed it to compete with English geographies then used in American schools. In a later edition he gave even more space to non-American areas. The book was an immediate success and was adopted at Yale as a text. European editions were published also, but in that day of pirating publishers, Morse received no foreign royalties. Ebeling, then the greatest European student of American history and geography, testified to the contribution of Morse "as the first who has cut a road through a vast wilderness."[50] A second edition, called *The American Universal Geography,* was published in two volumes, of which the first was mainly on America.

Morse's books sold so widely that his financial success became a topic of good-natured gossip among his contemporaries. Hazard wrote to Belknap that Morse was the only successful author in their triumvirate, and added with mild regret, "What a pity it is that *we* had not been geographers instead of *historians.*"[51]

Morse next brought out *The American Gazetteer* (1797), containing seven thousand separate articles. On an earlier occasion Morse had observed that Europeans had been the sole writers of American geography and were often inaccurate. "But since the United States have become an independent nation," he continued, "the rest of the world have a right now to expect authentic information." Much of Morse's historical matter was taken from Hazard's work, which was praised as the best collection of facts in American history.

Morse was also engaged in writing and compiling purely historical

[49] W. B. Sprague, *The Life of Jedidiah Morse* (New York, 1874), 193.
[50] *Ibid.,* 205; 1793.
[51] Mass. Hist. Soc. *Collections,* 5th ser., Vol. III (1877), 361, January 14, 1796.

works. With the aid of Rev. Elijah Parish, he wrote *A Compendious History of New England* which went through several editions. It is worth noting that the authors began their history with the Reformation, not with Columbus or some earlier figure; the next step of the historians, who in this respect approached more nearly the modern point of view, was to continue the narrative with the Pilgrims in Holland. One hundred years before J. T. Adams spoke critically of New England's part in the Pequot War, Morse had written: "This is a dismal section of our history. The time has been, when pious Christians had so lost sight of their Saviour's precepts and example as to engage in unnecessary war." Probably Morse's pleasant experience as missionary to the Indians helped dictate his indictment of the early brutality. On the whole this co-operative volume was well written and adequately proportioned. (Hannah Adams indignantly charged the authors with plagiarizing her own work.)

In 1824 Morse brought out his *Annals of the American Revolution* . . . , which included, in its varied features, biographies of the war heroes. He was a tired man by this time and had little interest in the book, saying it was "professedly a compilation," its issue timed to coincide with Lafayette's widely publicized return to America. The most interesting part of the volume was the section which included the letters of Franklin and Adams on the causes of the Revolution. John Adams' letters had been written some years earlier in answer to Morse's inquiries. Though Morse was not proud of his poorly arranged work, Americans had nothing better for many years to come.

JOHN MARSHALL

War heroes were beginning to be commemorated by grateful contemporaries. No one so dominated the American consciousness as did Washington. Chief Justice Marshall's study was classified as a biography, but his five-volume work was in reality a political history of America during the life of the first President. Indeed, the first volume of *The Life of George Washington* . . . (1804–1807) was complete in itself as a history of the colonies. Marshall's public and private associations gained him access to materials that few people of that day could have secured. Bushrod Washington, the President's nephew, urged Marshall to write the biography, and the latter's need for money at the time was one of the impelling causes for undertaking it.[52]

The volume on the colonies was compiled from the few standard authors used by most historians; the writer covering the years to the reign of William and Mary, said Marshall, needed little in addition to George Chalmers. Marshall himself appreciated the inconclusive character of his own work, but he believed there was a place for it in the absence of any other. He was apparently justified, for a reviewer in the Boston *Monthly Anthology* noted that it was the "first attempt to give a connected history of the various states."[53]

Some of the observations made by Marshall anticipated by many years later studies of the colonial period. He referred, for example, to the resolutions of the New York Assembly, in 1711, against taxation without consent: "This strong assertion of a principle, the controversy concerning which afterwards dismembered the British empire, passed away without notice. It was probably understood to be directed only against the assumption of that power by the governor."[54] In speaking of another legal problem, Marshall pointed out that no accurate definition had ever been made of the degree of authority exercisable by the mother country over the colonies: "In Britain, it had always been asserted, that Parliament possessed the power of binding them in all cases whatsoever. In America, at different times, and in different colonies, different opinions had been entertained on this subject." Marshall then went on to present a very good discussion of this question, and in somewhat the temper of the modern student he wrote of the rise of animosity against new taxation. His sentiment on England's retention of the tax on tea has since been echoed many times: "Never perhaps did a great and wise nation adopt a more ill-judged measure than this."

Marshall's tone throughout was restrained, and even when he came to write on the Declaration of Independence he was much more moderate than the later Bancroft and James Grahame. Marshall's last volume contained an excellent chapter on the causes that led to a change in the government of the United States and the adoption of a stronger central power, which emphasized the role of Washington in promoting sentiment for a vigorous national government. This whole critical period was, of course, presented from the Federalist standpoint. The biography

[52] A. J. Beveridge, *The Life of John Marshall* (4 vols., New York, 1916–19), III, Chap. V.

[53] *Monthly Anthology,* Vol. V (1808), 267.

[54] See E. Channing, *History of the United States* (6 vols., New York, 1905–25), II, 310.

became a history of national politics and of diplomatic relations, but at the conclusion of his work Marshall gave a sound estimate of Washington's character. The remark of one reviewer was just; his complaint was "not that there is too much history, but that there is too little biography."[55]

The political associations of Marshall had an adverse effect on the sale of the work. Only eight thousand of the anticipated thirty thousand subscriptions materialized. The price was high, and Republicans spread the rumor that it was a Federalist history of the United States, written as propaganda for use in the election of 1804. Jefferson, in a letter urging Joel Barlow to write a history of the United States, referred to Marshall's biography as "that five-volumed libel."[56] Madison was not so hostile, but he did think the last volume (1783–99) was inaccurate, and he suggested, too, that Marshall "would write differently at the present day [1827] and with his present impressions."[57] That staunch Federalist, Chancellor James Kent, however, thought the fifth volume was "worth all the rest," considering the work as a whole "an excellent History of the Government and Parties in this country."[58]

Unfortunately for Marshall's reputation as a biographer, a recent student has discovered that the Chief Justice was guilty of extensive plagiarism throughout his work. For the Revolution he was content to copy from Gordon and from the plagiarist's paradise, the *Annual Register*. Had Marshall been willing to exercise his creative imagination on the original materials available to him, he might have made a contribution of prime significance to American historical literature.[59]

PARSON WEEMS

The Revolutionary era and its leading figures were memorialized in rather sober histories, which created for the serious reader a more or less realistic pattern of our past. A construction of different design was sketched for a larger audience by the famous Parson Weems. The books

[55] *Monthly Anthology*, Vol. V (1808), 261.

[56] J. B. McMaster, *History of the People of the United States* (8 vols., New York, 1883–1913), V, 294; Beveridge, *Marshall*, III, 267 .

[57] Adams, *Jared Sparks*, II, 37.

[58] Beveridge, *Marshall*, III, 265.

[59] W. A. Foran, "John Marshall as a Historian," *American Historical Review*, Vol. XLIII (October, 1937), 51–64.

by Weems were a particularly colorful culmination of the literature of the Revolutionary period; from them countless Americans received an indelible impression of those stirring years. The publications of Mason Locke Weems were better known than those of any other American in the first half of the nineteenth century.

Weems was born in Maryland in 1759, and at an early age, tradition tells us, he was in an atmosphere conducive to the glorification of Washington's name. Weems studied medicine abroad, but it appears that he practiced little. His healing was of the soul rather than of the body, for in 1784 Dr. Weems became Parson Weems of the Anglican church. Not long after, he became a writer and itinerant bookseller, serving in the South as agent of the famous Philadelphia publisher Mathew Carey. "For thirty years there was no more familiar figure on the roads of the Southern States than this book peddler and author who . . . gipsy-like . . . travelled his long route year after year, sleeping in wayside inn, farmhouse or forest, fiddling, writing [and] selling books."[60]

With the publication of the *Life of Washington* in 1800, Weems came into his own as an author. It was written as an antidote to Marshall's marble figure, which was too austere even for men with conservative tastes. John Adams called Marshall's biography "a Mausoleum, 100 feet square at the base, and 200 feet high." Weems, a Jeffersonian Republican, was also anxious to prevent Federalists from monopolizing Washington's fame; *his* Washington, he said, was no aristocrat, "but a pure Republican."[61]

For more than two decades after publication of the *Washington,* Weems reaped the rewards of being the foremost American writer of juvenile literature. Large numbers of adults as well as children by the tens of thousands read his books, which were designed to inculcate the prized virtues of industry, temperance, and frugality. The story of Washington and the cherry tree (which first appeared in the fifth edition of the biography) became part of the national folklore. Despite his many inaccuracies, his simple writing was so warm with enthusiasm that it brought to life figures already grown austere and remote.

"George," said his father, "do you know who killed the beautiful

[60] L. C. Wroth, *Parson Weems* (Baltimore, 1911).

[61] W. A. Bryan, *George Washington in American Literature 1775–1865* (New York, 1952), 14, 15.

little cherry-tree yonder in the garden?" This was a tough question and George staggered under it for a moment. . . .

"I can't tell a lie, Pa, you know I can't tell a lie. I did cut it with my hatchet."

"Run to my arms, you dearest boy," cried his father . . . "glad am I, George, that you killed my tree; for you have paid for it a thousand fold. Such an act of heroism in my son is more worth than a thousand trees, though blossomed with silver, and their fruits of purest gold." The style of the biographer was the style of the preacher, and in an age which admired oratory Weems waxed eloquent indeed.

In his *Life of General Francis Marion,* Weems produced a historical romance that later received the praise of so good a writer as William Gilmore Simms. His accounts of military events, though described with partisanship, were fairly dependable. In other respects his biographies drew more from his imagination than from the lives of his subjects. The spontaneity that characterized the biographies of Washington and Marion was absent, however, in Weems' life of Franklin. The author's fondness for the Franklinian virtues was not enough to color the work richly; it was not easy to write glowingly of industry, temperance, and frugality.

Weems crusaded against drunkenness and gambling; the moralist was consistently true to himself, as biographer or writer of moral tracts —he was first and last an uplifter. And many listened; over a million copies of his books were sold. "As a 'Maker' of history," remarked Channing, Weems "vies with the household poets." Long stretches of Longfellow's *The Courtship of Miles Standish* or Whittier's *Barbara Frietchie* were no nearer the facts of history than was the *Washington* of Weems; and the latter "has had equal or greater influence on succeeding generations of Americans than any of these." It might not be too much to say that generations of historical scholars have been unable to modify seriously the popular picture Weems created of our Revolutionary heroes.

V

Gathering the Records–Awaiting the National Historian

THE STIRRING events of the two score years which followed 1760 were a stimulus to historical composition and the collection of documentary materials. It is therefore surprising that so little was done on a comprehensive scale. Old John Adams complained to his fellow revolutionist, Thomas McKean: "Can you account for the apathy, the antipathy of this nation to their own history? Is there not a repugnance to the thought of looking back? While thousands of frivolous novels are read with eagerness and got by heart, the history of our own native country is not only neglected, but despised and abhorred." To Elbridge Gerry the former President also complained of the "total ignorance and oblivion of the revolution" among the younger generation.[1]

Conditions were not quite so bad as Adams declared. He himself, in the midst of the war years, had written to Mrs. Warren of a plan to retire and spend his leisure hours in writing a history of the Revolution, "and with a hand as severe as Tacitus, I wish to God it was as eloquent, draw the portrait of every character that has figured in the business. But when it is done, I will dig a vault, and bury the manuscript . . . not to be opened till a hundred years after my death."[2] Alas, Adams never wrote the manuscript, but he carried on a correspondence for years with a number of individuals whose interest in the Revolution was whetted by his memories.

While the Revolution was still in progress Gerry had moved, in Congress, that each state should designate an official to collect memorials of the period. Had the motion been adopted, said Adams in 1813, "we should now possess a Monument of more inestimable Value than all the

[1] Adams, *Works,* X, 62, August 31, 1813; 37, April 14, 1813.
[2] *Ibid.,* X, 475–76, December 15, 1778.

Histories and Orations that have been written." In recalling old times McKean told Adams that he had often been asked to write a history of the American Revolution, Benjamin Rush having been especially insistent.[3] Rush himself had contemplated writing such a history and had gathered materials for it while the war was in progress. Joel Barlow, too, had prepared documents to write a history of the Revolution, and in his collection were the papers of General Gates.[4]

When Jedidiah Morse was seeking original materials on the Revolution he turned to Adams, who sent him long and revealing letters. "A history of military operations from April 19, 1775, to the 3d of September, 1783, is not a history of the American Revolution," said Adams. "The revolution," he said, "was in the minds and hearts of the people, and in the union of the colonies; both of which were substantially effected before hostilities commenced." The Revolution began, said the aged correspondent, with the Writs of Assistance in 1761. Pamphlets, newspapers, handbills from 1761–74, the letters of the committees of correspondence—a study of all these was necessary to understand the growth of union. "Here sir," said Adams, "opens an extensive field of investigation, even for a young historian, who might be disposed to undertake so laborious an enterprize." The real American Revolution, Adams reiterated, was the "radical change in the principles, opinions, sentiments and affections of the people" toward Great Britain. He suggested that young men of letters in all the states, especially in the original thirteen, should collect the historical materials bearing on the Revolutionary period. To Hezekiah Niles, who later compiled a useful book of documents, Adams was writing in the same vein, although he was doubtful that "the true history of the American Revolution" could be recovered.[5]

The lively history of the American Revolution by the Italian, Carlo Botta, evoked questions from various quarters. "Who shall write the history of the American Revolution?" Adams asked McKean. "Who can write it? Who will ever be able to write it? The most essential documents, the debates and deliberations in Congress, from 1774 to 1783, were all in secret, and are now lost forever." In reply McKean said that Major General James Wilkinson had written the history of the Revolu-

[3] *Ibid.*, X, 17, January, 1814.
[4] Adams, *Jared Sparks,* II, 49; I, 499.
[5] *Works,* X, 274, January, 1818; February 13, 1818.

tion, but Adams retorted in words he had already used—the history of the war was very different from a history of the American Revolution.[6]

At this same time Jefferson and Adams were also discussing these issues, and the Virginian likewise questioned whether anyone could write the history of the Revolution. He felt that the task could not be performed adequately because its external facts alone were known, "all its councils, designs and discussions having been conducted by Congress with closed doors, and no members, as far as I know, having ever made notes of them. These, which are the life and soul of history, must forever be unknown." Jefferson thought Botta's history better than any yet written, allowing for his invented speeches and his "fancying motives of action which we never felt." Wiser than Adams, who insisted that the Revolution began with the Writs of Assistance, Jefferson said that it would be as difficult to name the moment when the "embryo becomes an animal, or the act which gives him a beginning" as to say when the Revolution began "and what incident set it in motion."[7]

The elder statesmen were busy in their last years looking over old papers and answering all sorts of queries. Madison wrote to Edward Everett that he was putting together his notes on the Constitutional Convention.[8] "It has been the misfortune of history," wrote Madison, "that a personal knowledge and an impartial judgment of things rarely meet in the historian. . . ." If the materials of America's history should fall into proper hands, he added, "the American History may be expected to contain more truth, and lessons, certainly not less valuable, than those of any Country or Age."

To William Tudor, editor of the newly established *North American Review,* Adams wrote of various incidents in the Revolution, and in these and other retrospective letters he suggested so wide a scope of inquiry that historians a century later had not yet filled in his outline.[9] Although Adams was more than eighty, his energy never flagged, and his dimming eyes visioned broad areas for research. To younger men was communicated the enthusiasm of Revolutionaries still alive; and

[6] *Ibid.,* 17, July 30, 1815; 176, 180, November 20 and 26, 1815.

[7] P. Wilstach, *Correspondence of John Adams and Thomas Jefferson 1812–1826* (Indianapolis, 1925), 114, August 10, 1815; 159–60, May 5, 1817; 161, May 17, 1818.

[8] G. Hunt (ed.), *The Writings of James Madison* (9 vols., New York, 1900–1910), IX, 128, March 19, 1823.

[9] Adams, *Works,* X, 230, *passim,* especially letter of November 16, 1816.

to the expansive national spirit that came after the War of 1812, Jefferson, Adams, Madison, and old soldiers contributed their reminiscences of the founding of the nation.

Tudor was one who came under their influence, and through the pages of the *Review* he stimulated historical research. His scholarly maturity was evident in his urbane attitude toward early Puritan historians, particularly Cotton Mather.[10] Tudor's historical interests were of long standing, for in *The Monthly Anthology*, a predecessor of the *Review*, he had included articles on colonial historians. More than any other force the *Review* stirred the slow stream of intellectual life to a swift-flowing current.

Biographies of Revolutionary heroes were read carefully by the old guard, who conserved jealously the reputations of their dead comrades. "American History," wrote Adams to a friend, Dr. Benjamin Waterhouse, "whether in Fable, Allegory, Painting, Sculpture, Architecture, Statuary, Poetry, Oratory, or Romance: which forgets to acknowledge James Otis to have been the Father of the American Revolution, will be nothing but a Lie."[11] Tudor published a biography of Otis (1823); in recommending it highly to a friend, George Ticknor wrote: "There is nothing like it in print—that I have ever seen—among our materials for future history, nor could such a book be made twenty years hence for then all the traditions will have perished with the old men from whose graves he has just rescued them."[12] William Wirt drew from Jefferson his remembrance of Patrick Henry, and when Wirt's biography of the famed orator appeared, letters praising and censuring it were exchanged among the Revolutionary leaders. Thomas Jefferson Randolph's *Memoirs, Correspondence and Private Papers of Thomas Jefferson* (1829) provoked intense public discussion, helping to fix in the American mind the liberal image of the great Virginian. "The age of commemoration" had been ushered in; "We are no longer the new men of the new world," said one New Englander, "We have a noble inheritance in the fame of our ancestors."[13]

[10] *North American Review*, Vol. VI (January, 1818), 257.

[11] W. C. Ford (ed.), *Statesman and Friend* (Boston, 1927), 137, August 17, 1817.

[12] George S. Hillard (ed.), *Life, Letters and Journals of George Ticknor* (2 vols., Boston, 1876), I, 338; R. M. Dorson (ed.), *America Rebels: Narratives of the Patriots* (New York, 1953).

[13] M. D.. Peterson, "The Jefferson Image, 1829," *American Quarterly Review*, Vol. III, No. 3 (Fall, 1951), 204–20.

The last survivors among the signers of the Declaration of Independence and of the Constitution were conscious of a certain unity among themselves; Jefferson once spoke of the "Declaration-men."[14] They were aware of their unique position in American life. A few months before he died Jefferson wrote to Adams, introducing his grandson, T. J. Randolph: "Like other young people, he wishes to be able in the winter nights of old age, to recount to those around him what he has heard and learnt of the heroic age preceding his birth, and which of the Argonauts individually he was in time to have seen."[15]

In the summer and in the winter nights of their own old age these Argonauts spun tales of their heroic era and bemoaned the fact that no one had written its history. But the time was near at hand when materials for it would be systematically gathered. McKean regretted that the United States possessed no Thucydides, Tacitus, Hume, Robertson, or Gibbon, yet, he said, "we have gentlemen of great talents, and capable of writing the history of our Revolution with at least as much regard to truth as any of them has exhibited."[16] Doubtless there were some then capable of writing the history of the American Revolution; many years were yet to pass, however, before the task was seriously attacked.

GATHERING THE RECORDS

Before any large-scale history could be written, the materials had to be assembled. There was no lack of materials, for New Englanders, as George Bancroft pointed out, "have always been a documentary people."[17] In fact, an overwhelming number of authors who wrote history or biography or compiled annals came from New England. Jared Sparks pointed out in 1826, however, "No work approaching to the character of a complete history of America, of the United States or of the American Revolution, has yet appeared." Sparks, who was soon to go abroad to search for historical materials, said that "the colonial history of America is shut up in the office of the Board of Trade and Plantations in England."

Sparks, anxious to improve every aid to historical research, was

[14] P. L. Ford (ed.), *Writings of Thomas Jefferson* (10 vols., New York, 1892–99), X, 191, August 17, 1821.

[15] Wilstach, *Correspondence of Adams and Jefferson*, 195, March 25, 1826.

[16] Adams, *Works*, X, 177, November 20, 1815.

[17] *North American Review*, Vol. XLVI (April, 1838), 476.

critical of America's poor library facilities; he could number but seven libraries "in which a whole stock of books relating to America may not be ranged in the corner of a single case."[18] George Ticknor measured the influence of his education in Europe by the different perspective it gave him upon the resources of the Harvard Library. "When I went away," he said, "I thought it was a large library; when I came back, it seemed a closetful of books."[19]

At the time when Sparks was complaining of difficulties that beset the American historian, they were beginning to be overcome. Hezekiah Niles published the *Principles and Acts of the Revolution* . . . in 1822; he made it clear that he was presenting documentary evidence "to show the *feelings* that prevailed in the revolution not to give a *history of events.*" Between 1827 and 1830 Jonathan Elliot brought out the four-volume (a fifth was added later) *Debates . . . in Convention on the Adoption of the Federal Constitution.* Publication of the *American State Papers* came not long afterward. The introductory note to the first volume (1833) said that "in this compilation the future historian may find a body of authentic materials ready prepared for his hand."

Extensive work by Sparks and others had been in progress for some time. Historical literature promised greater rewards, including financial, than any other branch of writing. America's past had been glorious, and her future promised to be even more brilliant. With the zeal of the missionary, the new generation fused memories of hallowed traditions with glowing expectations for the years ahead. Every type of old record was diligently explored. *The Journals of each Provincial Congress of Massachusetts in* 1774 *and* 1775 . . . , edited by William Lincoln, (1838) announced that its primary object was "to *perpetuate materials* for the history of a glorious era in our national existence." Francis L. Hawks, lawyer, clergyman, and historian, was commissioned by the Episcopal Church to collect materials on its history in the colonial period. He went to England and brought back a mass of documents which he used in his *Ecclesiastical History of the United States: Virginia* (1836) and in a volume on Maryland. Similar activity further South was represented by Bartholomew R. Carroll's compilation, the *Historical Collections of South Carolina* (2 vols., 1836).

A very notable effort to collect sources on the Revolution was begun

[18] *Ibid.*, Vol. XXIII (October, 1826), 276–92.
[19] Hillard (ed.), *Life of George Ticknor,* I, 72.

in 1822 by Peter Force, a journalist and printer, in partnership with Matthew St. Clair Clarke, clerk of the House of Representatives. As their plan developed it became far more comprehensive in scope, projecting the publication in many volumes of an enormous body of sources on the history of the colonies. After many delays, the first volume was published in 1837, with the title *American Archives.* . . . "The undertaking in which we have embarked," said Force, "is emphatically, a National one; National in its scope and object, its end and aim." Their work, the compilers said, was in harmony with "the tendency of the present age [which] has been justly and philosophically designated as historick." Publication of national records in Europe had been supported by government aid, and Force called for similar assistance by the United States.

Between 1837 and 1853, nine volumes of *American Archives* (concentrating on the Revolutionary era) were published with government aid to the amount of $228,000; publication then ceased. Force also brought out four volumes of *Tracts and other Papers relating to . . . North America.* Bancroft hailed the *American Archives:* "Here are the clay and the straw, everything necessary but the forming hand" for historical composition.[20]

In addition to preserving many materials for the use of historians, Force was a focus of the historical interests of the country.[21] He found time to participate in the activities of a short-lived American Historical Society, in Washington; he was, in fact, its most vital spirit. Collectors and authors wrote to him seeking information and encouragement; when Bancroft wanted information on the attitude of American newspapers toward the Stamp Act, he sought it from Peter Force. A list of the latter's correspondents would almost exhaust the names of Americans who were then interested in the writing of history. In 1867 Force's remarkable library of some fifty thousand titles, perhaps the best collection of Americana in existence, was bought for the Library of Congress.

At the very time that Sparks was complaining of poor library facilities a decided improvement was getting under way. Public and private li-

[20] Bancroft, in *North American Review,* Vol. XLVI (April, 1838), 486.

[21] Force Papers, Vol. XXI, January 4, 1847, Library of Congress; Bassett, *The Middle Group of American Historians,* Chap. V; *The Historical Magazine,* Vol. IX, No. 11 (November, 1865), 337.

braries were being developed on a grand scale. A great addition was made to the Harvard Library with the purchase of the Americana collected by the German historian Christoph D. Ebeling. The Library of Congress was founded in 1800 and, after a slow start, grew rapidly in importance, especially after the acquisition of collections like the books and papers of Jefferson and Madison. As early as 1829 Sparks was urging that a "copy of every book and manuscript in existence relating to America" be secured for the library.[22] Booksellers John R. Bartlett in New York, improvident Obadiah Rich, a transplanted American in Europe, and especially Henry Stevens, Jr., performed valuable services for libraries and prosperous scholars in uncovering rare Americana. The British Museum, said Sparks, had been made one of the best places in the world for American historical research, due largely to Stevens.[23] The collections of John Carter Brown, of Providence, Rhode Island, and James Lenox, of New York were of surpassing excellence. Older historical societies were reinvigorated, and new ones founded everywhere in the country. Unfortunately, few of them functioned actively.

Through the efforts of some of the earliest Americans who had studied in Germany—Joseph G. Cogswell, George Ticknor, and Edward Everett—historical scholarship was greatly advanced. It was Cogswell who helped Harvard get the Ebeling collection, and at a later date he became the adviser to John Jacob Astor when the latter was building up his library in New York.[24] Ticknor, the historian of Spanish literature, was an inspiration to Prescott. Ticknor's famous Spanish collection —the best in the world, he thought—was enshrined in a palatial home which was a favorite meeting place for Boston's intellectual élite. Above the mantel in the library hung the portrait of Sir Walter Scott, whose romantic spirit hovered over that whole generation. Ticknor's friend Everett also was interested in the advancement of American scholarship, especially history. Herman E. Ludewig, a recent immigrant from Germany, was one of the most indefatigable bibliographers of the period. Among his publications was *The Literature of American Local History: a Bibliographical Essay* (1846), dedicated to Peter Force.[25]

[22] *North American Review,* Vol. XX (October, 1829), 432, n. 1.

[23] Adams, *Jared Sparks,* II, 522, n. 1; see L. W. Dunlap, *American Historical Societies 1790–1860* (Madison, 1944).

[24] A. E. Ticknor, *Life of Joseph Green Cogswell* (Cambridge, 1874), Chaps. XXI–XXVI.

Through the efforts of a few enthusiasts several of the states eventually published vast quantities of materials. No one individual was responsible for it, but the movement had its distant origins in the work of Hazard, in the correspondence of the Fathers, and more immediately, in the patriotic impulse to preserve the historical records of the nation. Several states made efforts to get copies of historical materials in British depositories.

New York was more successful than others in gathering the sources of her history. Governor DeWitt Clinton spoke of the need to set the State's records in order and to copy from European archives those materials bearing on New York's colonial period. In asking public support for these researches even in the midst of war (1814), Clinton wrote with great dignity: "Genuine greatness never appears in a more resplendent light, or in a more sublime attitude, than in that buoyancy of character which rises superior to danger and difficulty; in that magnanimity of soul which cultivates the arts and sciences amidst the horrors of war."

The state legislature supported Clinton's plea, and in the following years many volumes of Dutch records in local archives were translated by Dr. Francis A. Van Der Kemp. This request of 1814, which resulted in the organization and exploration of the New York State archives, was followed by another in 1839, asking legislative support for an investigation of documents in Europe. With the passage of an act defraying the expenses for the collection of materials from archives in England, Holland, and France, John Romeyn Brodhead was named agent. After a stay of three years in Europe, Brodhead returned in 1844 with eighty volumes of documents. His homecoming was an event of the first importance to historical societies in New England and the Middle Atlantic states, who sent representatives to a dinner at which Brodhead was an honored guest. In his characteristic style Bancroft said that Brodhead's ship "was more richly freighted with new materials for American history than any that ever crossed the Atlantic."[26]

[25] *The Historical Magazine,* Vol. I, No. 2 (February, 1857), 33–34. See Alex Ladenson, "Herman Ernst Ludewig 1809–1856," *The Library Quarterly* (April, 1944).

[26] Philip Hone's *Diary* (ed. by B. Tuckerman, 2 vols., New York, 1889), II, 236–37; E. A. and G. L. Duyckinck, *Cyclopedia of American Literature* (2 vols., New York, 1856), II, 595.

Brodhead's collection, while still in manuscript, was of immediate service to historians, but it became more widely useful when it was published in *The Documentary History of the State of New York* (4 vols.), and in *Documents relative to the Colonial History of the State of New York* (15 vols.). Other states added to their own published records, and some acknowledged the impulse communicated by New York. Samuel Hazard in his *Annals of Pennsylvania* (1850) expressed his gratitude to New York for permission to see the recently collected manuscript materials. In his *Pennsylvania Archives* (1852) the same compiler noted that "the States of New York, Massachusetts, New Jersey, Maryland, Virginia and other members of the Union have commenced the publication of their Colonial and Revolutionary history."

One writer, announcing "A Great Historical Enterprise," proposed that historical societies in the United States undertake the publication of a general index to all documents in English archives referring to the American colonies, thus anticipating by forty years the series issued by the Carnegie Institution of Washington.[27] Sparks had long been urging that transcripts be made of materials in European libraries for deposit in Washington, where they would be accessible to historians.[28]

Thus the amassing of materials went on apace, but the historian who had been eagerly awaited did not make his appearance until 1834. It was then that George Bancroft published his first volume. Wholly apart from his proper mixture of rhetoric and fact, so necessary to the success of a historian in that day, the acclaim that greeted him was in large measure due to the intense need of Americans for a national historian. Shortly before Bancroft's work appeared, a writer in the *American Quarterly Review*, 1827, had expressed the national longing: "A matured work of genius" on American history, he said, "would be of incalculable value." Prescott welcomed Bancroft's history as the first native work likely to supplant those written by Europeans. He reminded fellow-Americans that they had to go to the work of the Italian, Botta, for "the best history of the Revolution," and to the Scotsman, James Grahame, "for the best history of the Colonies. Happily the work before us bids fair, when completed, to supply this deficiency." Although Prescott conceded the merit of the histories written by foreigners, still he insisted they

[27] *The Historical Magazine*, Vol. IV, No. 10 (October, 1860), 314–15.

[28] R. Wolcott, *Correspondence of William Hickling Prescott* (New York, 1925), October 19, 1840.

were written by men who could not enter into the sympathies nor comprehend "all the minute feelings, prejudices, and peculiar ways of thinking which form the idiosyncrasy of the nation."[29]

On the eve of Bancroft's publication, William Ellery Channing discussed the quality of national literature: "We think that the history of the human race is to be rewritten. Men imbued with the prejudices which thrive under aristocracies and state religions, cannot understand it. . . . It is plain, that history is already viewed under new aspects, and we believe that the true principles for studying and writing it are to be unfolded here, at least as rapidly as in other countries." With these sentiments Bancroft was in perfect harmony. In the year in which his first volume appeared he wrote to Sparks that Americans had a history worth knowing, and that "a vein of public feeling, of democratic independence, of popular liberty, ought to be infused into our literature."[30]

Bancroft lived so long that he became a tradition before his death. For a half-century he dominated historical scholarship. His patriotic spirit, celebrating the triumphs of democracy, touched a prideful people and was welcomed by the great majority. In a more restrained manner a small minority established a tradition of a critical approach, but not until a later generation did its view find firm support. Charles Francis Adams wrote in the *North American Review,* 1831: "In this country . . . we are fond of celebrating the virtues of our forefathers . . . by festive anniversaries and eloquent panegyric. . . . Yet it is much to be feared, that this is not the right way to come at that real history, and those cool and rational conclusions which can alone be supposed likely to confer permanent benefit." He observed, too, that the "modern fashion of what is called philosophical history is attended with one great disadvantage, in the ease with which it admits of the perversion of facts, to suit the prejudices of each particular writer."

Despite the criticism of Adams, who was ahead of his time and against the tide of contemporary historical writing, "philosophical" history was to be written and read for some time to come. The *American Review* reported that "the great English historians are to be found in our huts and farmhouses, and editions of them are multiplied without number." Twenty thousand copies of Macaulay's history were reported

[29] W. H. Prescott, *Biographical and Critical Miscellanies* (New York, 1845), 308–10.

[30] Adams, *Jared Sparks,* II, 192, n. 1.

sold in the United States in 1849.[31] It was an exultant reviewer who acclaimed Bancroft as "our western Macaulay."[32] The volumes that Bancroft, Prescott, and Motley wrote were well suited to the romantic taste of the public; historians had not yet begun to write largely for one another.

ABIEL HOLMES

The transition from the historians of the colonial and Revolutionary years to the writers of the full-flowering national period was effected by Abiel Holmes. His was the first important attempt to comprehend American history in its entirety. Ezra Stiles and others in the eighteenth century had talked of such a project, but its fulfillment was delayed until Holmes took up the task.

Abiel Holmes, father of Oliver Wendell Holmes, belonged in the long line of New England ministers who wrote history; his particular contribution was *American Annals* . . . (2 vols.), in 1805; (a second edition under a slightly different title appeared in 1829). Holmes, who was the son-in-law of Stiles as well as his literary executor, wrote a biography of the Yale President (1798). The study of the many papers left by the older man stimulated him to write his own history.

Holmes observed that, though local histories of particular portions of America had been written, "no attempt has been made to give even the outline of its entire history." He set himself that task: "It has been uniformly my aim to trace facts, as much as possible to their source. Original authorities, therefore, when they could be obtained, have always had preference." Although Holmes had wished that his book might be better than a chronology, it proved to be little more; it belonged to the school of Thomas Prince.

The dryly factual character of the *Annals* was occasionally lightened by a personal observation—on the witchcraft episode, for example. His was the critical attitude of the Enlightenment: "This part of the history of our country furnished an affecting proof of the imbecility of the human mind, and of the potent influence of the passions." He took an enlarged view of the subject, embracing Europe, his remarks being an interesting precedent for the position taken by George L. Kittredge a

[31] Quoted in F. L. Mott, *The History of American Magazines 1741–1850* (New York, 1930), 178, 399.

[32] *The Historical Magazine,* Vol. VI, No. 2 (February, 1862), 41.

hundred years later in his apologia for the Puritans. When Holmes came to write on the Revolution his work partly realized his aim to compose narrative history. Holmes' pride in his country's past was matched by his confidence in her future.

The *Annals,* despite its many deficiencies, was a significant advance in American historiography. In a summary of American historical writing, by Bancroft in the *North American Review,* 1838, it was said of Holmes that all students of our history owed him gratitude. He was the link that connected "the men of an earlier generation, Belknap, Hutchinson, Stiles, Trumbull, and the rest with the scholars of our own." Sparks said the *Annals* was the "best repository of history, chronology, and biographical knowledge respecting America that can be found embodied in one work."[33] Long years afterward careful students still turned to it with confidence.

While the historian's research was admirable, his writing lacked distinction. When Holmes was a student at Yale he contributed to a publication, *Clio,* edited by Juliana Smith, who once remarked of his writing: "The Pegasus he rides is a sorry steed that has lost its wings and is badly shod." His descendants, Oliver Wendell and Justice Holmes, happily, were in this respect more gifted.[34]

TIMOTHY PITKIN

In 1828 Timothy Pitkin brought out a two-volume work, *A Political and Civil History of the United States of America . . . 1763 to . . . 1797,* five chapters of which summarized colonial history to 1763. Over a hundred pages of sources were appended to the volumes, and similar matter was frequently imbedded in the body of the text.

Pitkin said that Americans were sufficiently acquainted with the military events of the Revolutionary period. He believed it, therefore, desirable to present a "connected view of the political and civil transactions of our country, unmixed with military events, except so far as the latter had an influence on the former." He specifically disclaimed the intention of writing "a philosophical history."

At the end of his introductory chapters Pitkin had a few lines, still

[33] *North American Review,* Vol. XX (October, 1829), 429–41.

[34] H. E. Smith, *Colonial Days and Ways* (New York, 1900), 282–83; see, however, M. A. De Wolfe Howe's ascription of the epic poem "Yaratildia" (1796) to Holmes, Mass. Hist. Soc. *Proceedings,* Vol. LXII (1930), 155. See memoir of Holmes in Mass. Soc. *Collections,* 3d ser., Vol. VII (1838), 271–82.

worth reading, on the difference between European and American character. "Though the motives and views of those who settled in the different colonies, were different, yet their situation in their new places of abode, being, in many respects, similar, naturally produced in all an energy of character, and a spirit of independence, unknown, in the great mass of the people they had left in Europe. . . . Every man was a freeholder, and his freehold was at his own disposal. . . . This independent condition of the colonists . . . combined with that equality which existed among them, arising from an equal distribution of property, a general diffusion of knowledge, and a share which all had in the government, naturally produced a love of liberty, an independence of character, and a jealousy of power, which ultimately led, under divine Providence, to that revolution, which placed them among the nations of the earth."

Pitkin, adhering to his promise to confine the annals of military events to the barest minimum, gave much space to the negotiations between the colonies and England, between the new states and France, the formation of the Confederation and the internal difficulties of the fledgling American governments. Pitkin's strong interest in finance led him to stress the subject of public credit. He wrote as a Hamiltonian Federalist: "The general government . . . was totally inefficient, and the authority of the state governments greatly weakened, and in some instances almost destroyed. . . . The only remedy that promised relief, was an essential alteration in the national compact." Then followed the Constitutional Convention, which was called, said Pitkin, largely because of Shays' Rebellion: "This open and formidable opposition to the laws threatened not only the destruction of the government of that state, but of the union. . . . Fortunately the state of Massachusetts . . . was able to suppress the insurrections, without the aid of the Federal arm," which had already been promised.

The chapter on the convention at Philadelphia, which discussed, among other matters, the public reaction to the proposed new form of government, can still be read with profit. The policies of the Federalists, designed to strengthen the national government, were praised by the historian. His history ended with Washington's Farewell Address, an "inestimable legacy which the father of his country" left to the Americans.

Pitkin's work ranked far beyond most of the histories published up to that time, showing a power of organization and discrimination in choice of material that few could match. He did place a disproportionate emphasis on New England. Although his history contained no writing of an inspired character, it was not heavy reading, and its observations often showed the mark of a shrewd intelligence. There were many books, written long years after on the same period, which added little to what Pitkin wrote.

Pitkin's concern with economic questions led him to publish *A Statistical View of the Commerce of the United States of America . . .* (Hartford, 1816). It was an admirable work, still useful, expressive of the growing spirit of commercial enterprise after the War of 1812. Its sentences reflected characteristic national pride in material growth: "no nation, it is believed, had ever increased so rapidly in wealth as the United States." Pitkin's fame as a statistician has eclipsed his reputation as a historian, but his achievement in writing history deserved a better fate.

THREE EUROPEAN HISTORIANS OF AMERICA

That American history interested Englishmen in the eighteenth century was, of course, not surprising—the colonies were part of the empire. But even after that link was broken English interest continued, thanks to a common background, the similarity of institutions, and curiosity about developments in the young republic. Students of other lands, Germany and France particularly, were also drawn to a study of American history, for the new country was a powerful stimulus to the historical imagination. Probably the most important of the works published by Europeans were those of Ebeling, Grahame, and Botta, the last being the best known. It was unfortunate that Ebeling and Grahame were generally ignored for they might have greatly benefited American students.

Christoph D. Ebeling, professor of Greek and history in Hamburg, labored for forty years on various works relating to the New World. To a friend he confided that he had spent a good part of his life, all his money, and even much of his health collecting materials on the United States. He was said to have the best collection of eighteenth-century American newspapers in existence. Ebeling, who referred to himself as a "Cosmopolite," had a wide circle of correspondents in the United States, including Ramsay, Belknap, Morse, Stiles, Holmes, and the learned William Bentley.[35]

[35] "Letters of C. D. Ebeling," American Antiquarian Society *Proceedings,*

Ebeling's interest in America was not only to write a better history than was then in existence, but also to furnish for the benefit of a reactionary Europe a "faithful picture of a truly free republic." Between 1793 and 1816 his *Erdbeschreibung und Geschichte von Amerika* appeared in seven bulky volumes. It was the most inclusive work done on America by any one up to that time, European or American. But the great mass of materials it contained were largely inaccessible to Americans since few could read German, and those who could found his work had no literary charm to attract them. A small number of historians, including Bancroft, did find Ebeling's work helpful in their research.

Ebeling was also associated with other literary ventures relating to America—the *Amerikanische Bibliothek,* which stressed geography, and the *Amerikanisches Magazin,* which acquainted Germans with American constitutional documents, books, and miscellaneous news of life overseas. Ebeling's great library and collection of maps, purchased by Harvard in 1818, made the college the foremost native repository of American history. His material proved of real value to Abiel Holmes, and others used it also. Thus, through his writing and his collections, this German scholar, working under a severe handicap thousands of miles from the scene of his intellectual interests, ultimately did contribute to the development of American historical writing.[36]

Charles W. Botta, born in 1766, was a Piedmontese whose medical practice was sidetracked by his interest in politics and history. To Americans he was best known as the author of a *History of the War of Independence of the United States of America,* originally published in Italian in four volumes, 1809. An Italian edition was reviewed in a Philadelphia magazine which spoke of it as the best history of the Revolution ever written.[37] Translated in 1820, it immediately became the subject of extensive correspondence among Americans. In later life Botta explained that a discussion had arisen in a Parisian salon as to the most suitable theme for an epic poem. All agreed that the only event worthy of such

---

Vol. XXXV, Part 2 (October, 1925), 310, 413. See also E. E. Doll, "American History as Interpreted by German Historians from 1770 to 1815," American Philosophical Society *Transactions,* n. s., Vol. XXXVIII, Part 5 (1949).

[36] Mass. Hist. Soc. *Collections,* 2d ser., Vol. VIII (1826), 270–75; 6th ser., Vol. IV (1891).

[37] *Analectic Magazine,* Vol. V (May, 1815), 385; see Adams' discussion, *Works,* X, 171–72; J. D. Fiore, "Carlo Botta," *Italica,* Vol. XXVIII, No. 3 (September, 1951), 155–71.

treatment was the American Revolution. If suitable for a poem, Botta thought it was equally so for a history.

The Italian historian followed classical models by putting speeches into the mouths of characters who may or may not have uttered them. As was seemly for a European, Botta gave much space to the world-wide ramifications of the American Revolution. Irish discontent was related to the struggle, and other episodes attracted Botta to such lengths that at one point he interrupted himself by saying that "it is time to return upon the American continent."

Americans, of course, were delighted with Botta's enthusiastic republicanism; Jefferson thought his work would become the "common manual of our Revolutionary History." Apparently it did, for ten American editions were printed in the following years. Jared Sparks, who met Botta in Paris, in 1828, testified to the latter's careful workmanship.[38] Madison thought that Botta's work would give a strong impetus to a more critical study of the Revolution, but he did note its flaws, especially the failure to credit John Adams with a proper share in the debates on the proposal for independence.[39] Despite its obvious defects, not until Bancroft's volumes appeared was there an American narrative that could compete with the fame of Botta's history of the Revolution.

At the time when Americans were complaining to one another about the lack of interest in their history, a Scotsman, James Grahame, was writing a history of the colonies which, when published, was to be accepted by critical authority as the best in the field before Bancroft began writing. It has been pointed out by more than one critic that Bancroft never adequately recognized Grahame as his predecessor.[40] Grahame's love of the spirit of liberty had turned him to a study of American history. In his diary, June, 1824, he wrote: "The subject seems to me grand and noble. It was not a thirst of gold or of conquest, but piety and virtue, that laid the foundation of those settlements." The Revolution in America, Grahame went on to write, was not promoted by infidelity as that in France; on the contrary, the American Revolution in large part was caused by religious men.

It was in 1824 that Grahame began the composition of his history.

[38] Adams, *Jared Sparks,* II, 93.

[39] *Letters and Other Writings of James Madison* (4 vols., Philadelphia, 1865), III, 177, July 3, 1820; also 203–204, January, 1821.

[40] *The Historical Magazine,* n. s., Vol. I, No. 2 (February, 1867), 102–105.

"History is everything," he wrote to a correspondent. "Religion, science, literature, whatever men do or think, falls within the scope of history. I ardently desire to make it a religious work, and in writing, to keep the chief end of man mainly in view." Taking his task very seriously, he went to Göttingen where, he said, books were available that he could not get in England. The first two volumes of *The History of the United States of North America* . . . were published in 1827; they carried the narrative to the Revolution of 1689. Although his work was neglected in England, Grahame went on with his history.

The first significant welcome accorded his history was that extended by Charles Francis Adams in 1831, in the *North American Review*. Grahame's book, he said, was the "best that has anywhere appeared upon the early history of the United States." John Quincy Adams spoke with similar enthusiasm to Jared Sparks about Grahame, but Sparks was not impressed by the Scotsman's work.[41] In 1836 the remaining two volumes of Grahame's history appeared, to be met again with ill-merited neglect. Curiously, Grahame never visited the United States, and his friendships included but few Americans.

The historian wrote with intense devotion to American principles, adopting throughout a high moral tone. He once said that "the depths of my heart are with the primitive Puritans and the Scottish Covenanters," though he was opposed to their advocacy of close relations between church and state. Grahame was no blind admirer of all things American: "I am far from thinking . . . that every part of the conduct of the American states . . . was pure and blameless."

He gave a fair description of the policy of the Navigation Acts, not unlike that given by American historians many years later. English colonial policy, he said, "on the whole, was much less illiberal and oppressive than that which any other nation of Europe had ever been known to pursue." Grahame, who was trained as a lawyer, paid especial attention to the laws when he came to write the social history of the colonies. A very interesting appendix was added to the second volume. It dealt with the state and prospects of the North American provinces at the close of the seventeenth century, and included opinions of colonists respecting the sovereignty and policy of Great Britain. (The later Bancroft and Osgood, in their volumes on the seventeenth century, included similar surveys.)

[41] Adams, *Jared Sparks*, I, 554; II, 217.

In the eighteenth century, said Grahame, "British oppression and intolerance, which had founded most of the North American colonies, still continued to augment the numbers and influence the sentiments of their inhabitants." He was particularly conscious of American discontent with the mother country's religious policies. Long before other historians, who seemed in after years to rediscover the fact, Grahame showed how the British intention to introduce the episcopal establishment in the colonies aroused intense opposition in New England.

The historian's insights were sharp: "Even although no other subject of quarrel had presented itself, the commercial restrictions alone must in process of time have occasioned the disruption of the American provinces from the British empire." There was a careful examination of the constitutional aspects of the Stamp Act controversy, with a reference to a phase of history in this period which attracted Carl Becker and Arthur M. Schlesinger many years later. "The supporters of colonial rights in the higher classes of society at New York," said Grahame, "were struck with alarm at the riotous outrage committed by their townsmen [in the Stamp Act riots], and perceived the expediency of constituting prudent leaders for the management and control of the multitude." Grahame saluted the Declaration of Independence with a fervor matching that of native Americans: "While European sovereigns were insulting and violating every sanction and safeguard of national right and human liberty by the infamous partition of Poland, a revolutionary principle of nobler nature and vindictive destiny was developed in the earnest and wondering eyes of the world, in America."

Grahame's work was praised by competent American critics, but some held that because it was the work of a foreigner it could not have penetrated to the heart of their history. The alien vigorously replied to this contention, maintaining that a foreigner might well be fitted to write a country's history more impartially than a native. He died in 1842, three years before a second edition of his history appeared with an appreciative memoir by Josiah Quincy. There were some Americans who held it no bar to excellence, in writing their history, that a historian should have been born in Scotland.

VI

Patriots, Romantics–and Hildreth

THE LONG WAIT of Americans for native historians came to an end when Sparks and Bancroft appeared. More than any others they established American historical writing on a firm footing. They told the American people what they wished to hear about their past. In their many volumes, Sparks, Bancroft, and later Palfrey narrated in great detail the settlement of a new land, and the victories won by the colonists in behalf of political and religious freedom. Important factors in our early history, including the economic, were, however, inadequately considered by these filiopietistic historians. In their writings the ideals of freedom which they praised flowered unrelated to the soil from which they sprang. Hildreth, more perceptive than his fellow writers, had a clearer understanding of the forces at work in American history.

JARED SPARKS

Jared Sparks was born in the poverty of a small farm in Connecticut, in 1789, but his early brilliance at school opened the path to a richer life. It was his reading of Franklin's autobiography, he said, that first inspired him. Friends made it possible for him to get an education at Phillips Academy, in Exeter, New Hampshire, and then at Harvard. His study of theology brought him into the Unitarian fold as pastor in Baltimore; his chief interest, however, was literary, leading him to become an editor of the *North American Review*. During his stay in Baltimore he had served as chaplain of the House of Representatives, and this acquaintance with the leading public figures of his day was to be of real value in his later career as historian.

Sparks became the owner of the *North American Review* in 1823, and he quickly sought to lift it out of its New England provincialism. His attempt to make it more representative of the whole country was not very successful, however, for it continued to reflect, in the main, Boston tastes. Among Sparks' innovations was the practice of paying for articles, at the rate of one dollar a page. For a long time the *Review* continued to be the leading magazine in the country, exercising great power over the fate of new authors. In his editing of the magazine, as in his later editing of the letters of famous men, Sparks revealed a fatal weakness—he was timid about offending those in high places.

In the summer of 1823 Sparks wrote in his diary: "Meditating on the importance of having a new history of America . . . I would go to the foundation, and read everything on the subject." The next year Charles Folsom, who was running a press in Cambridge, asked Sparks for assistance in publishing a complete edition of Washington's writings. Sparks communicated with Supreme Court Justice Bushrod Washington, in whose care at Mount Vernon were thousands of historic letters. After much anxious waiting Sparks was given the coveted permission to study the great collection. Because he focussed attention on these papers the government bought them and added them to the growing collections of the Library of Congress.

The first president's letters launched Sparks into a number of enterprises of a historical nature, on all of which he worked while preparing the edition of Washington. During these years he thought of editing the papers of Hamilton, Lafayette, and John Jay. Meanwhile he had become interested in the whole field of the Revolution, and for months in 1826 he traveled through the Atlantic states, inspecting archives for material bearing on his great theme. He was more than ever convinced of the necessity for a study of the Revolution. "I have got a passion for Revolutionary history," he wrote, "and the more I look into it the more I am convinced that no complete history of the American Revolution has been written. The materials have never been collected; they are still in the archives of the states, and in the hands of individuals."[1]

Sparks continued in European archives his quest for documents bearing on the Revolution; his visit to England in 1828 made him one of the earliest Americans to examine the British side of the Revolutionary struggle. He also went to Paris, where he worked under difficult

[1] Adams, *Jared Sparks,* I, 509.

conditions to unearth from the archives the story of French participation in the American War of Independence. Lafayette was Sparks' host for a few weeks, and every morning, as the old general recounted his memories of Washington and the Revolution, the historian made note of them.[2]

The following twelve years were the most productive in Sparks' life. He published the *Life and Travels of John Ledyard,* the famous Connecticut traveler, in 1828; *The Diplomatic Correspondence of the American Revolution,* in twelve volumes, came right after, in the next two years. The latter work, done under a federal contract by which the government took a large number of copies, proved profitable to Sparks. In 1832 he brought out three volumes on *The Life of Gouverneur Morris,* which was one of his lesser achievements. These and other historical labors Sparks looked upon as contributions to his major interest—the history of the American Revolution, a task he never finished.

Between 1834 and 1837 the twelve volumes of *The Life and Writings of George Washington* were published. There was a note of relief in Sparks' journal, July 22, 1837: "Finished the 'Life of Washington' and sent the last sheet of the manuscript to the printer. The whole work . . . is now completed."[3] One volume contained the biography, the others included Washington's letters and public papers. Sparks disclaimed any intention of writing a "historical biography"; Marshall's work, he thought, made another such publication superfluous. He took a dig at some of his competing Washington biographers: "I have seen many particulars of [his life] which I knew not to be true, and others which I did not believe. These have been avoided; nor have I stated any fact for which I was not convinced there was credible authority. If this forbearance has been practised at the expense of the reader's entertainment, he must submit to the sacrifice as due to truth and the dignity of the subject."

Sparks wrote with more thoughtfulness than did many others, yet his Washington failed to fathom truly the nature of the general's greatness. Nevertheless, some of his remarks on the character of Washington were very appropriate: "Wisdom, judgment, prudence, and firmness were his predominant traits. . . . He deliberated slowly, but decided surely; and when his decision was once formed, he seldom reversed it, and

[2] *Ibid.*, II, 117.
[3] *Ibid.*, II, 278.

never relaxed from the execution of a measure till it was completed.... It is the happy combination of rare talents and qualities, the harmonious union of the intellectual and moral power, rather than the dazzling splendor of any one trait, which constitute the grandeur of his character." But Sparks' work did not seem much different from Marshall's "Mausoleum." As Artemus Ward expressed it, Washington still appeared to be "a human angil in a 3 kornered hat and knee britches."

Before the last of the Washington set was off the press, the first volumes of *The Works of Benjamin Franklin* were in process of publication. Between 1836 and 1840, ten volumes appeared, of which nine were devoted to letters and papers, and one reserved for a life of Franklin. In this biography, adjudged Sparks' best work after his *Washington,* a new characterization of the Philadelphia patriarch emerged. Formerly Franklin had been presented as a cunning, insincere individual, whereas in Sparks' hands he became a wise, honorable, and patient soul. The biography carried on where Franklin's autobiography ended. Franklin, said Sparks, "possessed a perfect mastery over the faculties of his understanding and over his passions . . . in every sphere of action through a long course of years his single aim was to promote the happiness of his fellow men by enlarging their knowledge, improving their condition, teaching them practical lessons of wisdom and prudence and inculcating the principles of rectitude and the habits of a virtuous life." It waited, however, for later biographers to make both Washington and Franklin more understandable to the mass of mankind.

Edward Channing in after years praised the two biographies as a "monument" to Sparks' industry and "historical insight." However, despite his energy neither the edition of *Washington* nor *Franklin* was complete. In justice to Sparks it should be mentioned that he foresaw the possibility of more papers being unearthed. But many years elapsed before more inclusive editions of the writings of the Revolutionary leaders were published.

While Sparks was busy publishing the biographies and correspondence of the Fathers, he was also engaged in editing a series of ten volumes in *The Library of American Biography.* He had written in his journal, July 28, 1832: "I have been thinking of a project for a new publication to be entitled 'A Library of American Biography.' " This was to be a series of prominent lives, serving in a measure as a connected history of the country. John Quincy Adams with his usual tartness pointed out to Sparks that Sanderson's *Lives of the Signers of the Declaration of Independence* were all eulogies: "Is it intended that [yours] should be so?"[4]

Sparks was too good a historian to echo the blatancy of Sanderson, but he catered sufficiently to patriotic taste to insure success for his venture. He followed it up with a second series of fifteen volumes likewise written for popular consumption. Sixty biographies, of which Sparks wrote eight, were included in these twenty-five volumes. In theory, the editor had a high standard of the art of biography. The subject, he said, was to be kept before the reader always. This type of writing, as distinguished from memoirs, was rather difficult, wrote Sparks, because it required "a clear and spirited style, discrimination in selecting facts, and judgment in arranging them so as to preserve just proportions."

At a later time, 1853, Sparks issued another publication which had been planned years earlier, the *Correspondence of the American Revolution; being Letters of Eminent Men to George Washington* (4 vols.). It had been projected when the editor was looking over Washington's papers, and required little preparation when the time for publication arrived.

It was clear to his contemporaries (as well as to later students) that much of the work done by Sparks as editor was impermanent. Progressive as he was in many ways, he clung to a custom that more farsighted editors were abandoning—dressing up the words of eminent men, lest the curious public see their idols in dishabille. It is unfair to compare Sparks with Parson Weems, who presented much fiction in the guise of history, yet fundamentally their purposes were somewhat similar. For both authors the lives of great men, particularly Washington, were sermons exhorting lesser mortals to nobler personal achievement. Not all aspects of Washington's life, nor all his words, were fit to be sacred sermons, and rather than exhibit Washington in all his humanity, Sparks excised or altered his language to fit the character created by a worshipful America. A number of critics, who were also acquainted with the original Washington letters, engaged Sparks in controversy over his "embellishments" of the language of the first president. Another accusation leveled against Sparks' edition of Washington was that he left out of the letters expressions unfavorable to New Englanders.

Sparks' frailties as an editor were clearly seen in the *Diplomatic Cor-*

[4] *Ibid.*, II, 189, 193.

respondence of the Revolution. When a new edition of this correspondence was proposed some twenty years after the death of Sparks, it was found that he had not included letters that referred to a projected substitution of Marshal Broglie for Washington as commander-in-chief in 1776–77.[5]

Most of Sparks' work was of an editorial nature. His creative writing had many shortcomings, for clearly he did not belong by temperament to the New England school of literary historians, which included Bancroft, Prescott, and Motley. However, the heavy emphasis that Sparks placed on original sources, particularly manuscript materials, drew praise from Prescott, who noted Bancroft's lesser dependence on such references. Bancroft, said Prescott privately, "is sketchy, episodical, given to building castles in the air," while Sparks, he said, was "on *terra firma*."[6]

The volumes Sparks published were widely circulated; over 600,000 copies of his books were sold in his lifetime.[7] In public appeal history vied with fiction. Sparks was well rewarded when he picked the subject that yielded the most fertile returns—Revolutionary history. Here was rich drama—struggles for liberty and conquest of new lands—that was also to provide themes for Bancroft, Prescott, Motley, and Parkman. They wrote when sagas of liberty and conquest were not dimly-remembered tales of half-forgotten ancestors, but when these epics were part of the very fabric of their lives. In their own day America was in process of winning vast new regions beyond the Mississippi, and Americans were giving welcome to liberty-loving revolutionaries fleeing European reaction.

Sparks' contributions to scholarship won him appointment to Harvard as McLean professor of history, the first chair distinctly devoted to that subject in the United States. He gave a course of lectures on the American Revolution; he had no real interest in his college teaching, however, preferring research. In 1849 he became president of Harvard, but he was unhappy in this post and resigned after four years. He seemed to enjoy not only writing but speaking to large audiences on historical topics; his courses of public lectures on the Revolution were popular enough to attract two thousand people.[8]

[5] F. Wharton, *The Revolutionary Diplomatic Correspondence of the United States* (6 vols., Washington, 1889), I, Preface.

[6] Adams, *Jared Sparks*, II, 292–93, n. 1, February 1, 1841.

[7] W. R. Dean, in *The Historical Magazine*, Vol. X, No. 5 (May, 1866), 146–56.

[8] Adams, *Jared Sparks*, II, 419.

In his later years (he lived till 1866) Sparks was kept busy answering many inquiries that frittered away his energies. Not all his correspondence, however, was inconsequential. Historians and public figures wrote to him for advice and information, and younger authors sought the guidance that came so willingly from the older man. John Gilmary Shea dedicated to him *The Discovery and Exploration of the Mississippi Valley,* and accepted his suggestion that he write the history of the early Catholic missions in Canada and the West; "It is a noble subject," said Sparks some years before Parkman illumined its nobility.[9] Sparks was generous in his praise of William Henry Trescot, of South Carolina, who published an essay on the *Diplomacy of the American Revolution* . . . (1852).[10] Trescot was advised to go on with a diplomatic history of the administrations of Washington and Adams; he did so, and sent Sparks the completed work in 1858. He was then urged to continue the diplomatic history of the United States to the Treaty of Ghent and beyond, but he did no more, and the task was left for Henry Adams.

In the enthusiasm of younger years Sparks had once written to Bancroft: "My absorbing passion is for books, knowledge, and thought; I would not exchange it for all the wealth of the Indies." The anticlimactic character of his last years of diverted energy was a sad commentary on the impermanence of youthful fire. In the days of his vigor, however, his work in behalf of American history had been prodigious. The library of nearly seventy volumes associated with his name accounts for his high station in American historiography. The few volumes of Abiel Holmes, Timothy Pitkin, David Ramsay, and William Gordon available before Sparks began publication indicate the vast gaps that he filled. Though his work was eventually superseded, the vast range of his activity altered completely the character of our historical literature and indicated the direction that much contemporary and later research was to take. His place is secure as a noted pioneer in American historical scholarship.[11]

[9] *Ibid.,* II, 557, and n. 2.

[10] *Ibid.,* II, 558–59; *see also* Trescot MSS. in Library of Congress, letters from Richard Rush.

[11] In addition to Adams, *Jared Sparks,* see Bassett, "Jared Sparks," *Middle Group of American Historians;* M. A. De Wolfe Howe, *Life and Letters of George Bancroft* (2 vols., New York, 1908); and Wolcott, *Correspondence of Prescott.*

GEORGE BANCROFT

The life of George Bancroft (1800–91) encompassed a great part of the whole first century of the American Republic, the spirit of which he faithfully mirrored. His father, the Rev. Aaron Bancroft, was a well-known liberal clergyman leaning to Unitarianism, and was the author of one of the many biographies of Washington which appeared during the years immediately following the President's death. It was written, said the elder Bancroft, not "for men of erudition, but for the unlettered portion of the community." The son succeeded better than the father in reaching that public.

George Bancroft was a promising youngster; when he completed his studies at Harvard he was not yet seventeen. One of his instructors, Edward Everett, who had gone to study at Göttingen, advised that Bancroft be sent to the German university. Through the generosity of a few Harvard men Bancroft was able to spend four years in Europe, gaining his doctor's degree in 1820.

Soon after his return he accepted the position of tutor in Greek at Harvard, but his unconventional character, strengthened by the acquisition of foreign manners, antagonized influential people. Ralph Waldo Emerson was more discriminating in his judgment. Bancroft, said Emerson, "needs a great deal of cutting and pruning, but we think him an infant Hercules. All who know him agree in this, that he has improved his time thoroughly at Göttingen. He has become a perfect Greek scholar, and knows well all that he pretends to know...."

Along with George Ticknor, who had also studied at Göttingen, and was a fellow-member of the Harvard faculty, Bancroft began a campaign to reform teaching methods at the college. Germany had inspired these younger men with newer pedagogic ideas with which they rashly hoped to supplant the uninspiring student recitations. Conservatism had its way, however, leaving Bancroft sick at heart: "Our hopes of a reform at college have pretty much blown over," he wrote to a friend; "I am heartily glad that the end of the year[1823] is coming so soon." In his own classes Bancroft did institute changes to the advantage of learning, but it was evident that he and Harvard would soon be parted.

With Joseph Green Cogswell, formerly a student at Göttingen and now working in the Harvard Library, Bancroft formed a partnership to found a school based on the model of the German Gymnasium. "It is our schools," they said, "which cry out most loudly for reformation." The aim of the new Round Hill School at Northampton, Massachusetts, wrote Bancroft, was to contribute to "the moral and intellectual maturity of the mind of each boy we take charge of; and the means are to be first and foremost instruction in the classics. . . . We might indeed assume a pompous name, speaking of instituting a gymnasium; but let the name be modest. I like the sound of the word Schoolmaster." For eleven years (1823–34) the school attracted attention and support as a worthy educational experiment. Bancroft himself left the school in 1831, convinced of his own limitations as a teacher, but in many ways he was now a different personality from the highly imaginative, excitable young Harvard tutor of nine years before. For one thing, he was already concerned with the very practical and great game of politics, but literary interests took precedence.

The earliest publication of the future historian was a slender volume of *Poems,* in 1823, a youthful indiscretion he lived to regret. As part of his work at the Round Hill School he had prepared adaptations of the better German textbooks for his English-speaking students. One of the books he translated was that of his old Göttingen master, Arnold H. L. Heeren, *Reflections on the Politics of Ancient Greece.* During these years, and in later life as well, Bancroft was an important agent in spreading a knowledge of German culture in the United States.

In 1828 Bancroft wrote to President Kirkland of Harvard describing a projected course in history. The volumes of Heeren were recommended for use wherever appropriate. For the portion dealing with the United States Bancroft offered to write the necessary "outlines" himself. That same year Bancroft translated Heeren's *Geschichte des Europaischen Staatensystem,* altering the title to suit American taste: *History of the Political System of Europe and its Colonies, from the Discovery of America to the Independence of the American Continent.* It is not unlikely that here lay the genesis of the future *History of the United States.*

In this period Bancroft was writing articles and reviews for the *North American Review,* but he was sometimes deeply hurt because editor Sparks took unusual liberties with the blue pencil. When Sparks made many changes in his article on Goethe, Bancroft wrote him: "If I mistake not the character of the American public, there is no need of keeping back any truth from it. The public is willing to be shocked." Despite much bickering, the two remained good friends, and the older man felt privileged to offer advice to Bancroft: "You must not work yourself to death, nor be too greedy after the treasures of this world. But you are doing great things, and the fruits of your labors are to appear not in the present time only, but in the future ages." His remarks were to the point, for Bancroft was already determined that wealth as well as fame should be the rewards of a literary career.

Writing was not divorced from politics in Bancroft's view; indeed he made each support the other. His normal association with New England Federalism was soon abandoned for the principles of Jefferson. In a Fourth of July oration, 1826, he declared his credo: "We hold it best that the laws should favor the diffusion of property and its acquisition, not the concentration of it in the hands of a few to the impoverishment of the many. We give the power to the many in the hope and to the end, that they may use it for their own benefit. . . ." It was Bancroft's article in the *North American Review,* 1831, on the Bank of the United States, which largely determined the course of his political life. He supported Jackson against the Bank, and thenceforth he was marked for high preferment among Democratic politicians, who well knew how to use his literary talents.

In 1834 Bancroft ran for the Massachusetts legislature on the workingmen's ticket. Though defeated and bitterly attacked by the Whigs, he attracted wide attention. That same year the first volume of his history brought him national distinction, and he was soon exchanging letters with such prominent political figures as William L. Marcy and Van Buren. In 1837 he was named collector of the port of Boston, in which office he remained until the Whigs ousted him four years later. He was by now, however, an acknowledged member in the national councils of the Democratic party. Though active in politics he did not neglect his history.

Bancroft announced his first volume with a flourish: "I have formed the design of writing a History of the United States from the Discovery of the American Continent to the present time. . . . I am impressed more strongly than ever with a sense of the grandeur and vastness of the subject. . . . I have applied, as I have proceeded, the principles of historical skepticism, and, not allowing myself to grow weary in comparing witnesses, or consulting codes of laws, I have endeavored to impart originality to my narrative, by deriving it from writings and sources which were the contemporaries of the events that are described." He was critical of those American historians who, he said, had taken on faith statements of earlier writers, failing to consult the sources themselves. He had not forgotten the training he had received in Germany. In discussing the credibility of various contradictory sources, in one instance, Bancroft referred to memory as "an easy dupe," and tradition as "a careless story teller." "An account," he continued, "to be of highest value, must be written immediately at the time of the event. The eyewitness, the ear-witness often persuade memory into a belief of inventions." The long note on the speech of James Otis on the Writs of Assistance was an excellent example of Bancroft's critical evaluation of the sources.

Bancroft lost no time in stating his theme: "The spirit of the colonies demanded freedom from the beginning." This, his main theme, and variations thereof echoed and re-echoed throughout his work. He glorified the Republic: "The United States constitute an essential portion of a great political system, embracing all the civilized nations of the earth. At a period when the force of moral opinion is rapidly increasing, they have the precedence in the practice and the defence of the equal rights of man." To Bancroft, the United States was the leader among all nations; no spokesman of the young Republic ever wrote with greater assurance.

This first volume treated the expansion of Europe into America, carrying the history of the colonies to the restoration of the Stuarts. In writing of the establishment of St. Augustine, the historian said that "it sprung from the unrelenting bigotry of the Spanish king.... In its transition from the bigoted policy of Philip II to the American principles of religious liberty" it was of striking interest to Americans. "Its origin should be carefully remembered, for it is a fixed point, from which to measure the liberal influence of time; the progress of modern civilization; the victories of the American mind, in its contest for the interests of humanity." Though Bancroft's history abounded in rhetorical excursions, he could sometimes write simply and impressively, as in his reference to the failure of Raleigh to plant a colony: "If America had no English town, it soon had English graves." As might be expected, Roger Williams was assigned an especially distinguished place in the historian's list of worthies. So too, the Quakers, whose New England persecutors were taken to task by this descendant of Puritans: "The fears of one class of men are not the measure of the rights of another."

During the next thirty years more volumes appeared, until ten in all were published, carrying the narrative through the Revolution. The title of the first volume had promised a history to the "present time," but for such a task life was too short—even for the long-lived Bancroft —and the later volumes bore the title *History of the United States from the Discovery of the American Continent.*

Though the second volume brought the story only to 1689, Bancroft was already preoccupied with the American Revolution. Writing of the hanging of the regicide Hugh Peter "for opposition to monarchy," Bancroft observed: "The blood of Massachusetts was destined to flow freely on the field of battle for the same cause; the streams were first opened beneath the gallows." At another point he paused to write in the same vein: "The Navigation Act contained a pledge of the ultimate independence of America"; at still another: "Bacon's rebellion . . . was the early harbinger of American independence and American nationality." Bancroft liked sweeping phrases, using them more skillfully than has generally been acknowledged: "Tyranny and injustice peopled America with men nurtured in suffering and adversity. The history of our colonization is the history of the crimes of Europe."[12]

Bancroft concluded his second volume with a summary, "The Result thus Far." There was a note of pride in the sentence: "Thus have we traced, almost exclusively from contemporary documents and records, the colonization of the twelve oldest states of our Union." In these pages Bancroft presented views strikingly similar to those of later scholars. He dimly anticipated Freeman and the latter's disciples, Herbert Baxter Adams and John Fiske, who believed that the roots of American institutions were to be found in Germany's primitive communities. ("Of the nations of the European world," said Bancroft, "the chief emigration was from that Germanic race most famed for the love of personal independence.") Like younger contemporaries, Bancroft celebrated the glories of the Anglo-Saxon mind. Another sentence anticipated Thomas C. Hall, who stressed America's indebtedness to the Lollards. "When America traces the lineage of her intellectual freedom," wrote Bancroft, "she acknowledges the benefactions of Wickliffe." The volume concluded with the statement: "We have written the origin of our country; we are now to pursue the history of its wardship. The period through which we have passed shows why we are a free people; the coming period will show why we are a united people."

[12] Cf. Voltaire's phrase, "The history of great events in the world is scarcely more than a history of crimes."

The third volume professed to cover the period from 1689 to 1748, but there was very little on the eighteenth century except an account of Indian civilization and colonial wars. The disproportionate amount of space assigned to the Indians partly reflected contemporary American interest of the 1840's in the life of the red man, who was still a vital factor in our history. This portion of Bancroft's work was much inferior to the first two volumes. It had no central theme, and the author wandered from one subject to another. For many years to come this was to remain the neglected period of our colonial history.

The next volume in the series, introducing the first epoch of the American Revolution, had for its subtitle *The Overthrow of the European Colonial System, 1748–1763*. There was a distinct speeding up of the tempo, with Bancroft's tendency to look toward the future more marked than ever: "The hour of revolution was at hand, promising freedom to conscience and dominion to intelligence. History, escaping from the dictates of authority and the jars of insulated interests, enters upon new and unthought-of domains of culture and equality, the happier society where power springs freshly from ever-renewed consent." The author quoted John Adams to the effect that "the history of the American Revolution is indeed the history of mankind during that epoch." Scattered through his pages were many observations that indicated how superior his concepts of historical writing were to those of Prince and Abiel Holmes. He insisted, for example, that it was the idea of continuity "which gives vitality to history. No period of time has a separate being; no public opinion can escape the influence of previous intelligence."

In writing the history of the American Revolution, Bancroft felt that he was "bound to keep faith with the ashes of its heroes." This conflict was "a civil war" in which men of the same ancestry were pitted against one another, "yet for the advancement of the principles of everlasting peace and universal brotherhood. A new plebeian democracy took its place by the side of the proudest empires. Religion was disenthralled from civil institutions. . . . Industry [freed from restrictions] was commissioned to follow the bent of its own genius."

The fifth volume, *How Great Britain Estranged America*, indicated that the work was to become far more detailed, for it covered only three years, to 1766. The first part was devoted to a picture of eighteenth-century life in Europe, with particular stress on the English aristocracy and its remoteness from American thought. Bancroft's approach, which emphasized the difficulty of mutual understanding between England and the colonies, was not unlike that of the later Charles M. Andrews in his *Colonial Background of the American Revolution*. The volume covered the storm over the Stamp Act and the debates in Parliament on taxing America.

The succeeding volume, the sixth, completing the history of the causes of the American Revolution, carried the narrative to May, 1774. The penal acts of that year, said Bancroft, "dissolved the moral connection between the two countries, and began the civil war." From the papers of Samuel Adams, with their revelation of the network of Committees of Correspondence, Bancroft drew his most valuable material for this period: "they unfold the manner in which resistance to Great Britain grew into a system, and they perfectly represent the sentiments and the reasonings of the time." As the chief engineer of revolution, Sam Adams was accorded a high place, while Hutchinson was treated with scorn.

The seventh and eighth volumes, *America Declares Itself Independent,* were detailed narratives of the two years to July 4, 1776. The rising tide of patriotic sentiment and the spirit of the Revolution were described with skill and proportion; probably no general historical work has ever done the task better. Contrary to conventional opinion of Bancroft's work, the historian was by no means eager to give offense to England. Discussing this very subject of animus, he wrote: "The tone of our writers has often been deferentially forbearing; those of our countrymen who have written most fully of the war of our revolution, brought to their task no prejudices against England, and while they gladly recall the relations of kindred, no one of them has written a line with gall."

The last two volumes took the story to the treaty of peace. While these, as well as the other volumes on the Revolution, were mainly a narrative of military hostilities, Bancroft did set aside chapters on the constitutions and internal history of the American states. His awareness of the international aspects of the struggle was reflected in his large-scale study of European intervention. The title of one chapter—"The King of Spain Baffled by the Backwoodsmen of Virginia 1778–1779"—revealed an interesting aspect of Bancroft's mind: he always tried to lift events out of their provincial setting to give them international significance. When he came to write on the causes that made the French alliance possible, Bancroft thought that "the force which brought all influences harmoniously together was the movement of intellectual freedom. We are arrived at the largest generalization thus far in the history of America."

Bancroft's first volume created an immediate sensation. Edward Everett wrote to him with unrestrained enthusiasm: "You have written a work which will last while the memory of America lasts; and which will instantly take its place among the classics of our language. It is full of . . . life and power. You give us not wretched pasteboard men, not a sort of chronological table . . . after the manner of most historians: but you give us real, individual, living men and women with their passions, interests and peculiarities."[13] Emerson declared: "It is noble matter, and I am heartily glad to have it nobly treated"; while Prescott placed Bancroft with the "great historical writers of the age."[14]

European praise was tempered with reservations. Heeren wrote from Germany, praising Bancroft's regard for sources, and expressing amazement at the mass of materials he had used: "You have chosen a great subject, it is a life work." Carlyle liked the color of the history but added "all things have light *and* shadow." Guizot qualified his praise with the reference that the work was "très démocratique." Even some Americans, at least in private, were keenly critical of Bancroft's achievement. John Quincy Adams noted in his *Diary* that the historian's treatment of the Navigation Act of 1651 was a "very lame account," and he disapproved also of his "florid panegyric." Bancroft's morality, said Adams, was "ostentatious," but "very defective"; yet his "transcendent talents" and "brilliant imagination" deserved acknowledgment.

The faults which Adams saw were transformed into virtues by Bancroft's idolatrous public. It hailed with delight this full-blown expression of Jacksonian democracy. Bancroft's history at once became the standard work on the United States; within ten years ten editions of the first volume had appeared. This and subsequent volumes ran through twenty editions or more before 1875. His history made him wealthy, but his expenses for books, manuscripts, and research assistance totaled over $100,000. A modern generation, however, knows scarcely more of his history than the author's name. Careful scholarship is dissatisfied with "his loud and uncritical Americanism" and with his omission of many phases of

[13] Howe, *Life and Letters of George Bancroft,* I, 205–206.

[14] W. H. Prescott, *Biographical and Critical Miscellanies,* 337.

colonial history. Where he wrote on the internal development of the colonies or on their relationship to the mother country his story was weak. His treatment of the early decades of the eighteenth century was also very sketchy, showing no real understanding of imperial administration. The colonists in their struggle with king and Parliament were right, and their opponents always wrong. Bancroft belonged to that school of historians which came to be called "prosecuting attorneys."

What invalidates most of Bancroft's material on the colonial period was the point of view which he adopted as a clue to America's history. His underlying theme was that even the early colonial years revealed a marked tendency to independence. Like most students of his day, he was interested in colonial history not so much for its own sake as for a background of the Revolution. Critical opinion encouraged that view. "What Mr. Bancroft has done for the Colonial history," said Prescott, "is, after all, but preparation for a richer theme, the history of the War of Independence, a subject which finds its origin in the remote past, its results in the infinite future." Jared Sparks, then the most erudite student of American history, made a similar approach, but with deeper understanding. "The more we look into the history of the colonies," he wrote, "the more clearly we shall see that the Revolution was not the work of a few years only, but began with the first settlement of the country; the seeds of liberty, when first planted here, were the seeds of the Revolution; they sprang forth by degrees; they came to maturity gradually; and when the great crisis took place, the whole nation were prepared to govern themselves, because they always had in reality governed themselves."[15]

In answer to later "scientific historians" who were critical of Bancroft's lack of objectivity, it should be remembered that he wrote at a time when history was something more than an investigation into the past—it was supposed to give instruction. The philosophic historians of the eighteenth century, in whose tradition Bancroft was largely reared (he read Gibbon daily), were not interested in history for history's sake.[16] These historians, as J. B. Black remarked, desired that history should "prove something," should "take us somewhere," should "provide us with a view of the world and human life." The idea of "progress" animated the thought of this school, and Bancroft was an apt pupil. He saw in the United States the goal to which civilization everywhere should

[15] Adams, *Jared Sparks*, I, 494.

[16] See J. B. Black, *The Art of History* (London, 1926).

aspire. "The inference that there is progress in human affairs is . . . warranted. . . . The trust of our race has ever been in the coming of better times." Bancroft in other respects, too, was akin to these eighteenth-century spirits who fancied that the moral world was "swayed by general laws. . . . Event succeeds event according to their influence . . . they form the guiding principle of civilization," arranging "checkered groups in clear and harmonious order." One could not, however, know "the tendency of the ages" intuitively, but must learn it by disinterested research.

Bancroft's kinship to earlier and to later writers—to Lord Acton, for example—was found in his notion that "as a consequence of the tendency of the race towards unity and universality, the organization of society must more and more conform to the principle of freedom."[17] In after years, when Bancroft was minister to Germany, Ranke told him that in his classes he referred to his history "as the best book ever written from the democratic point of view." In response Bancroft said: "If there is democracy in the history it is not subjective, but objective as they say here, and so has necessarily its place in history and gives its colour as it should."[18]

Bancroft's efforts to make his history a work of art often resulted in oppressing the reader. The stately rhythm of his writing became monotonous; the grand manner, too long sustained, grew boresome. Bancroft, in later life, took Carlyle's criticism to heart and rewrote his history. Although he dimmed, somewhat, the brilliance of the "light," he was never able to see any "shadow" in the history of his native land. The tone of the history became more moderate as the volumes succeeded one another, improving, too, in craftsmanship, but they continued "to vote for Jackson." That "cutting and pruning" which Emerson had thought necessary to Bancroft's development when he was still a young man should have been urged upon him all his life.

During the years Bancroft was writing his history, he was also active in politics, holding several appointive positions. Polk named him secretary of the Navy, in which position his chief contribution was to establish the Naval Academy. His next post was as minister to England (1846), where he took advantage of opportunities to collect materials for his history. With the growing ascendancy in his party of the Southern

[17] *The Necessity, the Reality, and the Promise of the Progress of the Human Race,* an address to the New York Historical Society, 1854.

[18] Howe, *Life and Letters of George Bancroft,* II, 183.

Democrats, Bancroft, opposed as he was to their proslavery sentiments, was shunted aside. His re-entrance to active political life was in part the reward for having written the message which President Johnson sent to Congress in December, 1865. Bancroft was given the congenial ministerial post in Berlin, where he remained from 1867 to 1874.

In the German capital the friendship of Bismarck gave Bancroft added distinction. The Jacksonian of the 1830's became the Junker of the 1870's. Yet there had always been a contradiction between his private life and his political philosophy. He liked the distinctions of the aristocracy, while heatedly defending the idea of American democracy. As early as 1823 he had written: "I love to observe the bustle of the world, but I detest mixing in it. I like to watch the shouts of the multitude but had rather not scream with them." Literary men in the romantic era often sentimentalized over the aspirations of mankind, but the behavior of man in the mass could be as suspect to "democratic" historians as it was to the most critical of conservatives.[19]

After Bancroft's diplomatic career was over, he decided to continue his history down to the adoption of the federal Constitution. In 1882 he published two volumes, the *History of the Formation of the Constitution of the United States of America.* The historian, now past eighty, continued to write in very much the spirit of the young author of thirty. "In America," he said, "a new people had risen up without king, or princes, or nobles, knowing nothing of titles and little of landlords, the plough being for the most part in the hands of free holders of the soil. They were more sincerely religious, better educated, of serener minds, and of purer morals than the men of any former republic. . . . [Their constitution] excelled every one known before; and . . . secured itself against violence and revolution by providing a peaceful method for every needed reform." (Bancroft, having lived through the Civil War, evidently had no desire to remember its violence when he was writing history.)

Many students, though recognizing merits in Bancroft's work on the Constitution, have marked its weaknesses. It was innocent of skepticism and too much of importance was omitted, notably the economic factors operating to influence political events. Bancroft perpetuated the conventional conservative treatment of Daniel Shays as a danger to prop-

[19] Cf. E. F. Goldman, "Democratic Bifocalism," in George Boas (ed.), *Romanticism in America* (Baltimore, 1940), 1–11.

erty rights, failing to understand the reasons for agrarian discontent. Perhaps as valuable as the text itself were the appendices of hitherto unprinted materials which comprised half of the two volumes.

Although Bancroft made many transcripts of papers in European collections, rigorous critics have pointed out that he did not always use them wisely in his history. Following the practice of his day he ran together disconnected reports making them into unified speeches, which he then put into the mouths of his leading characters. One excessively harsh critic, Sydney G. Fisher, said of Bancroft: "His researches for material both in this country and in Europe are described . . . as the most remarkable ever made. . . . But strange to say, we see no result of this in his published work. Nor can any subsequent investigator profit by his labors . . . many of his opinions are difficult to support with the evidence which the investigators are able to find."[20] Certainly some of the British papers he used should have given Bancroft another side of the controversy that preceded the outbreak of the Revolution.

Down to his death, in 1891, Bancroft was everywhere acknowledged to be the greatest historian of America, but younger men had already established a newer standard of scholarship which dated his volumes. The new generation of scholars, under the influence of the "scientific" school of history, pre-eminently exemplified by Ranke, went to extremes in ridiculing Bancroft and in making apologies for him. But Bancroft's faults should be measured, not merely counted. He was, in many respects, a characteristic spokesman of his age, which witnessed both in Europe and in America the publication of important nationalist histories. It was surely inconsistent to criticise Bancroft for the very fault which was often overlooked in German historians who were the idols of his American detractors. Bismarck thought that "next to the Prussian army, it was the German professors of history who had done the most to create the new Germany."

Bancroft, with all his weaknesses, brought order out of the records of America's past and placed the history of his own country in some sort of definite relation to that of Europe. That nearly everything he wrote has been rewritten is no very serious indictment—each new generation rewrites the past. A biographer suggested that the permanent value of

[20] S. G. Fisher, "Legendary and Myth-making Process in Histories of the American Revolution," American Philosophical Society *Proceedings,* Vol. LI (1912), 69.

Bancroft's history "may well be found to be as much in its presentation of the American point of view in the period in which it took form as in its record of an earlier time." Bancroft has often been spoken of as "the Father of American History." It is to the credit of modern historians of America that even before the third generation they had learned to avoid the sins of the father. But it is ungracious of them to ignore his virtues.[21]

JOHN GORHAM PALFREY

That last decade of the eighteenth century, which saw the birth of Sparks and Bancroft, produced a writer who was to become pre-eminently the historian of New England. That man was John Gorham Palfrey, born in Boston in 1796, and graduated from Harvard with his classmate Sparks. From his youth, said Palfrey, he was deeply devoted to the past of New England; his commencement oration dealt with the history of the Republic.

The first three volumes of Palfrey's *History of New England,* with the subtitle "during the Stuart Dynasty," appeared between 1858 and 1864. The historian had two main objectives: to trace in detail the interrelations among the New England colonies, and to write a narrative of those concurrent events in the homeland which affected the lives of the colonists.

The emigration to New England and the establishment of a social system in the new surroundings were the themes of the first volume. The historian, writing two hundred years after the events, fought again the political and theological battles that had disturbed his ancestors: "The name of Mrs. Ann Hutchinson is dismally conspicuous in the early history of New England." Toward the events of 1689 Palfrey exhibited the traditional provincial attitude which constantly interpreted the relations between the colonists and the crown as a conflict between "patriots" and "tyrants." He wrote apologetically of the witchcraft episode, seeking to palliate it by referring to similar conditions in Europe.

Palfrey brought out a fourth volume in 1875. In his history, he said, he was describing "the strenuous action of intelligent and honest men

[21] *Harvard Graduates Magazine,* Vol. XVI (June, 1908), 652; M. A. De Wolfe Howe, *Life and Letters of George Bancroft;* J. S. Bassett, *The Middle Group of American Historians;* N. H. Dawes and F. T. Nichols, "Revaluing George Bancroft," *New England Quarterly,* Vol. VI (June, 1933), 278–93; J. F. Jameson, *The History of Historical Writing in America* (Boston, 1891); R. B. Nye, *George Bancroft* (New York, 1945).

in building up a free, strong, enlightened and happy state.... Each generation trains the next in the lessons of liberty, and advances it to farther attainments; and when the time comes for the result of the modest process to be disclosed, behold the establishment of the political independence of America, and the boundless spread of principles which are working for good in the politics of the world." Thus in his eightieth year, the historian was expanding his commencement oration, "Republican Institutions as affecting Private Character."

Palfrey's anxiety to see in the events of the period, 1689–1740, indications of the later Revolution was a fault common to most of his contemporaries. Like others, too, he skimped the first half of the eighteenth century in his hurry to reach the Revolutionary era. The work concentrated heavily on politics, largely ignoring social and economic history.

"The plan of my work," said Palfrey, in a pathetically hopeful mood, "would be accomplished by the completion of one more volume, bringing down the narrative to the opening of the War of Independence." Despite his fears, Palfrey was able substantially to finish the manuscript of his last volume, the fifth, before his death in 1881; but it was not published until 1890. It was apparent that the declining vigor of the historian, already evident in the fourth volume, barely enabled him to carry on the research necessary for his last effort. This fifth volume (1740–75) was more like the old-fashioned chronology; it lacked the comparatively good organization and consecutive narrative of the earlier volumes.

In a tribute to Palfrey a fellow-New Englander said of him: "His excellence as the historian of New England and of her people is largely due to the strong flavor that was in him of the soil and the race." From his researches in England, Palfrey was able to get much valuable information in state papers, reports, correspondence, and other documents, and yet, what he had once said of Hutchinson and his history might with greater appropriateness be said of his own work: "All the details of his subject were vividly before him; [but] he did not understand his subject." Palfrey had once said, in a historical discourse: "The founders of New England left a rich inheritance to their children, but in nothing so precious as in the memory of their wise and steady virtue. May there never be baseness to affront that memory!" It was his self-appointed task to exalt that memory by patient, scholarly investigation. But, as another New Englander, Charles Francis Adams, wrote, Palfrey was devoid of skepticism, was "a victim almost of that terrible New England conscience" that guided his pen. This leading representative of the filiopietistic school of historians set up an impermanent monument as a token of his ancestor worship.[22]

RICHARD HILDRETH

Bancroft's fame so overshadowed other historians of America that their writings were almost completely eclipsed. The works of some of his contemporaries, however, fared better than his own at the hands of a critical posterity. One of these historians was Richard Hildreth, whose writing was strongly opposed to the prevailing temper of romantic nationalism. This Harvard graduate of 1826 had thought of writing a history of the United States in his student days; the work he eventually wrote was published in 1849. In the interim he had been editor of an influential Boston paper, the *Atlas,* and had written a successful antislavery novel as well as a campaign biography of Harrison.

The History of the United States of America . . . 1497–1789 was published in three volumes. Hildreth's opening words stated his view in unambiguous language: "Of centennial sermons and Fourth-of-July orations, whether professedly such or in the guise of history, there are more than enough. It is due to our fathers and ourselves, it is due to truth and philosophy, to present for once, on the historic stage, the founders of our American nation unbedaubed with patriotic rouge, wrapped up in no fine-spun cloaks of excuses and apology . . . often rude, hard, narrow, superstitious, and mistaken, but always earnest, downright, manly and sincere. The result of their labors is eulogy enough; their best apology is to tell their story exactly as it was."

The proud author called the reader's attention to the fact that, in 1849, "no other work on American history, except mere compends and abridgments, embraces the same extent of time." (It will be remembered that Bancroft had as yet published but three volumes, which brought him only to the middle of the eighteenth century.) "Nowhere else," said Hildreth, "can be found in the same distinct completeness the curious and instructive story of New England theocracy, the financial, economical, and political history of the colonies and the Revolution . . . the progressive, social, and intellectual development of our people."

[22] E. R. Hoar, Mass. Hist. Soc. *Proceedings,* Vol. XVIII (1881), 422–23; Palfrey, "A Discourse," Mass. Hist. Soc. *Collections,* 3d ser., Vol. IX (1846), 165–88; Adams, "The Sifted Grain and the Grain Sifters," *American Historical Review,* Vol. VI, No. 2 (January, 1901), 221.

The latter statement, however, was not completely justified in the text of Hildreth's work. The narrative was in the main, political history, although he did touch on education, immigration, religion, and social customs. His writing was often hardheaded and matter of fact. Unlike many other writers, he refused to be enthusiastic about the Quakers: "Their divine illumination superior to reason," was "in fact, but a whimsical, superstitious, ill-informed, passionate, narrow, ill-regulated reason, right no doubt, upon many important points, but often exaggerated; unwilling or unable to justify itself by argument or fact."

Hildreth's remarks on the effect of the revolution of 1689 were very interesting in the light of subsequent research: "By strengthening the Parliament, and increasing the influence of the manufacturing class, it exposed the American plantations to increased danger of mercantile and parliamentary tyranny, of which, in the acts of trade, they already had a foretaste—a tyranny far more energetic, persevering, grasping, and more to be dreaded than any probable exercise of merely regal authority." The historian did not like Cotton Mather, whose "application," he said, with a dig at Bancroft, "was equal to that of a German professor." During the witchcraft episode, Mather's "eagerness to believe invited imposture. His excessive vanity and strong prejudices made him easy game." Hildreth's caution, however, prompted him to remind his readers of contemporary belief in animal magnetism, and the like, lest they "hurry too much to triumph over the past."

When he came to describe the events of the 1760's, he told them in an unsensational manner, in some instances from a point of view that found later approbation. Writing of the Stamp Act, this contemporary of Bancroft said: "As commonly happens on such occasions, the immediate actors in these scenes were persons of no note, the dregs of the population." Their "revolutionary acts, designed to intimidate," were "melancholy forerunners of civil war." He spoke of the Boston Massacre, "for so it was called, exaggerated into a ferocious and unprovoked assault by brutal soldiers on a defenseless people." Hildreth had no love for the tales of war, then so frequently the staple of historical writing. He thought that war checked "the intellectual development of the people, or rather, turned that development almost exclusively into military and political channels. Of statesmen and soldiers, men great in action, we shall presently find enough. Thinkers are the product of quieter times." A contemporary (in *The Christian Review,* 1850) praised the historian for not catering "to the morbid relish for the disgusting details of battles."

The critical temperament of Hildreth was not betrayed into emotional excesses when he reached the stirring events of 1775: "There were in all the colonies many wealthy and influential men, who had joined indeed, in protesting against the usurpations of the mother country, but who were greatly disinclined to any thing like a decided rupture." The historian harbored no animosity against England. He took note, however, of "the domineering spirit of the British ministry and nation," at the same time paying quiet tribute to the New England yeomanry, "full of the spirit and energy of freemen," who "fought for their farms and firesides."

Hildreth handled impartially the question of the loyalists, but his interpretation of Shays' Rebellion and the events leading up to 1787 was strongly Federalist. The Constitutional Convention, he wrote, "represented in a marked manner, the talent, intelligence, and especially the conservative sentiment of the country. . . . The public creditors, especially, demanded some authority able to make the people pay. . . ." Although some eminent men opposed the Constitution, more numerous among its opponents were "the advocates of paper money, and of stop and tender laws," who "took the same side, as did all those whose ruined and desperate circumstances led them to prefer disturbance and revolution to the preservation of social order."

In 1851 Hildreth brought out a second series of three more volumes which continued the narrative to the Missouri Compromise. "In dealing with our colonial and revolutionary annals," he said, "a great difficulty had to be encountered in the mythic and heroic character . . . with which in the popular idea, the fathers and founders of our American Republic have been invested. . . . To pass from these mythical and heroic times to those which form the subject of the present volumes is like suddenly dropping from the golden to the brazen and iron ages of the poets." He noted that some conspicuous personages during the Revolution were described as possessed of "superhuman magnanimity and disinterestedness," who became later "mere ordinary mortals, objects of sharp, bitter, and often unmerited obloquy."

Though Hildreth again disavowed the use of "meretricious rhetoric" in writing his history and denied that his book was fashioned to fit "any partial political theory," his friendliness for the Federalists was clearly evidenced. Their leadership he thought superb: In Washington, Hamilton, and Jay, America had "a trio not to be matched, in fact, not to be approached, in our history, if indeed, in any other." Hamilton, "the real leader of the Federal party," was described as "a very sagacious observer of mankind, and possessed of practical talents of the highest order." He was wise in recognizing that the greater danger to the Union lay in the "resistance of the states to federal power than executive usurpation," but Hildreth thought Hamilton mistaken in believing that a president and senate chosen for life would strengthen the government. Jefferson was painted unsympathetically: "To sail before the wind as a popular favorite [was] the great object of his ambition." John Adams, on the other hand, wished "rather to guide public opinion than merely to sail before it."

In a very interesting examination of party divisions, Hildreth spoke of America's "natural aristocracy," comprised of the judiciary, lawyers, large landowners, merchants, and capitalists, the "clergy and the leading members of the great religious sects"; these generally supported Hamilton's measures. The "natural democracy" consisted mainly of small landholders, "men who cultivated their own farms with their own hands." Political divisions in the United States, as elsewhere, remarked Hildreth, "have arisen not so much from any direct contest between the principles of aristocracy and democracy, as from the factions into which the natural aristocracy has split; the democracy chiefly making itself felt by the occasional unanimity with which it has thrown itself into the scale of one or other such contending factions." Usually, however, there is no such unanimity, but a majority of the "natural democracy" under the influence of the "natural aristocracy" has been won to the side of the latter.

In a discussion of the international complexities of the late 1790's Hildreth's sympathies were with the Federalists and England: French "insults and injuries which, coming from Great Britain, would have set the whole country on fire, were submitted to with all the patience and even pleasure with which an overfond lover sometimes allows himself to be trampled upon and plundered by an imperious and profligate mistress." Again, referring to events a few years later, he wrote: "The manly resistance made by the Federalists to the insults and aggressions of France seemed to give them a hold upon the public mind such as they had never possessed before."

When the Republicans came to power, despite their earlier criticisms, said Hildreth, they immediately adopted most of the governmental machinery established by the Federalists, "testimony as irrefragable as it was reluctant, that however the so-called Republican leaders might excel the Federalists in the arts of popularity, the best thing they could do, in the constructive part of politics, was humbly to copy the models they had once calumniated." The New England historian referred to the "years of vexatious and ruinous commercial restrictions" in Jefferson's administrations, followed by the War of 1812, a "most disastrous and aimless war, ending in a near approach to national bankruptcy, and seriously threatening, had it not been unexpectedly brought to a close, the dismemberment of the Union." Hildreth said that the conflict was "an offensive war, voluntarily undertaken on the part of the United States to compel Great Britain, by the invasion and conquest of her Canadian territories, to respect our maritime rights."

On the question of Missouri's admission to the Union Hildreth, a Whig and always bitterly hostile to slavery, gave a decidedly Northern interpretation. The leaders of the Hartford Convention, he claimed, had a just provocation: "the provocation on the part of the South was their not being allowed to spread what they admitted to be a terrible evil over the whole territory west of the Mississippi." In Northern men this action was termed "moral treason," he said bitingly, but "in Southern representatives was but a manly refusal to submit to a domineering interference with constitutional rights." It was from the Missouri question, wrote Hildreth in 1851, that "recent American politics take their departure." During the last few years of his life Hildreth, worn out from his failure to achieve financial success as a writer, watched the American political scene from Trieste, whither he had been sent as consul by President Lincoln. He died in Italy in 1865.

Hildreth's forthright statements, right or wrong, were always refreshing. Self-consciously he wrote of the offense he gave to New England, "region of set formality and hereditary grimace," by his "undress portraits of our colonial progenitors." He was proud of "bursting the thin, shining bubble so assiduously blown up by so many windy mouths, of a colonial golden age of fabulous purity and virtue." Harvard's refusal to name him professor of history sharpened his hostile pen. In another work, *Despotism in America,* he referred to the "moral oligarchy" in early New England, and he anticipated later students with the observation that "the history of the contest in New England between Democracy on the one hand and the priestly and legal alliance on the other, has never been written." He noted that because of its apparent lack of dramatic episodes it had not attracted the attention of historians, who supposed that the progress of American democracy had been "quiet, silent and almost unresisted," whereas it was a "most violent and bitter struggle."[23] Theodore Parker, one of America's ablest critics, was on the whole favorably impressed by Hildreth's historical work though he objected to its lack of philosophy.[24]

Hildreth's formal history indicated his acceptance of the Federalist party program, but his other works revealed his opposition to their social philosophy. In these writings he sought to probe the factors—intellectual, moral, political, and economic—which operated in society. He brought out a thoughtful volume, the *Theory of Politics* (1853), in which the economic interpretation of history was more clearly elaborated than in his large-scale narrative. He had wide knowledge of leading European thinkers, and his analysis of the causes of revolts and political alignments was very keen. Though he did not regard wealth as the sole element of political power, he did consider it to be the most important, able to buy up all the needed props for its own perpetuation. The few rich could easily combine "to act together with energy and effect," paralyzing the opposition by bribing the leaders of the mass of the people. The only hope for the latter, he said, was for a split among the aristocracy, and then alliance with one of the factions.

In a reference to the French Revolution of 1848, Hildreth spoke of the socialist demands for the full return to labor of the value of the product created. If labor were the sole source of wealth, he asked, "why should not the wealth thus produced go exclusively to those whose labor has called it into existence, instead of sticking to the fingers of capitalists and speculators?" He went on to point out that rather than fight the socialists, property holders preferred the establishment of the Second French Empire.

His concluding chapter, "Hopes and Hints as to the Future," was largely Marxian in its argument. "The clergy, the nobles, the kings, the burghers have all had their turn. Is there never to be an Age of the

[23] *Despotism in America . . .* (1854), 13–14. In this work it is worth noting that Hildreth was very friendly to Jefferson as a democrat but hostile to him as a plantation owner with slaves.

[24] See essay on Hildreth in Theodore Parker, *The American Scholar* (Boston, 1907).

People—of the working classes?" asked Hildreth. "Is the . . . middle of this current century . . . destined to be that age?" It was emphasized that the distribution of the annual returns of labor was much more important than the distribution of the actually accumulated wealth. "But no redistribution even of that—though it might sweep away the existing comfortable class," he continued, "would suffice, very materially to elevate the condition of the great body of the people." What was really needed was a "great increase in the amount both of accumulated wealth and of annual products."

Hildreth was, however, more of an Owenite than a Marxian; he believed in a process of social change which was evolutionary and not revolutionary. He warned the rulers of society that "this socialist question of the distribution of wealth once raised is not to be blinked out of sight" nor "settled by declamations and denunciations, and mutual recriminations any more than by bayonets and artillery." Hildreth urged restraint upon the party of progress, advising it not to act, "for which it is at present disqualified by internal dissensions." The student of radical thinking in America might well turn to this and other little-known writings of Hildreth; indeed, increased attention has recently been given to him for his stimulating essays based on the utilitarian philosophy of Jeremy Bentham. To most scholars, however, his half-dozen volumes of history are apparently his chief claim to remembrance.

So critical a student as Channing, writing as late as 1917, said that Hildreth's work "remains to this day the most satisfactory account of the administrations of Washington and John Adams . . . it gives the facts accurately and in usable form." But it is well to remember that in his last three volumes he saw most of America's history from the view of Washington; he rarely left the Atlantic coast, and then not to go west but east to Paris and London.

Many writers in after years owed a large debt to Hildreth for the organization of his material and the philosophic grasp he displayed. College students were familiar with his work, using it as a text in the last decades of the nineteenth century, but thereafter Hildreth's volumes, along with those of Bancroft, were allowed to gather dust upon the shelves. New viewpoints on American history, as well as changed ideas as to the proper content of historical narratives, outmoded these distinguished historians.[25]

[25] A. M. Schlesinger, Jr., "The Problem of Richard Hildreth," *New England*

THE SOUTHERN VIEWPOINT

Historical writing in the South never showed the continuity of vigor apparent in New England. Southerners who might have been expected to write history sometimes excused their inactivity with the remark that they were so occupied with the tasks of governing that they had no time to pore over the records of the past—"they who are acting history themselves, care not to read the histories of other men."[26] The number of publications in the South was, however, not small. Near the close of the first third of the nineteenth century there was a reawakening of interest in historical writing. This was part of a general movement observable throughout the country at the time, but it was also an indication of the South's desire for independent intellectual expression.[27] This desire gained strength as the sectional division grew sharper in the next three decades when the South sought economic and cultural independence.

All the Southern states had their historians, who were particularly anxious to celebrate the achievements of their communities in the Revolutionary struggle. Major General William Moultrie wrote his *Memoirs of the American Revolution* (1802), as it was fought in the Carolinas and Georgia. A fellow-Revolutionist, the famous Light-Horse Harry Lee, also gave to posterity his interesting *Memoirs of the War in the Southern Department of the United States* (1812). These works contained more than the record of the authors' personal experiences, for they were fairly extensive historical narratives. Hugh McCall wrote the *History of Georgia* (1811, 1816); the versatile doctor, Hugh Williamson, published a *History of North Carolina* (1812), which was not highly regarded. Maryland had a historian, John L. Bozman, who, in 1837, recorded in great detail the colony's first thirty years. Another history of South Carolina was written in 1840 by one of the South's most distinguished literary figures, William Gilmore Simms. Historians had already appeared in the newer states to the west—John Haywood, in Tennessee, 1823, and

Quarterly, Vol. XIII, No. 2 (June, 1940), 223–45; D. E. Emerson, "Richard Hildreth," Johns Hopkins University *Studies in Historical and Political Science,* ser. LXIV, No. 2 (1946); M. M. Pingel, *An American Utilitarian: Richard Hildreth as a Philosopher* (New York, 1948).

[26] E. M. Coulter, "What the South Has Done about Its History," *Journal of Southern History,* Vol. II, No. 1 (February, 1936), 5.

[27] See *Southern Literary Messenger,* Vol. I, No. 1 (August, 1834).

Humphrey Marshall, in Kentucky, 1824.[28] Some periodicals, the *Southern Literary Messenger, DeBow's Review,* and the *Southern Quarterly Review,* published much historical material. But the South did not have the zest for history that New England and the Middle Atlantic states had. No one had yet surveyed the South as a whole nor had anyone there written the history of the nation.

GEORGE TUCKER

It was a source of some dismay that no Southern Bancroft had appeared, but finally George Tucker attempted to satisfy the need with *The History of the United States* . . . (4 vols., 1856). Tucker, who had been born in Bermuda and educated at the College of William and Mary, was a person of such talented versatility as to rank him one of the brightest intellectuals in the Old South. He had been a member of Congress, a professor of ethics in the University of Virginia, a writer on economics, and a biographer of Jefferson, before he turned to the history of the United States when he was seventy-five years old. He had known many of the prominent figures in American life, who helped enlighten him on the course of American history. In later life his Whig ideas and his belief in the ultimate extinction of slavery alienated him from the South, forcing him to move to the more congenial environment of Philadelphia.

Tucker's historical concepts were broad. The modern historian, he once said, unlike the earlier writer who treated only of politics and war, "aims to make us acquainted with the progress of society and the arts of civilization . . . everything indeed, which is connected with the happiness or dignity of man."[29] When he finally came to write his own history, however, he wrote in much the same manner as the historians whom he had thought were outdated.

Tucker rapidly disposed of the colonial period in order to reach the Revolution. He took the occasion to defend slavery, and furnished a useful corrective to contemporary writing by pointing to the similarities, rather than the differences, among the colonies on the eve of the Revolution. He wrote in praise of parties to whose clashing tendencies, he said, the United States "owe the highest civil freedom which is compatible with the salutary restraints of law and order." In a fair analysis of Jeffer-

[28] See R. L. Rusk, *The Literature of the Middle Western Frontier* (2 vols., New York, 1925), I, 242–49, for historical writing in this period.

[29] *Southern Literary Messenger,* Vol. I, No. 8 (April, 1835), 408–20.

son and Hamilton, Tucker said that the influence of Hamilton's political principles had almost disappeared, whereas the Virginian's had gained greatly in prestige.

Extended treatment was given to Jackson's administrations, on which Tucker wrote shrewdly and well. The most striking feature of these administrations, he said, was "that its presiding officer was unceasingly engaged in a series of angry controversies, which, whatever was their origin, always assumed more or less of a personal character." It could hardly be doubted, said Tucker, that Jackson's popularity "was rather increased than diminished by his belligerent propensities."

Though aiming at impartiality, Tucker laid no claim to being free of party prejudices. In an interesting concluding chapter, he defended the right of the South to deal with the slave question without interference from the North. While speaking of the South's intention to guard its institutions, he uttered a pathetic hope that the Union might continue. Depressed by fears of oncoming strife, he died in April, 1861, the guns of war already firing as he was buried on the grounds of the University of Virginia.

Tucker's history, written from the Southern point of view, naturally emphasized problems that had a sectional bearing, but it was probably as dependable as contemporary works written by Northerners, whose accent was on their region. It is one of history's minor ironies that Tucker's volumes were largerly ignored by the audience he addressed, who continued to read their own history as written by Northerners.[30]

CHARLES E. A. GAYARRÉ

The finest historian the South produced before the Civil War was probably Gayarré. Charles E. A. Gayarré, of Spanish and French descent, was born in 1805, in New Orleans, where his family had played an important part in the affairs of the old colony. As a young man he was sent to Philadelphia to study law, later being admitted to the bar. He was active in public life, both as judge and as United States senator, but ill health caused his retirement.

In his own community, Louisiana, Gayarré had before him the example of Judge Francois Xavier Martin, who had compiled a *History of Louisiana.* Gayarré translated and adapted Martin's history, bringing it

[30] L. C. Helderman, "A Social Scientist of the Old South," *Journal of Southern History* (May, 1936).

out in 1830 with the title *Essai Historique sur la Louisiane*. This historical romance—for it was not conventional history—covered the period to 1815. It displayed a literary skill that was to be an outstanding characteristic of all Gayarré's work. While regaining his health in France he prepared his *Histoire de la Louisiane,* which was published in two volumes, 1846–47. Partly under the inspiration of Sir Walter Scott, who was a great favorite in the South, Gayarré turned to the popularization of history. Fiction and history were closely interwoven in *The Poetry, or the Romance of the History of Louisiana* (1848) written in English to attract a larger audience. This dealt with the region's earlier years, but Gayarré had already been preparing materials on the later periods. Subsequent volumes on the French and Spanish domination of Louisiana (1854) fixed his place more firmly as an accurate and gifted writer. A final volume on Louisiana's history under American domination was published in 1866. Other productions came from his pen, including a suggestive study of Philip II of Spain, and an autobiographical novel.

Gayarré's volumes, written to a large extent from original documents, were as good as any work then being done in the United States. The volume on the Spanish domination, perhaps his best, treated a period that was congenial to him. He said that people enjoyed living in Louisiana under Spain; the colorful years 1769 to 1805 contained material well suited to his literary powers. The *American Domination* described the introduction of American institutions to a Europeanized Louisiana. This volume, on which Gayarré expended much care, covered the period 1803–16, and a supplementary chapter briefly sketched the years to 1861. The historian had tied his personal fortunes to those of his beloved state during the Civil War, and it was with a deep sense of tragedy that he issued this volume on the American domination: "My task . . . is done," he wrote, "but my love, as thy son, shall cling to thee in poverty and sorrow."

George Bancroft, in a note to Gayarré, said the latter had given his state "an authentic history such as scarce any other in the Union possesses. I have for years been making ms. and other collections," wrote Bancroft, "and the best that I have found appears in your volumes." In the long-drawn-out period from the Civil War to his death in 1895, Gayarré eked out a difficult living—sad epilogue to a valuable, productive life. "It is my horrible fate," he wrote to a friend, "to be compelled, for the sake of picking vile pennies, to live in the turmoil of a world of which I am so sick that I would become a monk if I could." The work of his earlier days placed him with American writers of the first rank; not until the twentieth century was the South favored with historians of similar distinction.[31]

BIOGRAPHY

In the second quarter of the nineteenth century American interest in biography as well as history was intensified. In addition to the many individual volumes issuing from the press, practically all periodicals included extensive sections of biographical material. Such was the eagerness with which readers awaited this literature that the *New York Mirror* called it "biography mania."[32] Unquestionably the memoirs of old Revolutionaries stimulated this interest, though biographical writing had, of course, a long tradition in colonial America, reaching at least as far back as Cotton Mather.

In 1810 *The Monthly Anthology* ran a discussion of biographical dictionaries, which included John Eliot's and William Allen's, both issued the year before. Some time later, in the first number of the *American Quarterly Review* (1827), an article on American biography listed four more biographical dictionaries in addition to Eliot's and Allen's. John Sanderson's *Biography of the Signers to the Declaration of Independence* (9 vols., 1820–27) was an especially noteworthy publication, but its excessively eulogistic tone irritated the critical mind.

Biographies were often criticised for being too long or too idolatrous. One reviewer said the modern biographer included everything in his work: "He prefixes an historical introduction, and happy it is, if his retrospect do not extend to the Deluge, or sweep over the civilized world." The biographer, it was complained, "rarely leads you into the private lodgings of the hero—never places before you the poor reasonable animal, as naked as nature made him; but represents him uniformly as a demigod." Jared Sparks, though not practicing what he preached, also was critical of fulsome biographies. "Should the future historian

[31] Louisiana Hist. Soc. *Publications,* "Gayarré Memorial Number," Vol. III, Part IV (March, 1906); *Louisiana Historical Quarterly,* Vol. XII, No. 1 (January, 1929), 5–32, contains Gayarré autobiography and bibliography; letters of Gayarré to E. A. Duyckinck, New Orleans, January 23, 1867, *Louisiana Historical Quarterly,* Vol. XXXIII, No. 2 (April, 1950), 237.

[32] 1830, quoted in Mott, *History of American Magazines,* I, 421.

rely on these alone for his authority," he wrote, "our descendants . . . will have the pride of looking back upon the most immaculate chapter of statesmen and heroes that have adorned the annals of any nation."[33]

Sparks took advantage of the public interest in biography to issue *The Library of American Biography,* and in announcing it he expressed the commonly accepted belief that "biography is only another form of history. . . . It admits of no embellishments that would give it the air of fiction," he said, with an implied rebuke to Parson Weems and others, "and yet its office is but half done, unless it mingles entertainment with instruction"—and thus he was less removed from Weems than he supposed. Washington Irving likewise agreed that "one of the most salutary purposes of history [was] that of furnishing examples of what human genius and laudable enterprise may accomplish."[34]

WASHINGTON IRVING

The career of the first president inspired many biographers in the early part of the nineteenth century, including the most famous literary personage of his day—Washington Irving. Before Irving had started on this project, however, he was drawn off in 1826 on an exciting biographical quest of another figure who was of perennial interest to Americans —Christopher Columbus.

Alexander H. Everett, minister to Spain and a student of history, suggested to Irving that an English version of Navarrete's collection of materials on Columbus "by one of our own country would be peculiarly desirable." Martín Fernández de Navarrete, perhaps the most learned student of the era of exploration, was then publishing a series of volumes on the Spanish voyages and discoveries. Irving seized the opportunity, preparing himself for his task by making his home with the great bibliographer, Obadiah Rich, then acting as American consul in Spain. Irving soon saw that the English-reading public would not be so much interested in a translation of Navarrete's documents as it would in a popular biography of Columbus. He worked industriously and seemed to enjoy it: "And so ends the year 1826," he wrote in his diary, "which has been a year of the hardest application and toil of the pen I have ever passed. I

[33] *North American Review,* Vol. XXX (January, 1830), 4.
[34] Irving, *Christopher Columbus,* 1850 ed., I, 56.

. . . close this year of my life in better humor with myself than I have often done."[35] After two years he completed the work, and in 1828 *The History of the Life and Voyages of Christopher Columbus* was published. Later, he brought out another book on the companions of Columbus.

Irving claimed to have used a wide variety of sources in the *Columbus,* but in the main it was based on Navarrete. Its vigor and charm substantiated his statement that he enjoyed writing it. His admiration for the discoverer was obvious; the description of the great voyage was well done, while the narrative of the return and reception at Palos was particularly moving. Irving's success was immediate and long lasting.

He now returned to the biography of Washington after abandoning a plan for a history of the United States. A good book on the first president, he said, "must be a valuable and lasting property. I shall take my own time to execute it and will spare no pains. It must be my great and crowning labor."[36] For many years thereafter the *Washington* kept Irving busy, but he did not work on it as conscientiously as he had on the *Columbus;* not until 1855 did the first volume appear. It dealt with Washington's life before the Revolution, but this, like succeeding volumes, was in reality a history of the times in which the subject of the biography lived. Although the work was not Irving's "crowning labor," it did on occasion reveal keen insight. The early popularity of Washington, he noted, "was not the result of brilliant achievements, nor signal success; on the contrary it rose among trials and reverses, and may almost be said to have been the fruit of defeats."

Despite the length of his biography, five volumes, Irving added very little to the earlier studies by Marshall and Sparks; in fact, he did not pretend to tap unused sources. Sparks found the volumes entertaining and instructive but did not think they should be passed off as a life of Washington. "Indeed," he said, the work "can scarcely be called history; it is rather a delineation of striking events, adorned with amusing incidents and anecdotes."[37] Although Irving's *Washington* was not greeted with much enthusiasm, his *Columbus* long remained a favorite with the general public and scholars. Even when, in after years, much

[35] P. M. Irving, *The Life and Letters of Washington Irving* (New York, 1862–64), II, 254.

[36] *Ibid.,* II, 424–25, December 18, 1829.

[37] Adams, *Jared Sparks,* II, 508–509.

new material had been unearthed, Henry Harrisse and Edward G. Bourne, two of the leading students of the literature of discovery, had kind words for Irving's Columbus.[38]

THOMAS HART BENTON

In the period before the Civil War few of the men making history also wrote it. On occasion they recorded the passing scene in letters or diaries, but they rarely produced a consecutive narrative. One of the era's most important publications, combining autobiography and history, was Thomas Hart Benton's *Thirty Years' View; or A History of the Working of the American Government . . . 1820 to 1850* (2 vols., 1854, 1856). Benton, who had been in the Senate, worked on these volumes in his retirement, and historians have recognized them as of the first importance. He also completed another useful work, the *Abridgement of the Debates of Congress from 1789 to 1856* (1857–61).

Benton said that as an active member of the Senate he "had an inside view of transactions of which the public only saw the outside." He could see how measures were promoted or thwarted; the secrets of "wirepulling" were open to him. His *Thirty Years' View,* he said, was not a "regular history," but "a political work, to show the practical working of the government."

The modern historian who wishes to look beneath the surface of events and get clues worth pursuing can find no better guide than Benton. In analyzing legislation relating to the disposition of public lands, a problem in which he was vitally interested, Benton said that many members of Congress then (1820) debating relief from debts contracted in land speculation were themselves "among the public land debtors, and entitled to the relief to be granted." In discussing the tariff bill of 1828, he quoted the remarkable speech of Representative McDuffie in opposition: "Do we not perceive at this very moment," said McDuffie, "the extraordinary and melancholy spectacle of less than one hundred thousand capitalists . . . exercising an absolute and despotic control over the opinions of eight millions of free citizens, and the fortunes and destinies of ten millions?" Benton went on to refer to the many allusions "coupling manufacturing capitalists and politicians in pressing this bill." He pointed out that the South, which had once been very prosperous, later grew

[38] S. T. Williams, *The Life of Washington Irving* (2 vols., New York, 1935), I, Chap. XIII; II, 227–31, 296–308.

slowly, whereas the North grew rapidly until it became "a money lender to the South."

Benton had promised Jackson, his hero, that he would write a review of his administrations. Much of his narrative was devoted to the Bank of the United States and his own opposition to it. In a reference to foreign affairs, he pointed to the interesting fact that in this sphere, where Jackson's impetuosity was most to be feared, the President was successful. In sketches of fellow-members of Congress, Benton presented excellent characterizations; that of John Randolph, of Roanoke, was notable. Throughout his work he digressed to point out alleged flaws in Tocqueville's estimate of American democracy.

Benton was deeply troubled by the South's discontent with her lagging prosperity, which she attributed to unfair federal legislation. It was this belief of "an incompatibility of interest," said Benton, "which constitutes the danger to the Union, and which statesmen should confront and grapple with"; he maintained there was "no danger to slave property, which has continued to aggrandize in value. . . ." Dissatisfaction with the distribution of wealth as effected by the laws "was the point on which Southern discontent broke out—on which it openly rested until 1835, when it was shifted to the danger to slave property." His appeal to the North to preserve the Union was largely based on the pecuniary advantage to be derived from it.

There was a cry of exultation in the chapter, "Last Notice of the Bank of the United States." For ten long years, wrote Benton, "the name of this bank had resounded in the two Halls of Congress . . ." and for the first time (1841) a session passed in which its name was not once mentioned. "Alas," said this bitter foe, "the great bank had run its career of audacity, crime, oppression and corruption." On another subject, the Oregon Territory, Benton quoted the prophetic remarks of Calhoun who spoke, in 1843, of the advantages of the region in trading with China and Japan. Markets would be opened for European and American trade, and, concluded Calhoun, "what has taken place in China, will, in a few years, be followed in Japan and all the eastern portions of that continent."

Because of Benton's Jacksonian bias he hardly did justice to the opposition. Nevertheless his work fulfilled his original intention—that it be a guide to the practical working of the government. Checked against other sources, it still retains great value.

VII

Francis Parkman

THE STANDARD of historical writing in America in mid-nineteenth century compared favorably with that of European contemporaries. On both sides of the Atlantic the nationalist, romantic school of historians predominated. The next generation looked back upon it and, ignoring its virtues, scolded it for its limitations—its obvious national, regional, and racial bias, its devotion to "drum and trumpet" history, its tendency to concentrate on colorful episodes and glamorous leaders. What the scornful critics neglected to note were the literary power and narrative skill which marked the best of the rejected historians. The "romantics," it should also be said, were usually as careful in the use of sources as were their self-styled "scientific" successors—they were, however, attracted to different types of materials. The "scientific" historians won out, only to lose the wide public devoted to the "romantics."

Francis Parkman, historian of the Anglo-French conflict for control of North America, was nurtured in the romantic tradition, but his books were not allowed to die as were those of Bancroft. Their faults were fewer, their virtues more numerous. Parkman's scrupulous care in using sources has not been surpassed by later writers, while his literary gifts have been the envy of a host of historians.

Parkman, born in Boston in 1823, was graduated from Harvard in 1844, but his education seemed to have been largely self-directed. He loved fine writing and read widely in the established English classics; his favorite books, however, were those on American Indians—Cooper rivaling Scott and Byron in his list of preferred authors.

At an early age he indulged his love of the forest, which was to be a main theme in his life work. In an autobiographical note, written late in life, he said: "Before the end of the sophomore year my various schemes had crystallized into a plan of writing a story of what was then known as the 'Old French War'—that is, the war that ended in the conquest of Canada." Here was stirring drama which his superb artistry was to recreate. Later, he indicated, he enlarged his plan "to include the whole course of the American conflict between France and England, or, in other words, the history of the American forest; for this was the light in which I regarded it. My theme fascinated me, and I was haunted with wilderness images day and night." Two ideas possessed him: "One was to paint the forest and its tenants in true and vivid colors; the other was to realize a certain ideal of manhood, a little medieval, but nevertheless good." He once explained to a fellow-historian how he had come to write the history of the French in America; it had come, he said, from two tastes—books and the forest.

Parkman took long walks through his beloved woods, tracing the battle lines that still scarred the now peaceful forest. The notes that he made in his student diaries were the historical materials of his riper years. On July 17, 1842, he wrote: "I went this morning to see William Henry. The old fort is much larger than I had thought; the earthen mounds cover many acres . . . the lines of Montcalm can easily be traced." In the fall of 1843 his health, which had not been too robust and had been injured "by numerous drenchings in the forest of Maine," was such that it was considered more advisable to send him to Europe than back to Harvard. In Italy his personal contacts gave him deep respect for Catholicism, traditionally opposed by his Puritan forbears. This close acquaintance with Catholics served him usefully when he came to write of their church in America.

For a brief moment, under family pressure, Parkman turned to law, but he could not keep his mind away from the Indians. He confessed he had "Injuns on the brain." Stealing time from law studies, he wrote Indian tales for the *Knickerbocker* magazine, all the while planning his great project. "In the way of preparation and preliminary to my principal undertaking," he said, "I now resolved to write the history of the Indian war under Pontiac, as offering peculiar opportunities for exhibiting forest life and Indian character." In the summer of 1845 on a trip to the West he gathered much material that went into *The Conspiracy of Pontiac*. He wormed information out of old settlers, talked with Indians, and studied the topography of the region near Detroit. His correspondence on historical subjects was already very extensive, as he had decided to devote himself almost entirely to history. His desire to see the Indian in his native state unchanged by contact with white civilization, "as a necessary part of training for my work," he said, brought him farther west in 1846. Although the trip was in preparation for historical writing, it incidentally resulted in a notable book of travel and adventure—*The Oregon Trail.*

Parkman's health was worse after his Western trip, and from then on it was always in an uncertain state. Few people, however, were aware of his suffering. Only after his death did it become generally known that he began the volume on Pontiac at a time when his health was particularly poor, and when his eyesight was so affected that he used a frame constructed like a gridiron to guide his black crayon: "For the first half year the rate of composition averaged about six lines a day." As time passed, his health improved so that he worked faster, completing the history in two and one-half years.

The Conspiracy of Pontiac appeared in 1851. The manuscript had been read by Jared Sparks, whose comments furnish something of a measure of the difference between the standards of the older and newer historians. The *Pontiac,* wrote Sparks, "affords a striking picture of the influence of war and religious bigotry. . . ." But he wished that Parkman would draw moral lessons in his history: "I am not sure but a word or two of indignation . . . at unnatural and inhuman developments of the inner man . . . would be expected of a historian, who enters deeply into the merits of his subjects."

Parkman requested criticism from his friend Theodore Parker. The latter's observations were keen and are worth noting because of many misconceptions which persist about Parkman's understanding of the Indian. "You evidently have a fondness for the Indian," said Parker, "not a romantic fondness, but one that has been tempered by sight of the fact. Yet I do not think you do the Indian quite justice . . . you bring out the vices of the Indians with more prominence than those of the European—which were yet less excusable. . . . It seems to me that the whites are not censured so much as they deserve for their conduct toward the Indians in these particulars"—rum, women, treachery, and cruelty.

Parker also made some helpful remarks on the technique of writing. "It always enriches a special history," he said, "to drop into it universal laws or any general rules of conduct which distinguish one nation from another. The facts of history which you set down seem generally well chosen. The historian cannot tell all; he must choose such as, to him, most clearly set forth the Idea of the nation—or man—he describes. Bancroft chooses one set of facts, Hildreth another, & how different the N[ew] E[ngland] of Bancroft from H.'s N. E."

The Conspiracy of Pontiac, while only a section of Parkman's large canvas, suggested its main outlines. "The conquest of Canada," he wrote, "was an event of momentous consequence in American history. It changed the political aspect of the continent, prepared a way for the independence of the British colonies, rescued the vast tracts of the interior from the rule of military despotism, and gave them, eventually, to the keeping of an ordered democracy. Yet to the red natives of the soil its results were wholly disastrous." To rescue from oblivion their struggle against the menace of the advancing colonists was the object of his work: "It aims to portray the American forest and the American Indian at the period when both received their final doom."

The difficulties that Parkman faced in writing this, as well as the other volumes of his series, were made clear in language fitting his subject: "The field of history was uncultured and unreclaimed, and the labor that awaited me was like that of the border settler, who, before he builds his rugged dwelling, must fell the forest-trees, burn the undergrowth, clear the ground, and hew the fallen trunks to due proportion."

The character of the Indian, as Parker had noted, received less than a just appraisal at the hands of the historian: "Ambition, revenge, envy, jealousy, are his ruling passions." It was a proud white man who wrote these words on the Indian: "He will not learn the arts of civilization, and he and his forest must perish together." After an examination of Indian civilization, Parkman studied the English and French rivals: "Canada, the offspring of Church and State . . . languished, in spite of all [support] from the lack of vital sap and energy. The colonies of England, outcast and neglected, but strong in native vigor and self-confiding courage, grew yet more strong with conflict and with striving, and developed the rugged proportions and unwieldy strength of a youthful giant. . . . In every quality of efficiency and strength, the Canadian fell miserably below his rival; but in all that pleases the eye and interests the imagination, he far surpassed him."

Pontiac, the leading chief of the Ottawas, determined to make war upon the victorious English, who were now spilling over into the diminishing lands of the Indians. The Indian chief, "though capable of acts of magnanimity . . . was a thorough savage. . . . His faults were the faults of his race; and they cannot eclipse his nobler qualities." The modern reader, further removed from the Indian than was Parkman, will question the justice of the remarks that Pontiac was "the Satan of this forest Paradise"; the implication of innocent white Adams and Eves was scarcely warranted.

The cries of warriors, the attacks on frontier posts, and the sickening details of border warfare filled most of the pages of *Pontiac*. The chieftain's long but futile siege of Detroit meant disaster to the Indian leader. Gradually his allies fell away, leaving him to make his peace with the English.[1]

Although Parkman planned immediately to get to work on the beginnings of his story of the Anglo-French struggle, ill-health again intervened to delay him. Not until 1865 was *The Pioneers of France in the New World* published, but Parkman had already written large parts of other volumes in his series. "Each volume," he said, "will form a separate and independent work." It was very probable that the uncertainty of his health caused him to arrange for publication in this way; it was his ultimate intention to remold his monographs into a continuous narrative.

Parkman wrote that the earlier volumes of his proposed series would be devoted to " 'France in the New World'—the attempt of Feudalism, monarchy and Rome to master a continent. . . . These banded powers, pushing into the wilderness their indomitable soldiers and devoted priests, unveiled the secrets of the barbarous continent . . . and claimed all as their own. New France was all head. Under King, Noble, and Jesuit, the lank, lean body would not thrive. Even Commerce wore the sword, decked itself with badges of nobility, aspired to forest seignories and hordes of savage retainers."

Against this combination "an adverse power was strengthening and widening with slow, but steadfast growth, full of blood and muscle—a body without a head." It was a case of "Liberty and Absolutism, New England and New France." When writing of the failure to plant a Huguenot colony in Florida, Parkman added: "To plant religious freedom on this Western soil was not the mission of France. It was for her

[1] H. H. Peckham, *Pontiac and the Indian Uprising* (Princeton, 1947), checks Parkman on several points and is friendlier to the Indians.

to rear in Northern forests the banner of Absolutism and of Rome; while among the rocks of Massachusetts, England and Calvin fronted her in dogged opposition." The historian, New England born, could see, however, the faults in his ancestral home: "Politically, she was free; socially, she suffered from that subtile and searching oppression which the dominant opinion of a free community may exercise over the members who compose it . . . in defiance of the four Gospels, assiduity in pursuit of gain was promoted to the rank of a duty, and thrift and godliness were linked in equivocal wedlock."

The Pioneers of France in the New World was divided into two parts, the Huguenots in Florida and Champlain in Canada. The bitter struggles between the Spaniards and the French for Florida were detailed in all their horror of massacre and countermassacre: "This pious butcher [Menéndez] wept with emotion as he recounted the favors which Heaven had showered upon [his] enterprise. . . . It was he who crushed French Protestantism in America." The vengeance that Dominique de Gourgues visited upon the Spaniards was described in milder language; in fact, his exploit was termed "romantic," but his courage, said Parkman, was sullied by "implacable cruelty."

The historian felt a deep kinship with all the chivalrous characters whose burning enthusiasm glowed in his pages. His view of history was close to Carlyle's belief that overshadowing personalities directed the course of events. Parkman spoke feelingly of Champlain, who "belonged rather to the Middle Age than to the seventeenth century." "The *preux chevalier,* the crusader, the romance-loving explorer, the curious knowledge-seeking traveller, the practical navigator, all claimed their share in him."

The high praise with which the *Pioneers* was received was repeated with even more emphasis when subsequent volumes appeared. Shorter intervals separated their publication—*The Jesuits in North America in the Seventeenth Century,* 1867; *La Salle and the Discovery of the Great West,* 1869; *The Old Regime in Canada,* 1874; *Count Frontenac and New France under Louis XIV,* 1877; *Montcalm and Wolfe,* 1884. The last work indicated that Parkman had leaped over a half-century to write the final act of his great drama, which he considered more important than the intervening period.

In the *Jesuits* the historian sought to "reproduce an image of the past with photographic clearness and truth." Sketches of individual

Jesuits, the trials and tortures they endured for their faith, made up the core of the narrative. In particular, Parkman singled out Isaac Jogues, "one of the purest examples of Roman Catholic virtue which this Western continent has seen." In the chapter, "Priest and Puritan," Parkman returned to his frequent comparison of the two competing civilizations, with the usual advantage on the side of New England. The Jesuits eventually failed to extend French influence: "The guns and tomahawks of the Iroquois . . . were the ruin of their hopes." The defeat of the Jesuits meant that the West would not be settled under the auspices of the French, and hence "Liberty," typified by New England, would ultimately triumph.

La Salle was revised and rewritten when much new material on the explorer was published by Pierre Margry, director of the Archives of the Marine and Colonies in Paris. The character of La Salle had a powerful attraction for Parkman, who admired his strong personality. The Frenchman "would not yield to the shaping hand [of the Jesuits] and . . . could obey no initiative but his own"; always he had an "intense longing for action and achievement." La Salle's aims were in conflict with the plans of the Jesuits, who set themselves implacably against him, regarding him as their most dangerous rival for control of the West. The Jesuits, in La Salle's scheme of things, were to restrict themselves to the Great Lakes region, while the English were to be kept behind the Alleghenies; "it was for him to call into light the latent riches of the great West."

Parkman's rich language painted the climactic voyage down the Mississippi: "Again they embarked; and with every stage of their adventurous progress the mystery of this vast New World was more and more unveiled. More and more they entered the realms of spring. The hazy sunlight, the warm and drowsy air, the tender foliage, the opening flowers, betokened the reviving life of Nature." The journey was ending in April's second week, 1682. As La Salle "drifted down the turbid current, between the low and marshy shores, the brackish water changed to brine, and the breeze grew fresh with the salt breath of the sea. Then the broad bosom of the great Gulf opened on his sight, tossing its restless billows, limitless, voiceless, lonely as when born of chaos." Parkman took leave of the leader, slain by conspiring subordinates, with the epitaph: "He belonged not to the age of the knight-errant and the saint, but to the modern world of practical study and practical action. . . . His whole life was a fight with adversity. . . . America owes him an enduring memory; for in this masculine figure she sees the pioneer who guided her to the possession of her richest heritage."

In *The Old Regime in Canada,* Parkman's purpose was to show how the French monarchy attempted to fasten its hold on its American colony, its partial success, and its eventual failure. "In the present book we examine the political and social machine; in the next volume of the series we shall see this machine in action." Ordinarily, Parkman was less interested in the slow process of establishing a civilization than he was in its unusual, colorful incidents. In this volume, however he came closest to modern interests in social history with such chapters as "Paternal Government," "Marriage and Population," "The New Home," "Trade and Industry," and "Morals and Manners." Though the material was well organized, the writing in these sections necessarily had less of the glow that lit the pages of frontier battles.

"One great fact stands out conspicuous in Canadian history," wrote Parkman in conclusion, "the Church of Rome. More even than the royal power, she shaped the character and the destinies of the colony. . . . The royal government was transient; the Church was permanent." The historian's pride of Anglo-Saxon ancestry dictated the concluding words: "A happier calamity never befell a people than the conquest of Canada by British arms."

The next volume, *Count Frontenac,* celebrated the deeds of "the most remarkable man who ever represented the crown of France in the New World." The first important struggle between the rival powers came under his rule. He organized a "grand scheme of military occupation by which France strove to envelop and hold in check the industrial populations of the English colonies." Parkman aimed to "show how valiantly, and for a time how successfully, New France battled against a fate which her own organic fault made inevitable. Her history is a great and significant drama, enacted among untamed forests, with a distant gleam of courtly splendors and the regal pomp of Versailles."

Montcalm and Wolfe, which followed, was acclaimed by the public as the finest book in the series, a judgment in which Parkman himself concurred. "The names on the title page," said the author, "stand as representative of the two nations whose final contest for the control of North America is the subject of the book." The historian explained that: "the subject has been studied as much from life and in the open air as the library table," a statement which was true of most of his work.

Parkman again compared the combatants and found "that in making Canada a citadel of the state religion . . . the clerical monitors of the Crown robbed their country of a trans-Atlantic empire. New France could not grow with a priest on guard at the gate to let in none but such as pleased him . . . France built its best colony on a principle of exclusion, and failed; England reversed the system, and succeeded." The historian was a master at generalization: "Pennsylvania was feudal in form, and not in spirit; Virginia in spirit, and not in form; New England in neither; and New York largely in both." The English colonies represented the future fighting against the past which was typified by French Canada—"moral and intellectual life" against "moral and intellectual torpor." It was a fatal struggle of "barren absolutism against a liberty, crude, incoherent, and chaotic, yet full of prolific vitality."

Throughout his work Parkman kept an eye on the European aspects of the colonial conflict. The glitter of Versailles cast a remote light in the darkness of the American woods; and the figure of imperial-minded Pitt, "this British Roman," loomed large in the Anglo-French struggle. Parkman, as was his way with his favorites, described the character of Wolfe at some length. The historian's own fondness for the military attracted him to the young commander, who seemed "always to have been at his best in the thick of battle; most complete in his mastery over himself and over others. . . . Wherever there was need of a quick eye, a prompt decision, and a bold dash, there his lank figure was always in the front." The long siege of Quebec wasted his frame, but "through torment and languor and the heats of fever, the mind of Wolfe dwelt on [its] capture." No writing could be more dramatic and more filled with suspense than the description of the successful attempt to scale the heights of Abraham. On the Plains of Abraham, two gallant soldiers, Montcalm and Wolfe, gave their lives for their rival sovereigns.

Toward the very close of his narrative, referring to the broad scale of military operations, Parkman mentioned what modern students wish he had elaborated further: "Now [1762] more than ever before, the war appeared in its true character. It was a contest for maritime and colonial ascendency; and England saw herself confronted by both her great rivals at once. . . . With the Peace of Paris ended the checkered story of New France; a story which would have been a history if faults of constitution and the bigotry and folly of rulers had not dwarfed it to an episode."

Praise from those fitted to speak came in abundance when *Montcalm and Wolfe* was published. "The book puts you in the front rank of living English historians," wrote Henry Adams. "Of its style and narrative the highest praise is that they are on a level with its thoroughness of study. Taken as a whole, your works are now dignified by proportions and completeness which can be hardly paralleled by the 'literary baggage' of any other historical writer in the language known to me today." E. L. Godkin, editor of *The Nation,* said he had never "been so much enchained by a historical book. . . . No one else does nearly as much for American literature." The aged George Bancroft paid a warm tribute, while Theodore Roosevelt asked permission of Parkman to dedicate to him his own work *The Winning of the West.*

In 1889 Parkman wrote to his friend the Abbé Casgrain, the Canadian historian, that although his health was better, "it is still an open question whether I shall ever manage to supply the missing link between the *Montcalm and Wolfe* and its predecessor *Count Frontenac.*" Fortunately he was able to return to his task; in 1892 *A Half Century of Conflict* was published. "The long day's work was done."

Of his last work Parkman wrote: "The nature of the subject does not permit an unbroken thread of narrative, and the unity of the book lies in its being throughout, in one form or another, an illustration of the singularly contrasted characters and methods of the rival claimants to North America." This book had less of the vibrant writing of the other volumes, and one sensed the author's hurry to finish his task; he was now a tired man. Parkman always liked to spin his story around some central character, and because he had none in his last installment, he was probably not much interested in it.

Although Parkman meant to be fair to the French, whose political and religious system he believed to be mistaken, his Anglo-Saxon view pervaded his writing. A French critic, whom Parkman thought unjust, said the latter saw "Canadian defects through a microscope, and merits through a diminishing glass." He did not mind sectarian criticisms of his work: "Some of the Catholics and some of the Puritans sputter at the book [*Jesuits*]—others take it very kindly only regretting that the heretical author will be probably damned."[2]

Parkman's sympathy for his aristocratic heroes, who were cast in a

[2] D. C. Seitz, *Letters from Parkman to E. G. Squier* (Cedar Rapids, 1911), 45, October 24, 1867.

medieval mold, stemmed from his own political convictions. "I do not object to a good constitutional monarchy," he once wrote to a correspondent, "but prefer a conservative republic [with restricted suffrage], where intelligence and character, and not numbers hold the reins of power." He thought the nineteenth century "too democratic and too much given to the pursuit of material interest at the expense of intellectual and moral greatness." To Pierre Margry he spoke with glee of the conservative victory in a municipal election: "Fortunately the low and socialistic elements—for we have them thanks to the emigration of 200,-000 Irish to Boston—have suffered a defeat."[3] Parkman's love of the pageantry of war came from deep within him; the military instincts, he said, "are always strongest in the strongest and richest nature." Even as a youth on his first trip to Europe he wrote in his diary: "Here in this old world I seem, thank Heaven, to be carried about half a century backwards in time. . . . Above all, there is no canting of peace. A wholesome system of coercion is manifest in all directions."

Godkin correctly placed a high estimate on the value of Parkman's contribution to American literature: for historians the New Englander's inspiration has an undying quality. "Faithfulness to the truth of history," he once wrote, "involves far more than a research, however patient and scrupulous, into special facts. Such facts may be detailed with the most minute exactness, and yet the narrative, taken as a whole, may be unmeaning or untrue. The narrator must seek to imbue himself with the life and spirit of the time. He must study events in their bearings near and remote: in the character, habits, and manners of those who took part in them. He must himself be, as it were, a sharer or a spectator of the action he describes." Plainly, history, he thought was "resurrection."

John Fiske was probably right when he said of Parkman: "Of all American historians he is the most deeply and peculiarly American, yet he is at the same time the broadest and most cosmopolitan." Later students argued that Parkman's volumes, written in the glow of Byronic romanticism, did not quite fulfill the highest ideal of historical writing. Surely one of his serious faults was neglect of social forces whose pressure in affecting the course of history may well have been as weighty as that of his dominant leaders. Nevertheless, though details of his narrative may be altered by supplemental studies, the main structure of his

[3] "Letters of Francis Parkman to Pierre Margry," Smith College *Studies in History,* Vol. VIII, Nos. 3–4 (1923), 165, December 15, 1875.

work seems built for permanence. It was a half-blind historian who made us see the heroism and villainy that stained with blood the green-carpeted wilderness he loved as much as life itself.[4]

[4] H. D. Sedgwick, *Francis Parkman* (Boston, 1904); C. H. Farnham, *Life of Parkman* (Boston, 1900); of many centennial appreciations, see Joseph Schafer, *Mississippi Valley Historical Review,* Vol. X, No. 4 (March, 1924), 351–64; W. L. Schramm, *Francis Parkman* (New York, 1937); Mason Wade, *Francis Parkman: Heroic Historian* (New York, 1942); O. A. Pease, *Parkman's History* (New Haven, 1953).

VIII

The Rise of the "Scientific School"

When Bancroft died in 1891, he had outlived his own school of historical writing by more than a decade. In a survey of American historical teaching in the 1880's, Francis N. Thorpe wrote: "Bancroft and Hildreth are our historians, but our history is yet to be written. The revival of historical studies in our generation is a step toward that consummation—the production of a complete history of America." Changes in historical writing were in abundant evidence in the 1880's—restrained expression, caution in statement, and a broader consideration of the social and economic background of American history. With the passing of the romantic school went a certain exuberance and spontaneity whose charm made literature of history. More than one observer regretted the passing of our younger days, fearing that our "matured" history writing might die of old age.

Historical studies began to enter deeply into the public consciousness. On the elementary level in the pre-Civil War era a hundred textbooks in American history had been published. In the heat of the nationalism that came as the aftermath of the Civil War, North, South, and West joined in prescribing American history in the schools.[1] Compilers of children's books, following the example of Noah Webster, substituted materials on American history for the conventional biblical stories that had been staple reading matter. About this time, Benson J. Lossing and Thomas W. Higginson were satisfying popular historical tastes with many articles in magazines. Lossing, in his *Pictorial Field Book of the Revolution,* sketched in pictures and in prose those incidents and scenes dear to American memory.

[1] B. L. Pierce, *Public Opinion and the Teaching of History* (New York, 1926), Chap. II; R. E. Thursfield (ed.), *The Study and Teaching of American History* (Seventeenth Yearbook of the National Council for the Social Studies, 1946), Chap. II by W. H. Cartwright.

The expansive growth of historical societies and the vitalizing of those that had existed almost in name only were other marked features of this generation of historiography. The creation and publication of collections of documents by these societies were of great aid to scholars. Contemporary with vast collections of sources then being made in England, Germany, France, and Spain, materials were being gathered in the United States to illumine the early history of the Republic. The published volumes of Peter Force's unfinished enterprise had revealed the wealth that lay at hand for the historical craftsman. State publications of colonial records were better organized than Force's work and proved a blessing to historians. *A Bibliography of the various Historical Societies throughout the United States* (1868) showed how much work had already been done in publishing documents and in writing local history.

STUDY OF THE ERA OF DISCOVERY AND EXPLORATION

Collections on the era of discovery and exploration—"the great subject," as the munificent collector John Carter Brown called it—were of special importance. For the first time American scholars, as a group, dug to the foundations of a subject, uncovering original sources upon which they based their narratives. Abandoning the preconceptions of earlier writers and speaking with caution, these scholars marked a transition from the older to the newer historical school. The interest of Americans in the period of discovery and exploration was but the local manifestation of a similar scholarly activity then in progress in Europe and Latin America.[2]

Noted collectors, like Brown, James Lenox, and Samuel L. M. Barlow, were enthusiastic bibliophiles who made available to students their rare materials. A number of writers turned their attention to episodes in the early history of the New World. John G. Shea made studies in early French exploration, editing the *Jesuit Relations* (1857–66). James C. Brevoort brought out his *Verrazano,* in 1874; and the following year

[2] F. Weber, *Beiträge zur Charakteristik der älteren geschichtschreiber über Spanish-Amerika* . . . (Leipzig, 1911), 22–27. See article by J. C. Brevoort, "Spanish-American Documents Printed or Inedited," *Magazine of American History,* Vol. III, Part 1 (1879), 175–78, showing the vigorous effect on scholarship caused by the publication of these documents.

the noted collector Henry C. Murphy discussed another phase of the same subject in *The Voyage of Verrazano*. The learned Harvard librarian and cartographer, Justin Winsor, wrote a biography of Columbus (1891), and then brought out in rapid succession three volumes on the exploration and settlement of the Ohio and Mississippi valleys. Winsor's interests were not those of Parkman; he was concerned rather with maps and documents for their own sake. A work of much value, whose publication was largely the result of Parkman's vigorous aid, were the six volumes of sources on French colonial history edited by Pierre Margry.[3] Even more important than these writings were the contributions of Henry Harrisse, which extended over some forty years.

Harrisse was born in Paris in 1830, came to the United States as a child, and secured his college education in the South. He qualified for the bar and moved to Chicago, where he vainly tried to earn a living. Eventually he left for New York, in which city he became a close friend of Barlow, who inspired in him a love for the study of the period of discovery. "Next to Christianity," thought Barlow, "the discovery of the New World was the greatest event of our era."[4] He was constantly emphasizing the necessity of consulting the original sources. "Even if there is . . . only one of our fellow-beings who longs to know the truth regarding the discovery and historical commencements of the New World, the book should be written," said Barlow. And then Harrisse wrote, in reference to himself: "Mr. Barlow made one proselyte, and . . . the task will be continued to the last."

Harrisse, who saw a magnificent theme for the pen of a historian in the rise, decline, and fall of the Spanish empire in America, recognized that bibliographical studies had first to be made. His *Notes on Columbus* (1866) was a good beginning. Encouraged by collectors, he undertook a more ambitious project, the *Bibliotheca Americana Vetustissima—A Description of Works relating to America* (1866); it made known to the student over three hundred items on the period 1492–1551. Harrisse said he had unearthed rarities in various parts of the country, sometimes finding them "in the dusty garret of a dilapidated church," where he pored "over them when the thermometer stood below zero."

[3] P. Margry, *Découvertes et établissements des Français dans l'ouest et dans le sud de l'Amérique Septentrionale 1641–1754* (1876–86). See Rev. John P. Cadden, *The Historiography of the American Catholic Church* (Washington, 1944), Chap. II, for Shea's work.

[4] H. Harrisse, *The Late S. L. M. Barlow* (New York, 1889), 11.

Although the great importance of his work was recognized by a small circle, the general reader was uninterested, and in disgust Harrisse moved to Paris. There, at last, financial success as an international lawyer made it possible for him to devote most of his time to his studies. Moreover, French scholars, among them Ernest Renan, heartened him with their warm welcome.

The fruits of Harrisse's labor were amassed in thirty volumes and many pamphlets, throwing light on various phases of his chosen subject. Six years after his bibliography of Americana was published, he issued a volume of *Additions* (1872), which revealed how eagerly he had combed the libraries of Europe for material. He found to his surprise that no library in Europe could compare with some private American libraries in the collection of books on his favorite period.

Harrisse had said of Humboldt's work, the *Examen Critique,* that it was "the greatest monument ever erected to the early history of [America]." A similar tribute by a distinguished scholar was later paid to his own publication, *The Discovery of North America* (1892).[5] Edward G. Bourne, who was well qualified to pass judgment, said that Harrisse's work was "the greatest contribution to the history of American geography since Humboldt's *Examen.*" Harrisse's lavish volume was a critical, documentary, and historical investigation, its careful analyses of conflicting evidence reflecting the author's legal turn of mind.

The discoverers who claimed most of Harrisse's attention were Columbus, Cabot, and Vespucius. His *Christophe Colomb* (1884) was an advance over earlier studies because of the publication of new documents and the author's customary sharp criticism of the sources. This, like his other works, was less a narrative than a study in historical criticism. In *John Cabot: The Discoverer of North America and Sebastian His Son* (1896), the son was held up to scorn: "Sebastian Cabot was a man capable of disguising the truth, whenever it was to his interest to do so." Harrisse gathered much material on Vespucius and worked up some of it; but he did not live to present it in a form comparable with his other publications. He had once written, long before his death in 1910, that his "task will be continued to the last," and with monkish

[5] José T. Medina, the great bibliographer and historian, said Harrisse was the real founder of the modern school of historians of the era of discovery and exploration, *Bibliotheca Hispano-Americana, 1493–1810* (Santiago, Chile, 1898–1907), VI, cxvii.

zeal he held to his vow. While subsequent students have not accepted all his conclusions, no one in his day was more familiar with the literature of discovery and exploration than the peppery lawyer-scholar Harrisse.[6]

IMPETUS TO HISTORY FROM THE CIVIL WAR AND THE CENTENNIAL, 1876.

The age of exploration aroused interest in historical writing among a limited few. A more general incentive was the Civil War, which stimulated interest in the whole field of American history, especially in the national period. Some escaped from the passions of war by returning to study the foundations of the Union which had just been preserved. Even during the war, in 1862, *The Historical Magazine* wrote that it was closing publication of that year's volume, "in the midst of a struggle which will for the next century be a matter of historic research and examination, and which in its overwhelming importance seems to banish for a season the study of the past." Yet, said the editor, "our past history, now more than ever claims, and is receiving, the attention of thinking men."

In the same magazine, soon after the war, a contributor made some acute observations. "It is really only now," he said, "that we are beginning to know for certain what were the undoubted facts in our revolutionary history of 1776. It will require fifty years of painstaking and painful waiting—fifty years of a new conscience and the . . . disrobing of passion" before the true history of the war of secession will appear.[7] While the war was still in progress, William H. Trescot, the historian of American diplomacy, was thinking of preserving materials for the future student. "It is only by a rigid and impartial scrutiny of all the testimony," he said, "that the future historian can reach the positive

[6] For biographical details, A. Growoll, *Henry Harrisse* (New York, 1899); H. Cordier, in *Bulletin du Bibliophile et du Bibliothécaire* (1910), 489–505; letters to Ildebrando Rossi, in *La Bibliofilia*, Vol. XXVIII (1927), 258–67; autobiographical letter to Barlow, 1884, MS in New York Public Library; R. G. Adams, *Three Americanists . . .* (Philadelphia, 1939); J. A. Borome (ed.), "Interview of Justin Winsor with Harrisse, 1891," *Hispanic American Historical Review* (August, 1952).

[7] *The Historical Magazine*, Vol. X, No. 5 (May, 1866), 166–67.

truth." The manuscript that he wrote in 1861 he referred to as "only a contribution to the materials of that future history."[8]

Memoirs of leading participants in the Civil War intensified public interest in history. Colonel Alexander K. McClure published a series of articles by military personalities in the *Philadelphia Weekly Times;* other editors likewise ran such articles in their journals. The most famous series of all was that in the *Century* (1885–88), under the editorship of Clarence C. Buel. These articles, later brought together in book form with the title, *Battles and Leaders of the Civil War,* were immensely popular, arousing widespread discussion.[9]

The approach of the centennial in 1876 was another impetus to historical writing. Moses Coit Tyler was most annoyed because his volumes on the history of American literature would not be ready for that date. Carl Schurz told Samuel Bowles, the famous newspaper editor, that a publisher had asked him to prepare a political history of the United States in time for the centennial year.[10]

Periodicals exclusively devoted to history—the *Magazine of American History* (1877) and the *Pennsylvania Magazine of History and Biography* (1877)—reflected the rising interest of Americans in their past. These journals, stimulated by the centennial, had been preceded by *The Historical Magazine* (1857–75), in whose editing Henry B. Dawson and John G. Shea had a large share. This publication came nearest to satisfying the need later filled by the *American Historical Review.* Samuel G. Drake, the Boston bookseller, antiquarian, and editor, was another force influential in stirring interest in history; not least among his labors was his editorial supervision of the early volumes of the *New England Historical and Genealogical Register.* The self-consciousness of the West was reflected in the establishment of the *Magazine of Western History,* which ran from 1884 to 1895.

BIBLIOGRAPHY AND SPECIALIZED HISTORY

The bibliographical activity of these decades was of transcendent importance, the names of Harrisse, Joseph Sabin, Paul L. Ford, and Justin Winsor standing to the fore. The prospectus of Sabin's *A Dictionary of*

[8] Trescot Papers, Library of Congress, August, 1870.

[9] Century Collection, MS letters, New York Public Library.

[10] F. Bancroft (ed.), *Speeches, Correspondence and Political Papers of Carl Schurz* (6 vols., New York, 1913), III, 113–15, November 27 and December 3, 1874.

Books Relating to America was announced in 1866, and two years later the first volume of this classic bibliography appeared. "Should I wait to make this bibliography as full and exact on all points as I trust it will generally be found, I should never complete it," he said. Sabin did not live to complete it, but Robert Vail and Wilberforce Eames, the dean of American bibliographers, eventually finished it. Another great work in this field was the *American Bibliography,* compiled by Charles Evans; twelve volumes were published, which included items down through 1799. A large task and one of inestimable aid to research in early American history was completed in 1947 when Clarence S. Brigham published his *History and Bibliography of American Newspapers,* 1690–1820 (2 vols.).

Improved studies of the individual states began to multiply, while narratives and collections of documents in religious history shed much light on the whole area of America's development. Very important work along these lines was done by Francis L. Hawks and William S. Perry. The latter's *Historical Collections relating to the American Colonial Church* (5 vols., 1870–78) brought to the attention of students many papers hitherto inaccessible. Charles W. Baird wrote on *The History of the Huguenot Emigration to America* (2 vols., 1885). John G. Shea dealt with the Catholic church in America; Abel Stevens published three volumes on Methodism (1858–61); and Henry M. Dexter, a learned scholar, compiled a valuable bibliography on the literature of Congregationalism. A work of great usefulness on all Protestant sects was the *Annals of the American Pulpit* (10 vols., 1856–68), edited by William B. Sprague.

A re-examination of certain aspects of the Revolutionary era had already begun. A friendlier interpretation of the Tories was presented by critical historians, notably Lorenzo Sabine in the *American Loyalists* (1847).[11] An interesting preliminary essay examined the classes in colonial society and their political allegiance. Sabine's book, which appeared in an enlarged and revised edition in 1864, had a significant influence on later writers who rescued the Tories from traditional obloquy. A century of America's history was better understood because of the pub-

[11] *The Life of Peter Van Schaack* (New York, 1842), by his son, H. C. Van Schaack, was called "the first attempt to present to the public of the United States a justificatory memoir of one of the Tories in the Revolution." See C. F. Adams, *North American Review,* Vol. LV (July, 1842), 99.

lication of the *Works of John Adams* (10 vols., 1850–56) and the *Memoirs of John Quincy Adams* (12 vols., Philadelphia, 1874–77). The indications are many that interest in the nation's past was at a high level, and that new forces were at work influencing the character of historical writing in America.

HISTORY TEACHING IN THE COLLEGES

More important than any of the factors hitherto mentioned in promoting a newer historical writing was the change that occurred in the teaching of history in American colleges and universities. The influence of these educational institutions was such that historians whose misfortune it was to live outside college walls were looked upon with condescension. Nevertheless, until nearly the end of the nineteenth century, many of the narratives read by the public were written by nonacademic historians—Bancroft, Hildreth, Prescott, Motley, Parkman, Rhodes, and others. Not until the last few years of the century did the academicians exert a preponderant influence on American historiography.

Colleges and universities had for some time, however, been affecting the teaching and writing of history. In earlier years Sparks at Harvard, William Dew at William and Mary, and Francis Lieber at South Carolina (later at Columbia) had given historical lectures of high quality, but these were isolated instances. Because of their intellectual pre-eminence in history and constitutional law Sparks and Lieber acted as clearinghouses for the ideas of contemporaries.[12] They realized the need, too, for better historical texts, and Lieber sought to fill that need. Little progress was made, however, and throughout America pedagogy was in a sorry plight. Even gifted professors taught history by having their pupils repeat from memory the dates in a manual or by having them recite its words.

The complaint which William Ellery Channing uttered in 1830 in his *Remarks on National Literature* had not lost its point. He granted that Americans were generous in spreading elementary education, but, he added, "we fall behind many in provision for the liberal training of the intellect, for forming great scholars . . . [who] can alone originate a commanding literature. The truth ought to be known. There is among

[12] C. B. Robson, "Papers of Francis Lieber," Huntington Library *Bulletin*, No. 3 (February, 1933), 147; see also Frank Freidel, *Francis Lieber* (Baton Rouge, 1947).

us much superficial knowledge, but little severe, persevering research . . . little resolute devotion to a high intellectual culture. . . . Few among us can be said to have followed out any great subject of thought patiently, laboriously, so as to know thoroughly what others have discovered and taught, concerning it, and thus to occupy a ground from which new views may be gained."

It was from Europe that Americans drew their inspiration for a fuller intellectual life. American and European intellectual relations had always been close, but never more so than in this period. What we need, said Henry Adams, writing home from London to his brother Charles, "is a *school.* We want a national set of young men like ourselves or better, to start new influences, not only in politics, but in literature, in law, in society, and throughout the whole social organism of the country—a national school of our own generation. And that is what America has no power to create. In England the universities centralize ability and London gives a field. So in France, Paris encourages and combines these influences. But with us, we should need at least six perfect geniuses placed, or rather, spotted over the country and all working together; whereas our generation as yet has not produced one nor the promise of one. . . . One man who has real ability may do a great deal, but we ought to have a more concentrated power of influence than any that now exists."[13] The "geniuses" that Adams so ardently desired for America very soon appeared.

Andrew D. White and Daniel C. Gilman had gone abroad in 1853 to study European educational methods. White, after three years' absence, during which he heard lectures under French and German masters, went to the University of Michigan to institute the first history courses in an American school that represented the modern trend. The path to change at Michigan had been eased by the higher standards already instituted by the progressive president, Henry P. Tappan. The young White read to his students the original sources from the rich library he had begun to collect. It interested them, he said, "far more than any quotation at second hand could do." History was placed at the forefront of studies at Michigan and, when White accepted the presidency of the newly established Cornell University, he carried there his enthusiasm for his favorite subject. "The historical works of Buckle,

[13] W. C. Ford (ed.), *A Cycle of Adams Letters* (2 vols., Boston 1920), I, 196, November 21, 1862.

Lecky and Draper, which were then appearing," said White, "gave me a new and fruitful impulse; but most stimulating of all was the atmosphere coming from the great thought of Darwin and Spencer—an atmosphere in which history became less and less a matter of annals, and more and more a record of the unfolding of humanity."

Lecky's history of rationalism stirred progressive minds in America.[14] Henry C. Lea, the historian of the Inquisition and one of the greatest scholars the United States ever produced, thought that Lecky's book would aid in developing a school "in which history may be taught as it should be. We have had enough annalists to chronicle political intrigues and military achievements," said Lea, "but that which constitutes the inner life of a people and from which there are to be drawn the lessons of the past that will guide us in the future, has hitherto been too much neglected."

Auguste Comte, the founder of sociology, had thought it possible, by applying the methods of natural science to history, to discover the laws of historical development and thus direct social evolution. He criticized the earlier historians with their too colorful political episodes and romantic attachment to great personalities. He advocated instead a study of society as a whole, believing that all peoples had a mass psyche which underlay the group mores.[15] Buckle believed that Comte had done more than any other writer to raise the standard of history, and his support of the French scholar's point of view helped to strengthen the latter's hold in English-speaking countries.[16] John Stuart Mill, whom the young Henry Adams considered "the ablest man in England," also deeply affected American thought. Mill and Tocqueville were "the two high priests of our faith," confessed Adams.[17]

The influence of Buckle was particularly great, many distinguished intellectuals falling under his spell. Theodore Parker was one of his earliest American correspondents, while Moses Coit Tyler once wrote of having been "obsessed . . . for weeks together" by the English historian.[18]

[14] Elizabeth Lecky, *A Memoir of William E. H. Lecky by His Wife* (London, 1909), 51–52.

[15] For the early influence of Comte in America, see R. L. Hawkins, *Auguste Comte and the United States 1816–1853* (Cambridge, Mass., 1936).

[16] H. T. Buckle, *History of Civilization in England,* 1883 ed. (2 vols., New York), I, 5 n.

[17] Ford (ed.), *A Cycle of Adams Letters,* I, 253, 281.

Americans, reflecting on their own national experience, were decidedly attracted to Buckle's thesis on the relationship between environment and the development of humanity; one of their own scientists, John William Draper, had been studying and working on this theme independently of Buckle.

Buckle, Lecky, and Draper[19] were not the only forces opening new perspectives to the young student. Seminar study provided an exciting experience to Americans abroad and this new delight in scholarship infused their teaching with unwonted zest. Herbert Baxter Adams, recalling student days in Berlin, spoke of the seminar with particular warmth: "Authorities are discussed; parallel sources of information are cited; old opinions are exploded; standard histories are riddled by criticism; and new values are established. This process of destruction and reconstruction requires considerable literary apparatus, and the professor's study-table is usually covered with many evidences of the battle of books."[20]

Charles K. Adams, a former student of White, introduced a seminar at Michigan in 1869, two years before Henry Adams initiated one at Harvard. The work of Henry Adams was of great value despite his own disparagement of his seven years' stay at his alma mater. Several of his students were awarded Harvard's first Ph.D.'s, among them some whose names are well known in the literature of history and economics—J. Laurence Laughlin, Henry Osborn Taylor, and Edward Channing. Adams was proud of "baking" his first "batch" of doctors of philosophy in 1876. To one of them, Henry Cabot Lodge, he wrote: "I believe that my scholars will compare favorably with any others, English, German, French or Italian. I look with more hope on the future of the world as I see how good our material is." The volume of *Essays in Anglo-Saxon Law* (1876) by Adams and his students "was the first original historical work ever accomplished by American university students working in a

[18] John Weiss, *Life and Correspondence of Theodore Parker* (2 vols., Boston, 1864), I, 467ff.; H. M. Jones, *Life of Moses Coit Tyler* (Ann Arbor, 1933), 141.

[19] Draper, a professor of chemistry at New York University, was the author of a *History of the Intellectual Development of Europe* (New York, 1863), which had a wide influence because of its evolutionary approach to history; see Donald Fleming, *John William Draper and the Religion of Science* (Philadelphia, 1950), Chap. VIII.

[20] "Seminary Libraries and University Extension," Johns Hopkins University *Studies in History and Political Science,* Vol. V, No. 11 (1887), 445.

systematic and thoroughly scientific way under proper direction"—this, at least, was the observation of a co-worker, Herbert Baxter Adams, who was more familiar with academic activities in history than any other teacher of his day.[21] Gilman thought that this Harvard volume might have given H. B. Adams at Johns Hopkins the idea for his own later *Studies*.[22]

Most of the younger men in the 1870's and 1880's were under the strong influence of John Richard Green and Edward Freeman. Green's *Short History of England,* in particular, was a great success in America. Green, said Henry Adams, "was the flower of [his] generation." James Ford Rhodes believed that Green had more readers in America than any other historian except Macaulay, adding that his power to shape the opinions of the reading public ranked him with England's greatest historians.[23]

The whole range of knowledge in these years felt the impact of Darwinism, principles of relationship and continuity being sought in every subject. Edward L. Youmans, a champion of the new thought in America, wrote to Spencer in 1871, the same year in which the *Descent of Man* was published: "Things are going here furiously. I have never known anything like it. Ten thousand *Descent of Man* have been printed, and I guess they are nearly all gone. Five or six thousand of [Huxley's] *Lay Sermons* have been printed . . . the progress of liberal thought is remarkable. Everybody is asking for explanation."[24] Charles Francis Adams said "a new epoch in the study of history" dated from the publication of *The Origin of Species,* adding "human history has become part of a comprehensible cosmogony, and its area vastly extended."[25] Historians dreamed of winning immortality by successfully applying Darwin's method to human history.

As a result of attending the lectures of leading scholars in France and Germany, American students at this time laid great stress on the

[21] *Ibid.,* 451.

[22] *Herbert Baxter Adams: Tributes of Friends,* John Hopkins University *Studies in Historical and Political Science,* Ser. XX, Extra No. (Baltimore, 1902), 55.

[23] J. F. Rhodes, "John Richard Green," *Historical Essays* (New York, 1909).

[24] Quoted in Sidney Ratner, "Evolution and the Rise of Scientific Spirit in America," *Philosophy of Science,* Vol. III, No. 1 (January, 1936), 113.

[25] C. F. Adams, "Historians and Historical Societies," Mass. Hist. Soc. *Proceedings,* 2d ser., Vol. XIII (1900), 89–90.

history of institutions, constitutions, social organization, legal theory, public law, administration, and government. Adams, who introduced to Harvard the habit of emphasizing institutional history, was thus akin in spirit to his contemporaries, Maine and Stubbs, Waitz and Fustel de Coulanges. In the seminar of H. B. Adams, at Johns Hopkins, students read on the wall before them the statement of Freeman: "History is past politics and politics present history." They were surrounded by portraits of men whose ideas fecundated their own—Pertz, Freeman, and Bluntschli, that revered master of Adams at Heidelberg. Above all others it was Ranke who most deeply influenced European and American historical scholarship. The great German historian had, it was thought, worked out a scientific method to arrive at objective truth, the writer freed from preconceived ideas.

The discontent that Ticknor had felt fifty years earlier when he compared his attainments with those of Europeans was still being experienced by Americans. "Every day I feel anew," wrote Ticknor in 1815, "what a mortifying distance there is between a European and an American scholar. We do not yet know what a Greek scholar is; we do not even know the process by which a man is to be made one." Then he added, with prophetic insight, "I am sure, if there is any faith to be given to the signs of the times, two or three generations at least must pass away before we make the discovery and succeed in the experiment."[26] The generations had now passed, the discovery had been widely made, and the experiment had already met with some success. The wish that Ebeling, the German historian of America, had expressed in 1817 was now beginning to be realized.[27] Referring to the four Americans—Everett, Ticknor, Cogswell, and Augustus Thorndike—then studying at Göttingen, Ebeling wrote: "I hope they will be the means of a learned intercourse between the worthies of the United States and Germany."

In his later years Ticknor revealed to his friend, the eminent geologist Sir Charles Lyell, something of the intellectual excitement then stirring in the scholastic world. He referred to the establishment of the Museum of Comparative Zoology at Cambridge and his own interest in it: "I think such an institution will tend . . . to lay the foundation for a real university among us. . . . I had a vision of such an establish-

[26] Hillard (ed.), *Life of George Ticknor,* I, 73n.

[27] "Letters of C. D. Ebeling," American Antiquarian Society *Proceedings,* Vol. XXXV, Part 2 (October, 1925), to Joseph McKean, June 11, 1817.

ment forty years ago, when I came fresh from . . . Göttingen; but that was too soon. Nobody listened to me. Now, however, when we have the best law school in the country, one of the best observatories in the world, a good medical school, and a good botanical garden, I think the Lawrence Scientific School, with the Zoological and Paleontological Museum, may push through a true university and bring up the Greek, Latin, mathematics, history, philosophy, etc., to their proper level. At least I hope so, and mean to work for it."[28]

Flushed with confidence, young Americans came back from Europe to their colleges and universities, and, in the reorganization of curricula then being effected, they made an important place for history. In a report to the trustees of Cornell in 1872, President White had bemoaned the fact that an American had to attend the lectures of Édouard de Laboulaye at the Collège de France or of Karl Neumann in Berlin to learn the history of his own country.[29] But it was not long before American history came into its own on its native soil. Chairs for history were created, and new courses instituted. Tyler held the first professorship of American history, established in 1881 at Cornell. In these years, said Charles K. Adams, American universities were more advanced than Scottish universities, and hardly behind Oxford and Cambridge in the teaching of history. Indeed, James Bryce thought Harvard and Johns Hopkins were already superior to British universities in their teaching of history and political science.

Americans had come of age and could look back upon their past with adult eyes. With the sophistication that was common to other teachers of his generation, Henry Adams wrote gaily to his English friend Charles Milnes Gaskell: "I am reading hard for a new course in American colonial history . . . in which I am to expose British tyranny and cruelty with a degree of patriotic fervor which, I flatter myself, has rarely been equalled." Herbert Baxter Adams thought Americans need no longer (1887) go abroad for instruction in history; it was available at Harvard, whose work in this field, he said, rivaled that of a German university.

When native faculties were more firmly established, students began to be trained in the United States in larger numbers, especially at Johns

[28] Hillard (ed.), *Life of George Ticknor,* II, 422, May 17, 1859.

[29] Laboulaye published a three volume history of the United States (1862–66); Neumann also published one in three volumes in 1866.

Hopkins under Adams and at Columbia under John W. Burgess. J. Franklin Jameson spoke of the "revelation" that Johns Hopkins was in 1876. Entrance into its atmosphere, he said, was "like the opening of the Pacific before the eyes of Balboa and his men. Here were no dated classes, no campus, no sports, no dormitories, no gulf between teacher and student where all were students, no compulsion toward work where all were eager."[30] The lengthy bibliography printed in the memorial volume to Herbert Baxter Adams revealed the scope of the Hopkins influence in the last quarter of the nineteenth century. In a tribute to his teacher, Frederick J. Turner said of Adams that his importance lay not in keenness of scholarship nor in the critical character of his investigations, but in the power to inspire "men with enthusiasm for serious historical work and in bringing out the best that was in them."[31]

The works of many scholars were published in the Johns Hopkins *Studies in Historical and Political Science,* and in the Columbia University *Studies in History, Economics and Public Law.* Charles K. Adams brought to the student a guide to historical literature with the publication in 1882 of his *Manual.* The work of a librarian like Justin Winsor was of great value in supplementing the efforts of Channing and Hart to establish the high place of American history at Harvard. Channing and Hart, through their *Guide to the Study of American History* and their many publications of rare documents, mapped out huge fields of our history.

The editorial labors of Benjamin F. Stevens, Reuben Gold Thwaites, Worthington C. and Paul Leicester Ford, and Victor H. Paltsits were of great assistance to historical writing; their volumes also fixed more firmly a high standard of editing. Among the many services of J. Franklin Jameson to scholarship was his work in connection with the historical division of the Carnegie Institution of Washington. He was the most active spirit in pushing important projects, particularly the editing of valuable manuscripts and publishing guides to materials on American history in European depositories. Other projects proposed by Jameson and his colleagues included an atlas of American geography and a dictionary of national biography comparable with England's. Years passed

[30] "The Johns Hopkins Anniversary," *The Dial,* Vol. XXXII, No. 377 (March 1, 1902), 144.

[31] *Herbert Baxter Adams: Tributes of Friends,* 45; see also W. Stull Holt (ed.), *Historical Scholarship in the United States, 1876–1901, as Revealed in the Correspondence of Herbert B. Adams* (Baltimore, 1938).

before very much materialized, but eventually these and other publications came from the press.

The invigoration of intellectual life that America experienced after the Civil War resulted in the formation of a number of societies among scholars in the social sciences. The founding of the American Historical Association in 1884, the establishment of the *Political Science Quarterly* in 1886, and the publication of the *American Historical Review* a few years later were signs of the change that had come over our native historical writing. High standards of craftsmanship were promoted, and the vigorous criticism of recognized scholars was a healthy stimulus to their younger colleagues.

Books were to change in content when McMaster brought the "people" into his narrative. The aspirations and defeats of the multitude have become as much the legitimate theme of the latter-day historian as the intricate developments of constitutional theory had been to the historian of an earlier day. "Our history is not in Congress alone," wrote a colleague of McMaster's in 1887; "that is, indeed, a very small part of it. Our discoveries, our inventions, our agrarian interests, our settlements westward, our educational affairs, the work of the church, the organization of charities, the growth of corporations . . . are all sources for research."[32] Henry Adams was writing to a friend in similar vein: "Society is getting new tastes, and history of the old school has not many years to live. I am willing enough to write history for a new school; but new men will doubtless do it better, or at least make it more to the public taste." He told Parkman that their school of history would soon be antiquated: "Democracy is the only subject for history." Henry's brother, Charles, also thought "that the day of the general historian of the old school" was over, and he prophesied the increasing importance of the monograph.[33]

New points of view were suggested by Frederick Jackson Turner, stressing the influence of the frontier in American history. The near monopoly that New Englanders had in writing American history was broken; Middle Westerners and Southerners refashioned the traditional interpretations of the American past. "General United States history," said Turner, "should be built upon the fact that the centre of gravity

[32] F. N. Thorpe, "The Study of History in American Colleges and Universities," U. S. Bureau of Education, *Circular of Information,* No. 2 (1887), 252.

[33] C. F. Adams, Mass. Hist. Soc. *Proceedings,* 2d ser., Vol. XIII (1900), 89–115.

of the nation has passed across the mountains into this great region [the Mississippi Valley]. To give to our history the new proportions which this fact makes necessary, must be the work of the younger generation of students."

The economic interpretation of American history (not unknown to some early students) was reinforced by a reading of Karl Marx, although he had little direct influence on American historical writing. Economists, particularly Thorstein Veblen, were among the first of the American scholars to appreciate the significance of Marx. E. R. A. Seligman's *The Economic Interpretation of History* (1902) was an analysis of this approach and noted the applications that had already been made of it in English, French, and American historical writing. Although critical of a rigid economic determinism, Seligman spoke of its great importance, observing that "the entire history of the United States to the Civil War was at the bottom a struggle between two economic principles." Wherever one turns in the writings of recent historical investigation, he said, "we are confronted by the overwhelming importance attached by the younger and abler scholars to the economic factor in political and social progress." Few writers went so far in their strict Marxian interpretation as A. M. Simons, in his *Social Forces in American History,* Gustavus Myers, in *The History of the Great American Fortunes,* Herman Schlüter, in *Lincoln, Labor and Slavery,* or Lewis Corey, in his suggestive studies of American capitalism.

No one did more to impress his fellow scholars with the value of this approach than Charles A. Beard. One of Beard's teachers, Herbert L. Osgood, was aware of the difference between their two generations. "Men of my generation," said Osgood, "grew up in the midst of great constitutional and institutional debates and our interest turned to institutional history. Profound economic questions have arisen and students of the younger generation, true to their age, will occupy themselves with economic aspects of history."[34]

Osgood's forecast was correct. Indeed, men of his own generation, Andrews and Jameson, swelled the volume of such historical literature, the former with a study of the Boston merchants and the Revolution, the latter with a fine, short survey of *The American Revolution Considered as a Social Movement* (1926). The most important contribution to the economic interpretation of the Revolutionary era had been made

[34] *American Historical Review,* Vol. XLI, No. 1 (October, 1935), 81.

several years earlier by Arthur M. Schlesinger, in *The Colonial Merchants and the American Revolution* (1918). Beard's volumes, *An Economic Interpretation of the Constitution* and *Economic Origins of Jeffersonian Democracy,* transformed the whole climate in which investigation of the early years of the Republic would subsequently be pursued. Beard's views had been anticipated by J. Allen Smith, in *The Spirit of American Government* (1907), but it was the former's documentation which made his work so impressive. The Civil War, too, underwent re-examination, and new light was thrown on its background by students who saw more in it than a constitutional struggle. Episodes in the history of labor found historians more accurate than were Rhodes or Oberholtzer. Henry David, in *The History of the Haymarket Affair* (1936), J. W. Coleman, in *The Molly Maguire Riots* (1936), and Almont Lindsey on *The Pullman Strike* (1942), showed how distorted by antilabor sentiments were the interpretations of earlier writers.

The scientific developments of the nineteenth century, with their facile general principles that explained so much, stirred the students of history to seek a like universal generalization in their own field. Most historians, said Henry Adams of his contemporaries, "have, in the course of their work, felt that they stood on the brink of a great generalization that would reduce all history under a law as clear as the laws which govern the material world. . . . The law was certainly there . . . to be touched and handled, as though it were a law of chemistry or physics."

No one tackled the problem with greater virtuosity than Adams, who found in the second law of thermodynamics a destructive blow to current social thinking. As he expressed it: "It was absurd for social science to teach progress while physical science was committed to destruction."[35] But such efforts to relate history and science, valuable as they were, ran afoul of the fact that scientific truths change, thus historical theories resting on them have transitory bases. A recognition of the special character of the organism of human society made scholars wary of drawing analogies between it and other organisms in nature.[36]

A most significant approach to history was the "collective psychological," advanced by Karl Lamprecht. According to this school the

[35] *A Letter to American Teachers of History* (Baltimore, 1910).

[36] C. A. Beard and A. Vagts, "Currents of Thought in Historiography," *American Historical Review,* Vol. XLII, No. 3 (April, 1937), 460–83; W. S. Holt, "The Idea of Scientific History in America," *Journal of the History of Ideas,* Vol. I, No. 3 (June, 1940), 352–62.

historian can understand the historical development of any age only in the light of its collective psychology, and the burden rests upon him to uncover the factors "which create and shape the collective view of life and determine the nature of the group struggle for existence and improvement."[37] Lamprecht's influence turned scholars back to intellectual history, and, under the leadership of James Harvey Robinson, a number of valuable studies were published exploring the growth of man's reason. Carl Becker, in particular, greatly enriched our perception of the spirit of the eighteenth century by his study of the *philosophes* and his analysis of *The Declaration of Independence* (1922).

The "scientific history" of the nineteenth century had tended to strengthen conservatism. Historians, said Becker, generally "studied the past as an inevitable process which must in any case be submitted to, but which, once rightly understood, might at least be submitted to intelligently. 'What is the use of rebelling against historical right?' asked Ranke." But the divinity of "historic right" was no more respected than the divinity of kings, and the "new history" raised the banner of revolt. Intellectual historians, like their forerunners, the *philosophes,* called for a "reinterpretation of the past in the service of social reform."[38]

Historians increased enormously the scope of their narratives and measurably deepened their understanding of the past by levying upon the contributions of colleagues in archaeology, geography, anthropology, ethnography, economics, psychology, and, particularly, sociology. The line between the historian and the sociologist seemed to vanish; in fact, the dominant group writing American history was spoken of as the "sociological school of historians."[39]

The accumulation of vast quantities of source and monographic materials has made it more and more difficult for any one person to master the whole field of our history. It is the opinion of many that Edward Channing's survey of American history in its entirety will be the last large-scale effort attempted by a single individual. Unfortunately death stopped him before his narrative caught up with contemporary America. The trend has been steadily in the direction of co-operative

[37] H. E. Barnes, *The New History and the Social Studies* (New York, 1925), 36, 198–203.

[38] Carl Becker, *Everyman His Own Historian* (New York, 1935), 170–72.

[39] Carl Becker, "Some Aspects of the Influence of Social Problems and Ideas upon the Study and Writing of History," *American Journal of Sociology,* Vol. XVIII, No. 5 (March, 1913), 641–75.

enterprise, and we may look forward to a continuing series of comprehensive histories written by individuals treating separate periods. The result, however, is often little more than a group of monographs thrown together and serves to emphasize the need for an integrated synthesis of the whole of American history. It must be a courageous spirit who will dare, alone, to scan the whole of our history and set himself the task of writing its record.[40]

[40] C. K. Adams, "Recent Historical Work in the Colleges and Universities of Europe and America," American Historical Association *Papers,* Vol. IV, Part 1 (January, 1890), 39–65; this is the best survey of what happened after 1860. See also J. A. Woodburn, Illinois State Historical Society *Journal,* Vol. XV (1922), 439ff.; A. D. White, *Autobiography* (New Yorw, 1905; W. C. Ford (ed.) *Letters of Henry Adams, 1858–1891* (Boston, 1930); J. S. Bassett, "The Present State of History-writing," in *The Writing of History* (New York, 1926); W. A. Dunning, "A Generation of American Historiography," American Historical Association *Annual Report* for 1917 (1920), 345–54; C. M. Andrews, "These Forty Years," *American Historical Review,* Vol. XXX, No. 2 (January, 1925), 225–50; Maxwell O. White, "History of American Periodicals to the Founding of the *American Historical Review,"* (MS thesis, University of Iowa, 1946); H. H. Bellot, *American History and American Historians* (Norman, 1952).

IX

Henry Adams

HISTORIANS of the "scientific school" were trained for the most part in the university seminars of Europe and America, and by the 1880's and 1890's their writings began to assume real significance. Henry Adams may well be said to have inaugurated this period in American historiography. The fluency of his style placed him with the literary historians, while his vigorous critical standards, comparative objectivity, and influence over academicians prompt his classification with the later group. His own career marked the transition from the group of literary historians—Parkman, Prescott, Motley, and Bancroft—to the professional historians of the late nineteenth century. Adams' devotion to French masters—Michelet, Renan, Taine—contributed much to his style and his view of historical development.

The romantic historians stressed narrative, appealed to the emotions, selected colorful episodes, and immersed their readers in the past. Adams concentrated on the sources, appealed to the intellect, brought the past to the reader, and emphasized the evolution of societal institutions. "My own conclusion," said Adams, "is that history is simply social development along the lines of weakest resistance, and that in most cases the line of weakest resistance is found as unconsciously by society as by water."[1]

The Adams family has been lavish in its contributions to American political and literary life. Its most important gift to historical literature was the *History of the United States during the Administrations of Jef-*

[1] William Jordy, *Henry Adams: Scientific Historian* (New Haven, 1952), 22, a very important book on Adams; H. D. Cater, *Henry Adams and His Friends* (Boston, 1947), 126; Max I. Baym, *The French Education of Henry Adams* (New York, 1951).

ferson and Madison, by Henry Adams. This representative of the fourth generation, one of the most interesting of them all, was born in 1838. After Harvard, study in Germany, and aiding his father in the London ministry during the Civil War, he returned to America. He wrote historical articles for journals and dabbled in reform politics before accepting a call to teach history at Harvard

In 1871 President Eliot invited Adams to give a course on the Middle Ages. As Adams expressed it in the *Education,* "between Gurney's classical courses and Torrey's modern ones, lay a gap of a thousand years which Adams was expected to fill." Despite his own gloomy judgments of his work, he filled the gap well, according to the testimony of some of his illustrious students. "He was the greatest teacher that I ever encountered," was Edward Channing's tribute. But Adams was not satisfied with his work and left after seven years. In retrospect, he wrote to Jameson about his teaching: "I became over-poweringly conscious that any further pretence on my part of acting as instructor would be something worse than humbug unless I could clear my mind in regard to what I wanted to teach. As History stands, it is a sort of Chinese Play without end and without lesson."[2] In looking back, these academic years "seemed to him lost," but at the time of "baking" his batch of doctors of philosophy in 1876, Adams saw himself and the world in a rosier light.[3]

In his last year at Harvard, Adams gave a course in the history of the United States 1789–1840, from which it was believed came his later writings on this period. Lindsay Swift, an Adams student, recalled that his teacher would assign students to debate on selected subjects, asking the sons of Federalist ancestors to exchange sides with sons of Republican ancestors. "To this day," said Swift, "I do not know which side Henry Adams favored—Federalist or Republican."[4] Adams measured his views against Henry Cabot Lodge's conservatism and thought his own teaching tended toward "democracy and radicalism."[5]

[2] Quoted in R. F. Nichols, "The Dynamic Interpretation of History," *New England Quarterly,* Vol. VIII, No. 2 (June, 1935), 163–78, November 17, 1896.

[3] Ford, *Letters of Henry Adams,* June 30, 1876; S. Mitchell, "Henry Adams and His Students," Mass. Hist. Soc. *Proceedings,* Vol. LXVI (1942), 294–312; Ernest Samuels, *The Young Henry Adams* (Cambridge, 1948), Chap. VII.

[4] L. Swift, "A Course in History at Harvard College in the Seventies," Mass. Hist. Soc. *Proceedings,* Vol. LII (1919), 73.

[5] Cater, *Henry Adams,* 81.

As an Adams, he came by his interest in the early national history of the United States quite naturally. In 1877 he brought out the *Documents Relating to New England Federalism* 1800–1815, and in 1879 he published a biography of Albert Gallatin, which was a happy augury for more important work to come. Adams had genuine enthusiasm for Gallatin: "He was the most fully and perfectly equipped statesman we can show. Other men, as I take hold of them, are soft in some spots and rough in others. Gallatin never gave way in my hand or seemed unfinished. That he made mistakes I can see, but even in his mistakes he was respectable."[6] Less beneficial to Adams' reputation was the biography of John Randolph, a bitter enemy of his grandfather, John Quincy, whose prejudice was inherited by the grandson. "I am bored to death," wrote Adams to John Hay, "by correcting the proofs of a very dull book about John Randolph, the fault of which is in the enforced obligation to take that lunatic monkey *au sérieux*."[7]

After "ten or a dozen years to Jefferson and Madison," said Adams in the *Education,* he brought out (1889–91) his nine volumes covering their administrations. He had been gathering materials for the work in America and in Europe, and in May, 1880, he wrote to Lodge: "I foresee a good history if I have health and leisure the next five years, and if nothing happens to my collection of material. My belief is that I can make something permanent out of it, but, as time passes, I get into a habit of working only for the work's sake and disliking the idea of completing and publishing." He planned at first six volumes for the sixteen years: "If it proves a dull story, I will condense, but it's wildly interesting, at least to me—which is not quite the same thing as interesting the public." Adams, depressed by his wife's suicide in 1885, neglected his history for some time, but by 1888 he was able to write with some relief to a friend, "Midsummer has come, the straw-berries and roses have dropped and faded, my last half-dozen chapters are begun."[8]

Historical scholars immediately recognized this work as one of the most significant that America had produced. Adams, following the pattern of Macaulay, introduced his history with several remarkable chapters on the social and cultural state of the Union in 1800. The presenta-

[6] *Ibid.,* 125, Adams to S. J. Tilden, January 24, 1883; the work was prepared with financial assistance from the Gallatin family.

[7] Ford, *Letters of Henry Adams,* September 3, 1882.

[8] *Ibid.,* May 13, July 9, 1880; July 15, 1888.

tion of materials on social history has never been done more interestingly. "Among the numerous difficulties with which the Union was to struggle, and which were to form the interest of American history," said Adams, "the disproportion between the physical obstacles and the material means for overcoming them was one of the most striking." As for the intellectual climate, Adams stated that "the American mind, except in politics, seemed . . . in a condition of unnatural sluggishness." The Congregational clergy, while still possessing prestige, "had ceased to be leaders of thought." Though Adams' belief in democracy was not robust, he had no sympathy for the extreme conservatism of New England Federalism, which had led to a dead end: "the future direction of the New England intellect seemed already suggested by the impossibility of going further in the line of President Dwight and Fisher Ames." New York, said Adams, was less hidebound: "innovation was the most useful purpose [it] could serve in human interests, and never was a city better fitted for its work." Its society, "in spite of its aristocratic mixture, was democratic by instinct," Pennsylvania had gone beyond her sister states; she appeared to be "the model democratic society of the world."

The words with which Adams portrayed Jefferson described himself as well: the Virginian's "true delight was in an intellectual life of science and art," and "he shrank from whatever was rough and coarse." His subtlety and contradictions fascinated Adams, who preferred Jefferson to Hamilton: "I dislike Hamilton because I always feel the adventurer in him," he once wrote to Lodge.[9]

No one has written better than Adams on "American Ideals," and he posed questions which democracy has not yet answered. He thought that, in 1800, "American society might be both sober and sad, but except for negro slavery it was sound and healthy in every part." In winged prose Adams recreated the dream of every American to fashion humanity anew. When he was composing his manuscript, Adams said he did not intend to give "interest to the society of America in itself, but to try for it by way of contrast with the artificial society of Europe, as one might contrast a stripped prize fighter with a life-guardsman in helmet and breast-plate, jackboots and a big black horse."[10]

Very skillfully Adams assembled the important personages at Jefferson's inauguration, and then he went on to discuss the organization of

[9] *Ibid.*, May 15, 1876.
[10] *Ibid.*, May 21, 1881.

the new government. In a short time, said the historian, "the energy of reform was exhausted . . . and . . . complications of a new and unexpected kind began, which henceforward caused the chief interest of politics to centre in foreign affairs. . . . The essence and genius of Jefferson's statesmanship lay in peace," and the tenacity of his hold on this idea is the clue "to whatever seemed inconsistent, feeble, or deceptive in his administration."

Adams wound his way nimbly over the tortuous path of American, Spanish, and French diplomacy. "Between the Americans and the Spaniards," said Adams, "no permanent friendship could exist . . . their systems were at war, even when the nations were at peace," and it was the Americans who were the "persistent aggressors." As for the French, Napoleon's failure to crush the Negro revolt in Haiti forced him to give up plans of a colonial empire in America and led him to sell Louisiana to the United States. Adams lingered delightedly over the theatricals with which Napoleon invested the sale of the territory; it was always the historian's pleasure to watch the play of mind upon mind. The constitutional difficulties into which the purchase of Louisiana plunged the Jeffersonians seemed to amuse him but he felt sorry for Jefferson. Privately, he thought Jefferson "a character of comedy," a victim of circumstances, helplessly carried along by the stream of history.[11] With incisive strokes Adams reached the heart of the debate over Louisiana, whose acquisition "profoundly altered the relations of the States and the character of their nationality."

The historian remarked that Jefferson's "extraordinary success" in foreign affairs in his first administration was paralleled by domestic accomplishments. Blundering Northern opposition aided him, especially the conspiracy of Massachusetts Federalists to detach New England from the Union. Adams traced the far-flung conspiratorial web with patient skill. The historian, after appraising Republican achievements in internal improvements, wrote generously that Jefferson "might reasonably ask what name recorded in history would stand higher than his own for qualities of the noblest order in statesmanship." But Adams could not easily shed his New England inheritance. The national government, during Jefferson's and Madison's administrations, he said, "was in the main controlled by ideas and interests peculiar to the region south of the Potomac, and only to be understood from a Southern standpoint.

[11] *Ibid.*, to John Hay, September 3, 1882; Cater, *Henry Adams,* 126.

Especially its foreign relations were guided by motives in which the Northern people felt little sympathy."

Jefferson's "overmastering passion," said Adams, "was to obtain West Florida." Abetting him were Monroe and Madison, who could not "resist the impulse to seize it." But negotiations with Spain over Florida were soon overshadowed by grave difficulties with England. "To the world at large nothing in the relations of the United States with England, France, or Spain seemed alarming," wrote Adams. "The world knew little of what was taking place." With the will to know that always characterized him, Adams found out what had gone on behind the scenes, and described the drama vividly. The millions of lives affected by this diplomacy, however, did not appear on the stage, even in the role of extras. It all seemed very remote, as Adams viewed the scene with the detachment of a scientist watching insects.

It was characteristic that in writing on domestic affairs Adams should have been particularly concerned with the internal reaction to questions of foreign relationships. It was especially interesting to observe his emphasis on American concern with international affairs in spite of his remark that the "United States moved steadily toward their separate objects, caring little for any politics except their own." He wrote brilliantly on diplomacy and politics in a patrician age, but he had no feeling for the life of the mass of men. Nowhere did Adams more clearly reveal the gulf that separates him from later historians than when he wrote: "Every day a million men went to their work, every evening they came home with some work accomplished; but the result was matter for a census rather than for history." Historians, even in his own day, were inclined to think that the life and work of a people were as much the proper subjects of historical inquiry as were minute details of diplomacy.

Beginning with the incidents of the *Chesapeake* and the *Leopard,* the historian measured the increasing tension in Anglo-American relations leading to the imposition and eventual failure of the embargo. As a result of the attack on the *Chesapeake,* said Adams, "for the first time in their history the people of the United States learned, in June, 1807, the feeling of a true national emotion." A clue to the niggardly policy of the administration toward the navy was found in the fact that the President "did not love the deck of a man-of-war or enjoy the sound of a boatswain's whistle; the ocean was not his element."

Adams, who clung to the original meaning of the word history, "inquiry," restlessly sought to know the psychology of nations. England expected her opponents to fight, and if they would not, "she took them to be cowardly or mean." The American administration, he said, "had shown over and over again that no provocation would make [it] fight; and from the moment that this attitude was understood, America became fair prey." Mingled with English contempt, however, was a "vague alarm" aroused by American threats to British commercial and naval supremacy. One effect of the events of this period, said Adams, was to make the Federalists a "British faction in secret league with George Canning." Jefferson preferred the embargo to war, with its dangerous influence on government, but, noted Adams, "personal liberties and rights of property were more directly curtailed in the United States by embargo than in Great Britain by centuries of almost continuous foreign war." The chapter on "The Cost of Embargo" was a splendid example of Adams' philosophic approach to history. He never forgot his own exacting standard for historical writing. The historian, he said, "must be an artist. He must know how to keep the thread of his narrative always in hand, how to subordinate details, and how to accentuate principles."[12]

He carried the reader at a rapid pace through the further ramifications of American diplomacy with England and France, finally leading up to the War of 1812. John Hay, who was his closest friend (but not his severest critic), wrote that volumes five and six "take the cake. There is a gathering strength and interest in these later volumes that is nothing short of exciting. The style is perfect, if perfect is a proper word applied to anything so vivid, so flexible and so powerful." Adams touched briefly on the economic significance of the embargo and nonimportation acts: "American manufactures owed more to Jefferson and Virginians, who disliked them, than to Northern statesmen, who merely encouraged them after they were established." The shifting status of Anglo-American relations was thus summed up: "As Canning frowned or smiled, faction rose to frenzy or lay down to slumber throughout the United States." The English minister, George Canning, was the evil genius throughout these protracted maneuvers; the harm he did was "more than three generations could wholly repair."

Turning back to the domestic scene, Adams took note of Henry

[12] Quoted in Jordy, *Henry Adams: Scientific Historian,* 57.

Clay's maiden speech as a senatorial "war hawk"; it "marked the appearance of a school which was for fifty years to express the national ideals of statesmanship." Thereafter, "the Union and the Fathers were rarely omitted from any popular harangue." The historian, descendant of diplomats, moved with easy grace in Congressional halls, Napoleon's court, and the council rooms of Britain. He well understood how impulses originating in one place were communicated to the others, and he carefully measured these forces. There was a machine-like movement of the narrative, effect following cause in precise progression.

There was an Olympian viewpoint in Adams' writing which put to shame the scribbling of lesser historical gods. Here was his overture to 1812: "As in the year 1754 a petty fight between two French and English scouting parties on the banks of the Youghiogheny River, far in the American wilderness, began a war that changed the balance of the world, so in 1811 an encounter in the Indian country, on the banks of the Wabash, began a fresh convulsion which ended only with the fall of Napoleon. The battle of Tippecanoe was a premature outbreak of the great wars of 1812." The young Republicans, said Adams, "were bent on war with England, they were willing to face debt and probably bankruptcy on the chance of creating a nation, of conquering Canada, and carrying the American flag to Mobile and Key West." This New England historian, reflecting his region's hostility toward the war, wrote critically of it, saying that probably four-fifths of the American people thought it could have been avoided. Madison's first term ended with "the country more than ever distracted, and as little able to negotiate as to conquer."

Adams followed the trail of war on land and sea; the parliamentary and diplomatic battles that accompanied martial events hovered in the background of his pages. Napoleon, whose enigmatic character strongly attracted the author, played almost as important a part in Adams' interpretation of American history as did the President. The historian, at home on the sea, described with keen delight American naval successes, which he attributed to the superiority of American naval architecture. He suggested also that the privateers which inflicted great damage on English commerce "contributed more than the regular navy to bring about a disposition for peace in the British classes most responsible for the war." The incompetence of American leadership on land filled Adams with disgust.

In New England, opposition to the war was increasing. Adams estimated that by 1814 "nearly one half of the five New England states supported the war, but were paralyzed by the other half, which opposed it." The national government itself was approaching exhaustion because of the lack of money and men to carry on the struggle; the Massachusetts Federalists now felt they could stop it. In his treatment of the Hartford Convention, Adams was moderately critical, but he took pains to show the contributions of Massachusetts to the war in a light more favorable than most writers were accustomed to do. It seemed that in England, too, the "war had lost public favor." The treaty which was finally reached actually left all the points in dispute "to be settled by time, the final negotiator, whose decision they [the Americans] could safely trust."

"The long, exciting and splendid panorama of revolution and war, which for twenty-five years absorbed the world's attention and dwarfed all other interests, vanished more quickly in America than in Europe, and left fewer elements of disturbance." Prosperity in America "put an end to faction," but New England did not share much in this wealth. In fact, the end of the war brought distress to Massachusetts, whose influence in politics suffered a sharp decline, whereas the South and West gained rapidly in economic and political importance. The Americans of 1815 were far less interested in the Rights of Man, which had troubled them in 1801, than they were in the price of cotton. In 1800 there had been indifference to internal improvements; sixteen years later people everywhere were actively interested in them. Although population was doubling within twenty-three years, wealth was doubling within twenty. Americans "with almost the certainty of a mathematical formula, knowing the rate of increase of population and of wealth . . . could read in advance their economical history for at least a hundred years."

"The movement of thought," which interested Adams more than the "movement of population or of wealth . . . was equally well defined." In religion, excitement tending to emotionalism was clearly in evidence, except in New England, where "the old intellectual pre-eminence . . . developed a quality both new and distinctive" in Unitarianism. Although in religion society tended to develop more divisions, in politics public opinion slowly moved in a fixed direction of emphasis on national sovereignty. Harvard College was at this time stimulating intellectual activity in many directions; "the American mind, as far as it went, showed both freshness and originality." Americans, thought Adams, "had as a people little instinct of beauty; but their intelligence in its higher as in its lower forms was both quick and refined."

The historian found that "the difference between Europe and America was decided," and in his political character, the American "was a new variety of man." Adams, along with James Bryce, noted that "the South and West gave to society a character more aggressively American than had been known before." Although "the traits of American character were fixed" as was the rate of population growth, Adams observed that the concern of history thereafter was "to know what kind of people these millions were to be." For an answer he thought that "history required another century of experience." His own volumes, he said, were "merely an Introduction to our history during the Nineteenth Century and [were] intended only to serve the future historian with a fixed and documented starting-point."[13]

One of the reasons that prompted Adams to write American history was his desire to establish his favorite subject as an exact science. Throughout his volumes he used the terminology of the physicist, often with striking effect. "By rights, he [Adams] should have been a Marxist," he said in the *Education,* "but some narrow trait of the New England nature seemed to blight socialism, and he tried in vain to make himself a convert. He did the next best thing, he became a Comteist within the limits of evolution." Comte, indeed, had a profound influence on Adams' ideas for many years. But in the end Adams reversed his beliefs completely. Where he had once agreed with Comte that society's progress was steady and worth while, he ended by believing in the social tendency to degradation. It was his prediction that by 1950, "present society must break its damn neck."

Adams, almost alone among American historians, tried to develop in detail a philosophy of history. Adopting the law of the dissipation of energy to human history, he foresaw a loss of vital power to the point of ultimate social stagnation. And that time was not far distant; in fact, he fixed it for the second quarter of the twentieth century. But Adams' "scientific" philosophy of history, which once seemed so plausible, has been fairly discredited by the recent study of William H. Jordy. Dr. Jordy found that Adams' pretensions to deep knowledge of science were merely pretensions. Adams, in much of his study, both in science and in

[13] Cater, *Henry Adams,* 480, October 6, 1899.

art, was no more than a lively dilettante, though often acutely perceptive. In the splendid *History,* however, he was the most skilled of professionals.

Edward Channing, a vigorous critic, termed the work of Adams a "masterpiece" and paid it the tribute of abandoning his own plans to write on Jefferson when he saw advance sheets of the *History.* Most students have praised the handling of diplomatic questions by Adams, who had an excellent knowledge of domestic and foreign manuscript materials. It is almost equally true, however, that many students have found fault with his treatment of internal affairs, which generally ignored the West and showed only a slight perception of the economic motivation in politics. In fact, long stretches of the *History* were but a series of political episodes placed in executive chambers or in legislative halls in Europe and America. In his almost exclusive devotion to Congressional proceedings as an expression of American politics, Adams was not unlike Schouler, but he was infinitely superior to the latter in skill of composition and analysis. Like a dart of lightning his keen penetration illumined dark corners and instantly blasted reputations.

Adams has not gone unchallenged. Defenders of Burr and the Virginians have denied the validity of many of the historian's strictures. The sharpest criticism of his work has recently come from Irving Brant, the biographer of Madison, who felt that Adams (along with almost every one else) minimized the Virginian's role in American history after 1789. Adams, it was argued, "did not understand the policies of Jefferson and Madison at all. He saw weakness and national humiliation, in their failure to go to war over this or that outrage"—impressment, the *Chesapeake* affair, or the French decrees. Jefferson and Madison, said Brant, preferred to husband the nation's rapidly growing strength as they faced "three choices—war, submission, or economic pressure and negotiation. . . ." They chose the third, "well knowing that war was the ultimate and probable alternative. Adams and a host of other writers have construed this course as submission, and have treated the War of 1812 as evidence of its failure."[14]

Adams was at his best in treating individuals, but, like most of his family, he was uneasy and unsympathetic in handling masses. He was no Whitman to draw a turbulent democracy to his breast. "Democracies

[14] Irving Brant, "James Madison and His Times," *American Historical Review,* Vol. LVII, No. 4 (July, 1952), 853–70.

in history," he once wrote, "always suffered from the necessity of uniting with much of the purest and best in human nature a mass of ignorance and brutality lying at the bottom of all societies." Like Comte, Adams believed in the intellectual élite exerting beneficent leadership in guiding the masses in society, with himself holding a dominant position in the select hierarchy. But the reformist program of his own group of intellectual aristocrats—honesty in government, civil service reform, lower tariffs—was too tepid for a society seeking solutions to the vast problems created by the industrial revolution. The peace of Adams' aristocratic soul was troubled by the disquieting symptoms he observed in American life. In his reform period he wrote to his brother Charles that he was preparing an article on political "rings": "I am going to make it monumental, a piece of history and a blow at democracy."[15]

The later volumes of the *History,* it may be noted, were more critical than the earlier ones. "They were written . . . in a very different frame of mind from that in which the work was begun," Adams admitted. The work as a whole, he said, "belongs to the *me* of 1870; a strangely different being from the *me* of 1890."[16] The generous idealism and hope of reform of earlier years had given way to ennui, cynicism, and gloomy predictions of worthless humanity's impending doom. And yet his habit of reducing everything to ashes was often a pose (he called himself a "moral dyspeptic"). To his intimates he was warm and compassionate; his self-conscious rationalism covered a never vanquished romanticism. Many Americans like Adams retreated to inner exile to escape the repulsions of an uncongenial world. Inner exile was re-enforced by a flight in space, usually to Europe. Adams used both escapes, adding a third, a flight in time—return to the Middle Ages, the pilgrimage to piety. The mass economic, political, and physical pressures of the modern mechanized world, which affected society with a glacier-like determinism, were antipathetic to his artist's temperament.

In the *Education* Adams wrote that he had "published a dozen volumes of American history . . . to satisfy himself whether, by the severest process of stating, with the least possible comment, such facts as seemed sure, in such order as seemed rigorously consequent, he could fix for a familiar moment a necessary sequence of human movement"; but he complained he "had toiled in vain." The historian of today, who also

[15] Ford, *Letters of Henry Adams,* January 27, 1869.
[16] *Ibid.,* January 2, February 6, 1891.

knows how difficult it is to follow clues through seeming chaos, can sympathize with Adams; he is also grateful that Adams' volumes were written, for they mark one of the highest achievements in American historiography.[17]

[17] Much has been written on Adams; see H. S. Commager, "Henry Adams," in *The Marcus W. Jernegan Essays in American Historiography* (Chicago, 1937), 191–206; W. H. Jordy, *Henry Adams: Scientific Historian* (New Haven, 1952), with annotated bibliography; Thornton Anderson, *Brooks Adams: Constructive Conservative* (Ithaca, 1951), for influence of Brooks and Henry upon each other.

X

The Nationalist School

The generation that grew up after the Civil War and succeeding generations up to the present read insatiably about the great conflict. Historians looking for a fit theme turned away from the fields of colonial history, already harvested they thought, and eagerly seized upon the middle period. Some went back to the Revolution for a running start, but James Ford Rhodes, seeking an "epic" period, began with the year 1850. A Southerner had gloomily prophesied that to the South's overflowing cup would be added the bitter taste of having the history of the war written by Northerners. The publications, for many years after, verified his dour prediction.

Although many of the historians who wrote on this period were trained in the use of documents and the weighing of evidence, they did not feel their task completed with the mere statement of facts. They donned the judicial role also, and despite prior professions of impartiality, they passed sentence upon the offending South. These prosecuting historians, worshiping that new deity, the national state, and believing in the essential immorality of slaveholding, indicted the South on two counts—as the assailant of nationality and as the defender of a decadent civilization. When their narratives digressed to include materials on social and economic history, they generally revealed a basic conservatism. They identified progress with prosperity, and were cold to protests for social reform—except for abolition. Labor, when treated at all, was generally associated with "troubles," such as strikes and "agitators"; agrarian discontent was identified with malignant currency inflation. For the most part, however, histories written by the nationalists dealt with conflicting constitutional interpretations—the mingled shouts of slavery and antislavery forces, and the murmurs of compromisers seeking to stave off the armed struggle.

Deification of the national state was closely related to glorification of the role of Anglo-Saxon peoples in furthering political progress. Darwinism apparently sanctioned the spread of Anglo-Saxon civilization because it had seemed the fittest to survive, and it was to the advantage of other peoples to pattern themselves after this dominant group—or else succumb in the inevitable struggle between them.

Before Darwin and Spencer supplied scientific terminology to the literary world, American historians had already preached the superiority of certain groups over others. In the eyes of Bancroft, Parkman, and Motley, liberty—political and religious—and the orderly progress of modern civilization were largely due to the efforts of Anglo-Saxon Protestants. Social change among Anglo-Saxons, it was said, was orderly, and even their revolutions were relatively polite, unlike the murderous events of Celtic and Latin catastrophes such as the French Revolution. Peoples other than Anglo-Saxons, it was asserted, were obviously of inferior stock. Immigrants from Ireland and from southern and eastern Europe were often spoken of as "hordes of ignorant foreigners." The English historian Freeman claimed American support for his flippant remark that the United States would be a grand land "if only every Irishman would kill a negro, and be hanged for it."[1] On Freeman's coat of arms, said Dunning, "were emblazoned the Anglo-Saxon militant, the Teuton rampant, and the Aryan eternally triumphant."

John Fiske, an ardent disciple of Darwin, Spencer, and Freeman, was convinced that the most suitable practice of political organization—federalism—had been created by American Anglo-Saxons. Burgess, too, was a strong believer in the racial superiority of Anglo-Saxons and in their surpassing political wisdom. In his work, *Political Science and Comparative Constitutional Law* (1890), Burgess asserted that the Teutonic peoples, because of their pre-eminence in building national states, must "assume the leadership in the establishment and administration of states"—not only over backward, i.e., barbaric peoples, but also over any people politically incompetent. With less emphasis Von Holst and McMaster held the same ideas. Their histories gave coherence to the sentiment of nationalism, and in the books of Burgess and Alfred T. Mahan writers

[1] *Life and Letters of Edward A. Freeman* (New York, 1895), II, 242.

found an arsenal whose weapons, though literary, helped prepare the way in the 1890's for the real instruments of war.[2]

HERMANN VON HOLST

Hermann von Holst, whose history of the United States expressed an intense American nationalism, was born in 1841, in Livonia (now Estonia), a Baltic province of Russia inhabited by many Germans. He was trained at Heidelberg, where he took his Ph.D. in 1865. Hostile to the Russian regime, he sought the freedom of America two years later. In the New World he projected a work on the evils of absolutism, meanwhile participating actively in Republican politics in New York. He had not been in America long when his friends, the noted Professor Heinrich von Sybel and the well-known student of American life Friedrich Kapp, commended von Holst to Bremen merchants who commissioned him to write informative essays on the United States. From the small beginning of newspaper and magazine articles that von Holst wrote eventually came the *Constitutional and Political History of the United States* (7 vols., 1876–92). He returned to Europe, becoming a professor at the new University of Strassburg, lecturing on American history and constitutional law. Other academic posts followed, ending with the University of Chicago, where he stayed from 1892 to his death in 1904. The history he wrote was used for some time as a text, but the English translation did not always accurately reflect the original German. In addition to his history, von Holst wrote a study of constitutional law in the United States, as well as biographies of John Brown and of Calhoun, for whose ability he had great respect.

One who knew von Holst well said that he "valued history chiefly for its practical bearing on current problems," and a "stern morality" guided his judgments on the past and the present. He was no believer in the virtues of that "objective history" so much talked of in his day. He held it a distinct right of the historian to measure events and men according to his own political and moral beliefs.

With the confidence that most authors have in their own impartiality, von Holst wrote: "I venture to assert that among all the works covering about as large a ground as mine, there is not one to be found which has

[2] J. W. Pratt, "The Ideology of American Expansion," *Essays in Honor of William E. Dodd* (Chicago, 1935); also Edwin Mims, Jr., *American History and Immigration* (Bronxville, New York, 1950), Chap. II.

been written with as much soberness of mind." He felt, indeed, that he had an advantage over American historians because of his foreign birth. Though he did his own research in the sources, he probably was strongly influenced in his constitutional ideas and his attitude toward slavery by Hildreth.[3]

A brief section of von Holst's *History* covered the years under the Confederation, written from his nationalist standpoint. The objections of the "particularists" to Federalism were dismissed as absurd. In unfolding his narrative, he rested his argument on the debatable theses that the Union was older than the states, and that state sovereignty was non-existent at the nation's birth. The main thesis upon which his book rested was thus stated: slavery was "the rock on which the Union was broken to pieces." On the themes of slavery and national sovereignty versus state rights he constructed his work: "The slave holding interest knit mesh after mesh in the net in which it sought to entangle the Union, but men did not or would not see this." Von Holst, like a true Bismarckian, was of course a partisan of Hamilton. Jefferson, on the other hand, "was always ready to sacrifice much of his favorite theories to his feverish thirst for power and distinction." The historian, usually a staunch upholder of nationality, was, however, very lenient in his judgment of the Hartford Convention of 1814.

A discussion of "The Economic Contrast between the Free and Slave States" (later drawn upon by McMaster) gave a doleful picture of Southern life. "Everything was considered in reference to the 'peculiar institution,' " said von Holst, "and therefore hostile distrust of everything was felt, because this institution was in ever sharper contradiction with the spirit of the age." The different industrial systems in North and South drove them farther and farther apart. Turning to a long study of the nullification movement of 1832, von Holst, quoting Bismarck, wrote: "Conquered and conquerors brought punishment upon themselves because they did not understand one thing, or, if they understood it, would not live up to it; 'Sovereignty can only be a unit and it must remain a unit—the sovereignty of law.' "

Beginning with Jackson's administration the narrative became more detailed. The historian's characterization of Jackson won wide acceptance: "Since Louis XIV, the maxim, *l'état, c'est moi,* has scarcely found a second time, so ingenuous and complete an expression as in Andrew

[3] A. H. Kelly, "Richard Hildreth," *Jernegan Essays,* 42.

Jackson. The only difference is that it was translated from the language of monarchy into the language of republicanism." Although the author gave considerable space to the panic of 1837, he soon returned to the main interest of his study—slavery and the constitution. His comment on the election of Harrison was typical: "The person who wished to read the future of the country . . . should not have stopped at the electoral vote [and popular vote] which went beyond a million. Weightier than these were the not quite seven thousand votes cast for Birney and Earle, the candidates of the liberal party." In his treatment of the annexation of Texas, von Holst adopted the view, conventional with antislavery writers, that the expansionist movement was solely the result of Southern desires for more slave territory. With forced imagery, von Holst wrote of the Congressional process of annexation: "The bridal dress in which Calhoun had led the beloved of the slavocracy to the Union was the torn and tattered constitution of the United States."

The caption, "Polk Weaves the Warp of the Mexican War," indicated von Holst's approach. He suggested the effect of annexation on the growth of abolition sentiment: "The long struggle over annexation had opened many eyes which had hitherto been struck with blindness. The thorn of the political rule of the slave holding interest had been pressed deeper into the flesh of many, and a still greater number, by a louder and clearer condemnation of slavery 'on principle' sought refuge from their own consciences for having allowed or helped the slavocracy again to win a victory." The historian thus referred to the Southern domination of American politics: "Questions which had hitherto been hotly debated, were now settled, in accordance with the views of the South, almost without a struggle."

Von Holst's interpretation was that a vast conspiracy had been hatched by American political leaders. In preparing the war with Mexico, Congress and the President were "participants in the guilt of the dark work which had been so busily and cunningly carried on in the White House." Ethics and the writing of history were always closely allied for von Holst, who referred to the "bold immorality, with which the leading Democratic politicians . . . devised and carried to its conclusion the whole affair of the war." The narrative inevitably led up to the statement that Polk "purposely brought on the war," but the author added that Congress, too, was in accord "with his crooked policy."

In view of his whole approach, it was strange to find von Holst defending "manifest destiny" and writing that "history cannot decide . . . questions by the code of private morals." This son of a Bismarckian generation could write bluntly of an established law of historic growth—that "decayed or decaying peoples must give way when they clash in a conflict of interests with peoples who are still on the ascending path of their historic mission, and that violence must often be the judge to decide such litigation between nations."[4]

Von Holst again returned to a comparison of the North and the South and found once more that the latter was at a great disadvantage in economic strength. Intellectual life in the North, he said, was also superior to that in the South. He regarded as most significant, not the fact that in every respect the South was behind the North, "but that the forces which had caused it to remain so far in the rear still continue to operate, and it would therefore necessarily fall still farther behind." The historian was always the strong protagonist of urban capitalism, and to the end of his life he believed in a thoroughgoing *laissez faire* doctrine. The proletariat of great cities he accepted as a necessary evil that came with economic growth.

The six years that followed the Compromise of 1850 von Holst declared were "the most important in the development of the irrepressible conflict, between the North and the South." Politicians were powerless in these years, "in the presence of the progressive and sternly logical development of actual circumstances." Thus did American history move on toward the inevitable tragedy with the precision of Greek drama.

In great detail von Holst noted how deeply the disputes over the Compromise of 1850 had affected public sentiment nearly everywhere. As for the election of 1852, he concluded that Pierce won because "the great majority of the people had become possessed by the quietistic conservative spirit, and did not wish their repose to be disturbed by any further contention as to the price paid for it." Douglas with his "moral hollowness" was the villain in the drama of the Kansas-Nebraska Bill, whose "ultimate consequences . . . brought the Union and slavery face to face with the question of existence."

In the 1850's the slavocracy, said von Holst, continued to stir up sentiment for expansion, this time to the Caribbean. Although unable

[4] In the 1890's von Holst opposed American expansionist tendencies; E. F. Goldman, "Hermann E. von Holst," *Mississippi Valley Historical Review,* Vol. XXIII, No. 4 (March, 1937), 515.

to secure Cuba, "the progressive fraction of the slavocracy which grew from year to year in weight and numbers, awaited only a new opportunity to take up the frustrated annexation project again, and they were resolved to create the opportunity if it did not offer of itself."

The history of these years was described in phrases suggestive of military tactics. The South under all circumstances during this period was "certain that none of the positions it had won could be wrested from it, for no hostile resolution of the house of representatives would receive the assent of the senate or the sanction of the president." But the South, in order to be victorious, needed to be on the offensive and show a confidence in victory, "and assurance of victory was best manifested by its coming forward with new and bold demands." The Kansas troubles were all due to the slavocracy, which "in the name of law and order, and behind the protecting shield of the president . . . carried on [the propagation of slavery] with blood and iron, in the territorial domain of the Union." Von Holst's partisan prose threw a lurid glow over "Bleeding Kansas."

Buchanan's election had been bought by a more binding pledge to the slavocracy, and, added von Holst, the "declaration of the Republicans that the era of compromises was forever closed, was answered from the South by the declaration that the time when the continuance of the slave states in the Union could be purchased by concessions, was forever past."

After a brief treatment of the Dred Scott decision, which, in the author's view, was "the greatest political atrocity of which a court had ever been guilty," the narrative moved on to the Lecompton Convention. The scorching words with which von Holst indignantly castigated the slavocracy in Kansas have lost none of their burning quality since they were written. Through these pages Kansas stalks like Banquo's ghost. The historian heard the voices of unlaid ghosts of free-soilers threatening the slavocracy with an early grave. As the "irrepressible conflict" neared its climax, Lincoln "loomed up higher and firmer, while . . . fragments of Douglas' armor strewed the ground."

In his infrequent departures from Congressional history, von Holst took stock of the country's economic position in 1857, and he reflected on the low standard of morality in railroad finance in that decade. He noted, too, the growing opposition to immigration and Catholicism by the Know-Nothing party and, though unsympathetic to Catholics himself, von Holst pointed out the danger of Know-Nothingism to American institutions. He drew a distinction between Anglo-Saxon immigrants—in particular, the Germans, who surpassed all others—and the Irish, who belonged "to the lowest stage of culture." He suggested, too, that nativism, as typified by the Know-Nothing movement, was an attempt to divert attention from the slavery question.

When the Thirty-fifth Congress ended, said the historian, the "funeral bells of the democratic party were tolling and hence the history of the Thirty-sixth Congress could not but become the knell of the Union." The crowded months after Harpers Ferry were the subject of von Holst's last volume. The prose swung into poetic rhythm as it celebrated the man John Brown, with his "homely realism" and "great, ideal loftiness of soul." From the sublimity of John Brown the reader was dropped to the grossness of party politics in 1860. Four parties were in the field; "one with a national, single-faced head; two double faced ones with the same name, and one with no face at all."

Buchanan, who did not have "the moral courage to do his duty" in suppressing the insurrection, was the object of von Holst's severe criticism; his policy of noncoercion was thoroughly ridiculed. "His dread of assuming any responsibility," said the historian, "was as great as his delusion with regard to his own infallibility." With the failure to preserve the already broken Union by compromise measures, its restoration, concluded von Holst in characteristic language, "could be effected only by blood and iron."

In the great struggle between good and evil the latter was vanquished when the Republicans won in 1860. With Lincoln's inauguration "the restoration of a Union incomparably stronger, more majestic and richer in promise for the future, was beyond a question, for the corner-stones of the new foundation were to be the burial mounds of the three dark powers which unbound the furies of civil war: the doctrine of noncoercion, the slavocratic interpretation of state sovereignty, and slavery."

Von Holst, German even during his American university years, glowering at his class, "always striking hard, always striving to emphasize the great things," performed a pioneer task and stimulated much research. He was among the first to appreciate the significance of the records of Congressional debates, and he also made good use of newspapers when this kind of material was rarely referred to. One soon discovers that von Holst's work was really only a history of the slavery contest, with but few references to other phases of American life. As he saw it, slavery was the principal question before the American people after 1830. Even before the historian finished his last volume, his work had begun to lose its hold on the more critical generation of American historians. More than any other large-scale enterprise von Holst's represented the fullest flowering of the Federalist-Whig-Republican school of history—nationalist, Northern, antislavery. His obvious bias can do no harm to the modern student who has learned his history from other and more temperate sources. The decades since von Holst wrote have added dust to his unused volumes so that today they have become objects of archaeological excavation rather than tools of historical research.[5]

JAMES SCHOULER

When von Holst was preparing his history, James Schouler was also at work on the same period. His *History of the United States under the Constitution* began to appear in 1880, with the explanation that no comprehensive narrative existed "from which one may safely gather the later record of our country's career." He partially excepted Hildreth's history, praising it for its accuracy, but, Schouler said, he differed from him "in many particulars, and most widely as to estimates of our political leaders and their motives." Schouler wrote that he wanted to begin where Bancroft "had seemingly laid down his pen," and to "supply the connecting link between the American Revolution and the Civil War." It was his distinction to be the first historian to bridge the gap from the Constitution to the end of Reconstruction by a continuous narrative. He was also the author of biographies of Jefferson and Hamilton and of an excellent study on *Americans of 1776*.

Schouler's history began with some introductory remarks on the states under the Articles of Confederation. The Constitutional Convention, he said, was "the protest of liberty protected by law against liberty independent of it." The historian halted his narrative at various points to portray the founding fathers. He described Washington in a long passage imitative of a decadent classicism; Schouler was less sympathetic to Hamilton than was Hildreth; therefore, by the usual rules of American historical writing, he was more friendly to Jefferson.

[5] A. B. Hart, on von Holst, *Political Science Quarterly,* Vol. V, No. 4 (December, 1890), 677–87; *The Nation* (January 28, 1904); C. R. Wilson, "Hermann Eduard von Holst," *Jernegan Essays,* 60–83.

In many respects Schouler's arrangement of materials seemed to be nothing more than an enlargement of the older method of writing historical chronicles as practiced by Prince and Abiel Holmes. History, he once said, is the "record of consecutive events . . . of consecutive public events"; to his mind "the only clear law of history is that of motion incessantly onward."[6] His divisions were based upon the succession of presidential administrations. This made for difficulty in pursuing any one topic for long and reduced him to the clumsy expedient of using such an introduction as: "The slavery question deserves attention in connection with the angry debates of this [1790] session."

Schouler's attitude on slavery, which colored his later narrative strongly, was early revealed: "That an institution, both wasteful and unrighteous, should have been suffered by wise statesmen to fasten its poisonous fangs so deeply into the vitals of a republic whose essential foundation was freedom, is one of those political facts which only the theory of human imperfection can well explain, so inevitable must have been the final catastrophe." The Federalists were severely criticised for their party tyranny in sponsoring the Alien and Sedition Acts, but the historian paid a generous tribute to John Adams, who "was in closer sympathy with the people than most leaders of the party to which he belonged, and a more genuine American."

Schouler's statement that "Jefferson proceeded moderately, and by no means maliciously, in the matter of removals from office," was supported by later scholars. In a résumé of Jefferson's administrations, Schouler said they "had fixed immutably the republican character of these institutions, and vindicated this American experiment as never before." The country at the close of Jefferson's term of office was said to be living in a "miniature golden age"; the phenomenon of his administration "was undoubtedly the development of a West" whose population in the Mississippi Valley in after years was "to assert a great, if not the greatest, influence in national affairs." These pages broke fresh ground but plowed neither deeply nor widely.

With much zest Schouler swung back to his political narrative leading up to the War of 1812. " 'On to Canada' had been the cry of the war party for years." The author found that "the disaffection of the New England States is a sad episode of the war for history to contemplate,

[6] Schouler, "The Spirit of Historical Research," American Historical Association *Papers,* Vol. IV, Part 3 (July, 1890), 98–99.

nor can the impartial historian on that topic hope to escape controversy." In his discussion of changes in parties he revealed no deep understanding of political motivation; for him it was the old drama, perhaps melodrama, of bitter personal rivalries, "jostling ambitions, intrigues to overthrow one administration and bring in another."

Bancroft's literary mantle was seized by Schouler, who wore it ungracefully: "Proud in our annals was the year 1818, when the whole nation felt itself soaring upward in a new atmosphere, exhilarated and bold, like an eagle loosened from confinement." Through rose-colored glasses he viewed the end of Monroe's administration, when "the whole mechanism of society moved in perfect order. The democracy ruled, but it was a democracy in which jealousies found no root, and the abler and more virtuous of the community took the lead." Soon, however, "fiercer passions rule once more the hearts of men."

Jackson's victory four years later was a triumph "of popular principles, and in a sense of the military . . . spirit in politics"; Adams, "out of all the infamous abuse, scandal, and vilification heaped upon him . . . emerged pure as refined gold." Tocqueville was drawn upon for a discussion of American social history, 1830. Though Schouler wrote that "we are now at the portal of an epoch full of eager progress and the crowding, trampling ranks of humanity," that humanity remained but an abstraction. The West, scarcely mentioned up to this time by general historians, was given brief notice; "The phenomenon of American development was the growth of the great West." New England's influence, however, in fashioning and ruling Northern society was strongest; she "was a sort of education, a great generator of ideas for American society." It should be remarked, too, that Schouler was not unsympathetic to Southern society.

The historian's thoughts on nullification were clothed in language reminiscent of medieval chivalry: "These were glorious days for the constitution's allied defenders; the one matchless in debate, the other terrible in action and clad in popular confidence like a coat of mail." His whole treatment of the nullification controversy was strongly warped by a nationalist bias. Similarly, his introduction to a discussion of the annexation of Texas was characteristic: "A dark chapter opens in our national history." This whole episode was interpreted from the view of Southern desires for more slave territory. Over most of these pages, in fact, hung the heavy shadow of slavery.

From his usual position Schouler surveyed the struggle with Mexico: "The glory of the Mexican War was the glory of the South, like the Texan conquest before it . . . to add largely to the area of slavery by annexations from Mexico was regarded by slaveholders as a necessary means of strengthening their power against Northern encroachments." The conventional Whig disapproval of Webster's Seventh of March speech was thus expressed: "He . . . bargained away his moral conviction for the sake of national harmony." The military adventures in Central America and Cuba were, to Schouler, "that cormorant appetite for seizing weak sovereignties," a "misguided policy of robbery and subjugation which seeks to conceal its cruel features under the mask of manifest destiny." Franklin Pierce was excoriated for being "an abject devotee of the slave holders." John Brown was utterly "irrational," but his treatment revealed the slave master's "innate tyranny and cruelty towards an adversary."

Schouler was more temperate in his remarks about the Civil War. " 'Conspiracy,' 'treason,' were names at first applied, all too narrowly, to those who struggled to break from the Union. 'Rebellion' is a more enduring and appropriate word. . . . We must divest ourselves of the false impression [which Schouler himself does much to convey, however] that the crime of a few Southern leaders produced the real mischief."

His volume on the Civil War had the benefit of his own youthful impressions of the events he described. Although he tried "to do full justice" to the motives of both sections, he admitted that he had "not suppressed [his] personal convictions as to the real merits of this sanguinary strife, nor amiably shifted the ground of discussion." Formerly he had discountenanced the use of the word "conspiracy" in connection with the war, but he forgot his own injunction when he wrote, "There was something of a conspiracy, however, in the present Southern movement for breaking up the Union."

At the age of seventy-four Schouler picked up his pen again to add a seventh volume, on Reconstruction. His main purpose, he said, was to vindicate the "much maligned" President Johnson. Like his contemporary, Rhodes, Schouler severely condemned the military Reconstruction Act because it forcibly uprooted "State governments already advanced towards natural conditions of self-rule" and replanted them "on a new political basis utterly impracticable and ruinous." The volume itself was little concerned with the Southern side of Reconstruction.

Schouler was deeply interested in the election of 1876. Though a partisan of Tilden, he wrote: "Iniquitous as we must deem that electoral figuring which placed Hayes instead of Tilden in the White House, it was probably better, under all the circumstances, for the peace of the country."

Throughout his history Schouler had conventional heroes and villains; Lincoln, naturally, was one of his greatest heroes. Opposed to him was Jefferson Davis, a "gloomy despot." Aside from a few references to passing events in other parts of the country, Schouler's history might have been written from a spectator's seat in Congress; his interests were almost entirely in political and constitutional history. He was inclined to conservatism, protective of the *status quo,* though critical of predatory and ostentatious wealth. A stern Scottish morality pervaded his writing, and he once pleaded: "Whatever may have been my imperfections as a narrator of events . . . I trust it may be said of me that I have written with a constant purpose to be just and truthful." Schouler, one of "the terrible just," was in reality not as judicial as some of his contemporaries who had learned to look more dispassionately at American history.[7]

JOHN W. BURGESS

John W. Burgess is more likely to be remembered for his work in founding and building up the School of Political Science at Columbia University and his many years of teaching service than for his contributions to American history. He came from a family of Tennessee slaveowners who were Whig Unionists. The idea of American unity inspired him from his boyhood. America, he felt, "was a great creative and regenerative force for the welfare of mankind."[8]

Young Burgess served in the Union Army and then studied at Amherst and in Germany. With the patronage of George Bancroft he attended classes under Germany's greatest masters of history and public law—Mommsen, Curtius, Ranke, Droysen, and Rudolph von Gneist, the leading student of English law and government. Of these it was von Gneist who had the most profound influence in directing Burgess' career.[9] Amherst called him from Germany in 1873 to a newly established professorship of history and political science. Three years later he

[7] For autobiography, see Schouler's *Historical Briefs* (New York, 1896); L. E. Ellis, "James Schouler," *Jernegan Essays,* 84–101.

[8] W. R. Shepherd, in *American Masters of Social Science* (ed. by H. W. Odum, New York, 1927).

[9] J. W. Burgess, *Reminiscences of an American Scholar* (New York, 1934), 131.

went to Columbia to teach constitutional history and international law, beginning an academic association that lasted throughout his life.

Burgess was the author of a number of studies in political science, but his several volumes on nineteenth-century America were more important for the student of historical writing. The publishing house of Charles Scribner's Sons, believing that the time was ripe for a fairer treatment of the struggle between the North and the South, turned to Burgess as the man best suited by birth and training for the task. Considering it his "sacred duty," he fulfilled the obligation.[10]

Introducing his work with a volume on *The Middle Period 1817–1858* (1897), Burgess said that it was high time that the history of those years "should be undertaken in a thoroughly impartial spirit. The continued misunderstanding between the North and the South is an ever present menace to the welfare of both sections and of the entire nation." He saw no incongruity between his profession of impartiality and his statement that this history must be written by an American and a Northerner "and from the Northern point of view," because it is, in the main, "the correct view." The stern moralist thus spoke: "The time has come when the men of the South should acknowledge that they were in error in their attempt to destroy the Union and it is unmanly in them not to do so." Although his early environment made him sympathetic to the South, Burgess wrote that "not one scintilla of justification for secession and rebellion must be expected." The main theme in *The Middle Period,* as Burgess saw it, was the struggle between the Northerners, who wished to adapt the government to changing conditions, and the Southerners, who claimed they clung to the beliefs of the framers of the Constitution.

The Civil War and the Constitution 1859–1865 (2 vols., 1901) was largely a history of military events and some political questions raised by the struggle. The development of constitutional law towards nationalism in these years was of special interest to Burgess. Though the historian disliked extremists on both sides, especially John Brown, he continued to maintain that the cause of secession was "constitutionally and morally indefensible." The constitutional arguments of the secessionists, he said, were "from every point of view, a mere jugglery with words."

In *Reconstruction and the Constitution 1866–1876* (1902) Burgess was largely interested in an examination of the means used to recon-

[10] *Ibid.,* 289.

struct the defeated states. He had once asked the South to acknowledge secession as an error; he now asked the North to make amends for Reconstruction. The purpose of Reconstruction, "to secure the civil rights of the newly emancipated race," was praiseworthy, but "erroneous means were chosen." The South should have been placed under a territorial civil government, he said, until the whites could be "intrusted again with the powers of . . . government." Insisting that there was a "vast difference in political capacity between races," Burgess believed that it was "the white man's mission, his duty and his right, to hold the reins of political power in his own hands for the civilization of the world and the welfare of mankind." An epilogue to his historical trilogy was a small book, *The Administration of President Hayes* (1916), in which the executive was praised for re-establishing "constitutional normality."

Although Burgess was intensely nationalist in his writing, he saw the danger of excessive centralization in practice. In his volume on *The Reconciliation of Government with Liberty* (1915) he concluded: "It is high time for us to call a halt on our present course of increasing the sphere of government and decreasing that of liberty." Later historical investigation played havoc with Burgess' theses on the great sectional struggle. He had no conception of it as a conflict between two differing civilizations, and even in his own narrower view—that differences over constitutional interpretation lay at the base of the war—his work was surpassed by the more penetrating essays of his former student, William A. Dunning. Posterity's verdict has been that Burgess gave us not so much history as historians.

JAMES FORD RHODES

Schouler and Burgess wrote about the Civil War as they saw it from a Northern judgment seat. James Ford Rhodes' stand was nearer Mason and Dixon's line, but his sight, too, was obscured by the traditional point of view. Rhodes had very unusual opportunities to write the history of the period he chose for his theme. Noted Democrats were frequent visitors at the Rhodes' home in Cleveland; through such associations Rhodes was able to write much of his history at firsthand. A conversation with Judge E. R. Hoar, for example, enabled Rhodes to account for President Grant's personal honesty "while keeping such bad company."[11] The elder Rhodes was a delegate to the Democratic convention of 1860

[11] Letter to R. U. Johnson, October 22, 1908, Century Collection, New York Public Library.

in Charleston, and his influence was to make the son a "sturdy Democrat."

Rhodes' interest in history was aroused, he said, when he entered New York University in 1865 and attended the classes of Benjamin N. Martin. The latter suggested stimulating reading to the young scholar, who reveled in Buckle's *History of Civilization* and Draper's *Intellectual Development of Europe;* these two books, he said, marked an epoch in his intellectual life. As he read the last words of Buckle's famous volumes, the young student "resolved some day to write a history."

"One evening in 1877, while reading Hildreth's *History of the United States,*" Rhodes remarked in an autobiographical sketch, "I laid down my book and said to myself why should I not write a 'History of the United States'?" From then on, despite the cares of business, he kept elaborate notes of his reading. "I resolved that as soon as I should have gained a competence, I would retire from business and devote myself to history and literature." In 1885 Rhodes kept his resolution, retired from business, and then plunged into a heavy schedule of reading.

The two volumes which appeared in 1892 carried on their title pages *History of the United States from the Compromise of 1850.* Rhodes planned to carry his narrative to the inauguration of Grover Cleveland in 1885, which marked the return to power of the Democrats. This period, he said, "ranks next in importance to the formative period—to the declaration and conquest of independence and the adoption of the Constitution." For eleven years before the Civil War, Negro slavery "engrossed the whole attention of the country. . . . It will be my aim," said Rhodes, "to recount the causes of the triumph of the Republican party in the presidential election of 1860, and to make clear how the revolution in public opinion was brought about that led to this result." The election of Cleveland was thought to be a "fitting close of this historical inquiry, for by that time the great questions which had their origin in the war had been settled as far as they could be by legislation or executive direction."

The influence of slavery upon politics was a central theme in the work. The historian underestimated the danger of secession in 1850; studies that have appeared since 1892 have noted the serious nature of such a move. Like von Holst, Rhodes adopted an antislavery view and confessed that he had been "profoundly influenced" by the former's work. For Rhodes, too, Douglas was a deep-dyed villain. As a supporter of unionism against secessionist theory, Rhodes wrote from the standpoint of a nationalist, but *The Nation* reviewer, referring to the historian's treatment of slavery, said, "We doubt whether a fairer view of the subject can be met with. . . ." Burgess, however, thought Rhodes too strongly prejudiced against slavery and severely criticized him for the perpetuation of the John Brown cult.

The publication of these two volumes won for Rhodes a well-merited distinction throughout the country, and his position as a man of letters was assured to the end of his life, in 1927. He was always conscious of his style, studying to improve it, feeling he had need to make up for his earlier business years that had been lost to literature. But try as he would, his writing rarely achieved distinction; the skill of Parkman was denied him. He was proud of his acceptance in the best literary circles, but sometimes the reader senses his lack of assurance: "Please the élite, the rest will follow," he wrote in 1898; "I am aspiring for culture and wish to be a scholar." Even in later years Rhodes rather self-consciously spoke of acquiring culture.

"My history has grown on me," he wrote to a friend, "and I shall close the third volume in the blaze of glory of our victories of the early part of '62." He thought he might have reached the Emancipation Proclamation if it had not been for the material Sumner's biographer, Edward L. Pierce, had given him, "but that and my other studies have enabled me to give somewhat of freshness to my treatment of English sentiment, of which I am glad, as considerable of my work is commonplace enough from following the beaten track."[12] Rhodes was sensitive about his treatment of Southern leaders. "My estimate of Lee is wholly sincere," he wrote to Dr. Frederick Bancroft, "and I shall be sorry if it shocks many of my old friends who bore the brunt and burden of the war and to whom Lee's 'traitorous conduct' obliterated in their minds all his virtues."

Two more volumes carried the story another four years to 1866. It was a narrative largely of the military and naval events of the war, but the historian included chapters on society in the North and in the South. He confided to Charles Francis Adams that he had not sufficient knowledge to grapple with the question of sea power. When Adams wrote to him gently that "no well and philosophically considered narrative of

[12] F. M. Anderson, "Letters of James Ford Rhodes to Edward L. Pierce," *American Historical Review,* Vol. XXXVI, No. 4 (July, 1931), 778–85.

the struggle has yet appeared," the answer came that "a purely narrative historian should, so far as he can, put all philosophical conditions aside. His aim is to tell a story and leave philosophy to others."

Rhodes changed the original terminal date of his work, Cleveland's inauguration, to 1877, when the South recovered "home rule." The historian believed that questions other than the Southern issue must be treated after 1877, but he said that he "had a lack of basic knowledge" to attack the social issues involved. He closed his history on an optimistic note: It "has covered twenty-seven years of pregnant events; the compromise on slavery devised by great statesmen; its upsetting by an ambitious Northern Senator; the formation of the Republican party; the agitation of slavery; Southern arrogance and aggression; the election of Lincoln; the refusal of the South to abide by the decision of the ballot-box; the Civil War; the great work of Lincoln; the abolition of slavery; the defeat of the South; Reconstruction based upon universal negro suffrage; the oppression of the South by the North; the final triumph of Southern intelligence and character over the ignorance and corruption that so long had thriven under Northern misconceptions. . . . The United States of 1877 was a better country than the United States of 1850. For slavery was abolished, the doctrine of secession was dead, and Lincoln's character and fame had become a possession of the nation."

William G. Brown, well qualified to speak on the subject, said that Rhodes' seventh volume was "the best history yet written of Reconstruction" but criticized it for its digressions. Some of the historian's omissions were very serious. He paid little attention to the westward movement after the war and, curiously enough, despite his early business career, displayed no interest in economic history or in the relationship between economics and politics. There was nothing, for example, on the interplay of politics and federal grants for railroads in the 1850's. As for Andrew Johnson, he seems today a more important personality than Rhodes was willing to concede. The latter might have devoted less space to the failures of the Reconstruction period and given more to such successes as the institution of a public school system. Negro students of the Reconstruction period have claimed that Rhodes magnified the virtues and minimized the faults of Democrats, whereas for Republicans, especially when colored, he did the reverse.[13]

[13] J. R. Lynch, "Some Historical Errors of James Ford Rhodes," *Journal of Negro History,* Vol. II, No. 4 (October, 1917), 345–68.

Aside from its position as a standard treatment of a momentous era, the work of Rhodes had immense value as balm to bitter wounds. "It is a sign that our country . . . is really getting past the time when the differences of 1861–1865 serve as red rags," wrote Professor Dodd to Rhodes. "May I say I believe your masterly *History* has done more than any other historical agency—perhaps any other agency of any sort—to bring about this state of feeling?"

A Southerner, however, would have treated the years 1850–77 differently. "It is a history written from the Northern point of view," remarked Lester B. Shippee, "by one who was willing to acknowledge . . . the rights on the other side, but who saw in *slavery* a great moral evil which had corrupted the greater portion of a whole society."[14] Slavery, for Rhodes, explained "practically all the main currents of American national history down to the close of Reconstruction." It should be stated, however, that in the pages on Reconstruction, Rhodes approximated more nearly a truly nationalist viewpoint.[15]

In 1911 Rhodes was at work on the continuation of his history. "I am now living in the period 1877–1897," he wrote to a friend, "and have more original material at hand than I have eyes to read or brains to assimilate." His interest in historical writing was, however, ebbing fast. To Charles H. Firth, historian at Oxford, Rhodes said, "I published in 1917 a [one-volume] History of the Civil War which you will not care for, but I will send you . . . the continuation of my History telling the tale from 1877 to 1899. I shall go on with it if life and health be spared, but I am indifferent whether I publish any more or not." *The History of the United States from Hayes to McKinley, 1877–1896* was published in 1919 and was followed three years later by *The McKinley and Roosevelt Administrations, 1897–1909*.

It was a misfortune to publish these two volumes, for they were far below the standard set by Rhodes' earlier work. Without a central theme, which slavery had formerly been, the historian seemed to lose his way. He showed no understanding of the great economic and social changes that had come over the United States since 1877, and his strong property sense colored his view of the Populists and of labor. Even in his own

[14] L. B. Shippee, "Rhodes's *History of the United States*," *Mississippi Valley Historical Review*, Vol. VIII, Nos. 1–2 (June, September, 1921), 133–48.

[15] Cf. N. W. Stephenson, "Mr. Rhodes as Historian," *Yale Review*, Vol. X, No. 4 (July, 1921), 860–65.

chosen field of political history he exhibited no critical approach to the events and personalities that fell within the scope of the later volumes. He knew many of the leading characters in American life who were portrayed in these volumes, and his appraisal of their actions was warped by friendly indulgence.

Although Rhodes did not number his readers in the large figures accredited to Fiske and Bancroft, those that he had were people who contributed most to molding public opinion—teachers, editors, political leaders. He had a high conception of a historian's calling: "Natural ability being presupposed, the qualities necessary for an historian are diligence, accuracy, love of truth, impartiality, the thorough digestion of his materials by careful selection and long meditating, and the compression of his narrative into the smallest compass consistent with the life of his story." In his earlier years, at least, Rhodes tried to live up to his own expressed standards, and his position among the leading American historians is therefore, still secure.[16]

JOHN FISKE

John Fiske, whose career as academician and as public lecturer had in it elements of both the older and the newer schools of historians, ranged over the whole field of American history. He was essentially a literary, philosophical historian, but his work had some kinship with the "scientific" group. Fiske seems strangely outdated. The intellectual battles he helped fight and win have been largely forgotten by a generation that has taken its victorious heritage for granted.

He was born in Hartford, Connecticut, in 1842, and as a child was deeply interested in history. In 1860 he went to Harvard, where he quickly earned a reputation as an intellectual radical. Accidentally, he discovered the work of Herbert Spencer in a Boston bookshop that year and immediately subscribed for his volumes. For the rest of his life he remained an ardent follower of Spencer and Darwin, becoming an active champion of the theory of evolution. The English leaders in the fight for evolution were heartened by the support of Fiske, the leading exponent of these new ideas in America. When Eliot became president of Harvard, Fiske was invited to give a course of lectures on "The Posi-

[16] M. A. De Wolfe Howe, *James Ford Rhodes* (New York, 1929); Rhodes, *Historical Essays* (New York, 1909); R. C. Miller, "James Ford Rhodes," *Jernegan Essays,* 171–90.

tive Philosophy," from which grew his work *The Outlines of Cosmic Philosophy*. To the end of his days Fiske was still trying to harmonize his religious beliefs and ideals with the latest doctrines of science.

Opposition to Fiske's unconventional ideas prevented his appointment to the history department at Harvard. After serving the college as librarian, he left in 1879 to enter upon a career as lecturer in history that has no parallel in America. His successful series of lectures on "America's Place in History" in 1879, given in the Old South Church in Boston, determined the future course of his life.

Fiske saw in America's development an excellent illustration of the theory of evolution applied to the history of civilization, and he popularized his thesis in widely attended lectures. He had a clear perception of the contemporary appropriateness of such lectures. "The centennial has started it," he wrote, "and I have started in at the right time." He thoroughly enjoyed his experiences as a lecturer, writing after one appearance: "The applause was great. I had a sort of sense that I was fascinating the people and it was delicious beyond expression." In the year that he made his American debut, he gave the same series in London with astonishing success. Two years later, 1881, he was lecturing on "American Political Ideas" under the auspices of Washington University in St. Louis. These lectures appeared in book form in 1885.

In the winter of 1883–84 Fiske gave a course of lectures on "The American Revolution," followed shortly by a new series on the Confederation, which resulted in the publication of *The Critical Period of American History* (1888). He took account of the difficulties facing the new nation and sketched the leaders in the Constitutional Convention. The historian went on to discuss the motives that prompted the states to accept the Constitution, and he included a vivid description of Washington's inauguration. This volume was probably the best of Fiske's works from the standpoint of interpretation, though it lacked documentation. Contemporary readers received *The Critical Period* with much favor, but specialists quickly recognized its slight scholarship.

Fiske now planned to write a comprehensive history of the United States. Before long, *The Beginnings of New England* and *The American Revolution* were ready for the press. A considerable portion of the former book went far afield to explain why the world's political center of gravity shifted from the Mediterranean and the Rhine to the Atlantic and the Mississippi, from the Latins to English-speaking peoples. Love of the dramatic made Fiske give disproportionate space to some subjects, King Philip's War, for example. The outworn character of his point of view may be measured by a chapter with the heading "The Tyranny of Andros." Today the episode is described as an incident in imperial reorganization.

The American Revolution was largely a military history, revealing nothing of the internal developments in the colonies. In the traditional manner, George III was burdened with the chief responsibility for bringing on the war. The much-reviled king was to Fiske a typical villain; "Scantily endowed with human sympathy, and almost boorishly stiff in his ordinary unstudied manner, he could be smooth as oil whenever he liked.... He had little faith in human honour or rectitude, and in pursuing an end he was seldom deterred by scruples."

In 1890, at the Lowell Institute of Boston, Fiske gave a course of lectures on "The Discovery, Conquest and Colonization of America," which outlined the two volumes which appeared in 1892. This was Fiske's most careful work, and some critics have regarded it as his best, particularly because of his use of source material. Its documentation, alone among his many books, approximated modern historical standards, but in his usual digressive manner, Fiske referred to many details of small significance. Phillips Brooks thought the chapter on Las Casas "the finest piece of historical narrative in the English language," while Rhodes exclaimed with too much enthusiasm that "the *Discovery of America* is a great book; it is the greatest historical work that I have ever read by an American except the *Rise of the Dutch Republic*."

Fiske allotted a very large proportion of space to pre-Columbian civilization, which was a reflection of contemporary interest in primitive peoples. He said that it was his investigation of prehistoric Europe and of early Aryan institutions that led him to study American aborigines. He thought that he might thus shed further light on the conclusions of the Aryan school of anthropologists.

The uncritical character of much of Fiske's research was seen in his *Old Virginia and her Neighbors* (1897) and his volume on *The Dutch and Quaker Colonies in America* (1899). Osgood said that when Fiske "crosses the threshold of the eighteenth century, his narrative becomes so sketchy as to lose nearly all its value.... He can only express the pious belief that such and such things are so; the proving of them requires activity of an order different from that of telling a pretty story or sketching the results of earlier investigations."

New France and New England (1901) had very little documentation and, like the work on the American Revolution was largely a military history. *The Mississippi Valley in the Civil War* (1900), the result of another lecture series, was also a military history. Fiske obviously devoted much of his lecturing and writing to military history because that phase of the subject can be made most interesting to the widest number of people. Another work, *Civil Government in the United States,* was dominated by the outmoded evolutionary theory that traced the origins of the New England township to Greek and Roman institutions.

His fondness for playing with ideas sometimes led Fiske to unwarranted speculation upon the motives of men. Theorizing too often substituted for research, yet he had a wide acquaintance with monographic literature; his familiarity with primary sources was limited. It is well known that he frequently borrowed and summarized the research of others without acknowledgment; his *Critical Period,* especially, suffered from these frailties.

It is scarcely surprising that Fiske often showed little direct knowledge of the sources. His need for money, leading to hurried writing, prohibited leisurely examination of large masses of materials, and, besides, his grandiose view of history precluded close observation of any particular period. Fiske, however, had something of value to say on this subject. His remarks referred to Freeman, but they were probably intended also as a justification of his own wide range of historical writing. Freeman, he said, "was remarkably free from the common habit—common even among eminent historians—of concentrating his attention upon some exceptionally brilliant period or so-called 'classical age,' to the exclusion of other ages that went before and came after. Such a habit is fatal to all correct understanding of history, even that of the ages upon which attention is thus unwisely concentrated."

Fiske's political and economic views were similar to those of many fellow historians—currency inflation was dishonest and even blasphemous; governmental paternalism (which included a protective tariff) was a great evil as social Darwinism demanded the application of the principle of *laissez faire;* "backward races," including the Spanish, should give way to Englishmen and Americans, whose common mission it was to establish "throughout the . . . earth a higher civilization and more permanent political order than any that has gone before." In fact, as Fiske imagined the future, the world might yet see the consolidation of the "Teutonic race" ruling all mankind.

Fiske won high praise for his activities in bringing to Americans the products of advanced European thought. But in his historical as in his scientific writing he gave no indication of any great originality. Though he theorized about evolution applied to history, his writings were, for the most part, conventional political and military history. He was really an amateur in history, as well as in philosophy, with a zest for life that was infectious. He stimulated youthful Americans to a study of their own history; his picturesque writing "could enlist a hundred readers where ten had read before," said Schouler in tribute.

Charles M. Andrews, as a young scholar, felt the popular reaction to Fiske, who brought into a dull period of historical writing, provincial in tone, the volumes that captivated the American public.[17] "He vitalized it [American history], bringing it out of its isolation into touch with the forces of world history. He . . . accomplished a remarkable feat when he turned the American people from Prescott, Irving, *et al.*, whose subjects lay chiefly outside the limits of the present United States, and caused them to read with enjoyment books that dealt with their own origin and growth. Nothing that Fiske wrote is great history, but much of it is good history," concluded Andrews, "and his place in American historiography is one of great merit and dignity." Robert L. Schuyler summed up his contribution with precision: "Both in his philosophical and in his historical work he was rather the live wire that diffuses knowledge than the dynamo that generates it."[18]

WOODROW WILSON

Wilson, like Fiske, was a successful popular historian. He, too, sought some key to the nation's history and thought he found it in spiritual forces. Wilson is hardly remembered today as a historian whose volumes were once widely read, but his own attitude towards his historical work sufficiently accounts for the modern student's disesteem. His main in-

[17] Andrews, "These Forty Years," *American Historical Review,* Vol. XXX (January, 1925), 234.

[18] R. L. Schuyler, *Political Science Quarterly,* Vol. XXXIII, No. 3 (September, 1918), 433; J. S. Clark, *Life and Letters of John Fiske* (Boston, 1917); J. B. Sanders, "John Fiske," *Jernegan Essays,* 144–70; H. S. Commager, "John Fiske: An Interpretation," Mass. Hist. Soc. *Proceedings,* Vol. LXVI (1942), 332–45.

terests were primarily political; historical writing was always subordinate. He once wrote to Turner: "I love history and think there are few things so directly rewarding and worth while for their own sakes as to scan the history of one's own country with a careful eye and write of it with the all-absorbing desire to get its cream and spirit out. But, after all, I was born a politician." It is well to observe also that much of Wilson's historical work was written for magazines. "The editors of the popular monthlies offer me such prices nowadays that I am corrupted," he wrote in a light vein to Jameson, in 1900. He assured Jameson, however, that he would not alter the quality "to suit the medium."

Like others of his generation who were entranced by Green's *Short History of the English People,* Wilson sought to write a similar book on America. It was Green's glory, wrote Wilson, "to have broadened and diversified the whole scale of English history."[19] The Princeton University professor said that he wrote the history of the United States "in order to learn it," and his interest was less in knowing what had happened than in finding out "which way we were going." The history of nations appeared to him to possess a spiritual quality; it is a thing, he wrote once, "not of institutions, but of the heart."

Wilson was not satisfied that the facts of themselves constituted truth. The truth, he said on one occasion, "is evoked only by such arrangements and orderings of facts as suggest meanings." A colorless presentation of facts was not true to the picture, and it was the historian's task to use the facts dug up by original research workers to convey "an impression of the truth"; obviously everything cannot be told. He added that the historian must also be an investigator, knowing "good ore from bad." It was Wilson's belief that the history of every nation had a plan which it was the task of a historian to divine, and in writing of past generations he was to inject himself into their atmosphere, "rebuilding the very stage upon which they played their parts"; the historian should know no more of the period of which he wrote than the generation which then lived. It was the duty of historians to judge of the sincerity of men and the righteousness of their policies.

Wilson contended that picturesque writers of history have always been right in theory; they failed only in practice. Writing at a time when a reaction was beginning to set in against the dry, doctoral dissertation,

[19] Wilson, "On the Writing of History," *Century Magazine,* Vol. L (September, 1895), 791.

he concluded that the historian needed imagination as much as scholarship. "Histories," said this professor, who had a very large general audience, "are written in order that the bulk of men may read and realize."[20] He had studied under Adams at Johns Hopkins, and he resented concentration on facts to the exclusion of artistic interpretation; he was clearly not much of a believer in "scientific" objectivity.

Whatever the subject of his inquiry, Wilson sought to probe its inner spirit, always thinking of the practical bearing of his work. In his postgraduate years he had been attracted to government, finding in Walter Bagehot, who had written on English politics, a model to guide him in his study of American political institutions. He wanted to present them as living organisms and to write a work that would reform them. "I want to contribute to our literature, what no American has ever contributed," he said, "studies in the philosophy of our institutions"; no abstract philosophy, he insisted, but something immediate in its applicability.[21] The result was his justly famous *Congressional Government* (1885).

Wilson's most important historical contribution, *A History of the American People,* was published in five volumes (1902) after a popular reception had been accorded it as a magazine serial. The great number of illustrations, sometimes irrelevantly placed in the narrative, made it much bulkier than it needed to be. Something of that remoteness from reality which critics in after years found in Wilson as president was noticeable in the historian: "It was the spirit of liberty and of mastery," he wrote, "that made the English swarm to America." The stern morality of which his colleagues spoke at the Peace Conference in 1919 was also a characteristic of the professor.

Wilson's handling of political events leading up to the Revolution, especially the activities of Samuel Adams, was very good, but correspondingly poor was his treatment of economic factors. There was no presentation of the colonies, for example, as parts of an imperial system. Wilson did not attempt to utilize the work that Osgood and Beer had already done on this phase of the subject. It was interesting to observe that in this history, written mainly for popular consumption, a generous interpretation of the Loyalist point of view prevailed.

[20] *Ibid.,* 788–93.

[21] Letter to Ellen Axson, 1883, in R. S. Baker, *Woodrow Wilson; Life and Letters* (8 vols., New York, 1927–35) I, 211, 214.

The place of the West was given heavy emphasis in the chapters on the early national period: "The instant cry of hot protest that came out of the West [because of Jay's proposed surrender of the navigation of the lower Mississippi] apprised eastern politicians of the new world a-making there, the new frontiers of the nation." The second struggle with England was referred to as a "clumsy, foolhardy haphazard war." The nine volumes of Henry Adams on Jefferson's and Madison's administrations were compressed into swift-moving sentences that filled only a few pages in Wilson's history.

In the 1820's there was a new spirit in the land: "The new nation, its quality subtly altered, its point of view insensibly shifted by the movement into the West . . . for the first time chose after its own kind and preferred General Jackson." With a note of exultation, Wilson wrote: "The people's day had come; the people's eyes were upon everything, and were used in a temper of criticism and mastery. . . . Half the economic questions of that day of change," said the historian, "took their magnitude and significance from the westward expansion."

Wilson unreservedly acknowledged Turner's influence; the two were close friends and talked at length about the significance of the frontier: "All I ever wrote on the subject came from him," Wilson said on one occasion. At another time he wrote that our historical writing had suffered from having been done almost exclusively by Easterners. Historians from regions most shocked by Jackson's election spoke of it "as a period of degeneration, the birth-time of a deep and permanent demoralization in our politics. . . . But we see it differently now," said Wilson; it was "regeneration," with a change once and for all of the old order. It was the West that "set the pace," and there was to be found the true national spirit; the East, he said, was sectional.[22] Wilson's history was spiced with interesting generalizations and suggestive insights, but unfortunately he too often left them unsupported.

There was a gentleness in Wilson's treatment of his native South that contrasted strangely with the sternness of contemporary historians. In some respects his attitude antedated the similar approach of William E. Dodd and Ulrich B. Phillips. In a separate volume, *Division and Reunion 1829–1889* (1893), Wilson redressed the usual apportionment of space in historical writings by emphasizing the South and presenting

[22] Wilson, "The Proper Perspective of American History," *The Forum,* Vol. XIX (1895), 544–53.

its society in a sympathetic light. His contention that there was no American nation until after the Civil War profoundly affected historical interpretation. His judgment on the radical leaders, Stevens, Wade, and the rest, was bitterly severe. It is hard to acquit them, he wrote, "of the charge of knowing and intending the ruinous consequences of what they had planned." The voice of a Southern man who, as a boy, had known the dark days of Reconstruction, spoke in these pages, which were a vigorous indictment of the Republican party.

In the last volume of his history Wilson discussed the changed character of American industrial and agricultural life after the Civil War. His treatment of labor, particularly in the Pullman strike, was quite conservative. In fact, his history, generally speaking, showed little of the progressivism that marked his later career. Grover Cleveland was one of the author's heroes, and these two Democrats, temperamentally, had many things in common. In the 1890's "a new sectionalism began to show itself, not political, but economic," wrote Wilson, remembering his talks with Turner. But the analysis of events leading up to the election of 1896 was very thin. In view of Bryan's influence on Wilson's political career, it is interesting to note that the latter was not particularly friendly to the Nebraskan's candidacy in 1896. The historian's judgment did not appear to advantage when he discussed the Spanish-American War, or estimated its results.

Throughout his work Wilson delighted to characterize political leaders; he was not, however, very effective in accounting for social changes. His smooth-flowing language made of his materials, gathered from authoritative sources, an attractive piece of literary craftsmanship. No extended research was needed to write his history; yet it is of significance to note, as did Turner in his review of the volumes, that Wilson was "the first Southern scholar of adequate training and power to deal with American history as a whole in a continental spirit." His work, however, is no longer read, and one may with certainty conclude that Wilson will be remembered not as one who wrote history, but rather as one who made it.[23]

[23] M. L. Daniel, "Woodrow Wilson: Historian," *Mississippi Valley Historical Review,* Vol. XXI, No. 3 (December, 1934), 361–74; an essay by Wilson, "The Truth of History,"; L. M. Sears, "Woodrow Wilson," *Jernegan Essays,* 102–21; R. S. Baker, *Woodrow Wilson: Life and Letters,* I–V.

TWO HISTORIANS OF THE PEOPLE: MCMASTER AND OBERHOLTZER

While a number of writers in the last decades of the nineteenth century were conventionally narrating the political and constitutional history of the period following the Revolution, another historian emerged whose volumes were to have a remarkable influence on his own and the next generation. His work was called *A History of the People of the United States, from the Revolution to the Civil War.* It won for its author, John Bach McMaster, immediate recognition in and beyond the academic world.

McMaster was collecting historical materials in his undergraduate days at the College of the City of New York, from which he was graduated in 1872. He became an instructor in civil engineering in Princeton, but his interest in history persisted. It was while on a surveying trip to the West, he once related, that he was impressed "with the drama of the settlement of a new land, the creation of a new empire, and determined to write its history before the spirit of the period was gone."[24] When his first volume was published, in 1883, the University of Pennsylvania invited him to occupy a specially created chair of American history.

McMaster's volume, with its catholicity of subject matter, was a unique contribution to historical writing in America and was instantly recognized as such. Social history thus made a conspicuous and very successful debut. During the thirty years that followed eight volumes were completed by McMaster, and after a long interval another was added on Lincoln's administration.

The author fixed the attention of the reader instantly with his declaration: "the subject of my narrative is the history of the people." They "shall be the chief theme," although much will need to be written of political and military history. "It shall be my purpose," wrote the historian, "to describe the dress, the occupations, the amusements, the literary canons of the times; to note the changes of manners and morals." His history was to describe also the discoveries and inventions of a mechanical nature; "to tell how, under the benign influence of liberty and peace, there sprang up, in the course of a single century, a prosperity unparalleled in the annals of human affairs; . . . how by a wise system

[24] E. P. Cheyney, *American Historical Review,* Vol. XXXVII, No. 4 (July, 1932), 826.

of free education and a free press, knowledge was disseminated, and the arts and sciences advanced."[25]

In his early volumes McMaster largely fulfilled his promise. A cross section of American civilization in 1784 took up a large part of the first volume. "The Constitution before the People" was an excellent description of public opinion expressing itself on a matter of great importance. McMaster's discussion of Hamiltonian policies was friendly to the Federalists, while his pages on Shays' Rebellion were hostile to the debtors. The difficulties of organizing materials of social history were made vividly clear when one observed that descriptions of Noah Webster's spelling reforms and of John Fitch's steamboat were inserted in a chapter on "The Breaking up of the Confederation." The headings of chapters are in fact, very slight indications of their contents. Wander as he might, however, McMaster usually found his way back to the main thought of his chapter.

The historian credited the Federalists with responsibility for American prosperity in the 1790's. He denounced them, however, for their opposition to the Louisiana Purchase, calling them "mere obstructionists, a sect of the political world which of all other sects is most to be despised." McMaster's attitude toward Jefferson might have been dictated by his reading of Hildreth, for he wrote that Jefferson, on his return from France, "was saturated with democracy in its rankest form, and he remained to the last day of his life a servile worshipper of the people." Privately, the historian spoke of Jefferson as a "demagogue, a 'straddler,' a false friend . . . and I mean to show him up." In dealing with the Whiskey Rebellion, McMaster was friendlier to the insurgents than he had been to the rebels who followed Daniel Shays. The historian never showed much understanding of agrarian problems, though the "people" he was describing were mostly farmers. In his thinking and in his writing he generally identified the "people" with the middle class.

McMaster, in attempting to be impartial in his analysis of diplomatic questions, wrote that it "is perfectly true that the Federal party did show a singular affection for England, did submit with meekness while she

[25] Cf. Macaulay's *History of England:* "It will be my endeavor to relate the history of the people as well as the history of the government; to trace the progress of useful and ornamental arts . . . the rise of religious sects . . . the changes of literary taste . . . to portray the manners of successive generations, and not to pass by . . . even the revolutions which have taken place in dress, furniture, repasts and public amusements."

held their posts, impressed their seamen, condemned their cargoes and their ships; but it is likewise true that the Republican party exhibited a most infatuated love for France," where, they believed, a revolution similar to their own had been effected. At this point, McMaster, in a weird interpretation, revealed a racial bias characteristic of his contemporaries. He distinguished between Celtic revolutions, like the French, marked by violence and Saxon revolutions, like the American, "conducted with the sobriety, with the dignity, with the love of law and order that has ever marked the national uprisings of the Saxon race."

McMaster spoke of matters rarely before included in general history. In a description of town and country life at the end of the eighteenth century, he made an interesting suggestion: "There is not, and there never was, a text-book so richly deserving a history as the [New England] Primer." Shortly thereafter, Paul Leicester Ford wrote a history of that famous book. It should be mentioned, too, that McMaster was one of our earliest historians to take note of the West, and his lines on the pioneers have done service for many authors. The disposal of public lands interested him, but of special concern throughout his work were internal improvements; he rightly saw that transportation was the key to much of American history.

"No person could, in 1803, look over our country," said McMaster, "without beholding on every hand the lingering remains of monarchy, of aristocracy, of class rule. But he must indeed have been a careless observer if he failed to notice the boldness with which those remains were attacked, and the rapidity with which they were being swept away." There was little of democracy in the seaboard states, "but the leaven of Revolution was quietly at work," and restrictions were gradually removed. The opening of a new century brought with it "a great reform in manners, in customs, in institutions, in laws." The adoption of Ohio's constitution at this time, said the historian, "was another triumph for the rights of man."

As McMaster went along, he sometimes forgot his "people" and returned to conventional political and military history. Occasionally he forgot the meaning of his own material. Thus, despite his own pages on internal improvements, westward migration, economic and social growth, he wrote: "from 1793 to 1815 the questions which occupied the public mind were our neutral rights, orders in council, French decrees, impressment, embargoes, treaties." But he was more accurate in describing the nature of American interests after 1815: "Henceforth, for many years to come, the questions of the day were to be the state of the currency, the national bank, manufactures, the tariff, internal improvements, interstate commerce, the public lands, the astonishing growth of the West, the rights of the States, extension of slavery, and the true place of the Supreme Court in our system of government."

Monroe, said the historian, must have been convinced after his tour of the country that the questions facing him were "of home, not of foreign origin; and that in settling those questions the West would have a most decisive influence." There were illuminating pages on the westward rush in these years. Instead of looking toward Europe, the seaboard inhabitants "now on a sudden veered around and faced the Mississippi Valley," and "an era of internal improvements opened which did far more to cement the Union and join the East and West inseparably than did the Constitution and the laws." A very important chapter, "Pauperism and Crime," was related to the economic distress of the postwar years. This was a period of active humanitarian movements to mitigate the harshness of laws against debtors, to promote temperance, and to reform prison conditions.

"The condition of the workingman," he wrote, "stood in need of betterment. In the general advance made by society in fifty years he had shared but little. . . . Ten years of rapid industrial development had brought into prominence problems of urban life and municipal government . . . new and quite beyond solution in 1825." From a consideration of growing complexities in urban life, McMaster moved on to frontier life: "Common hardships, common poverty, common ignorance, and the utter inability to get anything more out of life than coarse food, coarse clothes, and a rude shelter, reduced all to a level of absolute equality which existed nowhere else." The historian inclined to the belief that because religion had a firm hold on frontier regions, "nowhere else was the standard of morality higher or more fully attained."

McMaster concerned himself at length with the industrial revolution, the status of Negroes, and the rise of a militant antislavery movement. While the North was vigorously cultivating "every art and science which could add to the wealth, increase the prosperity and comfort of the people, and develop the material resources of the country," the South was indifferent to these forces that were changing civilization. McMaster's main interest in the industrial revolution was to show how it operated in effecting a strong antagonism between North and South.

The culture of the masses was always an important theme for the historian, and in a long chapter on literature he gathered together materials on magazines, popular fiction, and "moral books," whose effect, he said, was "to inculcate a morality of the most unhealthy sort." His remarks on the charges of American literary subservience to England were sensible; the preference of American readers for English authors, he said, "was not subserviency, but sound literary judgment."

McMaster had hailed Jackson's election as "a great uprising of the people, a triumph of democracy, another political revolution the like of which the country had not seen since 1800, and no mere driving from office of a man or class of men." But he was critical, too, of his turbulent "people." "The era of mob rule had fairly opened and issues of every sort were met with force." The steady growth of the country continued, however, aided by European migration that began to increase rapidly. "Had it not been for the presence of the imported laborer great works of internal improvement could not have been built, and the early thirties were remarkable for the number of turnpikes, canals, and railroads constructed."

The Sixth Census provided McMaster with another opportunity for a view of society in the East, South, and West. As before, special attention was given to improved means of communication and America's rapid urbanization. The Atlantic migration was well handled, but interstate migration within the Union was disposed of too briefly. In the section on the South, which was largely given over to a description of plantation life and slavery, McMaster again drew a comparison between the North and South, with the former strongly favored. "Socially and industrially," he concluded, "the North and South were now two distinct peoples." A chapter, "Social and Political Betterment," rounded out his survey of the country. The vigorous humanitarian movement and the further extension of political democracy in the 1840's enlisted McMaster's enthusiasm, so that even though interpretations were missing in the author's vast accumulation of facts, the reader did enjoy the narrative.

As the historian told the story of the 1850's, his "people," who had formerly been engaged in varied social, economic, and cultural activities, were now mainly involved in great political debates. The core of his narrative dealt with the spirit of secession in 1850, "Bleeding Kansas," and the presidential elections. In his treatment of the Lincoln-Douglas debates, McMaster left no room for doubt as to his own position, referring to one of Douglas' speeches as "his usual biased and partisan review of the political situation. . . ." With an unwonted air of speed, McMaster hurried through the debates and maneuvers relating to secession to reach the election of 1860. Buchanan, of course, was strongly criticized for not meeting firmly the secessionist threat.

Politics did not entirely eclipse other activities, even in the seething 1850's. Once again McMaster referred to the problems created by the rapid growth of cities; and the more radical labor movement then arising was chronicled with special emphasis on the influence exerted by recent immigrants. The distress that came with the panic of 1857 was pictured realistically; no less interesting were the startling comments of Mayor Fernando Wood of New York on the crisis: "Those who produce everything get nothing," he said, "and those who produce nothing get everything."

In 1927, when McMaster was seventy-five years of age, he brought out a volume on Lincoln's administration. It was for the most part a story of people at war, with only brief sections on the nonmilitary aspects of American life during those years. In his treatment of Northern economy, he wrote: "Two years and a half of war had brought no economic or industrial suffering to the North." After the hardships of the first year, "the people soon adjusted themselves to war conditions and went on with their daily occupations more prosperous than ever." Although sympathetic to the stricken South, he was critical of the Black Codes which, he believed, were drawn "with cruel harshness and a deliberate intention to reduce the freedman as far as possible to his old state of slavery."

The pen that spilled so many words—literally millions—was busy on other works of a historical nature. Biographies of Franklin, Webster, and Stephen Girard are among the titles in McMaster's bibliography. He wrote texts that included far more of social history than similar books, and their success was spectacular; over 2,500,000 copies of his texts were sold. Pedagogically they did for American history what James Harvey Robinson's texts were then doing for the teaching of European history.

When McMaster was preparing his biography of Webster, he revealed a marked divergence from his usual attitude toward historical writing, which he had once regarded as involving only a minimum of interpretation. Now he said it was necessary to avoid earlier biographical studies: "None of them make it at all clear why Webster was a great man, they merely state the fact."[26] Unfortunately his own attempt at interpretation was not very impressive. A more successful achievement, both in organization of material and in interpretation, was his concise little volume, *The Acquisition of Political, Social and Industrial Rights of Man in America* (1903).

It is on his vast *History* that his reputation must ultimately rest. The historian glorified the common man. Personalities were rarely emphasized; they were subordinated to their environment. He had no heroes; indeed, he rather tended to belittle traditional figures. He spoke of Washington's "cold heart. . . . Time has dealt gently with his memory, yet his true biography is still to be prepared."

McMaster had a gargantuan appetite for historical facts; for him they were all created equal. His was not a critical spirit that could probe into American life with a nice discrimination and express its findings with an economy of phrase; he was content to pile page upon page of description. The ebullience of most of his own generation was reflected in his volumes which were pervaded with uncritical national enthusiasm. In a speech, in 1898, on "The Social Function of the History of the United States," in words reminiscent of Bancroft, he said: "Our national history should be presented to the student as the growth and development of a marvelous people. . . . We are a people animated by the highest and noblest ideals of humanity. . . . There is no land where the people are so prosperous, so happy, so intelligent, so bent on doing what is just and right, as the people of the United States." The historian's biographer rightly quipped that if Bancroft's history voted for Jackson, McMaster's voted for McKinley.

In his early years McMaster had chosen Macaulay for his model, but the farther he drifted from the influence of the English historian, the more accurate his own work seemed to become. The first volumes, in particular, contained many inaccuracies in quotations, in careless citation of sources, and in some of their sweeping generalizations. It is very probable that the less enduring parts of his work were the sections on

[26] Letter to R. U. Johnson, February 20, 1900, Century Collection, New York Public Library.

political history. As his work gained in accuracy, it seemed to lose something of its engaging, picturesque quality.

From first to last McMaster has had his admirers and detractors, but he lived to see a whole school of historians follow in his footsteps. Some of his sentences and paragraphs have been elaborated into monographs; McMaster himself, however, while exploiting newspapers intensively, made little use of monographic materials, even when he wrote his later volumes, by which time special studies were available. He was, perhaps, the first to emphasize the place of the West in American history, and in stressing economic factors he was a predecessor of Beard as well as of Turner. Roosevelt, whose *Winning of the West* owed much to McMaster, wrote of the latter's work to Henry Cabot Lodge: "If all of McMaster's chapters were changed round promiscuously it would not, I am confident, injure the thread of his narrative in the least. He has put much novel matter in a brilliant, attractive way; but his work is utterly disconnected. . . . In fact all he has done is to provide material for history." And students of both greater and lesser maturity these past seventy years have not hesitated to make good use of McMaster's bountiful offerings, beginning with John Fiske and ending with the latest novice in a class in American history. Bancroft, who was omitting footnotes in a new edition of his work, once advised McMaster to do likewise, because writers were in the habit of using these notes without acknowledgment. McMaster's friend Frederick D. Stone used to say, when a new volume of the history appeared, "Now we shall soon have something from John Fiske."[27]

Albert Bushnell Hart, who saw at firsthand the changes in historical fashions over a longer period than any other American historian, said that McMaster was "the founder of the modern school of [social] historians of the United States." The disciples have not followed McMaster uncritically, but they have accepted his lead in broadening immensely the boundaries of historical inquiry.[28]

[27] E. P. Oberholtzer, "John Bach McMaster," *Pennsylvania Magazine of History and Biography,* Vol. LVII, No. 1 (January, 1933), 25.

[28] W. T. Hutchinson, "John Bach McMaster," *Jernegan Essays,* 122–43; C. R. Fish, review of McMaster, *Mississippi Valley Historical Review,* Vol. I, No. 1 (June, 1914), 31–43; A. B. Hart, "The Writing of American History," *Current History,* Vol. XXXIII, No. 6 (March, 1931), 858–61; E. F. Goldman, *John Bach McMaster: American Historian* (Philadelphia, 1943).

ELLIS PAXSON OBERHOLTZER

Among the many students who passed through McMaster's classes at the University of Pennsylvania in the late 1880's was Ellis Paxson Oberholtzer. Under his teacher's influence the younger man turned in time to historical writing, as editor, biographer, and historian. He edited the series of "American Crisis" biographies, wrote a volume on *The Literary History of Philadelphia* (1906), and completed useful biographies of two of the most important financiers in the history of the United States —*Robert Morris* (1903) and *Jay Cooke* (1907). Oberholtzer had already published the first volume of *A History of the United States since the Civil War* when McMaster brought out the final volume in his own history, which covered the years of strife. Handing a copy of his book to Oberholtzer, McMaster said: "There, I have come up to you. It is for you to go on."[29]

Oberholtzer did go on, publishing four additional volumes which brought his narrative to the assassination of McKinley. Following in the footsteps of his predecessor, Oberholtzer wrote a social and political history of the years after the Civil War without attempting much in the way of interpretation. The same types of sources were used to depict the life of the people—newspapers, pamphlets, Congressional documents, and manuscript collections.

The most interesting chapters in the first volume were those on social conditions in various parts of the country. "The South after the War" was a tragic picture of misery and degradation, with but few signs of economic reconstruction. "The Triumphant North" described immigration, prices, and the material wealth of the region, striking in its contrast with the poverty of the South. In something of the spirit of the more modern student, Oberholtzer spoke of President Johnson laboring "with industry, tact and patriotism to heal the great sectional wound." From a study of the Johnson Papers, the historian concluded that the President had wide popular support. As might have been inferred from his attitude to Johnson, when the author came to write of the impeachment proceedings, he was hostile to the Congressional radicals. Economic and political despoilers—Gould, Fisk, Drew, Tweed—were the objects of his wrath, for he wrote with strong moral indignation. He

[29] Oberholtzer, "John Bach McMaster," *Pennsylvania Magazine of History and Biography,* Vol. LVII, No. 1 (January, 1933), 19.

had in his youth high regard for Godkin, editor of *The Nation,* whose "moral force" still influenced the writing of Oberholtzer years after.

Oberholtzer piled his details mass upon mass, but despite this accumulation of facts, the reader was not very much enlightened with respect to the passing scene. For example, in a reference to California, he said that the state "was in the control, economically and politically, of a small oligarchy of men enriched by mines, railroads and other enterprises." Another general statement was typical: "The entire nation came through the year 1876 with an enlargement of view in an economical, an industrial, an artistic and an ethnographic sense, as well as with a finer comprehension of American history, and the purpose and design of the government." Oberholtzer would have done better to develop these statements, instead of leaving them unsupported by detail.

The impartiality that generally characterized McMaster was absent in the writing of his disciple. Oberholtzer himself once expressed preference for the method of James Schouler, which would not be "impartial as between right and wrong, honorable and dishonorable conduct." His treatment of labor in particular revealed marked prejudice. He confused socialism with anarchism, referred to the Molly Maguires as "black-hearted men," and in his story of strikes was grossly unfair. Without revaluing the evidence in the Haymarket Affair, he was convinced that the anarchists "merited" their punishment. His bias was apparent, too, in his remarks on the Mormons, who were "polygamous fanatics." There was no attempt to present fairly the point of view of the cheap-money advocates of this period. His sense of proportion was poor; too much space, for example, was given to the Alabama Claims and to the complications arising from Chinese immigration.

The division of Oberholtzer's volumes followed the tradition of the old political chronology—presidential administrations and Congressional elections being the dividing lines. Thus the first part ran to 1868, the next to 1872, then there was a skip to 1878, and the fourth ended with the presidential year 1888. Historical writing as typified by McMaster and Oberholtzer has declined in favor, for the modern student prefers a synthesis of materials rather than a mere accumulation of facts.

JUSTIN WINSOR

The ferment in historical circles in the two decades following the Civil War indicated that the time was ripe for a comprehensive treatment of

American history. "What a boom in American history just now," wrote Edward Eggleston to Justin Winsor in 1882.[80] Winsor, who had ably edited *The Memorial History of Boston,* organized a more ambitious work covering the entire field of American history. He was well equipped to head so vast a project, for his knowledge of American history, according to Channing, was unrivaled.

Between 1884 and 1889 the *Narrative and Critical History of America* (8 vols.) was published under his editorship. There were thirty-nine contributors; Winsor himself wrote about half of the entire work, including chapters credited to others. Volumes one through five contained a history of North and South America to the eighteenth century; six and seven were on the United States, 1763–1850; the last volume continued with the later history of British, Spanish, and Portuguese America. It was a notable characteristic that Winsor did not think of America as exclusively the region comprising the United States.

The first volume, *Aboriginal America,* reflected the particular interest that students then had in earliest America. Winsor, whose specialty was geography and the early discoveries, gave full rein to his enthusiasms, writing on Joliet, Marquette, Hennepin, and Lahontan. The section on the American Revolution (Vol. VI) contained a chapter by Mellen Chamberlain which was a great advance over Bancroft's treatment of the causes of that crisis, for it laid particular stress on the Navigation Acts. The disinclination of nineteenth-century historians to treat recent history was notorious; the nearest Winsor's history got to mentioning the Civil War was the last line in a chapter on "The Constitution of the United States and Its History," by George T. Curtis. The volumes on the United States were the poorest of the eight. One can get no clearer picture of some of the differences between recent points of view on American history and those of seventy years ago than by comparing the sixth and seventh volumes with Channing's third, fourth, and fifth volumes. In an appendix Winsor, who was a great librarian as well as learned historian, brought together some of the notes of his vast collection on the manuscript sources of American history; he added, too, a list of printed authorities.

Winsor disclaimed any intention of offering "a model for the general writing of history, based on a co-operative and critical method.

[80] J. A. Borome, "The Life and Letters of Justin Winsor" (MS thesis, Columbia University, 1950), 404–37.

There is no substitute for the individuality of an historian," he remarked. He suggested that one great value of works of this nature was to make accessible to students a summary of scattered material and to furnish them with a guide to the sources; each chapter was accompanied by editorial notes and a critical essay on bibliography. To judge by the mere mass of notes one might say that it was these that were accompanied by the narrative chapters. As a matter of fact, it is the notes that still earn Winsor's volumes a place on the student's shelf. They unearthed a great treasure for historians, and they are still the open-sesame for many subjects in American history. Winsor, said Channing in gratitude, "made the scientific study of American history possible by making available the rich mines of material."[31]

Later readers hesitated to acquaint themselves with the forbidding volumes of the *Narrative and Critical History*. Winsor's own writing bore the mark of hasty composition and lacked grace. The work indicated the interests of older scholars of that day and was not representative of the views of the younger group of historians. The latter pointed to the preponderance of material on the period of discovery and exploration and noted also that the narrative did not extend beyond 1850. Younger scholars, dissatisfied with the existing state of historical writing and feeling the need for a work that would summarize the latest findings, were brought together at the turn of the century to produce the *American Nation* series.

THE *American Nation*

The *American Nation, A History,* edited by Albert Bushnell Hart, represented the work of the first generation of trained American historians. The previous generation which had co-operated to produce Winsor's *Narrative and Critical History,* were mainly skilled amateurs to whom history was an avocation—only two of them were professors of history. Contributors to the *American Nation* were almost entirely academicians.

The twenty-seven volumes of the *American Nation* were published between 1904 and 1908; a volume on the later period appeared some years afterward. Hart introduced the series by remarking that no one would deny "that a new history of the United States is needed, extending from the discovery down to the present time. . . . On the one side there is a

[31] Edward Channing, "Justin Winsor," *American Historical Review,* Vol. III, No. 2 (January, 1898), 197–202.

necessity for an intelligent summarizing of the present knowledge of American history by trained specialists; on the other hand there is need of a complete work, written in untechnical style, which shall serve for the instruction and the entertainment of the general reader." The co-operative method, it was said, was the only one that could meet the problems involved. Although several European historical enterprises had employed the division of labor, the *American Nation,* the editor asserted, was "the first attempt to carry out that system on a large scale for the whole of the United States." This series was to be something more than political or constitutional history; it must include, said Hart, "the social life of the people, their religion, their literature, and their schools . . . their economic life, occupations, labor systems, and organizations of capital." Wars and diplomacy were also to be given their due by the historians, whose volumes were to be written from original sources. Bibliographical apparatus, though not on so lavish a scale as in Winsor's series, was part of each volume.

The *American Nation* was divided into five groups: the first, "foundations of the nation," included five volumes that carried the story to about the end of the seventeenth century; group two, "transformation into a nation," began with *Provincial America,* by Evarts B. Greene, and concluded with *The Confederation and the Constitution*, by Andrew C. McLaughlin; the next group, the "development of the nation," reached down through *Jacksonian Democracy,* by William MacDonald, and included the excellent *Rise of the New West,* by Frederick J. Turner. These three groups of volumes on the whole presented a well-proportioned, continuous narrative and were generally superior to the later ones. Group four, "trial of nationality," heavily emphasized the Civil War. The last group, "national expansion," was scarcely adequate to meet its promise, although it did include the valuable *Reconstruction, Political and Economic,* by William A. Dunning.

In the first group Edward P. Cheyney's *European Background of American History* presented much fresh material; perhaps one of the most important of his chapters was "The System of Chartered Commercial Companies (1550–1700)." *Spain in America,* by Edward G. Bourne, was one of the best volumes in the series, giving as it did a more favorable picture of Spanish civilization in the New World than Americans were accustomed to find in their books. *Colonial Self-Government 1652–1689,* by Charles M. Andrews, represented the author's own findings on the Navigation Acts and the problem of imperial administration. Many of the ideas in this volume were novel to historians and general readers alike in the first years of the twentieth century. Two closing chapters insufficiently explored the "Social and Religious Life in the Colonies (1652–1689)," and "Commercial and Economic Conditions in the Colonies (1652–1689)"; however, the last chapter, for its time, was very good.

Before Greene wrote his volume, the period from 1689 to 1740 was known as the "forgotten half-century." Bancroft and Hildreth had not treated this era with as much detail as the earlier years; hence there was not even a general background available for the student of the first half of the eighteenth century. "Scholars generally agree that the subject matter of this volume has never been adequately treated as a whole," wrote the author. The interest of this period, he rightly asserted, "lies rather in the aggregate of small transactions, constituting what are called general tendencies, which gradually and obscurely prepare the way for the more striking but not necessarily more important periods of decisive conflict and revolution." Two outstanding features characterized the history of these years: the first was a great expansion in the area of settlement, as well as in industry and commerce; the second was "the interaction of imperial and provincial interests."

New perspectives and additional materials have outmoded the volumes on the Revolution. Claude H. Van Tyne, who wrote *The American Revolution,* turned to this subject again in later years, publishing two excellent books embodying the latest research. Van Tyne had an unrivaled knowledge of the manuscript and printed materials on the Revolution. McLaughlin, in his book on the Confederation, did a valuable service in pointing out that this government "was more creditable to the men of that time than posterity has been willing to allow . . . from its mistakes the framers of the Constitution learned wisdom." This was but one of the volumes on constitutional history that McLaughlin published after many years of close study. He later summarized his views in *A Constitutional History of the United States* (1935).

John S. Bassett's *The Federalist System* described the successful establishment of the new government, the organization of the Republican party, and the difficult problems faced by the young Republic in adhering to neutrality in the era of the French Revolution. Bassett fairly credited the Federalists with a great achievement in launching the new nation. Edward Channing's *The Jeffersonian System* had the benefit of the prior publication of Henry Adams' work, but, of course, independent research went into its composition. Garrison's volume, *Westward Extension,* described the region beyond the Mississippi, the causes for its settlement, and the development of sectionalism. Garrison was one of the relatively few Western scholars of this generation whose researches had made important contributions to American historical knowledge. Dunning's *Reconstruction* set a high standard that was not maintained in the volumes on the Civil War or on the later period.

The *American Nation* received on publication, and still receives, the gratitude of scholars for its services in co-ordinating the contributions of many different authors and in presenting the latest results of scholarship. A work of this magnitude, however, was expected to contain not only the summing up of the results of one period of research but also a forecast of the interests of the coming generation of scholars. This it failed to do. In the main the volumes, excepting Turner's, followed conventional lines of political history, with a chapter or two of "social" history thrown in as a sort of concession to the younger element in historical circles. When Hart called for a general history, he had pointed out that one of the most serious failings in scholarship was an insufficient knowledge of social history. The volumes he edited, however, did not go far to remedy that failing. In general, the facts were there, but little attempt at interpretation was made. And yet the *American Nation* was unquestionably a stimulus to historical writing, for it showed the many gaps that needed to be filled. It also improved the writing of those textbooks whose authors found short cuts to knowledge in Hart's series.[32]

EDWARD CHANNING

Edward Channing was one of the earliest and finest products of the "scientific school" of historiography in America. He combined in himself its best, as well as its worst, features. He was a strong nationalist, though no chauvinist; he could be objectively critical in weighing events and deliberately personal in measuring men. He heeded his master, Henry Adams, in cultivating keen analysis in the study of sources and exercising skepticism in treating tradition. But the pupil lacked the master's hand in shaping historical material.

[32] The forthcoming *New American Nation,* edited by H. S. Commager and R. B. Morris, should mark a new summing up of the scholarship of the past half-century.

Channing, temperamentally, seemed to be closely attached to the colonial era and the early Republic, but his field of interest came in time to embrace the whole of American history. In 1905 he brought out the first volume of *A History of the United States,* which he intended to complete in eight volumes. While at work on the seventh he died suddenly, in January, 1931, in his seventy-fifth year.

Channing was a descendant of New England's brightest intellectuals. An appropriate environment drew him to history soon after his graduation from Harvard in 1878, and five years later he was named instructor at his alma mater. A vigorous critic himself, the training he gave to students in dealing carefully with historical evidence was invaluable.

Among Channing's earliest studies was *The Narragansett Planters, a Study of Causes;* it illustrated his skepticism of accepted traditions and his desire to go to the sources for his narrative. His *Town and County Government in the English Colonies of North America* opposed the theory of Teutonic origins of New England towns. The first careful summary of the English Acts of Trade and Navigation affecting the colonies was made by Channing in a paper before the American Antiquarian Society in 1889. While he was still an undergraduate, Channing was taking notes for the history he was later to write. He once said that he felt he had to write a history of the United States from the sources, after listening to the dogmatic lectures of Henry Cabot Lodge and reading the biased history of Hildreth.[33]

In the preface to his principal work Channing wrote: "I have undertaken a new study of the history of the United States from the discovery of America to the close of the nineteenth century. . . . The growth of the nation will . . . be treated as one continuous development from the political, military, institutional, industrial, and social points of view. . . . I have considered the colonies as parts of the English empire, as having sprung from that political fabric, and as having simply pursued a course of institutional evolution unlike that of the branch of the English race which remained behind. . . . I have also thought that the most important single fact in our development has been the victory of the forces of union over those of particularism." The institutions and forces making for union were worthy of especial emphasis, said Channing, "for it is the triumph of these which has determined the fate of the nation."

[33] S. E. Morison, "Edward Channing," Mass. Hist. Soc. *Proceedings,* Vol. LXIV (1932), 250–84.

Channing's treatment of the colonies as part of the English imperial system was a novel and important feature for its time. It belonged to the school of colonial historians whose most distinguished representatives were Channing's contemporaries, Osgood and Andrews. Channing, descendant of Puritans, was more sympathetic to his ancestors than were some of his fellow historians. After noting that the first generation of New Englanders were very much like those who stayed behind in the mother country, the author wrote that, as a result of new conditions, "the Puritan creed only slowly assumed the sternness of aspect which made intellectual excitation save for religious purposes an impossibility." As for the Virginia settlers, Channing said, "They were the first heroes of American history."

In the closing pages of his first volume Channing returned again to the statement he had made in his preface: "The greatest fact in American history has been the union in one federal state of peoples living in widely separated regions under very different conditions of society and industry." This was effected because "the institutions and the political ideals of these communities had in them so much that was akin." While noting similarities to English precedents, the historian also stressed colonial divergences from them. His conclusion, however, was that the colonists in the seventeenth century "were still Englishmen in their feelings and prejudices, in their virtues and in their vices. Contact with the wilderness and freedom from the constitutional restraints which held down Englishmen in England . . . had not yet resulted in making the colonists Americans.

Channing's likes and dislikes were rather obvious: "Had the governors been persons of force, independent means, and character," he wrote, "they would have exercised an important influence upon colonial life and constitutional development. . . . Fortunately," he added, "they were usually persons of quite opposite qualities."[34] In the chapter "Beginnings of Constitutional Controversy" (Vol. II), Channing paid particular attention to New York, whose assembly fought out some of the issues later handled in more dramatic fashion by James Otis and Patrick Henry in a larger sphere.

By 1760, the historian stated, "changed climatic conditions and en-

[34] L. W. Labaree has strongly qualified this estimate of colonial governors in his *Royal Government in America* (New Haven, 1930).

vironments had already begun to alter the racial characteristics of the descendants of the first comers from England." Institutional ideas and commercial interests diverged in England and the colonies. "In all that constitutes nationality, two nations now owed allegiance to the British crown. The colonists were patient and long-suffering; only prolonged misgovernment on the part of the rulers of Britain compelled them to declare themselves independent of that empire from which they had sprung. . . .

"Commercialism, the desire for advantage and profit in trade and industry," said Channing, "was at the bottom of the struggle between England and America; the immutable principles of human association were brought forward to justify colonial resistance to British selfishness. The governing classes of the old country wished to exploit the American colonists. . . . the Americans desired to work their lands and carry on their trade for themselves." The historian went on to show how the colonists had drifted away from English political and social ideas. In contrast to older writers, said Channing, "the modern student sees in the third George no mere tyrant, no misguided monarch, but an instrument of a benign providence bringing, through pain and misery, benefit to the human race." Although the historian presented valuable information showing the burdensome taxes under which the colonists were laboring, his judgment on the Stamp Act was that it "was eminently fair and well constructed, the sole objection to it was in the mode of passage." By 1774 "America was united; not that all Americans thought alike or were opposed to England, but everywhere the radical party had come to the same conclusion." Leaders of that radical party, Samuel Adams and Joseph Warren, were classed "among the most astute politicians this country has ever seen."

The events of 1775 were introduced with a note of pride: "In Europe, war was a profession; in America it was only waged for life and family." The writer paid high tribute to Jefferson's work in drafting the Declaration of Independence: "Never in the whole range of the writings of political theorists has the basis of government been stated so succinctly." Although the ideas and even the words were Locke's, "the reader will go to Locke in vain for so lucid a statement of his ideas." In his treatment of the post-Revolutionary years, Channing differed from others who had painted a gloomy picture of economic life at the time the Constitution was adopted. Americans, he said, "had already regained their footing in the commercial world and were experimenting in many directions to effect a diversification of their means of livelihood."

Channing required three volumes to reach the establishment of the Union; three more carried him another seventy-five years through the crisis which threatened that Union. The generation after the adoption of the Constitution, he said, was "distinctly a period of transition from the old order of things to the new, from the modes of thought and action of the seventeenth and eighteenth centuries to those of our own times."

Channing discussed at some length the problems that confronted Washington, particularly those created by office-seekers. The author's comment was illuminating: "The 'spoils system,' . . . instead of being an invention of Jacksonian Democrats or Jeffersonian Republicans, was an inheritance from the Federalist Presidents and by them had been built up on colonial and English precedents." Channing's inclination was in the direction of the Federalists, especially the few leaders who, he asserted, "acted with a sagacity that the world has seldom seen." The historian, however, attempted to hold the scales severely equal, for elsewhere the Federalist party was described as "reactionary from start to finish," becoming "more aristocratic with each successive year." Hamilton was judged fairly: although "he made some of the cruelest blunders in our history," America's debt to him cannot be overstated. "He was the organizer of exploitation, the originator of monopoly; but he did his work at the precise moment that exploitation needed to be organized and human ingenuity required excitation by hope of monopoly."

In an analysis of "The Revolution of 1800," the historian took a fling at one of the many traditions he brushed aside in the course of his work: "A change of less than two hundred and fifty votes . . . would have given New York's vote to Adams and made him President with seventy-seven votes to sixty-one for Jefferson—of such was the Revolution of 1800."[35] Channing was rather friendly to Jefferson, and he was generous in praise of Gallatin's financial policy. Like his teacher, Henry Adams, Channing showed how the Louisiana Purchase played havoc with Jefferson's political theories. The international difficulties that arose during Jefferson's second administration had a strong fascination for Channing, who

[35] In answer to Channing, it should be observed that significant changes have often occurred even with small majorities.

had always been attracted to this period of history. The embargo, he pointed out, did not effect nearly so much injury, except in Virginia, as had been conventionally supposed. In fact, said Channing, "the extension of manufacturing in New England and in other States north of Maryland, went on throughout the period of commercial warfare; and thereafter was greatly stimulated by the conflict with England."

Channing's treatment of the Hartford Convention was more lenient toward New England than that of other writers. The war's end was greeted with delight, he wrote, and the American people with their back to Europe and their face to the West, now "addressed [themselves] to the solution of the problems of the Nineteenth Century."

"The American mind, which had concerned itself only with political organization," said the historian mistakenly, "suddenly turned to other problems of human existence and became renowned for fertility of invention, for greatness in the art of literary expression, and for the keenest desire for the amelioration of the lot of humanity." As for the West, Channing was not much impressed by Turner's ideas on the significance of the frontier: "It is remarkable," he said, "how evanescent has been the influence of these new conditions, for the American people is now and has been for some years among the most conservative of the nations of the earth."

The New England historian, heir to abolitionist traditions, looked upon extremists with disdain. He spoke with some feeling of his great-uncle, William Ellery Channing, who, in the abolition controversy, "took the middle path that satisfies no one, but sometimes is the path of wisdom." The later Channing, indeed, showed much sympathy for the owners of plantations: "It is by no means improbable . . . ," he wrote, "that the slaves were often happier than their masters."

The ferment in religion and education before the Civil War strongly interested Channing, who recorded at length the significant developments in each field. Though he duly recorded important gains in education, he was not greatly impressed with statistics: "There were more colleges and more secondary schools [1850] in proportion to the total population than there were in 1800 or in 1820, but so far they do not seem to have greatly affected the average intelligence of the American people, and it was the education of democracy and not the breeding of scholars that underlay the whole educational movement of that time.

Indeed, by 1860, the golden age of American scholarship was passed." It was in literature "that the renaissance of the American mind is most noticeable." Unlike narrower New England students of literature, Channing wrote that "the geographical distribution of writers, readers, and students shows that all sections of the country were interested in literature, using that word in its widest meaning." The conclusion of his discussion of literature was as exuberant as that on education was depressing: "This half-century in the United States in poetry, in fiction, and in history stands apart—it is without an equal since the days of Shakespeare, Francis Bacon, and John Milton."

While Channing's judgments on America's intellectual life were sometimes eccentric, he had a sure grasp of her political history. Of the period following the war of 1812, formerly considered barren of significance, he said that it was a formative era in domestic history "and in our international history of the greatest interest and of the highest importance." Forces were then "taking shape that were to determine the history of the United States down to the year 1865."

The historian accepted the general judgment that "the Missouri Compromise marked the end of the first chapter in the history of nationalism. From that time for forty years, the whole spirit of our development was towards dualism—for the Missouri Compromise practically marked the division of the country into two groups, having distinctly different economic interests." The highest praise was bestowed upon Webster's "Reply to Hayne," "probably the most famous speeches ever delivered in the national Senate." Channing closed his treatment of the period to 1848 with this question: "Would the Republic remain one united country, or would it be divided according to the social and economic desires of the inhabitants of the several sections into which it was geographically divided?"

The way in which the country answered that question was the theme of Channing's final published volume, *The War for Southern Independence*. The historian thus set the stage for the coming drama: "By the middle of the century, two distinct social organizations had developed within the United States, the one in the South and the other in the North." Had there been proper leadership, "peaceable secession might have been achieved in 1850." Few Northerners have been fairer than Channing in his analysis of the old South. He reminded his readers that "all treatments of Southern life by Northern writers gave an entirely false assessment of the weaknesses and the strengths of the slave system." Nevertheless he was forced to conclude: "Almost alone in the advancing modern world, the South stood still."

Channing's disagreement with Whig historiography was clear in his defense of Webster's "Seventh of March" speech against abolitionist censure. As for *Uncle Tom's Cabin,* it was credited with enormous influence in America and Europe; it "did more than any other one thing to arouse the fears of the Southerners and impel them to fight for independence." The eleven years before 1859 were termed the "most significant in our history, for it was then that the Southerners determined to have their own way within the United States, or else to leave the Union . . . ; and the people of the Northern States determined in their own minds that the time for concessions had passed and that there should be no more compromise with slave power."

A careful analysis of opinion, North and South, in the days preceding the open break between the sections was presented by the historian. But in this volume, as elsewhere, instead of pages devoted to unraveling some knotty problem of especial interest to the author, we might have preferred further elucidation of some interesting remarks, such as the following: "Looking backward, we can see that the people of the North in 1861 undertook to . . . use the legislative power that the absence of Secessionists from Congress placed in their hands to build up the manufacturing industries of the North and to extend its agricultural operations. . . . It may well be that the prolongation of the war for a year or more was distinctly a lesser evil than the retardation of Northern prosperity." In his closing lines Channing clearly indicated what his outlook on Reconstruction would have been had he lived to write the volume. "Well would it have been," he said, "had the reconstruction of Southern society been in the hands of these men [leading soldiers] and of others who respected one another and were guided by Abraham Lincoln."

It is difficult to find any philosophy of history in his volumes, although like others of his generation, he carried over into history the twin beliefs in evolution and the idea of progress. Providence, in Channing's view, also played its part in guiding the fortunes of the nation. He was, of course, aware of the writings of Karl Lamprecht and his school, as well as of economic determinists. Instead of especially emphasizing economic factors, he wrote, "now it is more often the case to emphasize the sociological or psychical change that is wrought by changed modes of living and by the general operation of economic factors. Possibly the best way to analyze the problems of progress or of changes in human outlook would be to combine all these various factors into one, for surely one's mode of living exercises a very important influence on one's mode of thinking." His own environment, he clearly understood, determined his point of observation on American history: "The time and place of one's birth and breeding," he acknowledged, "affect the judgment, and the opportunity for error is frequent."

It is not surprising that there has been very strong sectional criticism of what may well be the last of the important New England interpretations of our history. Critics have pointed out that in his treatment of the background of the Revolution Channing included nothing to suggest antagonistic views between the Atlantic coast and the back country, nor did he take account of sectional alignments in the post-Revolutionary period. Van Tyne remarked that this "historical account rarely leaves the Atlantic coast"; to the New England historian the Mississippi Valley was "Transappalachia." Channing's narration of the conflict with France and Spain for the great valley shared the weakness of older histories in revealing an Anglo-Saxon bias.

When, in some of his volumes, he emphasized social factors, these were not always related to political developments; he failed, for example, to link up economic questions with the call for a constitutional convention. Like his contemporary McMaster, Channing's treatment occasionally ranged over so wide a variety of materials as to cloud the specific objective of his chapters. Charles A. Beard's remark on Channing's volume dealing with the Civil War—that it told what doctors of philosophy thought of this period—was appropriate for the other volumes as well. The "Great Work," as the history was known to Harvard students, often seemed to be a series of seminar reports unrelatedly strung together. In the main it was a history for historians, and many specialists have found in Channing's contribution materials hitherto unknown to themselves. His work has had and will continue to have great influence on teachers and careful writers of our history.

The distinguished historian had no illusions about the permanence of a particular interpretation. He once wrote that "no historian can hope to live as can a poet or an essayist, because new facts will constantly arise to invalidate his most careful conclusions." His keenness of observation unsettled many judgments long thought permanent, and he stimulated much new research in many fields of American history.[36]

[36] C. R. Fish, "Edward Channing: America's Historian," *Current History,* Vol. XXXIII, No. 6 (March, 1931), 862–67; R. R. Fahrney, "Edward Channing," *Jernegan Essays,* 294–312; Beard's review in *New Republic,* Vol. XLIV, No. 571 (November 11, 1925), 310; J. A. DeNovo, "Edward Channing's 'Great Work' Twenty Years After," *Mississippi Valley Historical Review,* Vol. XXXIX, No. 2 (September, 1952), 257–74.

XI

The Imperial School of Colonial History

Long before Bancroft died, students were beginning to question the value of his work on the colonial era. Far too much emphasis, they said, had been laid on exploration, martial events, and the conflicts between personalities. Critics argued that Bancroft, Palfrey, and other older writers conveyed no understanding of colonial institutions, their development, and the relationship of the colonies to the rest of the empire. It was not surprising that at a time when Americans were finishing their studies in Europe they adopted a broader perspective in the writing of their own history. The American eagle had also begun to spread imperial wings, and it is thus no coincidence, perhaps, that in looking back over their past, American historians should have become conscious of broader horizons. Nor were they uninfluenced by the renewed interest of Englishmen in their own empire, as evidenced in the works of Sir Charles Dilke and Sir John Seeley.

Bancroft, we have seen, was not as provincial as his later critics thought him. Writers of the modern school, however, have altered so greatly our understanding of the past that American colonial history now appears as but an episode in the expansion of Europe. Osgood, Channing, Beer, and Andrews contributed much to this revision of our historical narrative; Andrews went farthest in reconstructing the view of colonial past from the vantage point of the English homeland. "The years from 1607 to 1783," he said, "were colonial before they were American or national, and our Revolution is a colonial and not an American problem."

To some degree these American historians were anticipated by several British writers. The works of Trevelyan and Doyle were quite provocative to their younger transatlantic contemporaries, as were the chapters on the American Revolution in William E. H. Lecky's *History of England in the Eighteenth Century* (1878–90). Moses C. Tyler recommended Lecky to his classes at Cornell because he considered the English historian's treatment "the very best means of getting the coming generation of American students out of the old manner of thinking upon and treating American history, which has led to so much Chauvinism among our people."[1]

MOSES COIT TYLER

Moses Coit Tyler, though primarily a historian of literature, helped to change the cultural climate in which political historians could shape a new view of colonial and Revolutionary history. Tyler had been trained for the ministry, but in his late twenties he resigned, explaining to a confidant, "I was not built for a parson." He preferred literature: "That is my passion and I think my mission." In his commonplace book he jotted down the thought of writing the history of American literature.[2] Although he gave up the ministry for a university career, his conception of the academician was somewhat akin to that of the ardent missionary. He once maintained "that while history should be thoroughly scientific in its method, its object should be practical. To this extent I believe in history with a tendency. My interest in our own past is chiefly derived from my interest in our own present and future; and I teach American history, not so much to make historians as to make citizens and good leaders for the state and nation."[3] Like so many other students of his day, Tyler felt the impact of Buckle, and he hoped to find the law of American development through her literature.[4]

During his career as professor of English literature at the University of Michigan, and later as professor of American history and literature at Cornell, Tyler found time to do a vast amount of research for his four volumes on America's literary history, to publish a biography of Patrick

[1] Elizabeth Lecky, *A Memoir of W. E. H. Lecky,* 185–86, A. D. White to Lecky, July 30, 1890.

[2] H. M. Jones, *Moses Coit Tyler,* 111.

[3] "The Study of History in American Colleges and Universities," U. S. Bureau of Education; *Circular of Information,* No. 2 (1887), 156.

[4] Jones, *Moses Coit Tyler,* 141.

Henry, and to make contributions to professional periodicals. His essay on the American Loyalists in an early issue of the *American Historical Review* was one of the first to strike the modern note in our changed attitude toward the Revolution.

In 1879 Tyler published *A History of American Literature* (2 vols.) to 1765. The arrangement of the work was intended to show how from "several isolated colonial centers, where at first each had its peculiar literary accent," there developed a "tendency toward a common national accent; until finally, in 1765 . . . the scattered voices of the thirteen colonies were for the first time brought together and blended in one great and resolute utterance" of defiance against England.

In a swinging prose that showed a lusty pride in his Anglo-Saxon heritage, Tyler described various writers in Virginia and New England. Tyler could speak with assurance upon the characteristics of colonial historians, poets, and theologians because a careful study of every book or pamphlet referred to had given him an intimate acquaintance with its writer. Although he could be severely critical of Puritanism, Tyler had a genuine affection for many of the writers who were nurtured in its faith. The prayers of the Puritan, he said, "were often a snuffle, his hymns a dolorous whine, his extemporized liturgy a bleak ritual of ungainly postures and of harsh monotonous howls, yet the idea that filled and thrilled his soul was one in every way sublime, immense, imaginative, poetic—the idea of the awful omnipotent Jehovah, his inexorable justice, his holiness, the inconceivable brightness of his majesty."

A number of individuals were rescued from oblivion by the tender mercies of Tyler, and in some cases were revealed to be writers of genuine worth. He referred to John Wise as "the first great American expounder of democracy in church and state," and he indicated the value of Nathaniel Ames, whose almanacs were superior to those of Franklin. These two volumes had an immense value when they appeared, bringing a much-needed organization to the study of American literature, but they seem less important today. Tyler was often too lenient in his criticism of poor writing and sometimes excessive in his praise of merely good writing.

No sooner was this history out of the way than he prepared for its successor. In his diary, August 7, 1879, he wrote: "Began work with reference to next volumes of American literature." Nearly a score of years were to pass, however, before they were published. The two volumes on *The Literary History of the American Revolution* 1763–1783 (New York, 1897) were Tyler's most valuable bequest to historians. With justifiable pride he said: "For the first time in a systematic and a fairly complete way, is set forth the inward history of our Revolution—the history of its ideas . . . in the various writings of the two parties of Americans who promoted or resisted that great movement." His plan was to let both parties "tell their own story freely in their own way." Light as well as sober literary forms—ballads, songs, and squibs—that shed illumination on the revolutionary era were included by Tyler.

This work was markedly different from other treatments of the Revolution. Tyler did not fix his eyes upon political or military figures or King George III. His interest, he said, was in "essayists, pamphleteers, sermon writers, song writers, tale tellers, or satirists, the study of whose work . . . may open to us a view of the more delicate and elusive, but not less profound or less real, forces which made that period so great."

A careful analysis was presented of the publications of noted political figures—John Adams, Daniel Dulany, Jonathan Mayhew—and John Dickinson, whose *Letters from a Farmer in Pennsylvania* were described as "the most brilliant event in the literary history of the Revolution." Tyler also brought to a larger public the story of the relationship between politics and religion in the prerevolutionary era. As a student of literature he was, of course, interested in the art of writing, but he was also concerned with the political significance of such writers as Francis Hopkinson, Philip Freneau, and John Trumbull.

In his study of the literature of the Loyalists, Tyler dispelled some hardy misconceptions about that unpopular group. He denied that the Tories were "a party of mere negation and obstruction," pointing out that they "had positive political ideas, as well as precise measures in creative statesmanship." It is erroneous, he said, to think of the Tories as "opposed either to any reform in the relations of the colonists with the mother country, or to the extension of human rights and liberties here or elsewhere." In a tone that put to shame persistent provincialism in our historical writing, Tyler said that it was an "error to represent the Tories of our Revolution as composed of Americans lacking in love for their native country." The outstanding Loyalists—Jonathan Boucher, Joseph Galloway, and Daniel Leonard—received extended consideration at the hands of the historian.

Nothing better has ever been done on the literary history of the Revolution, despite some defects of omission. Tyler failed, for example, to consider sufficiently the place of the newspaper in the Revolution, nor did he include some writers in England who were of American birth or who had resided in America, notably George Chalmers. He might also have given more space to Southern writers. The judgment of Paul Leicester Ford, however, that these volumes were "far and away the best treatment of the literature of those years of turmoil," is still true.

All writers on early America have had their labors considerably lightened because Moses Coit Tyler lived before them. In his younger days he had written that he intended to cover the whole of American literary history in three or four volumes. The fourth brought him only to the era of the Revolution. Ghosts of buried controversialists encounter their ancient adversaries in the lively pages of Tyler, and whatever of immortality has been granted to them came through the enthusiastic research of the historian. A splendid standard of historical scholarship was not the least part of the heritage Tyler left to posterity.[5]

GEORGE OTTO TREVELYAN

Histories of America written by Englishmen in the eighteenth century were well known on this side of the Atlantic. English historical studies of America, written in the nineteenth and twentieth centuries, continued to be read in the United States, but only a limited few aroused any enthusiasm. Scholarly English interest in America was uncommon; when it did exist, it was often vitiated by a bias for or against democracy. Despite a prejudice against studies of America written by Englishmen, Americans read with an almost morbid curiosity the innumerable books by British travelers who condemned or praised the United States. Of these Englishmen who wrote on America, most of them were strongly attracted to the drama of the Civil War, but some displayed an interest in the earlier period when the American colonies had been part of the British Empire. Two of the most important among them were Trevelyan and Doyle.

George Otto Trevelyan's history of the American Revolution remains one of the best-known works on America written by a European. Trevelyan was a nephew of Macaulay, whose influence was important in directing the younger man to the study of history. His concern with the American Revolution came by way of his study of Charles James Fox.

[5] For Tyler's diary, see J. T. Austen, *Moses Coit Tyler* (New York, 1911).

Family tradition and a personal sympathy with the customs of the late eighteenth century enabled Trevelyan to breathe life into his picture of that society which was the background for *The Early History of Charles James Fox* (1880). This volume, which fascinated the literary and political world, wrote the author's son, gave "the reader the entrée as an intimate member of a bygone aristocratic society."

To the regret of his friends, who used to say that a Parliamentary statute should be passed to force Trevelyan to finish his biography of Fox, the historian turned to write on the American Revolution. His justification was that Fox's life between 1774 and 1782 was "inextricably interwoven with the story of the American Revolution." The actions of British public figures in these years, said the historian, could only be understood in the light of what was then happening in the colonies. Over a period of fifteen years (1899–1914) six volumes on *The American Revolution* were published.

Trevelyan began his work with illuminating comparisons between English and American society in the eighteenth century, in which the latter came off very well. Commenting upon some temperamental differences, he said: "There could be no personal sympathy, and no identity of public views, between the governors in Downing Street and the governed in Pennsylvania and New England. . . . All who loved England wisely dwelt with satisfaction upon the prosperity of America."

The spirit of the historian's approach to the Revolution was suggested in the lines he quoted from Tennyson:

O thou, that sendest out the man
To rule by land and sea,
Strong mother of a Lion-line
Be proud of those strong sons of thine
Who wrench'd their rights from thee!

The Revolution was a civil war, and the differences were not exclusively between peoples on opposite sides of the Atlantic; there were divisions among Englishmen and hostilities among Americans themselves.

Trevelyan brought to life the leading protagonists with pen portraits of rare artistry, while his description of military operations upheld his reputation as a vivid and picturesque writer. Fox and Burke were his heroes; George III, Lord North, and Lord Sandwich were among his villains. Trevelyan's history was, obviously, a Whig interpretation of

English politics; also it did not attempt to discuss many of the internal American problems that arose during the Revolutionary years. Unfortunately the English historian neglected to use monographic studies that would have been more valuable than were Fiske or Lossing.

Englishmen have generally thought Trevelyan's narrative too favorable to Americans; even some Americans have thought so. Theodore Roosevelt, a nationalist historian if ever there was one, praised Trevelyan's work, but he said the historian "had painted us a little too favorably." Roosevelt liked especially the description of battles and characterizations of soldiers such as Washington and Morgan. In a typical burst of enthusiasm Roosevelt sent to Trevelyan a letter saying that he had "written the final history of our Revolution."

It was the opinion of the historian's son and biographer that Trevelyan depicted English civilization during the era of the Revolution "in a pleasanter and more intimate light than any to which American readers were accustomed." To learn that many Englishmen also had once despised George III soothed American tempers. Perhaps Trevelyan's work will be discussed in the future less as a contribution to historical literature than as a factor in improving Anglo-American relations in the early years of the twentieth century.[6]

JOHN A. DOYLE

John A. Doyle was an Oxford man whose interest in America appeared to have been awakened early. He won the Arnold Prize in 1869 with an essay on *The American Colonies Previous to the Declaration of Independence,* and a few years afterward wrote a textbook on United States history. In his essay Doyle wrote with vigor and insight, anticipating the views of Benjamin F. Wright, who maintained, as against Turner, that the colonists brought democracy with them and did not get it from contact with the frontier. Speaking of the Anglo-American empire in the middle of the eighteenth century, Doyle thought that in it "there was apparently little of the material for national unity. Its inhabitants were not of one race or one speech, still less were their institutions or worship the same. One thread alone bound them together—the common spirit of independence and self-government." Doyle concluded that "the whole key to the American Revolution lies in two facts;

[6] G. M. Trevelyan, *Sir George Otto Trevelyan: A Memoir by His Son* (London, 1932).

it was a democratic and a conservative revolution. It was the work of the people, and its end was to preserve, not to destroy or to construct afresh."

In the following years Doyle made the studies that eventually led to the publication in five volumes of his history of the colonies. In his first sentences he indicated his unprovincial approach to his subject: "I have preferred to regard the history of the United States," he said, "as the transplantation of English ideas and institutions to a distant soil, and the adaptation of them to new wants and altered modes of life." The process by which these institutions were developed was to be his main theme. In the spirit of the modern student, Doyle wrote of the significance of the transition from the period of exploration to settlement in the seventeenth century: "We pass, as it were, from a dreamland of romance and adventure into the sober atmosphere of commercial and political records, amid which we faintly spell out the first germs of the constitutional life of British America."

Doyle's treatment of New England was better and more detailed than that accorded the Southern colonies. His attitude toward New England was more detached than that of Palfrey, free as it was of any necessity to defend the actions of the Puritans. Doyle spoke of Mrs. Hutchinson's revealing in her trial "a conspicuous union of self-reliance with dignified sobriety and restraint." At least one of the Puritan leaders, Winthrop, earned Doyle's unstinted praise: "He is, on a narrower stage, the counterpart of Pym and Hampden, the forerunner of Washington and Madison."

Throughout, Doyle's work was informed by stimulating generalizations. He spoke, for example, of the need of the Puritans to modify in after years their "rigid system of public morality. . . . Fresh wants, material, intellectual, and spiritual, have to be satisfied; commerce brings with it gradations of wealth, intercourse with the outer world calls out new ideas and new tastes. The difference between the town and the country becomes wider. Men are no longer confined to a little circle, where the actions of each are open to the full view of his neighbors, and where all live under the pressure of an austere and exacting public opinion. To bridge over the gulf which severed the new life from the old, to modify Puritanism and to adapt it to fresh requirements, to secure change without risking disruption of violent reaction, this was the problem which new England had now to solve." In his examination of disputes with the governors, the Englishman offered a valuable corrective to the conventional, patriotic interpretation made by American historians.

In the year that Doyle died, 1907, his last two volumes were published; one was on the middle colonies, the other, *The Colonies under the House of Hanover,* treated the provinces as a unit down to the Revolutionary period. In his description of politics in the middle colonies, he was naturally concerned with the disputes between Governor Cornbury and the Assembly, and he took the opportunity to observe the similarity between executive attitudes then and sixty years later. "There is in Cornbury," he wrote, "the same dull obstinacy, the same narrowness of view that we see in Gage and Dunmore. Like George III, and too many of George's Ministers, Cornbury deals with the question as though it were a mere legal controversy. . . . He wholly fails to see that the very fact of their being dissatisfied and disaffected is in itself of importance."

The accession of the Hanoverians was a convenient point of vantage from which the historian could take a comprehensive view of the colonies. As Doyle expressed it, it was the internal history of the colonies which was of prime interest in the seventeenth century; in the next century it was external. "External pressure, exercised by the mother country, becomes the main factor in colonial history. . . . The result is an entire and important change in our point of view. Henceforth we can regard the colonies as an organic whole forming part of an administrative system."

In his treatment of the commercial relations between the colonies and England, Doyle took a position similar to that of George L. Beer, although he pressed his point too far when he said there was "no desire to sacrifice the colonies to the mother country." His handling of the general problem of imperial administration was inadequate. He failed to use the sources that lay close at hand in British depositories, depending rather on unsatisfactory printed materials. While Doyle's last volume was unsystematic, it contained a fairer interpretation of the Revolutionary period than historians were wont to make at that time. Doyle said that it was "the blind reliance of English statesmen on administrative methods whose doom had been plainly foretold" which was largely responsible for the eventual conflict.[7]

[7] For his critical approach to the Revolution, see an essay on Trevelyan in Doyle's *Essays on Various Subjects* (London, 1911).

Doyle's work was chiefly a political history, but on occasion he turned to other subjects. One of his best chapters was a general survey of institutions, manners, and the economic life of New England in 1650. The chapter on religion in his last volume was excellent and probably gave the contemporary reader the best short treatment of the subject then available. In his section on immigration Doyle revealed a very strong bias against the Irish, but on the whole he was not given to emphasizing his prejudices.

Charles M. Andrews referred to Doyle's volumes on the seventeenth century as "unquestionably the best that we have."[8] But the work of Americans—Osgood, Beer, and Andrews himself—soon superseded the volumes of Doyle, particularly in the handling of internal problems in the colonies and in unraveling the complexities of imperial policies. Doyle's allotment of four volumes to the seventeenth century, and one to the eighteenth was, of course, a serious distortion of the relative significance of each period for the whole development of colonial life. Although important when they first appeared, Doyle's volumes are rarely consulted today.

HERBERT LEVI OSGOOD

Until Osgood turned his energy to a study of the American colonies, there was no dependable, comprehensive treatment of this foundation period of American nationality. A new orientation was demanded, and Osgood was among the first to see that a large part of American colonial history must be told with reference to the British imperial system, of which the colonies were but a portion. American colonial history, he once wrote, needed to be taken out of its isolation and made to "appear as a natural outgrowth of the history of Europe." This departure from the conventional point of view, so orthodox today as to be part of all textbooks on early American history, was productive of important conclusions, particularly in making more understandable Britain's policy toward her colonies.

Herbert Levi Osgood was a student at Amherst when Julius H. Seelye and John W. Burgess were on the faculty. Burgess, then newly returned from study with the leading German historical scholars, directed Osgood's attention to what was soon to be his life work. Follow-

[8] C. M. Andrews, "American Colonial History, 1690–1750," American Historical Association *Annual Report* for the year 1898 (1899), 50.

ing the advice of Burgess, he left for the mecca of most young American scholars—Germany. There he was most deeply influenced by the aged master, von Ranke, to whom, he said, American scholars owed a debt of gratitude which could not easily be repaid. Within a few years of his return from Europe, Osgood was added to the strong faculty of Columbia University.

In looking over the fields as yet untilled by the methods of the modern historian, Osgood believed the development of American colonial institutions a theme worthy of a scholar's lifetime. An article on "England and the Colonies," in the *Political Science Quarterly* (1887), indicated the bent of his future study. Referring to the Revolution, he wrote that "the whole struggle was but an episode in the development of the English colonial system."

Osgood was one of the earliest to realize that to understand colonial history a deep study must be made of English commercial policy. No longer were the ministers of the King or George III himself to be at the mercy of prosecuting attorneys in the guise of historians; instead, their actions were to be judged in the light of a general imperial policy. In such a light English policy was found "blundering and vacillating" but not criminal.

Osgood had pointed out, in a critical review of Fiske's *American Revolution,* that a new environment had wrought a new people, so that soon after the middle of the eighteenth century "two political societies of quite different type were thus brought into conflict." The duty of the historian, he said, was "to do justice to the character and aims of both." Fiske, in Osgood's opinion, had done no better on this score than had his predecessors. The reviewer then went on to say: "The truth is until American historians cease the attempt to defend a dogma, and begin in earnest the effort to understand the aristocratic society which existed in England and the democracy which was maturing here, and the causes of conflict between the two, we shall not have a satisfactory history either of the colonial period or of the revolution. The Englishman too," he warned, "who carries his party prejudices into the work will reach no better results." On another occasion Osgood complained of the concentration of students on the seventeenth century and on the Revolution to the neglect of the period 1690–1760. Our historians, he said, "come up to that period with a fairly full and comprehensive narrative, and then they become scrappy, inconclusive, and largely worthless."

In the main Osgood's subject was to be the colonies as they were in themselves and their relation to the mother country. He thought that the history of the colonies fell into two phases: the system of chartered colonies and the system of royal provinces; and the change from one form to the other. This change, he wrote, "was the most important and significant transition in American history previous to the colonial revolt." From the beginning of the eighteenth century to the War for Independence, the royal province was the prevailing form of colonial government. He insisted that to understand the Revolution, the student must know the precedents that had been slowly established in the royal provinces.

The details of Osgood's history were presented in relation to the functioning of the state. Materials of a social, economic, or religious nature were used only in so far as they threw light on political growth. As Osgood's biographer, Dixon Ryan Fox, phrased it, "Land interests him not as something to till with spades and hoes, or to sell for profit, but as something that engenders controversy as to distribution and taxation by the different governments."

In *The American Colonies in the Seventeenth Century* (vols. I, II, 1904), Osgood stated that he had written "an introduction to American institutional history." His work had a double purpose: "To exhibit in outline the early development of English colonization on its political and administrative side"; it was likewise "a study of the origin of English-American political institutions." This meant that his attention was devoted to the continental colonies, and the plan of his work could not include extensive reference to the commercial and economic aspects of colonization.

For an understanding of American history it was necessary to know the varied forms English institutions took when reproduced in America, and how they were modified overseas. Osgood pointed out that the origins of American institutions were not to be found wholly in the Revolutionary period but in earlier forms that "had undergone steady development for a century and a half before the date of independence." Not until the earlier years had been thoroughly investigated, he said, could a satisfactory history of the Revolution be written.

In the first as well as the last of his volumes Osgood was at special pains to note intercolonial relations which were to weave close ties among the scattered colonists and prepare them for the needed co-operative activity of the Revolutionary era. At the close of his second volume Osgood added some interesting conclusions about American society at the end of the seventeenth century. He found that the colonists by this time "in their large relations . . . were [still] subordinate to Europe," but "their personal and local concerns were as distinct from those of contemporary Europeans as time or space could well make them. In their languages and in the type and traditions of their culture they were Europeans; but they were transplanted upon a new and distant continent, and felt chiefly the pressure of its environment. They had already become colonials in the full sense of the word but had not yet reached a developed American type." The characteristics of equality and uniformity in American society were by now clearly marked, especially in the corporate colonies. In this first century of American history "in their main outlines American institutions, both local and colonial, were fashioned. . . . If at any time the acquired rights of self-government of the colonies at large should be imperiled, that type of political theory which had its home in New England could easily be extended to fit conditions in the provinces." Conditions in America predisposed the colonists in favor of self-government, and in this temper they "faced the home government and any plans of systematic control which it might devise and seek to enforce."

A third volume (1907) on the seventeenth century was concerned with "Imperial Control: Beginnings of the System of Royal Provinces." For the first time, the author noted with justifiable pride, an attempt was made to trace the imperial system of control "as a distinct and separate feature of colonization. . . . Attention has been directed to the organs through which it was exercised, to the objects and ideals which were pursued, and to the obstacles which prevented their attainment." Osgood's most competent reviewer, Charles M. Andrews, said that this third volume completed "the most important interpretation of our colonial history that has thus far been made."

After taking the reader through the complicated and sometimes exciting events that made royal provinces of the colonies, the historian concluded with effective generalizations. The changes that came toward the end of the seventeenth century were "accomplished by a combination of executive and judicial action. It swept away assemblies and boundary lines, and aimed to undo the results of a half century of historic growth." For bringing about these changes, the Crown and Parliament were responsible. "Prerogative government over the colonies reached its high-water mark" in the reign of James II, wrote the historian, who added, "Never again was so much attempted or accomplished by this method. When, in later times, imperial pressure was again brought to bear, parliament was resorted to at every step."

At his death in 1918, Osgood left the manuscript, practically completed, of *The American Colonies in the Eighteenth Century,* which carried the narrative to 1763. After much delay it was published in 1924 through the bounty of a grateful student. Osgood had stated in 1898 that the two most important themes in our history during the eighteenth century were imperial policy and colonial resistance, and, because of their constant interaction, it was difficult for him to divide arbitrarily his material as he had done for the seventeenth century. Although several chapters dealt with the working of the imperial system seen from the distant view of London, most of the book was concerned with the internal history of the various colonies, and especially with the struggles between governors and assemblies.

With the beginning of the eighteenth century, wrote Osgood, "the controlling fact of the situation was the gradual coalescing of the colonies into one system, under the control of the British government." The historian faced the difficult task of following the individual growth of each of the colonies and making clear their position as part of the British Empire. The arrangement of the work was made to turn upon the succession of colonial wars and the intervals of peace in the struggle between the French and English. The author's problem in recording the history of the separate colonies was to "bring out their peculiarities and their uniformities." With pardonable pride Osgood wrote that "in scope and plan, as in much of its material, this is a pioneer work"; no longer would the decades it covered be called the "unknown period" of American history.

Because of the strategic position that the colony of New York had in the wars with the French, her place in the history of these years tended to be especially emphasized. Osgood's interest was not so much in the military events themselves as in their effects upon governmental institutions. He was at pains to show, for example, that the need for military appropriations increased the power of the New York assembly.

Among the significant pages in the second volume were those on the attitude of English officials toward commercial questions. Up to about 1730, said Osgood, "though the cabinet and parliament were much occupied with questions of trade no new principles were evolved, though the application of those already accepted was slightly extended. Of special importance is the fact that no wholesale changes in the administrative or fiscal policy of Great Britain toward the colonies were considered or probably even mentioned in those bodies which were really responsible for the conduct of the British government."

This work contained chapters of particular excellence on the English church and the Dissenters; "The Growth of the Spirit of Independence," 1749–63, was a very valuable section, including, as it did, material on the Great Awakening. Osgood was unsympathetic to that religious movement, which, he noted, had caused "no appreciable improvement in the morals of communities." In a discussion of planners of colonial union, the historian assigned Shirley a high place. The latter's services in this cause, he said, were paralleled only by those of Franklin.

Osgood gave careful attention to the problems created by the frontier; he associated the Albany Congress with westward expansion. In his final volume he discussed the fourth intercolonial war that was finally to settle the struggle for supremacy in favor of the English. His judgment on the capture of Quebec was restrained: the death of both commanders "lifted the event out of the realm of mere military success and defeat or of political change into that of sentiment. Wolfe in particular has been taken out of the category of ordinary men and raised to the rank of a hero. . . . But what really happened was that, backed by superior force and aided by fortunate circumstances, to which he contributed by good management, Wolfe . . . hit upon a plan which led to success, and it was crowned with a timely death."

Of *The American Colonies in the Eighteenth Century,* Andrews wrote that it was "not British history, nor yet American history in any narrow and exclusive sense of that term, but something between, more American than British and growing more and more American with every decade that passes." Unfortunately Osgood was not able to add to his volumes on the eighteenth century those illuminating generalizations with which he concluded his volumes on the previous century. These interpretive passages were excellent summaries and the writing in them was better than elsewhere. His style was never ornamental, nor was it easy reading for the student who liked his history romanticized. He wrote history for historians and did not think it was his function to make history fine literature, yet he was never obscure. Although he kept abreast of the published monographic material, much of it the outgrowth of his own seminar, the larger part of the historian's sources were in manuscript, particularly for his volumes on the eighteenth century.

Interest in social and intellectual history has so broadened the scope of research that Osgood's contribution, great as it was, left a large part of the colonial story untold. It is a fair statement to say that he paid insufficient attention to economic and social forces acting on the course of legislation. His work included no adequate study of the commercial policy of England toward the colonies, a theme left largely for other scholars, especially Beer and Andrews. Pioneer in the modern study of the political origins of the United States, Osgood lived to encourage other students to walk more easily over the path he had so laboriously hewn.[9]

GEORGE LOUIS BEER

George Louis Beer's work, said Robert L. Schuyler, "ranks as one of the major contributions to knowledge made by American historical scholarship in the present century." Beer was a student of Burgess, Seligman, and Osgood at Columbia University, and under Osgood's direction the young scholar turned to the study of colonial history. In 1893, when he was but twenty years old, he published his master's thesis on *The Commercial Policy of England toward the American Colonies,* which foreshadowed his later historical writing. This little book, on a subject hitherto largely ignored, heralded a new point of view in American history. Written with freedom from any patriotic bias, it gave a new slant to the relations of England with her colonies, whose inhabitants were no longer to be viewed as people subjected to tyranny but as participants in the mercantilist system. "Thus we can see," wrote Beer in the course of his argument, "that the laying of restrictions on colonial manufactures was a necessary consequence of the mercantilist system."

[9] D. R. Fox, *Herbert Levi Osgood* (New York, 1924); H. F. Coppock, "Herbert Levi Osgood," *Mississippi Valley Historical Review,* Vol. XIX, No. 3 (December, 1932), 394–413; E. C. O. Beatty, "Herbert Levi Osgood," *Jernegan Essays,* 271–93.

The score of years preceding 1776, he suggested, "must be regarded as transitional, as a period during which it was to be determined whether the colonies were sufficiently mature, not only to assert, but also to maintain their independence."

Beer looked forward to rewriting his essay on an extended scale at an early date, but teaching (which he did not like) and business postponed fulfillment of this intention for a decade. In 1903 his long-planned trip to London to study the needed documents materialized. He returned the next year to begin his immense task—"to describe and explain the origins, establishment, and development of the British colonial system up to the outbreak of the disagreements that culminated in the American Revolution; to analyze the underlying principles of British colonial policy [in] . . . trade and navigation." The details of his plan were concerned with the English fiscal system and the part of the colonies in it, colonial economic legislation that affected the relations to the mother country, the economic life of the colonies themselves, the British official system in America and how far the laws were enforced, and the relations of economics to the political system. In the part of the plan that he lived to complete, Beer gave us only that side of American history which was seen from the mother country. Far more definitely than Osgood, Beer "deliberately took the reader from the soil of America and set him down in the midst of those who were viewing the colonies from a position 3,000 miles away."

Beer wrote the last volume of his projected series first—*British Colonial Policy, 1754–1765* (1907), which remains the most widely known of his works. Its wealth of sources showed the impossibility of writing on this subject from the printed materials available in America; in fact, for all his volumes Beer drew largely from manuscripts.

The center of his interest, he said, was the British Empire, not the rise of the United States. Beer wrote that his book on its positive side was "a portrayal of British policy, a study in imperial history; on its negative side it is an account of the preliminaries of the American Revolution." The imperial administrative system was now tightened, he pointed out, because in these years the question of defense became one of the highest importance as a result of the struggle with France. In this volume Beer gave the first satisfactory treatment of the illegal trade carried on by the colonists. The long way that he had moved from the interpretation of nineteenth-century nationalist historians was revealed in his conclusion that the aim of the "purely commercial regulations of the years 1764–1765 . . . was to encourage and not to restrict colonial industry." This book, in which the author leaned backward in desiring to be fair to England, has played a large part in the revision that has been made of the history of the American Revolution.

Beer then turned back to the sixteenth and seventeenth centuries to seek the beginnings of the colonial system. His investigation resulted in the publication of *The Origin of the British Colonial System, 1578–1660* (1908). He showed that mercantilist principles were firmly established in practice long in advance of theorists who evolved the doctrines of mercantilism. Two more volumes appeared later (1912) as Part I of *The Old Colonial System,* covering the years 1660–88. Beer had planned an additional six volumes to carry the narrative to 1754, but he never found time to write on the early eighteenth century. Instead, he was brought up sharply against the twentieth century when the world war broke out in 1914, and he abandoned the past for the present. Anglo-American relations, which had once been an intellectual interest to the historian, became an absorbing passion to the publicist who labored in effecting the peace settlement.

Beer defined the term "colonial system" as "that complex system of regulations whose fundamental aim was to create a self-sufficient commercial empire of mutually complementary economic parts." One of his chief aims, he said, was to learn "precisely what the statesmen of the day sought to accomplish, what means they employed for their purposes, to what extent these instruments were adapted to the actual situation, and how the various parts of the Empire developed under these regulations." To Americans who nursed a grievance against the English, Beer brought the salutary reminder that the colonial system was not a one-sided one and that it was recognized as mutually advantageous by the ancestors of aggrieved descendants in the twentieth century. To compensate for colonial trade restrictions, England protected the colonies "and gave such of their products as were needed and wanted a monopoly of the home market."

Although Beer was much interested in economic history, he generally ignored the machinery of commerce and industrial organization; only incidentally were freight charges, insurance, prices, and the like included in his discussion. He underestimated the place of colonies as markets, for his emphasis was rather on these territorial possessions as sources of supply.[10] He tended to overemphasize the role of the "sea dogs" in colonization, whereas the English merchants were far more important. These were, however, minor flaws in a pioneer work. Beer's volumes did not entertain the general reader who preferred his history with a dash of the dramatic. They have rather served to instruct both English and American students of colonial history in rereading their common past. The version of that past as expounded by Osgood, Beer, and Andrews has, with some revisions, come to be the one accepted by the careful student of today.[11]

CHARLES MCLEAN ANDREWS

Charles M. Andrews had a long and distinguished academic career, most of it at Yale. As a young man he, like so many others who were to make valuable contributions to American culture, was drawn to the Johns Hopkins of the 1880's, aglow with the freshness of intellectual discovery. The favoring circumstances of birth and nurture—he was born and bred in New England—gave him the ideal background for a historian of the American colonies. "I am a Puritan of the Puritans," he once said in describing his ancestry.

The earliest publications of Andrews indicated the bent of his later major interests, especially his study of *The River Towns of Connecticut* (1889). Since the emphasis in the 1880's and 1890's was on institutional history, it was not surprising that he should have been strongly attracted to the field of colonial institutions. The young scholar was critical of the behavior of the early settlers: "In all their relations with their brethren and neighbors in the Connecticut valley, the Puritans," he said, "showed little of that austere honorableness for which they are famed." Andrews' intellectual independence also prompted him to dissent from the theses of Freeman and H. B. Adams, who had held that American political institutions took their origin in the ancient German village community.

Andrews, along with Osgood, made a plea for the study of American colonial history from 1690 to 1750. It was asserted that an understanding of the later years rested not on the era of settlement, but on the "middle

[10] See valuable article by Curtis Nettels, "Markets in the Colonial System," *New England Quarterly,* Vol. VI, No. 3 (September, 1933), 491–512.

[11] *George Louis Beer: A Tribute to his Life and Work* (New York, 1924); G. A. Cockroft, "George Louis Beer," in H. Ausubel *et al.* (ed.), *Some Modern Historians of Britain: Essays in Honor of Robert Livingston Schuyler* (New York, 1951).

period of conflict and experience."[12] This period, said Andrews, was "marked at its beginning by a strengthening of the old British colonial administration all along the line; an administration destined from this time forward to come more and more under the control of parliament and to pass from the hands of Crown and council who had hitherto directed colonial affairs. No writer," he continued, "has, however, made any proper attempt to emphasize this fact or tell us, by careful attention to details, how the experiment worked. Yet, so far as it concerned all the colonies together, it is the most important phase in their history after 1689." Andrews also drew attention to the value of including the Canadian and West Indian colonies in a study of the British North American group.

Much of his scholarly labor was devoted to exploring archives in America and England, which gave him an unrivaled knowledge of the sources of American colonial history. In 1908, in conjunction with Frances G. Davenport, he brought out a *Guide to the Manuscript Materials for the History of the United States to 1783 in the British Museum [and other Depositaries]*. "Notwithstanding the fact that for a hundred and fifty years our colonies were a part of the British empire," Andrews remarked, "no systematic attempt has ever been made by British or American historians to discover the extent and value of the material contained in British archives relating to American history."[13] Andrews subsequently published another guide to materials for American history in the Public Record Office of Great Britain. Osgood hailed the work of Andrews as "one among many signs that we have entered upon a new epoch in the study of American history. . . . It implies and will be followed by a more comprehensive and scientific treatment . . . than has been possible or even imagined. The era of partial views, and isolated efforts, whether in the collection of materials or the writing of history, is passing away."

While Andrews performed an immensely valuable service in providing these and other tools for research, he managed also on various occasions to give illuminating surveys of parts, and once, the whole, of the colonial period. He contributed a volume to the *American Nation* series,

[12] Andrews, American Historical Association *Annual Report* for the year 1898 (1899), 50.

[13] C. M. Andrews, "Materials in British Archives for American Colonial History," *American Historical Review,* Vol. X, No. 2 (January, 1905), 325.

and two volumes to the *Yale Chronicles,* the *Fathers of New England* and *Colonial Folkways.* These latter books, written for a more general audience, contained the distillation of his deep knowledge of colonial life. For the Home University Library, Andrews wrote an excellent volume on *The Colonial Period* (1912). He observed that earlier writers on this theme had emphasized the colonies to the exclusion of the mother country and had also neglected the relations between the two. It was his belief "that the balance should be restored." Thus he gave almost as much space to England as he did to the colonies, and in another departure from tradition he included in his survey Canada and the West Indies, as well as the original thirteen colonies: "No distinction existed between them in colonial times and none should be made now by the writer on colonial history."

In 1924, Andrews published a volume of essays on *The Colonial Background of the American Revolution.* It restated his earlier thesis on the dependence and interdependence of mother country and colonies which "determined to no small extent the attitude and policy" of each to the other. Again he reminded his readers that historians writing of the events from 1763 to 1775 have generally "failed to see that primarily they were but a part of the history of British colonization and should be interpreted in the light, not of the democracy that was to come years later, but of the ideas and practices regarding colonization that were in vogue in Great Britain at the time." Andrews contrasted the settled and smug ruling classes in England with the society then in the making in the colonies and found that a conflict was almost inevitable. The colonies, he concluded, were too far advanced to "be held in leading strings; . . . such constitutional concessions as would have satisfied the demands of the colonists, these British statesmen could not make, because they were barred by the mental limitations of their own time and class."

On another occasion the Yale historian said that immobility was the characteristic of the English official mind in the half-century before 1775.[14] Americans, meanwhile, were forming a new society. "The story of how this was done—how that which was English slowly and imperceptibly merged into that which was American—has never been adequately told," he said, "but it is a fascinating phase of history. . . . It is

[14] Andrews, "The American Revolution: An Interpretation," *American Historical Review,* Vol. XXXI, No. 2 (January, 1926), 221.

the story of the gradual elimination of those elements, feudal and proprietary, that were foreign to the normal life of a frontier land, and of the gradual adjustment of the colonies to the restraints and restrictions that were imposed upon them by the commercial policy of the mother country. . . . It is . . . the story of the gradual transformation of [colonial] assemblies from provincial councils that the home government intended them to be into miniature parliaments. At the end of a long struggle . . . they emerged powerful legislative bodies, as self-conscious in their way as the House of Commons in England was becoming during the same eventful years."

In 1934 and 1936, Andrews published the first two volumes of the long-awaited work, *The Colonial Period of American History: The Settlements.* The point of view adopted years earlier was again affirmed: "I have approached the subject from the English end, and have broadened the scope of my inquiry to include all England's colonial possessions in the west" during the seventeenth century. It was necessary to do so, he maintained, because "final conclusions must always rest upon the experiences England had with all, not a part of her colonies." The reader was warned to keep in mind the fundamental difference between the seventeenth and eighteenth centuries; the former "shows us an English world in America, with but little in it that can be strictly called American: the eighteenth everywhere presents to the view an Anglo-American conflict. . . . The colonial period of our history is not American only but Anglo-American."

Andrews gave an excellent picture of the temper of English life in the sixteenth century and the emergence of an ambitious middle class whose aspirations were intimately linked with settlements in far-flung places. In the first forty years of the seventeenth century, rapidly accumulating capital sought areas for operation other than those in the older region of European trade. The energetic men who founded companies to make settlements in the New World were members of an interlocking directorate whose aim was the creation of an empire. While the historian seemed to stress more the material than the religious motive for colonization, he did speak of the latter as an important factor in overseas migration. As in his younger days, he was not too kindly disposed to the Puritans. Andrews skimmed lightly over social and economic history; his main interest was institutional history, and his range of knowledge here was unsurpassed.

Through the complexities of conflicting materials on the early years of Rhode Island, Andrews picked his sure way, giving on the whole a friendly, yet dispassionately critical, estimate of Roger Williams. He demolished many timeworn traditions, proving, for example, that no question of a search for religious freedom entered into the founding of Connecticut, but rather "the allurement of a fertile valley." He also provided the reader with a much-needed corrective to the persistent misunderstanding of Puritan "democracy," observing that "the ideas of the Connecticut Puritans regarding the political and religious organization of society [were] far removed from the democratic ideas of later times." Andrews continually warned the student against accepting the older interpretations of Bancroft and his school, who saw in the seventeenth century the foreshadowings of the later American Revolution. Whatever rights and privileges the colonists claimed were the same that Englishmen everywhere were then claiming.

The historian's third volume (1937) closed his study of founding the colonies. The great work of settlement was now ended, and a new period in colonial history was at hand. The fourth, and last, volume in the series (1938), subtitled "England's Commercial and Colonial Policy," was a study of English efforts to administer the colonies in the interest of trade and revenue, and her attempt to work out more satisfactory commercial and constitutional relations with her overseas possessions.

What was elaborated between 1660 and 1696 constituted a code which for over a century guided executive policy respecting the economic organization of the empire. The English found that it was a never ending task to clarify the system to themselves, for the policy was fluid, "never reaching the stage of exact definition." Four decades, marked largely by failure, elapsed before any degree of "smoothness of operation" was achieved. Andrews' description of the operations of the agencies named to carry out the mercantile acts and effect a closer supervision of the colonies was a major contribution.

In his characteristic manner he modified or opposed conventional judgments, writing that the first navigation act of 1651, for example, "injured England's commerce more than it did the commerce of Holland." A study of vice-admiralty proceedings led to the conclusion that smuggling as a colonial pastime has been overemphasized by historians. Mercantile regulations were ineffective and the colonists' freedom of action was little hampered. An irrepressible conflict was in the making, for "just at the moment when the executive authorities were drawing together the bonds of control more tightly than ever before and becoming more insistent on enforcing their policy at any cost, the colonies themselves were feeling the urge for greater freedom and an overmastering determination to govern themselves."

In general Andrews' tendency was to present a conservative view of problems and people, denying, for instance, the existence of a proletariat in the colonies. Also, after marshaling the material supporting the thesis of economic conflict between the colonies and the mother country, he minimized it as a factor in bringing on the Revolution. The Revolution, he asserted, was primarily "a political and constitutional movement and only secondarily one that was either financial, commercial, or social. At bottom the fundamental issue was the political independence of the colonies, and in the last analysis the conflict lay between the British Parliament and the colonial assemblies."

The four volumes that Andrews lived to complete had an abundance of detail dealing with counting room and council room. The uncompleted portion of his work was to have presented other facets of colonial life, which the historian knew much about; and in it he intended to show how a more distinctively American civilization gradually emerged. When death intervened, the loss to historians was great. What Andrews did complete must rank as among America's ablest contributions to historical scholarship.[15]

NEW LIGHT ON THE NAVIGATION ACTS: LAWRENCE A. HARPER AND OLIVER M. DICKERSON

A chief concern of the imperial school of colonial history was the study of the manner in which the economic life of the colonies was regulated by the mother country in accordance with the principles of mercantilism.

[15] L. H. Gipson, "Charles M. Andrews and the Reorientation of the Study of American History," *Pennsylvania Magazine of History and Biography,* Vol. LIX, No. 3 (July, 1935), 209–22; some interesting biographical details are in Andrews' paper, "Historic Doubts Regarding Early Massachusetts History," Colonial Society of Massachusetts *Transactions,* Vol. XXVIII (1935), 280–94; see excellent essay by A. S. Eisenstadt, in Ausubel *et al.* (eds.) *Some Modern Historians of Britain: Essays in Honor of . . . Schuyler.*

Although Beer and Andrews had done much to shed new light on imperial regulations, there was still much that lay in shadow. Two students, Lawrence A. Harper and Oliver M. Dickerson, have explained how the Navigation Acts really worked and what their effect was on imperial economy. Harper's book, *The English Navigation Laws: A Seventeenth Century Experiment in Social Engineering* (New York, 1939), told historians clearly for the first time what these laws were, how they functioned, and their beneficial effects on English shipping. In other writings Harper carried on his studies of the impact of imperial economic regulations upon the colonies on the eve of the Revolution. In opposition to Beer, who did not believe these regulations weighed heavily upon the colonies, Harper concluded that, in the 1760's, they were burdensome and discriminatory.[16]

Dickerson's book, *The Navigation Acts and the American Revolution* (Philadelphia, 1951), is the most recent and most revealing study of this important theme. It followed several lines of investigation: the attitude of Americans and British toward the trade and navigation acts; how the acts worked in the colonies; the change in policy after 1764 and how it operated to destroy imperial unity. Dickerson found that as the Navigation Acts were not oppressive, smuggling did not tend to be excessive, most merchants preferring to operate within the existing structure of legislation. The trade and navigation system was in fact the "most important cement of empire" for one hundred years. Certainly, as the commercial system functioned, it did not seem to inhibit American prosperity. Indeed, to British visitors, America was wealthy and growing rapidly more prosperous. According to Dickerson it was Britain's envy and fear of this prosperity that led her merchants to back a change in commercial policy and thus help bring on the Revolution.

In the 1760's, the mother country, said the colonists, changed the rules of the imperial game, transforming regulations which formerly had been designed to protect and encourage trade into laws for raising revenue. It was then that Americans began to oppose them. A new body was set up—an American Board of Customs Commissioners—with headquarters at Boston, to administer the trade and revenue laws. This

[16] Harper, "Mercantilism and the American Revolution," *Canadian Historical Review,* Vol. XXIII, No. 1 (March, 1942), 1–15, and his essay in R. B. Morris (ed.), *The Revolutionary Era: Studies Inscribed to Evarts Boutell Greene* (New York, 1939).

body, said Dickerson, waged war "upon ships, seamen, merchants and commerce in the interests of revenue." John Hancock, it seems, was not at all a smuggler, but rather one of the board's victims; his was clearly a case of political "persecution." The establishment of this board, in 1767, with authority practically independent of both the crown and the colonies (their salaries were paid out of what they collected) was a disaster for imperial unity, for it divided the colonial empire administratively. The mistakes of the Customs Commissioners led to one crisis after another—the seizure of Hancock's sloop, *Liberty,* the "Gaspee" affair, the "Tea Party," the call for troops—until finally the empire was embroiled in civil war. The inevitable question which Dickerson's work suggests is this: Would the Revolution have occurred if the old system of trade and navigation, minus revenue-producing factors, had been permitted to continue after 1763?

CLARENCE WALWORTH ALVORD

The concentration of Eastern historians on the role of their area (to the exclusion of the West) in the Revolutionary era seemed mistaken to Westerners, especially to students of Turner. Among the many who sought to reinterpret American history with the Turner thesis as a key, none did better work than Clarence W. Alvord. Early in his career he established his claim to scholarly notice by his discovery of the records of the old French settlements in Illinois. He edited the *Kaskaskia Records 1778–1790* (1909) and, with Clarence C. Carter, also published *The New Regime 1765–1767* (1916). With Lee Bidgood, Alvord issued an important publication on *The First Explorations of the Transallegheny Region by the Virginians 1650–1674* (1912). This was the first attempt to tell the story of the discovery of this region by the Virginians, whose achievements had been unknown to Parkman and Winsor. Under Alvord's editorship, fourteen volumes of the Illinois Historical *Collections* appeared; he was the editor of one of the best state histories ever written —the *Centennial History of Illinois*—in which series he wrote the first volume.

Alvord's most noteworthy historical narrative was *The Mississippi Valley in British Politics* (2 vols., Cleveland, 1917); its subtitle described its contents: "A study of the Trade, Land Speculation and Experiments in Imperialism Culminating in the American Revolution." The author informed the reader that in his pages the conventional narrative of the events leading up to the Revolution was not to be found. "Whenever the British ministers soberly and seriously discussed the American problem," said Alvord, "the vital phase to them was not the disturbances of . . . Boston and New York, but the development of that vast transmontane region that was acquired in 1763 by the Treaty of Paris." Although his point of observation lay on the Western prairies, his work, he said, was not a history of the West. Rather, his eyes were fixed on the British ministry "in the hope of discovering the obscure development of a western policy"; for he thought it impossible to fathom the British-American policy unless contemporary British politics were thoroughly understood. The problems of Indians, land companies, fur traders, the rights of the various colonies in the West—all these had to be dealt with, and Alvord described the attempts made to solve them.

Like his fellow-writers of the imperial school of colonial history, Alvord was hostile to chauvinism. Indeed, like Beer, he seemed to lean backward in his attempt to be fair to Britain. Although he made mistakes in his description of British politics, Alvord's general interpretation did much to narrate more accurately the real scope of conflicting interests in the Revolutionary era.[17] Some of his material was especially good; in particular might be mentioned his chapter on "The Beginning of Western Speculation." By the 1770's, said Alvord, "British muddling in the West was doomed. By 1774 the colonists of the eastern seacoast . . . were already preparing to assert themselves. Thus there culminated at the same time two series of events, one eastern and one western, which had for years run parallel, so closely interwoven that any attempt to understand the one without a knowledge of the other must inevitably fail."

In his anxiety to redress the balance of emphasis, Alvord minimized English public interest in the region of the Atlantic seaboard. Publications of all sorts, especially newspapers and magazines, reflected that concern which he underestimated; but once having made this qualification on his work, it should be granted that Alvord's volumes marked an important development in the historiography of the Revolution.[18]

[17] See L. B. Namier, *England in the Age of the American Revolution* (London, 1930).

[18] S. J. Buck, "Clarence Walworth Alvord, Historian," *Mississippi Valley Historical Review,* Vol. XV, No. 3 (1928–29), 309–20; Marion Dargan, Jr., "Clarence Walworth Alvord," *Jernegan Essays,* 323–38.

LAWRENCE HENRY GIPSON

Neither Osgood nor Andrews lived to carry their detailed narratives beyond the first half of the eighteenth century. The same revision they had made of colonial history up to that point was obviously needed for the subsequent period. The efforts of many scholars have been directed to refashioning an interpretation of the quarter-century preceding the Revolution. No one, however, attempted it on a scale comparable to that of Osgood and Andrews until Lawrence H. Gipson set himself the enormous task.

Gipson is an enthusiastic disciple of Andrews, carrying over into his own studies views he learned from the master. A thorough grounding in colonial and imperial history prepared him to initiate his plan for a vast work on *The British Empire before the American Revolution* (1936-49). To the present time he has published seven volumes which have brought him to the victory of Britain in 1760.

The first three volumes were a survey of the empire in the middle of the eighteenth century. Going a step farther than Andrews, Gipson broadened his investigation to include not only the North American colonies, but also the mother country and Africa, arguing that "Guinea carried the empire." The British Empire of this period, with its tremendous vitality, "was undoubtedly the most imposing politico-economic structure that the world had ever known." In Gipson's view it was mainly private enterprise, not state planning, which had expanded the bounds of empire. The British Empire, he said, was a "world of literate people devoted to freedom and opposed to governmental regulation."

Gipson's canvas continued to be large in his succeeding volumes; his intention was to trace the history of the empire by "beating its bounds." The fourth and fifth volumes, *Zones of International Friction 1748–1754,* described the imperial conflict in all quarters of the globe, but the heart of the narrative was the rivalry for America. The historian tried to keep his eye not only on the center of empire in London but also on the colonies at the same time, in order, as he put it, "to view the operation of British imperial dynamism at its various sources of manifestation." That dynamism, as expressed in the Albany Plan of Union, was described in great detail in some of Gipson's best chapters.

The sixth and seventh volumes narrated the years of defeat and victory in the Seven Years War, which Gipson preferred to call "The Great

War for the Empire," believing that name lifted the conflict out of the narrower setting established by other historians. Contrary to earlier interpretations he argued that traditional European techniques of carrying on war were more important than the practices of frontiersmen in winning the struggle in America. It was really, he said, "a European conflict in a New World setting." It was British superiority in several categories —her navy, her heavy industry, and colonial agriculture ("turned to warlike purposes")—which ultimately beat the French.

Gipson has offered no challenge to Parkman's artistry, but he has succeeded in reminding scholars of problems and policies of empire which the great nineteenth-century historian never considered. While enlarging the scope of historical inquiry—attempting to spin a web of empire such as others had not done before—he has not always been successful in keeping his various strands in touch with one another. As he has told the story thus far, the American colonies were less weighty in the scheme of empire than has usually been believed. Possibly in too strong a reaction to the old excessive patriotism he has minimized the role of the American colonists in the struggle with France. Then too, like Andrews before him, it may be that in an effort to look at colonial conditions through English official eyes, the subtleties of American political expression in the direction of democracy may have escaped him. It is possible that in Gipson's volumes to come a better balance may be struck. What we already have is evidence of the most comprehensive expression of the imperial school of colonial history.

XII

The Frontier and Sectional Historians

HISTORIANS HAVE WRITTEN works of major importance dealing with sections of the United States, and frequently in so doing they have cast new light on the history of the country as a whole. The vastness of the country, with its distinctive geographical divisions equal in size (and in economic significance as well) to entire European nations, has made it necessary for careful writers to spend the better part of a lifetime mastering the material pertaining to one section. Histories relating to New England alone have a tradition reaching back to the colonial period; in the South the histories that were written dealt mainly with single states. George Tucker and Lyman Draper were interested in the history of the West, but in their day that region was still in the making; not until the West was well settled did students arise to survey its history comprehensively, and as a result of the efforts of Turner and his co-workers our national history has been recast. In recent years there has been a great emphasis on cultural regionalism, in part an attempt to pick up the broken thread of a tradition once full of vitality, and in part a revulsion against a too nebulous national pattern. In all the arts the renaissance of regionalism has resulted in outstanding contributions to the composite national culture. The writing of history, too, has been stimulated in this invigorating atmosphere. *Regionalism in America* (ed. by Merrill Jensen, Madison, 1951) was a stimulating appraisal of the diversity of expression in the national life.

The West

HUBERT HOWE BANCROFT

"I cannot imagine anyone's writing about the history of the West without constantly referring to Bancroft," said Bernard De Voto.[1] Bancroft's massive contribution to the history of the Far West had developed in an unusual manner. Early in life he worked for a bookseller, and in 1858 he founded his own publishing and mercantile firm in San Francisco, whither he had moved from the East. It was about this time, the garrulous Bancroft tells us in his *Retrospection,* that he began to bring together all the books in his stock on California. He extended his field gradually to include the western half of North America from Alaska to Panama, including Mexico and Central America. He collected every scrap of material he could on this vast territory, made trips everywhere, employed copyists for years to build up the collections, took down the stories of surviving old pioneers, and bought libraries in Europe and America. After a decade of extensive and intensive collecting—he gathered some sixty thousand volumes in all—Bancroft set to work to write the history of the Coast.[2] Because his training had been exclusively for business, Bancroft remarked he could apply only business methods to the task of historical composition: "I became satisfied," he said, "that in no other way could anything have been made out of the situation."[3] About a dozen writers worked in Bancroft's library under his managerial direction, and the assignment of credit for the composition of the various volumes is not always an easy matter. Bancroft's own contributions as writer made up some four volumes of the history.[4]

It was Bancroft's original intention to start with Central America, inasmuch as the first of the continental discoveries were made there. But because the natives who occupied the territory before the discoveries played so large a part in the early story of the whole region, he had

[1] Quoted by J. W. Caughey, "Hubert Howe Bancroft, Historian of Western America," *American Historical Review,* Vol. L, No. 3 (April, 1945), 468.

[2] Bancroft, *The Works of Hubert Howe Bancroft* (39 vols., San Francisco, 1882–90), XXXIX, *Literary Industries,* 197.

[3] "Methods of Writing History," *Retrospection, Political and Personal* (New York, 1912), 328.

[4] W. A. Morris, "The Origin and Authorship of the Bancroft Pacific States Publications: A History of a History," *Oregon Historical Society Quarterly,* Vol. IV (March-December, 1903), 287–364.

to give much space to them. Thus there appeared, in 1875, the first of the long series of volumes, *The Native Races of the Pacific States of North America* (5 vols.), which anthropologists still find useful. Then over a period of fifteen years came others—*Central America* (3 vols.); followed by the *History of Mexico* (6 vols.), with a separate publication reserved for the *History of the North Mexican States and Texas* (2 vols.); later came the *History of California* (7 vols.); *Arizona and New Mexico;* the *Northwest Coast* (2 vols.); *Oregon* (2 vols.); *Washington, Idaho, and Montana; British Columbia; Alaska; Utah; Nevada, Wyoming and Colorado.*

The history proper thus embraced twenty-eight volumes. To the reader who wondered at the need for such bulk, Bancroft retorted that his great trouble was how to condense without injuring the work. Subsequent volumes on *Popular Tribunals* and miscellaneous essays, six in number and largely written by himself, nearly completed the catalog of this group of publications appearing under Bancroft's name; later in life (he died in 1918) he published additional works. His success in marketing his vast and expensive series was remarkable—six thousand sets were sold at a gross return of $1,000,000.

The stamp of the factory system of production that marked Bancroft's work should not make the student insensitive to his real achievement. In the first place he did amass a great collection of material (it eventually went to the University of California at Berkeley), and he also had a vision of a broad historical approach rarely realized then or since. In an essay on "History Writing," he remarked that great men deserve their place in history, but not in the foreground.[5] He urged historians to see how nations originate and develop, to study ecclesiastical as well as civil government, family relationships, "the affinities and antagonisms of class, occupation, and every species of social phenomena," including labor, industry, the arts, the intellect—"in short the progress of man's domination over nature." Perhaps in self-defense Bancroft went on to say that a writer of history need be no genius—"indeed, genius is ordinarily too erratic for faithful plodding"—but he must have good judgment, common sense, broad experience, and a wide range of knowledge. Bancroft did render a great service to historical literature, and his histories, although marred by flaws, were generally dependable. Later students corrected them in various details, but his biographer as-

[5] *The Works of Hubert Howe Bancroft,* XXXVIII, 84–85.

serted that they still remain "the largest and the basic [contribution] to the history of Spanish North America."[6]

REUBEN GOLD THWAITES

One of those who made possible the writing of a fuller history of the region beyond the Appalachians was Reuben Gold Thwaites, who had gone west from Massachusetts to Wisconsin. Thwaites became associated with the Wisconsin Historical Society, and as editor of its publications, following in the footsteps of Lyman Draper, he made them a model for other societies.

The productivity of Thwaites was tremendous; in a period of some twenty-five years he wrote 15 books, edited and published over 160 volumes, besides writing articles and making addresses. His historical writing was, on occasion, good, but of far greater value was his work as editor. He, perhaps, understood wherein lay his superior accomplishments, for in one instance he wrote: "An editor of historical sources cannot with propriety comment upon the character or the motives of the actors in the drama outlined upon his pages; sufficient that . . . he presents materials from which philosophical historians may construct their edifices."[7] His weak critical ability marred his writing as well as his editing, but the numerous volumes issued under his name made it possible for others to study many phases of Western history. His most important edited publications were the *Jesuit Relations,* the *Original Journals of Lewis and Clark* (8 vols., New York, 1904–1905), and the reprints of *Early Western Travels 1748–1846* (32 vols., Cleveland, 1904–1907).

The *Jesuit Relations* was a monumental series of seventy-three volumes. Most of these documents were either rare printings or were still in manuscript. Thwaites had great admiration for the Jesuit missionaries, whose work he termed "one of the most thrilling chapters in human history." Some of the explorers, notably Champlain, left their own narratives, but it was the Jesuits who provided most of the information that remains concerning the frontiers of New France in the seventeenth century. From annual reports (1632–73) made by missionaries, which eventually reached France, a series of volumes was issued under the

[6] J. W. Caughey, *Hubert Howe Bancroft: Historian of the West* (Berkeley, 1946).

[7] *Jesuit Relations* (73 vols., Cleveland, 1896–1901), LXXII, Preface.

title *Jesuit Relations*. They have proved to be as useful to geographers and anthropologists as to historians.

The *Early Western Travels,* collected in one vast publication, presented through the eyes of many travelers a panorama of the steady flow of settlers into the American wilderness, the quick formation of societies, and their evolution into urban settlements. Because of Thwaites' labors, documents and rare books which had been in the possession of a few individuals or libraries were now made available to a wide number of students, and his volumes gave a definite impetus to the study and writing of Western history.[8]

THEODORE ROOSEVELT

It is not surprising that Theodore Roosevelt, who was one of the men most influential in promoting an expansionist sentiment in the United States in the latter years of the nineteenth century, should have become interested in the early westward movement. Roosevelt had lived on the far Western frontier for some time before writing his volumes on the pioneers. "The men who have shared in the fast-vanishing frontier life of the present," he wrote in his preface to *The Winning of the West,* "feel a peculiar sympathy with the already long-vanished frontier life of the past."

Roosevelt's interest in history was aroused very early. As an undergraduate, he said in his autobiography, "I was already writing one or two chapters of a book I afterwards published on the Naval War of 1812." He found this subject far more to his liking than the topics assigned to him by his professors at Harvard. His methods would not always be considered orthodox by the professional guild as, for example, on the occasion when he wrote to Henry Cabot Lodge (half in jest, perhaps): "I have pretty nearly finished Benton [a biography in the *American Statesmen* series] mainly evolving him from my inner consciousness."[9]

To his friend Lodge, Roosevelt wrote in August, 1888: "I continue greatly absorbed in my new work [*The Winning of the West*], but it goes very slowly. . . . I shall try my best not to hurry it, nor make it

[8] F. J. Turner, *Reuben Gold Thwaites, Memorial Address* (Madison, 1914); C. W. Alvord on Thwaites, in Mississippi Valley Historical Association *Proceedings* for the year 1913–14, Vol. VII (1914), 321–33.

[9] June 7, 1886.

scamp work." Consciously, he patterned his history after Parkman, weaving his narrative around prominent leaders and dramatic episodes. In accordance with his promise to his publishers, Roosevelt had the first two volumes ready the next year. He first sketched in the groups who contended for possession of the region between the Alleghenies and the Mississippi—the English-speaking peoples, the French, and the Indians. He had the frontiersman's view of the Indians, whose cunning, stealth, "and merciless cruelty" made them "the tigers of the human race." But the historian was also critical of many of the whites who committed "deeds of the foulest and most wanton aggression." Although most of Roosevelt's work was concerned with the spectacular events of territorial expansion (he was at his best in narratives of frontier fighting), he also gave some very interesting descriptions of the backwoodsmen in their more peaceful moments. The Americans had gained a firm foothold in Kentucky by 1775, he wrote, for "cabins had been built and clearings made; there were women and children in the wooden forts, cattle grazed on the range, and two or three hundred acres of corn had been sown and reaped." Some three hundred men in Kentucky were "surrounded by an overwhelming number of foes" with whom a "death struggle" impended.

By 1783, with the coming of peace, a large immigrant tide flowed into Kentucky. "The days of the first game hunters and Indian fighters were over," and the herds of buffalo in this region were nearly gone. Churches, schools, mills, stores, race tracks, and markets told of the planting of a new civilization. In Tennessee, also, a new civilization was in the making, but Roosevelt paid scant attention to the frontier of the Southwest. The backwoodsmen were spread now almost to the Mississippi, and they had increased to some twenty-five thousand. "Beyond the Alleghenies," wrote Roosevelt, "the Revolution was fundamentally a struggle between England, bent on restricting the growth of the English race, and the Americans, triumphantly determined to acquire the right to conquer the continent."

Within a few years after the Revolution, said Roosevelt, "the rifle-bearing freemen who founded their little republics on the western waters gradually solved the question of combining personal liberty with national union." Separatist movements were nullified, and by 1790 the commonwealths beyond the Alleghenies "had become parts of the Federal Union." The pages on the struggle between the Spaniards and the

Americans for the navigation of the Mississippi revealed Roosevelt's strong chauvinism. He convicted the Spaniards of "systematic and deliberate duplicity and treachery" in opposing "their stalwart and masterful foes." The spirit of the Elizabethan buccaneers blustered through his writing, especially in his remarks on the "Ethics of Territorial Conquest." Here was the Bismarckian philosophy of "blood and iron" and "the end justifies the means." In his history as in his politics, however, Roosevelt's bark was not accompanied by much of a bite.

In late December, 1895, Roosevelt wrote to Lodge, "The 4th volume of my *Winning of the West* is done." It covered the period beginning with the wars against the Northwestern Indians, who had defeated St. Clair, and closed with the acquisition and exploration of the territory secured through the Louisiana Purchase. The graphic pages on the rout of St. Clair's army were followed by the story of Mad Anthony Wayne's victory over the Indians. But there was more to Roosevelt's story than the sound and fury of frontier warfare. In his chapter "Tennessee Becomes a State 1791–1796," he included some important items on land speculation, a subject then generally neglected by historians. The section on "Men of the Western Waters, 1798–1802" contained Roosevelt's best pages on economic and social history. "The pioneers stood for an extreme Americanism, in social, political, and religious matters alike," he concluded. "The trend of American thought was toward them, not away from them. More than ever before, the Westerners were able to make their demands felt at home, and to make their force felt in the event of a struggle with a foreign power." It was clear that the influence of Turner on Roosevelt was deep.

Turner said that Roosevelt's history "rescued a whole movement in American development from the hands of unskilful annalists." His emphasis on American controversies with England and Spain relating to the frontier was of value for a fuller understanding of the "truly national history of the United States—a work that remains to be accomplished," added Turner. The dramatic and the picturesque, rather than the institutional, usually interested Roosevelt, and because of that very fact his work had much to offer the general reader. The special student who looks for more careful research, especially in the materials of foreign countries bearing on the questions arising from the settlement of the Mississippi Valley, will prefer to consult the volumes of Samuel F. Bemis, Arthur P. Whitaker, Verner W. Crane, and others.

Roosevelt was always scornful of scholars ("day laborers," he called them) who allegedly concerned themselves with minor matters, slowly accumulating carefully ascertained facts, but presenting them without literary skill. Just before the annual meeting of the American Historical Association in 1912, he wrote to Lodge in his characteristic manner: "I am to deliver a beastly lecture—'History as Literature.'" (It was the presidential address.) None of the members of the association, he added, "believe that history is literature. I have spent much care on the lecture, and as far as I know it won't even be printed anywhere." Roosevelt's desire to make history literature was commendable. His tendency to make it the vehicle of American imperialism, however, marred the value of his otherwise signal achievement.[10]

FREDERICK JACKSON TURNER

When Frederick Jackson Turner was growing to manhood, historical interests in the United States were still centered for the most part in a few communities close to the Atlantic coast. Even when historians did enlarge their narratives to survey more of the country than the Atlantic coast, they were wont to pass over Western sections hurriedly or to write of them with but little understanding of their relationship to the areas eastward; for the most part it was a kind of enlarged New England which was then described.

A few students, however, watching the West of the mid-nineteenth century in the process of growing, were aware of the place of the frontier in American development. Godkin, editor of *The Nation,* McMaster, and James Bryce understood the meaning of the frontier. Bryce, in his chapter on "The Temper of the West" in *The American Commonwealth,* spoke of the West as "the most American part of America; that is to say, the part where those features which distinguish America from Europe come out in the strongest relief. What Europe is to Asia, what England is to the rest of Europe, what America is to England, that the Western States and Territories are to the Atlantic States, the heat and pressure and hurry of life always growing as we follow the

[10] Roosevelt-Lodge letters are in *Selections from the Correspondence of Henry Cabot Lodge and Theodore Roosevelt 1884–1918* (2 vols., New York, 1925), I, August 12, 1888, December 23, 1895, December 26, 1912; H. J. Thornton, "Theodore Roosevelt," *Jernegan Essays,* 227–51; R. C. Miller, "Theodore Roosevelt, Historian," *Medieval and Historiographical Essays in Honor of James Westfall Thompson* (ed. by J. L. Cate and E. N. Anderson, Chicago, 1938).

path of the sun." Not until Turner began writing, however, was a clearly formulated expression of the place of the frontier in American life presented to students of American history.[11]

Turner was born in Portage, Wisconsin, a region that was not yet out of the frontier stage of development. In an autobiographical note, he said that he hunted and fished among Indian neighbors who came to town "to buy paints and trinkets and sell furs. . . . Is it strange that I saw the frontier as a real thing and experienced its changes?" On his mother's side he was descended from preachers. "Is it strange that I preached of the frontier?" he remarked with a smile.[12]

Turner studied at the University of Wisconsin and then went on to Johns Hopkins, where he took his Ph.D. in 1890. At Wisconsin he studied with William F. Allen, who had an important influence upon him, directing his attention to economic and cultural factors in history, and to the role of western expansion in American development. It was at Wisconsin, where Turner was a member of the faculty until 1910, that he did his most effective teaching. When Carl Becker, then a freshman, saw Turner in 1893, he was a young professor, so zestful and buoyant that he lifted students to new realms of the intellectual life. From no other man, said Becker, did he "ever get in quite the same measure that sense of watching a first-class mind at work on its own account . . . the most delightful sense in the world of sitting there waiting for ideas to be born; expectantly waiting for secret meanings, convenient explanatory hypotheses to be discovered, lurking as like as not under the dullest mass of drab facts ever seen." As a teacher he was not given to passing on to his students final judgments, and he was equally reluctant to do so in his writing. Born with a really intellectual curiosity, he had a mind that was ever alert, fresh, and independent, which sought its own answer to the many problems that face a historian. "I have had a lot of fun exploring, getting lost and getting back, and telling my companions about it," he once wrote to Becker.[13]

In his earliest, little-known writings, and in his teaching, Turner suggested such broad areas of research which looked at American his-

[11] H. C. Nixon, "Precursors of Turner in the Interpretation of the American Frontier," *South Atlantic Quarterly*, Vol. XXVIII, No. 1 (January, 1929), 83–90.

[12] Letter to C. L. Skinner, March 15, 1922, in *Wisconsin Magazine of History*, Vol. XIX, No. 1 (September, 1935), 91–103.

[13] Carl Becker, "Frederick Jackson Turner," in H. W. Odum (ed.), *American Masters of Social Science*, 281–82; Avery Craven, "Frederick Jackson Turner," *Jernegan Essays*, 252–70.

tory with so wide-angled a vision that it scarce does him justice to speak of him only as a "sectional" or "frontier" historian; he had strong objections to being labeled "primarily a Western historian." He certainly thought of himself as a truly nationalist historian, and indeed he believed that even for international organizations (such as the League of Nations) his knowledge of American frontier and sectional experience enabled him to contribute suggestions of significance. And yet because of his major writings and through the distorted emphasis of his overzealous students, his name has been associated with a narrower, a "Western," view of American history.

Dissatisfied with the overemphasis of Herbert Baxter Adams' "germ theory of politics," which traced American political institutions back to primitive German custom, Turner sought an explanation in terms of American environment. Thus in his earliest published work, *The Fur Trade in Wisconsin,* he posed the question which in one way or another he tried to answer ever afterward. "The exploitation of the Indian is generally dismissed," he observed, "with the convenient explanatory phrase, 'the march of civilization.'" And then came his troubling question: "But how did it march?" Confining his researches to America to illustrate this social process (although Adams had said that American institutions had already been sufficiently studied), Turner foreshadowed his own later approach when he wrote of the effects of the trading post upon the white man: "In every country the exploitation of the wild beasts, and of the raw-products generally, causes the entry of the disintegrating and transforming influences of a higher civilization."[14] And in studying American civilization Turner was particularly interested in finding out what gave it the particular stamp that served to differentiate it from an older European civilization.

The West appealed to him as a factor in the creation of American life. While Rhodes and von Holst were immersed in the slavery struggle, and other historians—Roosevelt, Winsor, and Thwaites—were attracted to the epic period of the West, Turner was "trying to see it as a whole . . . on its institutional, social, economic and political side." He saw "that there was a persistent persuasive influence in American life which did not get its full attention from those who thought in terms of North and

[14] Turner, "The Character and Influence of the Indian Trade in Wisconsin," Johns Hopkins University *Studies in Historical and Political Science,* Vol. IX, Nos. 11–12 (Baltimore, 1891), 74–75.

South, as well as from those who approached the West as fighting ground, or ground for exploration history." He was less interested in the West as a region in itself than as an illustration of the process of American development.[15]

Turner's ideas gradually matured, and he presented them, in 1893, before the annual meeting of the American Historical Association in an essay, "The Significance of the Frontier in American History." In his first sentences he referred to the closing of the frontier and then added: "Up to our own day American history has been in a large degree the history of the colonization of the Great West. The existence of an area of free land, its continuous recession, and the advance of American settlement westward, explain American development."[16] Because of contact with each new frontier in its movement westward, American social development was in constant process of being reborn, and it was this "continuous touch with the simplicity of primitive society" which furnished "the forces dominating American character. . . . The true point of view in the history of this nation is not the Atlantic Coast," said the professor from Wisconsin, "it is the Great West."

In transforming the wilderness, the pioneer was at first barbarized, but slowly he and the wilderness were changed, and in that change a new personality was created which was distinctly American. The advance of the frontier, said Turner, "has meant a steady movement away from the influence of Europe, a steady growth of independence on American lines. And to study this advance, the men who grew up under these conditions, and the political, economic, and social results of it, is to study the really American part of our history." Unlike the Atlantic seaboard, where the population was predominantly English, the frontier was a region where immigrants became "Americanized, liberated, and fused into a mixed race English in neither nationality nor characteristics." It was the frontier with its vast public domain that conditioned "the growth of nationalism and the evolution of American political institutions," but most importantly the frontier profoundly affected the growth of individualism and democracy. Frontier life determined the type of religious organization built up in the United States and also had a marked effect in shaping intellectual characteristics—the inventive mind, often coarse and strong, with a comprehensive grasp of

[15] Letter to C. L. Skinner.

[16] Essay reprinted in *The Frontier in American History* (New York, 1920).

material things, and exhibiting an unquiet, nervous energy. The disappearance of the frontier in 1890, said Turner, marked the closing of the first period of American history.

With the passing of the frontier came a gradual approach to social uniformity in the United States, and as Turner watched this change, he endeavored to comprehend the play of forces in the country. To understand the contemporary scene, he sought light in the past; and in several essays he expounded the idea that the United States was a federation of sections whose rival interests created tensions which were eased by compromise in Congress.[17]

In a manuscript found among his papers after his death in 1932, Turner explained how he led up to his last studies: "Looking back over my work as a university teacher, which ends this year," he wrote in 1924, "I find that the central interest of my study has been that of . . . maps of population advance—not as a student of a region, but of a process. From cave man to the occupation of a planet. Study of American advance required examination of the geographic, economic, social, diplomatic advances of the frontier," in all of which Turner engaged. It led him also "to examination of the sectional aspects of the advance into new geographic areas, which compelled [him] to study conditions in the various Atlantic Coast regions leading to migration, and into the effects of the newer regions upon these older ones, and to study the special geographical problems into which the various zones of advance brought new societies—the interaction of the various migrating stocks, each in its particular geographic province, adjusting to new social types, and the resulting play of sectional forces in American politics as the old and the new sections found in Congress and in party the need of adjustment or the impulse to conflict. As a result," added Turner, he had "been led to a study of the various sections of the United States, both internally and in their mutual relations with each other and the federal government." He was interested, too, in the way frontier forces acted upon foreign relations, and his studies in American diplomacy indicated the value of this approach.

Turner noted again and again the analogy between American sec-

[17] See collected essays in *The Significance of Sections in American History* (New York, 1932); Fulmer Mood, "The Origin, Evolution and Application of the Sectional Concept, 1750–1900," in M. Jensen (ed.), *Regionalism in America* (Madison, 1951).

tions and the nations of Europe; America, he believed, should be thought of in continental, not in national terms alone. But unlike European countries, which must compose their clashing interests peacefully by conferences or violently by war, the sections of the United States may compose theirs by parliamentary procedure. He was certain that sectionalism was not likely to disappear. Turner was careful to note that neither physical geography nor economic interests were the only factors in sectionalism; the inherited habits of thought of various stocks was likewise of great importance. "We must shape our national action," he said, "to the fact of a vast and varied Union of unlike sections."

Over a period of forty years Turner continued to study his great theme and occasionally to publish essays and monographs illustrating his ideas. Once, by dint of persistent editorial persuasion, he was inveigled into writing a volume, the *Rise of the New West 1819–1829,* for the *American Nation* series (1906). The rise of the new West, said the author, "was the most significant fact in American history in the years immediately following the War of 1812." Turner referred to the strongly national and democratic character of the West: "By the march of the westerners away from their native states to the public domain of the nation, and by their organization as territories of the United States, they lost that state particularism which distinguished many of the old commonwealths of the coast. . . . It was a self-confident section, believing in its right to share in government, and troubled by no doubts of its capacity to rule."

Turner's writing did not often have the form of a continuous narrative. The fact of the matter is that he rarely concerned himself with history in the conventional sense of a narrative of events chronologically arranged. As Becker expressed it, Turner's writing "is all essentially descriptive, explicative, expository." Because his writing was of such a character, students of history waited in vain for the comprehensive work that was never written. The illuminating generalizations that Turner worked out compressed much material into few pages. In his last years he was a research associate at the Huntington Library in California, and while there he brought almost to completion *The United States, 1830–1850: The Nation and Its Sections;* it was published posthumously, in 1935.[18]

[18] Max Farrand, "F. J. Turner at the Huntington Library," Huntington Library *Bulletin,* No. 3 (February, 1933), 157–64.

Turner had long believed that the period 1830–50 offered "the best opportunity for a new work," the West in particular needing special study, "which as yet it hasn't received." But the book went on slowly. "I find it very hard to write," he told a friend, "and suspect that I need to break for the wilderness and freshen up—rather than tie myself to the chair."

In many ways the most satisfying chapters were those describing the various sections of the country. Although Turner's bias was always in favor of the West, he constantly referred to the great influence that native and transplanted New Englanders, as well as New Yorkers, had in the life of this period. The generalizations that enriched his other writings were found scattered in this volume also, and now, more than before, Turner inclined to an interpretation in terms of a class struggle. In speaking of the New York Locofoco party, for example, he said that "the movement was a landmark in the rise of organized demands of the common people for the control of government in the interests of their own economic and spiritual welfare. It presaged a succession of later movements (strongest in the western sections to which New England and New York sent settlers) that included the organization of Anti-Monopolists, Grangers, Populists, and the whole group of later progressive parties." In a discussion of the Bank and the failure to renew its charter, Turner said: "The severance of official connection between the national government and the capitalist was one of the most important steps in American history. Thenceforth the industrial interests were obliged to act by underground methods and by the lobby."

This score of years appeared to Turner as one of fundamental importance in the history of the country, for the very character of its population was then changing because of increased immigration. In its economic, political, and intellectual life it was striking out in new directions: "Between 1830 and 1850 there was . . . a cycle of change in American ideals and in the composition of the people."

The search for the meaning of American life was ever in the heart of Turner, and there was a warm pride that ran through much of his writing—the pride of frontier birth. In his later years he was deeply troubled by the question of the reconciliation and application to civilization in the twentieth century of frontier ideals of individualism and democracy. But the exuberance and vitality of his writing and teaching reflected, in the main, a natural optimism.

In the process of developing his frontier thesis Turner more than once halted to ask himself, and his friends as well, whether he had overemphasized it. Scarcely any well-formulated criticism was directed at the thesis in his lifetime, although Channing, his Harvard colleague, voiced skepticism of its value. Then, in a sudden rush, a flood of vigorous statements were made against the Turner doctrine. An obvious shortcoming of the frontier interpretation of national development was its disregard of the fact that the growth of American democracy was part of the progress of Western civilization as a whole. "The proper point of departure for the discussion of the rise of democracy in the United States," said one critic in his counterblast, "is not the American west but the European background."[19] The religions—Brownism, Puritanism, Quakerism, and Presbyterianism—brought over by most of the colonists had "relatively decentralized and democratic forms of organization." It is therefore incorrect to ascribe to frontier conditions a primary influence in determining the type of the institutions planted there. "The customs and ideas brought by the settlers from an older civilization," said B. F. Wright, "are of vastly more importance in shaping the history of the new lands."

It should be remembered also that the years after Jackson's election coincided with the period of revolt and unrest everywhere in the Western world, and the agitation for social and political change in America was related to similar movements in Europe. It was the machine-age civilization that was more responsible than the disappearance of the frontier for the emphasis on social rather than individualist democracy. And, as in other respects, Europe went through these developments earlier than America, which followed in its wake.

Other critics have observed that the closing of the frontier line in 1890 meant little, for a large acreage still lay open for settlement. More damaging testimony was that the lands which presumably were the safety valve for the discontented of the East rarely came into their hands. Speculators and railroads generally got them first. One critical observation was that frontier areas were usually settled by people living on adjoining lands—that is, farmers—and not those who were dissatisfied in urban communities. Another critic offered evidence that for the discontented farmer the pull of the city was greater than the lure of more

[19] B. F. Wright, "American Democracy and the Frontier," *Yale Review,* Vol. XX, No. 2 (December, 1930), 349–65.

distant land. Sometimes, instead of going west, the unemployed went out of the country entirely to seek a livelihood. Critics have noted a certain vagueness in Turner's use of the words "frontier," "democracy," and "nationalism." He seems also to have followed the unsafe practice of applying to the whole West generalizations that had greater validity for his own region of the Old Northwest.

Despite the valuable correctives that have been made of the Turner thesis, it has not been completely demolished by any means. Europeans corresponding in circumstances to those living in America were often different in temperament: they differed in concepts of equalitarianism and, above all, were usually poles apart in hopefulness. The frontiersman was generally a democrat in action before the existence of the fact was translated into a political franchise. There was a lift of the spirit (after the first heartbreaking toil was over) that impressed the European visitor deeply. Even if Turner did exaggerate the role of the frontier in the promotion of democracy, his general thesis that the movement westward profoundly affected the course of American history and greatly influenced the formation of traits of the national character was valid. Students of European, Canadian, and Latin American frontiers have applied the Turner thesis to these areas. Many writers in their study of literature, religion, law, economics, political science, history, and sociology have accepted its validity. While sometimes, in their ardent discipleship, they pushed to extremes the thesis of the master, they nevertheless produced fruitful works. The seminal teaching and writing of Turner resulted in a rich growth, and his school of historians has flourished like the green bay tree.[20]

HERBERT EUGENE BOLTON

The way to the frontier has not always been from East to West; in the very earliest days of our history it was from South to North. In the study of New Spain's contribution to American history no one has done more important work than Herbert Eugene Bolton. Beginning with the

[20] The literature on Turner has become too extensive to be listed here. The best bibliography is in R. A. Billington, *Westward Expansion* (New York, 1949), 760–62; note especially the writings of Fulmer Mood, the most learned student of Turner's career; see also Merle Curti, *Frederick Jackson Turner,* Instituto Panamericano de Geografía e Historia: Comisión de Historia (Mexico, D. F., 1949); also *The Turner Thesis,* G. R. Taylor (ed.), *Problems in American Civilization* (8 vols., Boston, 1949), II; H. N. Smith, *Virgin Land* (Cambridge, Mass., 1950), is very stimulating.

exploration of Mexican archives, he enlarged the field of investigation to include materials of the homeland in Spain to round out his story of the Spanish borderlands in North America. Going beyond his preceptors, McMaster and Turner, Bolton proclaimed the epic of a greater America in which the essential unity of American history, North and South, has been stressed; his has been literally a history of the Americas, not merely the story of the expansion of the thirteen colonies into a nation. His researches in anthropology, cartography, and history took him all over lands once part of Spain's empire in North America. His long list of publications include *The Spanish Borderlands, An Outpost of Empire* (Berkeley, 1930), *Rim of Christendom: A Biography of Father Kino* (New York, 1936), *Coronado On The Turquoise Trail* (Albuquerque, 1949), and volumes of edited writings. A disciple of Bolton, Lawrence Kinnaird, thus expressed the spirit of the school which has its center in California: "Many of the best-known students of the American frontier have failed to see that the proximity of Spanish territory to the United States had any bearing upon their subjects. Documents of vital importance to the understanding of American expansion have remained unused in Spanish and Mexican archives while old-school historians, apparently oblivious of their existence, have attempted to write and rewrite early United States history."

In a textbook, *The Colonization of North America 1492–1783* (New York, 1920), written with Thomas M. Marshall, Bolton gave the key to his point of view. More emphasis was placed on non-English colonies and on those English colonies which were not among the original thirteen: "By following the larger story of European expansion it becomes plain that there was an Anglo-Spanish and a Franco-Spanish, as well as a Franco-English struggle for the continent, not to mention the ambitions and efforts of Dutch, Swedes, Russians, and Danes." Bolton stimulated many students to follow paths he trod himself, and the historian who would gain more than an Anglo-American viewpoint on our history must read the works of this teacher and his disciples.[21]

[21] See Charles W. Hackett *et al.* (eds.), *New Spain and the Anglo-American West: Historical Contributions Presented to Herbert Eugene Bolton* (2 vols., Los Angeles, 1932); also Bolton's presidential address before the American Historical Association, "The Epic of Greater America," *American Historical Review,* Vol. XXXVIII, No. 3 (April, 1933), 448–74; Adele Ogden and Engel Sluiter (eds.), *Greater America: Essays in Honor of Herbert Eugene Bolton* (Berkeley, 1945).

OTHER HISTORIANS OF THE WEST

The number of students working on the history of the Mississippi Valley and on regions farther west increased greatly following the early days of George P. Garrison at Texas and of Turner at Wisconsin. The vigor of the *Mississippi Valley Historical Review* and other periodicals is a reflection of the vitality of students of this area, whose contributions are of great importance to American historiography.

In the revision that has been made of Turner's interpretation of the frontier as a region where economic equality and democratic institutions generally prevailed, Thomas P. Abernethy's work has been genuinely significant. His book *From Frontier to Plantation in Tennessee: A Study in Frontier Democracy* (Chapel Hill, 1932), indicated how inequalities had been transmitted to the frontier or had quickly developed there; in 1787 only one-eighth of the adult whites in west Tennessee were landowners. Poor farmers went to the back country or were dependent on wealthy landlords. In Abernethy's view, Tennessee's famed citizen, Andrew Jackson, was no "real leader of democracy"—not at least in the state, where he and his friends usually took the conservative side of public issues. The real interpreter of popular sentiment from that community, said the historian, was Andrew Johnson, "the only true and outstanding democrat produced by the old South."

In a subsequent volume, *Western Lands and the American Revolution* (New York, 1937), Abernethy continued Alvord's study of the West as an area for speculative activity. The chief object of his work, said Abernethy, was "to investigate the political consequences of conflicting claims to western lands." This book, like its predecessor, was at pains to modify traditional interpretations of Western democracy. Most of the Western lands, said the author, fell into the hands of speculators. Leadership on the frontier, as in older communities, was concentrated in a few hands, and the general run of men in the West had much in common with the rank and file in the East. Unlike Turner, Abernethy found no clear cut sectional alignment between the East and the West. In all his studies, including his *Three Virginia Frontiers* (Louisiana State University Press, 1940), Abernethy reflected Tocqueville's view of American democracy—that along with its virtues there were dangers in the power of the majority. Democracy and liberalism, he reminded his readers, were not necessarily one and the same.

The movement westward of the older Eastern stock was the subject of Lois Kimball Mathews' *Expansion of New England 1620–1865* (Boston, 1909). It was more than the physical transplanting of peoples that she described, for the migrants carried with them their culture pattern, which implanted a distinctive Puritan character on the regions of the Middle West. An important analysis of emigration based on study of hundreds of individuals was made by L. D. Stilwell, *Migration from Vermont, 1776–1860* (Montpelier, 1937). The territory settled by these emigrant New Englanders was described by Beverly W. Bond in *The Civilization of the Old Northwest . . . 1788–1812* (New York, 1934). In his anxiety to stress the "distinctive" aspects of civilization in this area, Bond seemed to minimize its ties with other parts of the United States—for example, with the South.

The era following that covered by Bond was the subject of a very detailed treatment by R. C. Buley, *The Old Northwest: Pioneer Period 1815–1840* (2 vols., Indianapolis, 1950). Here was no sentimentalizing of the pioneer; he was painted realistically. The successes and failures of the frontiersman's life, his work, his religion, his schooling, his politics—all were described at length in the fullest presentation yet of a Western section. Buley was interested in the mind and body of the first settlers, never losing sight of their dreams.

The next period in the history of this region was described by Henry C. Hubbart, *The Older Middle West, 1840–1880 . . .* (New York, 1936). Hubbart's volume, emphasizing the distinctive characteristics of this section which set it off from the East and South, was especially good on the Southern influence in this area, but he failed to treat adequately a subject fundamental to an understanding of life in this region—the changes associated with the growth of capitalism in the Middle West. The *History of Agriculture in the Northern United States 1620–1860* (1925), by Percy W. Bidwell and John I. Falconer, explained some of the reasons for the movement westward of New Englanders, but the work's real significance lay in its large collection of materials which laid a firm foundation for later historians of agriculture.

The whole physical development of the West was greatly clarified by the comprehensive work of Louis C. Hunter, *Steamboats on the Western Rivers* (Cambridge, 1949). It was a technological study which covered in thorough fashion the changing history of navigation in the interior of the United States. Along with the technical aspects of steamboating, Hunter described the economics of river traffic, the triumph of the railroads, and the replacement of the steamboat by the less glamorous towboat and barge.

The intimate relationship between railroads and Western settlement was the theme of a critical study by Paul W. Gates, *The Illinois Central Railroad and Its Colonization Work* (Cambridge, 1934). Gates avoided the conventional treatment of railroad history—its technical aspects and the spectacular struggles of financial speculators, usually associated with early railroad history—in order to study the social, political, and economic impact on the community of this new force in the life of the West. Gates has also written extensively on the agriculture of the West in the nineteenth century, and is unquestionably one of its most thoughtful students. He found the facts of land ownership were often far removed from the fanciful picture drawn by less skeptical historians. In the discovery of realities in the westward movement, Henry N. Smith's *Virgin Land: the American West as Symbol and Myth* (Cambridge, 1950), has been truly enlightening. It was a fine study of the manner in which the image of the West was created and implanted in the American mind, and the effect of that image on legislation and literature.

The discontent produced by technological and economic factors which perplexed the farmers, and which they sought to control, was the theme of an excellent volume by Solon J. Buck, the *Granger Movement* (Cambridge, 1913). Fred E. Haynes likewise treated this subject in his *Third Party Movements since the Civil War* (Iowa City, 1916), but its most comprehensive historian was John D. Hicks, author of *The Populist Revolt* . . . (Minneapolis, 1931). The farmer, said Hicks, was waging "a long and perhaps a losing struggle . . . to save agricultural America from the devouring jaws of industrial America." A continuation of this study was made in *Agricultural Discontent in the Middle West 1900–1939* (Madison, 1951), by Hicks and Theodore Saloutos. The book was especially strong on agrarian organizations and their efforts to improve the status of farmers.

Fred A. Shannon, a learned and iconoclastic student of American agricultural life, published an able study of *The Farmer's Last Frontier: Agriculture 1860–1897* (New York, 1945). He emphasized the effect of soils, climate, and nature's pests on the lives of Western farmers. In the course of his investigations he destroyed traditional interpretations of rural life. He discredited as a myth the "agricultural ladder" theory which assumed that farmhands and tenants readily rose rung by rung to independent land ownership. He showed, too, with convincing statistics, that the city was more of a safety valve for agrarian discontent than were distant farm frontiers.

Of the modern historians who have carefully studied frontiers to the South and Southwest no one has been more scholarly than Verner W. Crane, who has written of *The Southern Frontier 1670–1732* (Durham, 1928). It was the Indian trade that furnished the clue to the conflicts in this area, as in the Northwestern frontier in this period. Crane minimized the significance of Spain in affecting developments in this frontier, but other historians have stressed Spanish-American relations. In addition to the volumes of Bolton and his students, Arthur P. Whitaker made important contributions to this field with *The Spanish-American Frontier 1783–1795* (Boston, 1927) and *The Mississippi Question 1795–1803: A Study in Trade, Politics, and Diplomacy* (New York, 1934). The complexities of the acquisition of Louisiana, which have troubled many students, were greatly clarified by Whitaker. To unravel the tangle of American relations with foreign powers, including Spain, has been the main enterprise of Samuel F. Bemis. Beginning with *Jay's Treaty* (New York, 1924), he published other studies which were the basis for his comprehensive *A Diplomatic History of the United States* (New York, 1936).

For the region beyond the Mississippi a volume of the first importance was published in 1931 by Walter Prescott Webb, *The Great Plains*. With distinct literary skill and imaginative research he constructed a narrative that explained how the environment determined the character of the white civilization that finally triumphed over the native red man. The Colt revolver, barbed wire, and the windmill were the tools that helped in the conquest, and in the process "American institutions and cultural complexes that came from a humid and timbered region" were fundamentally altered.[22] The social history of the Northern Plains was told in attractive fashion by Everett Dick, in *The Sod House Frontier 1854–1890* (New York, 1937). The unending struggle to adjust to this

[22] See the sharp criticism of Webb's book in Fred A. Shannon, *An Appraisal of Walter Prescott Webb's "The Great Plains," Critiques of Research in the Social Sciences*, Vol. III (New York, 1940); see also J. W. Caughey's comment on the *Critique* in *Mississippi Valley Historical Review*, Vol. XXVII, No. 3 (December, 1940), 442–44.

elemental frontier was made vividly clear in Dick's wide selection of materials.

The regions farther westward have had innumerable chroniclers of particular episodes, but good, general accounts are still relatively few. Katharine Coman wrote one, *Economic Beginnings of the Far West* (2 vols., New York, 1912), which contained a large body of useful materials, and William J. Ghent, a careful student, gave us *The Early Far West, 1540–1850* (New York, 1931). Frederic L. Paxson, a close student of the West, dealt in his volume on *The Last American Frontier* (New York, 1910) with the period following that covered by Ghent. John W. Caughey, in his *California* (New York, 1940), avoided the usual overemphasis on the state's earlier period in order to describe more fully the years since it entered the Union. The area farther north, Oregon, Washington, and northern Idaho, has been treated in a scholarly survey by Oscar O. Winther, *The Great Northwest* (New York, 1947), a book that reveals the author's strong attachment to this rugged land. For an important part of their study all historians of this region are dependent upon H. M. Chittenden's *The American Fur Trade of the Far West* (3 vols., New York, 1902). In the trilogy by Bernard De Voto, *The Course of Empire* (1952, written last), *Across the Wide Missouri,* and *The Year of Decision,* the broad sweep of Western history from the days of Spanish Conquistadors to the Mexican War was encompassed. De Voto is an enthusiast about his subject and the vigor of his prose communicates the ardor of a dedicated author. His interest is generally more in the drama of Western exploration and conquest, and less in the toilsome task of settlement.

The manner in which the nation's rich resource, the public land, has been disposed of has attracted much critical scrutiny in recent years. The assumptions of earlier students that land was to be had for the asking and settled with little doing have been rudely shattered by later scholars. A summary of their findings was presented by Roy M. Robbins in *Our Landed Heritage: The Public Domain* (Princeton, 1942). The author made a successful effort to relate the history of land disposal with concurrent developments in American life.

A synthesis of the many materials embracing the whole field of the frontier was made by Ray A. Billington (in collaboration with James B. Hedges) in *Westward Expansion: A History of the American Frontier* (New York, 1949). Though recognizing the modifications that have been made in Turner's interpretation of the role of the West in American history, Billington was guided by the writings and teaching of the acknowledged master, as well as by the instruction of Frederick Merk, Turner's successor at Harvard. It was a useful summary of the latest findings on nearly every phase of the westward movement, and it explained with much success the effect of the frontier in creating the kind of civilization that ultimately developed in the newer regions.

One aspect of that civilization, and an important one, was covered in a painstaking study on *Manifest Destiny* (Baltimore, 1935), by Albert K. Weinberg. This study of the expansionist philosophy and its effects on American history belongs with the volumes of Julius W. Pratt, *The Expansionists of 1812* (New York, 1921), which emphasized a neglected factor in that struggle, and his *Expansionists of 1898* (Baltimore, 1936), which ascribed much of the strength of this movement to the activities of Alfred Thayer Mahan, Theodore Roosevelt, and Henry Cabot Lodge. Expansionism and the Monroe Doctrine ultimately became intertwined and, according to Latin Americans, interchangeable. The comprehensive history of the Monroe Doctrine by Dexter Perkins was the finest study ever made of that fundamental factor in American history.

New England

From the days when Increase and Cotton Mather urged the writing of a history of New England, a number of writers have essayed the task. Nearly all writers of her history have construed their subject in such a manner that they have dealt almost exclusively with Massachusetts, devoting comparatively little space to her neighbors. Charles Francis Adams wrote expressly on Massachusetts, but James Truslow Adams gave more attention than others have done to the Bay Colony's neighbors. A nineteenth-century historian, William B. Weeden, was a successful manufacturer before he turned to history. He was keenly aware of the social problems created by the Industrial Revolution, and though he had something of the Christian Socialist outlook of the 1880's, he was in the main a strong economic individualist.[23] In 1890 he published his *Economic and Social History of New England 1670–1789,* which was one of the first attempts to do for a section what McMaster was then doing for the nation as a whole. He consulted sources rarely used before

[23] See his *The Social Law of Labor* (Boston, 1882).

by historical scholars, and his chapters on money, lands, agriculture, fisheries, commerce, prices, and manners included materials that are still useful to the student. When he touched on political matters, such as the Navigation Acts, he gave an outmoded interpretation, but his volumes remain among the best of their type. A later, and excellent, investigation of the relationship between communications and communal growth was that of E. C. Kirkland, *Men, Cities and Transportation: A Study in New England History, 1820–1900* (2 vols., Cambridge, 1948).

Writers on New England have gone through cycles of pietism and of pitiless criticism. In that region's early days her glories were presented by seventeenth-century historians untarnished. Then with the growth of skepticism came a more detached view of ancestors, notably in the works of Hutchinson and Belknap. The filial piety of Palfrey expressed again the devotional spirit of Cotton Mather. A sharp reaction against the ancestor worship of Palfrey was revealed by Brooks Adams in the *Emancipation of Massachusetts* (1887), Charles Francis Adams, and James Truslow Adams. The latter, in particular, in his anxiety to redress the balance, erred seriously in his estimate of the Puritans. A sounder interpretation of the civilization of early New England was advanced in the works of Kenneth B. Murdock, Perry Miller, Clifford K. Shipton, and Samuel Eliot Morison. Murdock's literary studies and his biography of Increase Mather indicated a richness of Puritan culture apparently unknown to earlier students. Similarly the works of Miller (especially his *New England Mind in the Seventeenth Century* and his *Jonathan Edwards*) and Shipton's essays and biographical sketches of Harvard graduates have revealed a depth and variety in Puritan thought hitherto largely ignored. Morison heads the "revisionist" school, whose organ is the *New England Quarterly*.[24]

CHARLES FRANCIS ADAMS

America's royal family, the Adams', made regal gifts to their native land in public service, in scholarship, and in the creation of a critical tradition. A prince of the blood was Charles Francis, son of the Charles Francis Adams who served his country brilliantly as minister to Eng-

[24] Some stimulating remarks are found in C. M. Andrews, "Historic Doubts Regarding Early Massachusetts History," Colonial Society of Massachusetts *Transactions,* Vol. XXVIII (1935), 280–94.

land during the Civil War. While his brother Henry was acting as secretary to their father in London, Charles joined the Union Army, feeling that it was necessary that at least one member of the family offer deeds as well as words in behalf of his country. "For years our family has talked of slavery and of the South, and been most prominent in the contest of words," he wrote to his father, "and now that it has come to blows does it become us to stand aloof from the conflict?"[25]

Unlike Henry, Charles entered rather vigorously into the currents of American political and business life; for a long time his historical interests were not much more than an avocation. But in the twenty-five years that followed his retirement from association with the Union Pacific Railroad in 1890, he delivered many addresses on history and published several works, including *The Life of Richard Henry Dana, The Three Episodes of Massachusetts History,* a critical appraisal of New England historians in *Massachusetts: Its Historians and History,* and a volume of *Studies: Military and Diplomatic.*

In his autobiography, Adams spoke of two epoch-marking events in his life: one was the discovery of a book, the other was an invitation to deliver an address. The former occurred when he was in England in his thirtieth year, in 1865. "I one day chanced upon a copy of John Stuart Mill's essay on Auguste Comte," he wrote. "That essay of Mill's revolutionized in a single morning my whole attitude. I emerged from the theological stage, in which I had been nurtured, and passed into the scientific." It was the invitation to deliver an address some eight years later that had the effect of fixing more certainly the direction of Adams' intellectual life. He was asked by the citizens of the town of Weymouth to deliver a historical address on the two hundred and fiftieth anniversary of its settlement; out of so small a beginning he was led for forty years thereafter "through pastures green and pleasant places."

Of the harvests he reaped, none has been of greater value than the sheaf of papers gathered together in *The Three Episodes of Massachusetts History* (2 vols., Boston, 1892). These episodes were the settlement of Boston Bay at Weymouth in 1623, the Antinomian controversy, and a study of church and town government. Seventy years before Adams published his history, his great-grandfather, John Adams, had written to Jefferson about his own reading: "Controversies between Calvinists and Arminians, Trinitarians and Unitarians, Deists and Christians,

[25] Ford (ed.), *A Cycle of Adams Letters,* I, 10.

Atheists and both, have attracted my attention. . . . The history of this little village of Quincy, if it were worth recording, would explain to you how this happened."[26] The great-grandson decided that its history was worth recording.

The first episode was enlivened by the appearance of Thomas Morton, whose enigmatic personality, so un-Puritan in its characteristics, attracted Adams. The historian's examination of the treatment of Anne Hutchinson in the Antinomian controversy led him to write that her "so-called trial was, in fact, no trial at all, but a mockery of justice rather—a bare-faced inquisitorial proceeding." An Adams of the fourth generation was not likely to look at provincial events narrowly. The Antinomian controversy, wrote the historian, was much more than a religious dispute: "It was the first of the many New England quickenings in the direction of social, intellectual and political development—New England's earliest protest against formulas."

The Adams' were not accustomed to mince words when their minds were made up. Charles Francis Adams could not drop this subject without some caustic references to New England historians who had sought to palliate, or even to justify, their ancestor's actions. "In the treatment of doubtful historical points," he said, "there are few things which need to be more carefully guarded against than patriotism or filial piety." In his third episode, which is probably the most interesting to the present-day reader, Adams told of the mores of Quincy. The American unit, he said, was to be sought in the towns and their records; "the political philosopher can there study the slow development of a system as it grew from the germ up." Chapters on "Population and Wealth," "Social Life," "Town Meetings," and "Intemperance and Immorality," though pioneer efforts, still remain very useful.

In the opinion of Osgood, the work of Adams was "the most original and suggestive town history ever written in this country," and it set a precedent for critical treatment that James Truslow Adams and others remembered when they began to write on New England. Charles Francis Adams had a quiet satisfaction contemplating in retrospect his *Three Episodes*. "It may not be great, and certainly has not nor will it obtain a recognized place in general literature," he said, "but locally,

[26] Wilstach, *Correspondence of John Adams and Thomas Jefferson,* 68, July 18, 1813.

it is a classic." Posterity is not likely to quarrel with his own judgment of his book.[27]

JAMES TRUSLOW ADAMS

Writers outside of academic halls were once responsible for some of our finest historical writings. That tradition has thinned since Henry Charles Lea, Francis Parkman, and Prescott wrote their notable volumes, but it has been reinforced in recent years by the work of Douglas Southall Freeman and James Truslow Adams. The latter had no regret because of his lack of academic experience, indeed, he thought "too long an academic training and career" was "rather a detriment than a benefit to a historian."[28] Turning from a business career, he brought out a succession of volumes which made it possible once again for a historian to live by his writing. For himself, he fulfilled the ambition of Macaulay —that his volumes should replace the latest novel on the drawing-room table. No name was better known than his among the public that read history in America.

Adams came into prominence among the historical guildsmen with his *The Founding of New England* (1921). It was acclaimed by Morison as the "best short history of early New England that has appeared for a generation," but the justice of Adams' severe criticism of Puritan religious intolerance was widely questioned. It seemed to have been generally overlooked that only three years before, in his history of Southampton, Adams had been very sympathetic to the Puritans: "We should not sneer, as historians have some times done," he wrote, "at those who came to secure religious freedom and in turn denied it to some extent in others." He went on to a further defense: "Those engaged in the work of laying the foundations of a new civil and religious polity should not be blamed for refusing to passively watch others sap those very foundations which they were attempting to build up at the expense of so much they had held dear. Nor was their attitude either hypocritical or disingenuous." The work of the earliest settlers, wrote Adams, "was stern and their theology as well, but their lives, like ours, were filled with the satisfaction of honest work and with the sweetness of love for their wives, tenderness for their children, and the joys of friendship."

[27] See C. F. Adams, *Autobiography* (Boston, 1916).

[28] "Is History Science?" in *The Tempo of Modern Life* (New York, 1931), 205.

For some unknown reason, when he came to write on the New England Puritans, in 1921, he did not see their sweetness and tenderness, nor their joys. Rather he concentrated on their shortcomings, feeling perhaps the necessity of overcoming the influence of the filiopietistic school of historians as typified by Palfrey. Apart from this particular bias of Adams and the fact that his volume was almost exclusively a political history, *The Founding of New England* did merit high praise. It made excellent use of the work of Osgood, Beer, and Andrews in presenting the colonies as cogs in an imperial machine; a chapter on "The Theory of Empire" was especially good in this respect. What Fiske, in his *Beginnings of New England,* called "The Tyranny of Andros," Adams called "An Experiment in Administration." He emphasized the economic factors, rather than the religious, behind the mass migration in the 1630's. In examining the workings of the theocracy, he said that "the domestic struggle against the tyranny exercised by the more bigoted members of the theocratic party was of greater importance in the history of liberty than the more dramatic contest with the mother country." His iconoclasm was refreshing, even if his brand of orthodoxy set up a new cult—anti-Puritanism.[29]

The second volume in the series was *Revolutionary New England 1690–1776* (1923). The historian traced the beginnings of colonial grievances, the gradual development of revolutionary sentiment, and the rise of a radical party. From 1713 to about 1750, "we can see at work forces tending to develop democratic ideals in certain elements of the community, and foreshadowing the alignments and parties of a later time"; the ten years preceding 1750, he said, were "marked by an intense quickening of thought and action."

The historian studied the internal struggle for political and economic power between the mercantile aristocracy and the lower classes in the colonies, and he noted the growth in self-consciousness of these same lower classes. The modern attitude toward the Loyalists was given full expression by Adams, who referred to the Revolution as a "Civil War." In these two volumes Adams possibly exaggerated the isolation of New England from the rest of the colonies. It was the opinion of Leonard W. Labaree, whose *Royal Government in America* emphasized many features of the history of this period more lightly touched on by Adams,

[29] In opposition, see C. K. Shipton, "A Plea for Puritanism," *American Historical Review,* Vol. XL, No. 3 (April, 1935), 460–67.

that the latter's volume did not adequately explain the revolutionary movement.

The last of the trilogy was *New England in the Republic 1776–1850*. Its main theme, said the author, "may be considered to be the continued struggle of the common man to realize the doctrines of the Revolution in the life of the community." In keeping with his awareness of the aspirations of the rank and file, he gave a sympathetic review of Shays' Rebellion. In the conflict over the adoption of the federal constitution, the historian was especially interested in the struggle between the conservative element and the opposition, which was anxious to preserve and extend the liberal doctrines preached in 1776.

In keeping with studies like those of Beard, Adams maintained that, having achieved their object in gaining their independence from England, the conservative leaders in America strove to prevent the revolutionary movement from going further, thus altering the essential structure of American society. But once begun, the process of revolution was not easily stayed; the mass of the people had come to expect radical changes, "and for many decades after 1783," said Adams, "this struggle between these two groups constitutes the main interest of our history." He observed the conflict as it revealed itself in its various aspects—in business, politics, education, relations between capital and labor, religion, and in the debate over slavery. A subordinate subject was the gradual growth of sectionalism and its decline when the ties of union proved stronger. After 1850 nationalist forces "swept the New England states into the swift movement of what had by then become a genuinely national life."

Hostility to the Puritans was somewhat diminished in this study, and in his closing lines Adams did mild penance: "We thus end the story as we began, with the leaders of the New England people wrestling with a transcendent moral problem [in 1850 it was slavery]. . . . Perhaps, at times, in a reaction against the old point of view which regarded all Puritans and all Revolutionary soldiers and agitators as saints and patriots, we may have been tempted to stress the shadows rather than the lights. . . ."

"A small part of the public, God bless it, does want to know something about the past of our race," wrote Adams, "but it wants to be able to stay awake while it reads."[30] In his volumes on New England and in

[30] *The Tempo of Modern Life,* 212.

his very readable *Epic of America,* Adams kept many thousands awake while they enjoyed a stimulating interpretation of our past.

SAMUEL ELIOT MORISON

The tradition of historical scholarship in New England is the strongest in American literature, and its present representatives are worthy heirs. The foremost of them is Samuel Eliot Morison, who combines the exact scholarship of his master, Edward Channing, with the literary skill of Henry Adams. Morison's love of the sea led to a brilliant reconstruction of Columbus' voyage, in his *Admiral of the Ocean Sea* (2 vols., Boston, 1942). To Rear Admiral Morison was assigned the congenial task of writing the history of the navy's role in the Pacific during World War II.

Morison, in his re-examination of the earlier years of New England, has thrown much new light on a familiar subject. He began with a study of Harrison Gray Otis (2 vols., Boston, 1913), a distinguished Federalist who lived on long after his party had died. Morison then wrote on a subject fancied by many New England historians—*The Maritime History of Massachusetts 1783–1860* (Boston, 1921). The contents were much broader than the title would indicate, for in the period before the Civil War a large fraction of American commerce was handled by ships from Massachusetts. Thus the volume covered more than a provincial area; in fact, like the ships that sailed from New England's ports, it covered the world. And for the lover of the sea (as well as for the student of history) there was real tang in the gusty, swinging words that described the days of New England's glory.

After this volume Morison turned back to the years of the founders and in his *Builders of the Bay Colony* (Boston, 1930) wrote about the characters of the first generation who interested him most—men and a woman (Anne Bradstreet) who typified the varied aspects of the first fifty years of Massachusetts. Morison said that his "attitude toward seventeenth-century puritanism has passed through scorn and boredom to a warm interest and respect." In the sketches that made up this volume, the historian pictured a people rarely endowed by former students with a broad humanity and allegedly too little concerned with esthetics. The Puritans who emerged from his pages were real individuals whose characteristics belied the stereotype fashioned by superficial historians and cartoonists. Morison came out strongly for the thesis that the motive for the Puritan migration was religious and not economic. He pushed this view too far, perhaps, for while the leaders may have been thus largely motivated, the evidence is not convincing with respect to the mass of their followers.

The Puritan Pronaos (New York, 1936), studies in seventeenth-century intellectual history, again revealed the historian's broad knowledge of the Puritan mind. As in the earlier volume on the *Builders,* Morison showed the awareness of the Puritan to the world of his own day, and the clergy in particular were credited with being not merely the religious leaders of the community, but the political and intellectual guides as well. Morison modified or discarded many timeworn traditions about "reactionary clergy" who were drags on the progress of New England. Unlike other students who maintained that New England led a life apart from Europe, he showed how closely in many ways intellectual activity in the New World paralleled that in the Old.

Morison's history of Harvard is of the first importance for an understanding of the development of American education. Three volumes have already appeared, carrying the story to the beginning of the eighteenth century.[31] The first, *The Founding of Harvard College* (1935), gave in detail the European background and the first fifteen years of the college. Emmanuel College, Cambridge, training ground for many Puritans, exerted great influence in the creation of Harvard. The broad purposes of the charter providing for a general education were properly emphasized by Morison, in contrast to those who so often pointed to the narrowly ecclesiastical objectives of Harvard's training.

The sacrifices of the Puritans to make of their school a worthy institution, and the returns it gave to the community in intellectual and spiritual guidance were made clear by the historian, justly proud of his alma mater. A splendid composite "portrait" of the Harvard alumni concluded the third volume. With the completion of this work Harvard will have a history unmatched as yet by any other educational institution, and at the same time a contribution of the first order will have been made to the intellectual history of America.

[31] Morison edited a volume on the period since President Eliot's administration: *The Development of Harvard University, 1869–1929* (Cambridge, Mass., 1930).

The South

Historical studies received a marked impetus in the North and Middle West soon after the Civil War, but they lagged in the South. Problems far more pressing than the study and writing of history occupied the Southern states in the period of Reconstruction, but the publication of many war memoirs maintained the continuity with an earlier tradition of historical writing. Gayarré was still alive and influential among historical students, and one or two of the historical societies showed some signs of vigor. At the bar of history, the only tribunal available to the South, Southerners pleaded their cause. To Alfred T. Bledsoe, editor of the *Southern Review,* General Lee remarked: "Doctor, you . . . have a great work to do; we all look to you for our vindication." The Southern Historical Society, founded in 1869, had for its main purpose the preservation of materials bearing on the Civil War. It published a journal, the *Southern Historical Society Papers,* which brought to light many documents. The *Southern Bivouac* (1882–87) was one of the most important contributions to historical periodical literature in the post-Civil War era. At a later time, 1896, the Southern History Association, with wider interests than the former historical society, was formed. It was the new university, Johns Hopkins, that provided a more vitalizing force. As late as 1890, however, there was no great activity in history in the South.[32] But at this very time young men were publishing their first studies; it must also be remembered that students in other parts of the country were occasionally being drawn to Southern topics, even though Southerners at home might be negligent of them.

Herbert Baxter Adams and others were aware of the value of research in Southern history. A writer in *The Nation* (May 26, 1881), for instance, pointed out that the history of the local institutions of the South remained to be written: "It is a good field of investigation for the rising generation of students in that section of the country," he concluded. William A. Dunning, not long after, was to begin the teaching that created an excellent body of scholars devoted to Southern history, while William E. Dodd and John Spencer Bassett performed similar services.

[32] W. P. Trent, "Historical Studies in the South," American Historical Association *Papers,* Vol. IV, Part 4 (October, 1890), 57–65; D. S. Freeman, *The South to Posterity* (New York, 1939).

Woodrow Wilson was studying his native region with an eye that looked askance at the conventional Northern approach to Southern history,[33] while William G. Brown, cut off too early in his career, published a suggestive reinterpretation in *The Lower South in American History* (New York, 1902).

Co-operative works were published with more attention than was usually given to Southern points of view. *The History of North America* (20 vols., 1903–1907), edited by Guy C. Lee and Francis N. Thorpe, gave more space than did the *American Nation* series to the South, assigning, for example, a whole volume to the Civil War from a Southern standpoint.

A co-operative work more specifically the expression of Southern consciousness, and a reflection of the widening interest in its history, was *The South in the Building of the Nation* (12 vols. and index vol., 1909). The scholarship of some of the writers insured the high quality of their contributions. Philip A. Bruce wrote on Virginia, Bernard C. Steiner on Maryland, William K. Boyd and J. G. de Roulhac Hamilton on North Carolina, Ulrich B. Phillips on Georgia, and Walter L. Fleming on Alabama. The authors looked upon the South as something of a distinct political and economic unit, "with an interrelated and separate history." The eleven states that organized the Confederacy, the border states of Kentucky, Maryland, and Missouri, and the state of West Virginia fell within the scope of the history, the publication of which was justified on the ground that "no true history of the South has been written."

One volume was on the South as a whole, with a section, "The South in Federal Politics," making a valuable contribution. Another volume, on economic history from 1607 to 1865, was the first comprehensive attempt to compile such information in the South since De Bow's work in 1852. This volume, and a companion work which carried the treatment to 1909, broke new ground in research. In a useful section on "The Economic Causes of the Civil War," John H. Latané redirected attention too long focused on the constitutional and moral aspects of the struggle. The series was broad enough to include volumes on the intellectual life of the South, as well as her social activities. For many years students wishing quick access to materials on the South found it very advantageous to use this series.

[33] See Wilson's *Division and Reunion* (New York, 1893), especially 106ff.

PHILIP ALEXANDER BRUCE

One of the most prolific of Southern historical writers and one of the most important was Philip Alexander Bruce. In 1896 he brought out an exceedingly valuable *Economic History of Virginia in the Seventeenth Century* (2 vols.), in which he made use of hitherto unexplored manuscript collections. His was the first attempt, he said, "to describe the purely economic condition of the Virginia people in detail," and his volumes were filled with meticulous descriptions of manufactures and of the conditions of agriculture and labor. Bruce, of course, was too good a historian to accept the cavalier tradition of Virginia history, but he did say: "There are many evidences that a large number of the immigrants were sprung from English families of substance"; and in another connection he stated that "the moral influence of the large plantation was . . . extraordinary." Throughout Bruce's work the reader sensed his nostalgia for the spacious days of the old landed aristocracy.

In 1907 Bruce published another study, *Social Life of Virginia in the Seventeenth Century,* which was an inquiry into the origin of the planter aristocracy and a description of the manners and diversions of the people. Leaving aside slaves, the population of Virginia, he said, was socially a duplication of the smaller rural communities in England, although the physical surroundings of the New World had made for some modifications. In a subsequent work, *The Virginia Plutarch* (2 vols., Chapel Hill, 1929), Bruce paid tribute to the great Virginians, claiming for them the homage that is rightfully theirs.

In opposition to Bruce, Thomas Jefferson Wertenbaker minimized the influence of the aristocracy in Virginia's early history. In his *Planters of Colonial Virginia* (Princeton, 1922), Wertenbaker found that the colony was filled with comparatively small farms "owned and worked by a sturdy class of English farmers." These white yeomen were the most important element in the life of early Virginia until the spread of slavery in the eighteenth century transformed the colony "from a land of hard-working independent peasants, to a land of slaves and slave holders."

ALEXANDER BROWN

At the time when Bruce was initiating his investigations into Virginia's early history, Alexander Brown was unearthing the sources of her history and publishing them in important volumes. In 1890 he published *The Genesis of the United States* (2 vols.), covering the years from 1605 to 1616, "the period of the first foundation." He continued the *Genesis,* with some changes of opinions on men and events, in *The First Republic in America* (Boston, 1898), in which he criticized severely the writings of John Smith. Brown wrote about the enemies of the Virginia Company almost as though they were his personal opponents. His thesis was that James I frustrated the growth of democracy in Virginia, thus beginning the long history of royal tyranny that ended with George III.[34] Obviously, Brown's ability lay in collecting, not in interpretation.

EDWARD MCCRADY

Interesting as the history of colonial Virginia has been to the modern student, equally rich in charm and incident is the history of colonial South Carolina. Edward McCrady, a lawyer by profession and historian by avocation, wrote a four-volume *History of South Carolina* (1897–1902), which covered her story to the close of the Revolutionary War. Of special interest were several chapters captioned "1765–1775," which gave an excellent picture of the professions and the economic and social life of the colony on the eve of the Revolution. Although he treated rather fully social conditions in the eighteenth century, McCrady did not consider the interaction between social and political events. He also failed to make clear South Carolina's position in relation to the rest of the empire. The remaining two volumes covered the war period, and so well did McCrady carry out his task that his work has been recognized as one of the best state histories ever written.

WILLIAM ARCHIBALD DUNNING

William Archibald Dunning, who was a very sympathetic student of Southern history, was one of the many products of John W. Burgess' classes in Columbia University. He later joined his teacher on the faculty of that school, where he built up a whole group of scholars devoted to Southern history. The maiden effort of the young Ph.D. in 1885 was *The Constitution of the United States in Civil War and Reconstruction 1860–1867,* in which he showed an independence of judgment that remained always a distinctive characteristic. When writing of the plans

[34] For a good analysis of Brown's work, see Wesley F. Craven, *Dissolution of the Virginia Company* (New York, 1932), 12–21.

of Thaddeus Stevens and others for the confiscation of Southern property, Dunning said that "all such propositions were the passionate fancies of fanatics more extreme than the Southern fire-eaters who had precipitated the war." In his closing lines he stated his thesis—that in the revolution which had occurred "the written Constitution had been pronounced finished. It had held the fragments of the nation together till they should be welded inseparably in the white heat of war, but it had not itself escaped the blaze."

This concern with constitutional and institutional history was further manifested in his *Essays on the Civil War and Reconstruction* (New York, 1897). Unlike some recent students who have seen in the Reconstruction acts evidences of powerful Northern economic forces, Dunning wrote that their chief end was "purely political." He had high regard for the political and administrative capacity shown in the Reconstruction of the Southern states, judging it to be "one of the most remarkable achievements in the history of government"; his condemnation of the purpose of Reconstruction was equally straightforward. In his essay on the impeachment and trial of President Johnson, Dunning wrote: "The single vote by which Andrew Johnson escaped conviction marks the narrow margin by which the presidential element in our system escaped destruction."

To Dunning was assigned the volume in the *American Nation* series covering the years immediately following the Civil War; *Reconstruction: Political and Economic 1865–1877* instantly took its place as the foremost treatment of those troubled years. Instead of fixing his attention exclusively on the South during Reconstruction, as so many before him had done, the historian looked at "the period as a step in the progress of the American nation." In the record of the North in these years, he said, "there is less that is spectacular, less that is pathetic, and more that seems inexcusably sordid than in the record of the South." He did not draw the picture of those years in all white or all black, as many others have done, but he did try to make the reader understand more clearly the motives of the Southerners in undoing the plans of Reconstruction.

In 1914 a number of Dunning's former pupils inscribed to him a volume of *Studies in Southern History and Politics*. Some of the authors of this testimonial, which was a fitting commentary on Dunning's influence in the promotion of study of the South, were among the leading students of this section: Ulrich B. Phillips, Charles W. Ramsdell, J. G. de Roulhac Hamilton, William K. Boyd, and Holland Thompson. The writings of his many students of Reconstruction in the several states supplemented Dunning's own investigations, but the "Old Chief," as this stimulating lecturer was affectionately called, did more than anyone else to rewrite the history of the years following the Civil War. "He was the first," said Hamilton, "to make scientific and scholarly investigation of the period of Reconstruction."

ULRICH BONNELL PHILLIPS

Ulrich B. Phillips was one of the many students who had been advised to study with Dunning. In 1902 he published *Georgia and State Rights,* which owed part of its inspiration to Turner. The latter had helped Phillips see that local political divisions rested on economic differences stemming from variations in soil fertility. Phillips had originally intended to study the effect of nullification upon Georgia politics, but his work expanded to become a complete survey of the state's history before the Civil War. Phillips was himself a native of the cotton belt, Troup County, Georgia, and in picturing the region, he was anxious to correct historical misconceptions concerning it. "The contrast between the extremes of wealth and poverty in the South," he said, "has been exaggerated; . . . the social system was by no means rigid in the cotton belt."

Other works followed in due course: *The History of Transportation in the Eastern Cotton Belt* (1908) and *The Life of Robert Toombs* (1913). He edited two volumes on the *Plantation and Frontier 1649–1863* in the *Documentary History of American Industrial Society,* to which he prefixed valuable introductions. These volumes contained little-known materials on the South at work; his attempt, said Phillips, was to give a "reasonably full view of Southern industrial society." No one had a better knowledge of sources for the history of the South than Phillips, and his own library scarce had a rival. He was the author, too, of *American Negro Slavery* (1918), as well as of articles on politics and economics. In later years he was coeditor of *Florida Plantation Records* (1927), but the most important publication of his last days was his *Life and Labor in the Old South* (Boston, 1929), one of the best books yet published on the South as a whole.

This volume was the result of his own familiarity with conditions in the South and the distillation of minute knowledge gained from old manuscript collections. Phillips seems to have presented too favorably the position of the Negro under the slave system, but he was not guilty of willful distortion of the facts, as were many Northern writers on the South. (Frederic Bancroft's *Slave-Trading in the Old South,* published in 1931, gave a more somber picture than did Phillips.)

Phillips' concentration on his own region was so exclusive that he missed important factors that impinged on the South. Thus, concurrent Northern developments, such as the antislavery movement, never were integrated in his work. Even within his own region, his material was usually drawn from the records of large planters. Thus we get from him no satisfactory picture of the smaller planters with few slaves who were more typical of the South's economy. This segment of Southern society was the theme of an informative study by Frank L. Owsley, in his *Plain Folk of the Old South* (Baton Rouge, 1949). Owsley and others who have written on the yeomanry seem to have exaggerated their significance in the economy of slave society. As for the Negro's view of Southern life, it was beyond Phillips' comprehension. His understanding was that Negroes were innately inferior to whites, and thus, accustomed as they were to a lower status, slavery did not bear heavily upon them. The Negro's smoldering, and sometimes overt, hostility to slavery was something Phillips appeared to know nothing about. This militant aspect of slave society, though exaggerated by Herbert Aptheker in *American Negro Slave Revolts* (New York, 1943), had been neglected by earlier historians. In these and in other matters Phillips' interpretation of the Old South has undergone important revision. Nevertheless, the work that he did in his comparatively short career (he was only fifty-six when he died) bulks large in the intensified study of the South that this generation of scholars has been making.[35]

[35] See Fred Landon and E. E. Edwards, "A Bibliography of the Writings of Professor U. B. Phillips," *Agricultural History,* Vol. VIII, No. 4 (October, 1934), 196–218; Wood Gray, "Ulrich Bonnell Phillips," *Jernegan Essays,* 354–73; K. M. Stampp, "The Historian and Negro Slavery," *American Historical Review,* Vol. LVII, No. 3 (April, 1952), 613–24; R. Hofstadter, "Ulrich B. Phillips and the Plantation Legend," *Journal of Negro History,* Vol. XXIX, No. 2 (April, 1944), 109–24. See Fabian Linden, "Economic Democracy in the Slave South: An Appraisal of Recent Views," *Journal of Negro History* (April, 1946), for criticism of Owsley's interpretation.

WILLIAM E. DODD

Another scholar and teacher who contributed much in this field of research was William E. Dodd. Although he published few volumes, through them and through various articles and addresses, he educated his many readers and students to a better understanding of the old South. He was a man of wide interests, examining the characteristics of political leadership in his *Statesmen of the Old South* (New York, 1911), as well as in other biographies, and ranging at length over *The Cotton Kingdom* in a compact little volume that contained enough ideas for a shelfful of books. Still another work, *Expansion and Conflict* (Boston, 1915), anticipated other writers in pointing to the economic causes which operated to bring on the Civil War.

Dodd had as clear an understanding of the necessity for research in Southern history as any student in the field. In an article, "Profitable Fields of Investigation in American History 1815–1860," he suggested political, economic, and biographical studies, a study of the Illinois Central Railroad, a survey of the attitude of the churches to slavery, as well as other themes.[36] Taking to task McMaster and Henry Adams for confining their histories to a restricted area, Dodd said that a comprehensive work would include the debtor regions, West and South. On the theme of the Civil War, he maintained, contrary to conventional impression, that the abolitionists "were in no sense one of the great forces which shaped the national destiny"; they would have brought about a Northern secession had it not been for stronger economic and social forces opposing them. Powerful economic groups fought for mastery in the period from 1815 to 1860, and for a time the plantation owners dominated, but toward the end, Northern industrialists, the protagonists of nationalism, were victorious—a nationalism that protected its economic interests. Throughout his work in scholarship and in public life (he was named ambassador to Germany in 1933) Dodd avowed himself the disciple of Jefferson.

THE CIVIL WAR AND RECONSTRUCTION

Another Jeffersonian with less scholarship than Dodd but a more dynamic style, was Claude G. Bowers—journalist, orator, historian, and

[36] *American Historical Review,* Vol. XVIII, No. 3 (April, 1913), 522–36; a number of these studies have since been undertaken and published.

ambassador. In several volumes he presented a Democratic interpretation of important periods of our history. The first to appear was *The Party Battles of the Jackson Period* (Boston, 1922) which, in the main, glorified Jackson and Benton. Bowers then turned back to write *Jefferson and Hamilton: The Struggle for Democracy in America* (Boston, 1925), which revealed the depth of the author's devotion to the great Virginian. In his next work, *The Tragic Era: The Revolution after Lincoln* (Boston, 1929), Bowers followed the lead of Dunning and his students, and in colorful phraseology he severely indicted the radical Republicans, whose policy ruined the South. The whole approach of Bowers was through the conflicts of leading personalities who symbolized certain forces. His episodic treatment was a throwback to the narrative style of Prescott, with the significant difference that the latter had an essentially aristocratic view of history. Although Bowers did not present much that was novel, he did accent familiar episodes in a manner that gave them new vitality.

Within recent years Negroes have been producing valuable works on various phases of American history. *The Journal of Negro History* has published many significant articles and documents, and one of its editors, Carter G. Woodson, was himself the author of several useful volumes on Negro education and labor, among them, *The Education of the Negro Prior to 1861* (New York, 1905) and the well-known *The Negro in Our History*. W. E. Burghardt Du Bois, early in his career, published an excellent volume on the *Suppression of the Slave Trade* (1896). In later years he brought out *Black Reconstruction,* which advanced the thesis that the former slaves were well on the way to creating a better society in the period after the Civil War when they were defeated by reactionary forces. In fact, it was argued, there was a democratic movement in the North as well as in the South which was crushed by the combination of reactionary elements in both sections. Du Bois, noting that historians have generally emphasized the evils of the Reconstruction period, thus missing the constructive achievements of these years, vigorously redressed the balance. He claimed that because leading radicals—Thaddeus Stevens and Sumner especially—were genuinely interested in the welfare of the Negro people, white historians have vilified them and purposely distorted history. Among younger scholars, John H. Franklin, by his volume *From Slavery to Freedom*

(New York, 1947) and other writings, has shown himself to be among the most critical students now at work on the history of the South.

The thesis of Du Bois was given considerable support by Roger W. Shugg in his *Origins of Class Struggle in Louisiana* (Baton Rouge, 1939). Shugg showed that for a moment during and immediately after the Civil War the promise of a better existence floated before the eyes of Negroes and poor whites. It was not fulfilled, however, and the continuing depressed state of these people in the following decades caused them to join eagerly in the Populist movement.

C. Vann Woodward's *Reunion and Reaction: The Compromise of 1877 and the End of Reconstruction* (Boston, 1951), supported with a wealth of detail the position of previous authors who had spoken of an alliance between Northern and Southern conservatives to end the "cold war" that followed 1865. Part of the deal involved Southern votes for Hayes over Tilden and Congressional support for building Western railroads. The compromise, said Woodward, "revealed the party of Radical Reconstruction in alliance with ex-Rebels and ex-slaveholders; the party of emancipation and freedmen's rights abandoning the Negro to his former master." It assured the "dominant whites political autonomy and nonintervention in matters of race policy and promised them a share in the blessings of the new economic order."

The interest that was awakened in Southern history at the end of the last century has developed at an accelerated rate. Like students working in other fields, so too in this area scholars have invoked economic interpretations to clarify the history of the South. While more intense study has been given to the era of the Civil War than to any other period, some students went back to the early days of settlement to chart the fundamental factors in the evolution of Southern society up to that tragic conflict. Thus Avery O. Craven's *Soil Exhaustion as a Factor in the Agricultural History of Virginia and Maryland, 1606–1860* (Urbana, 1926) was a work of prime importance. Of more significance for agriculture as a whole was Lewis C. Gray's *History of Agriculture in the Southern United States to 1860* (2 vols., 1933), which pointed out, among other things, that slavery was not a dying institution on the eve of the war. This work was one of the finest collections of economic materials available to the historian. Part VII, "Geographical Expansion and Regional Development," was of particular significance for students of the generation preceding the Civil War. Robert R. Russel's *Economic Aspects of Southern Sectionalism, 1840–1861* (Urbana, 1923) and John G. Van Deusen's *Economic Bases of Disunion in South Carolina* (New York, 1928) detailed the interrelations between politics, agriculture, and finance.

The whole complex of Southern thinking in ante-bellum days revealed the erection of intellectual and psychological defenses for its way of life. W. S. Jenkins, in his *Pro-Slavery Thought in the Old South* (Chapel Hill, 1935), showed the development from apology to militant assertion that a slave society was the crown of civilization. Clement Eaton's *Freedom of Thought in the Old South* (Durham, N. C., 1940) indicated the growing constriction which choked that freedom in a society that was an anomaly in the Atlantic world of the nineteenth century. One of the strongest statements of the Southern view of the great crisis was Avery Craven's *The Coming of the Civil War* (New York, 1942).

Varied explanations—political, social, economic, ideological, and psychological—have been advanced to account for the war.[37] While the bitterness of Civil War antagonists was reflected in the books of their descendants to our own day, writers eventually emerged almost free of sectional patriotism. Historians, instead of concentrating upon constitutional differences or slavery as a cause of the war, emphasized, as did Charles and Mary Beard, economic forces, while others broadened their interpretation to speak of the diversity of civilizations as bringing on the "irrepressible conflict." In the revision that has been made of the history of the decade of the 1850's, Roy F. Nichols, in *Disruption of the Democracy* (New York, 1948), spoke of political rivalries, the sectionalization of parties, and hyperemotionalism leading up to the final break in 1861. Nichols drew especial attention to the effect of political developments within the states in shaping the national pattern. The figure of Douglas has been rescued from the despoilers, notably in the revealing studies of Frank H. Hodder and in the *Eve of Conflict: Stephen A. Douglas and the Needless War* (Boston, 1934) by George F. Milton. A distinguished survey of the prewar years, superseding

[37] See the excellent study by H. K. Beale, "What Historians Have Said About the Causes of the Civil War," in *Theory and Practice in Historical Study: A Report of the Committee on Historiography* (Social Science Research Council *Bulletin 54,* 1946).

Rhodes in many respects, was made by Allan Nevins in his *Ordeal of the Union* (2 vols., 1947) and *Emergence of Lincoln* (2 vols., 1950). While summarizing the best of previous findings, he added much that was unfamiliar on such important matters as the Compromise of 1850 and the role of Buchanan and Seward in the crucial winter of 1860.

Many studies of the states in war have been made in recent years, and through emphasis on such factors as states' rights and opposition to conscription, as well as the shortage of salt, the story of the failure of the Confederacy has been further clarified. In our age which has studied the history of the common man and has sought to understand the mass mind, it was natural to expect that, along with the generals, the rank and file would have their day. Bell I. Wiley, who wrote on the Negroes in wartime, presented the ordinary soldier in two informative works—*The Life of Johnny Reb* (1943) and *Life of Billy Yank* (1951). A useful synthesis of many of the new studies (which included the rehabilitation of Andrew Johnson) was made by James G. Randall, in his *Civil War and Reconstruction* (Boston, 1937).[38] Paul H. Buck's *The Road to Reunion* (1937) was a useful reminder that conciliatory forces were at work to make the nation one again.

A most ambitious project in Southern history, not yet completed, is *A History of the South.* Five volumes have already appeared, beginning with Wesley F. Craven's *The Southern Colonies in the Seventeenth Century.* These books are more than summaries of previous scholarship; they are, at their best, important contributions to knowledge. Thus Craven emphasized the relationship between the West Indies and the continental colonies to account for the culture pattern which developed in the South. Charles S. Sydnor, in *The Development of Southern Sectionalism 1819–1848,* stressed the influence of the debate over the Missouri Compromise in stimulating sectional thinking. E. Merton Coulter was the author of the two volumes on the Civil War and its aftermath—*The Confederate States of America 1861–1865* and *The South During*

[38] See F. L. Owsley, *State Rights in the Confederacy* (Chicago, 1925); A. B. Moore, *Conscription and Conflict in the Confederacy* (New York, 1924); Ella Lonn, *Salt as a Factor in the Confederacy* (New York, 1934); G. F. Milton, *The Age of Hate: Andrew Johnson and the Radicals* (New York, 1930); H. K. Beale, *The Critical Year: A Study of Andrew Johnson and Reconstruction* (New York, 1930); J. G. Randall, *Constitutional Problems under Lincoln* (New York, 1926); F. B. Simkins and R. H. Woody, *South Carolina During Reconstruction* (Chapel Hill, 1932); for critical comment see A. A. Taylor, "Historians of the Reconstruction," *Journal of Negro History* (January, 1938).

Reconstruction 1865–1877. Coulter was less successful than his colleagues in this project in freeing himself from sectional bias. This failing was particularly noticeable in the volume on Reconstruction, in which Coulter seemed to be under the necessity to defend the position of the "unreconstructed rebels."[39] One of the best works in the series was Woodward's *Origins of the New South 1877–1913*, for it explains, as no other volume does, the impact of a changing economy on the mind and map of the South. Woodward had earlier written a biography of *Tom Watson* (New York, 1938) which explained the foundering of popular leadership on the rock of racial intolerance. In no field of study is there greater vitality than in the history of the South, and her own universities are contributing largely to its vigorous growth.[40]

[39] See the astringent paper by J. H. Franklin, "Whither Reconstruction Historiography?" *Journal of Negro Education* (Fall, 1948), 446–61.

[40] See W. H. Stephenson, "The South Lives in History," *The Historical Outlook*, Vol. XXIII, No. 4 (April, 1932), 153–63. Obviously, only a small part of the vast literature on the pre-Civil War era can be mentioned here.

XIII

Biography

BIOGRAPHIES have always comprised a large part of the literary output in America. In colonial days they were often sketches of the lives of eminent clergymen, and in the early national period eulogistic prose celebrated the deeds of Revolutionary leaders. New Englanders, as George Bancroft once observed, were a documentary people; they left innumerable diaries and autobiographies. New Englanders, removed to other regions, retained the practice of keeping a personal record, and their descendants have followed the tradition. The mind of a typical, intelligent Puritan was disclosed in the diary of Samuel Sewall; the more cosmopolitan eighteenth-century spirit was fully revealed in the autobiography of Franklin.

All during the nineteenth century volumes of biography continued to flow from the press while periodicals also fed this interest in distinctive personalities. Nathan Sargent, a Whig (later Republican) journalist famous as "Oliver Oldschool," wrote his memories of *Public Men and Events 1817–1853* (2 vols., Philadelphia, 1875). His letters from Washington, with witty descriptions of Congressional proceedings, were widely published in Northern newspapers before the Civil War. A contemporary from Virginia, Henry A. Wise, left a narrative, *Seven Decades of the Union* (Philadelphia, 1872), which purported to cover the years 1790 to 1860, but it was mainly concerned with personalities of the Jacksonian period. Wise was a prominent figure in Virginia politics (he served as governor from 1855 to 1859), and his close association with John Tyler was reflected in his eulogistic treatment of the President.

Of first importance in biographical literature in the middle of the nineteenth century were the works of James Parton. He had a sound understanding of how biography should be written: "The art is to be short where the interest is small and long where the interest is great." He asked that biographers be forthright; we are ordinarily "too mild and forgiving," he told Bancroft; "we are so afraid of being savage, that we are apt to be soft."[1]

His first significant biography was *The Life and Times of Aaron Burr* (New York, 1858), which went far to rehabilitate the duelist whose memory had been execrated since the tragic death of Hamilton. The constructive aspects of Burr's career received their due recognition from Parton. In 1860 he brought out his *Life of Andrew Jackson* (3 vols.), which was his finest achievement. In his next work, *The Life and Times of Benjamin Franklin* (2 vols., New York, 1864), he reinforced the picture that Sparks had drawn of a versatile man, famed equally as a philosopher and statesman. Parton, always a democrat in his sympathies, was drawn to Jefferson, whom he warmly presented in a biography published in 1874.

Contrary to popular impression, Parton was not an uncritical worshiper of American democracy. He favored rather an aristocracy of intellect with democratic sympathies, which explained his natural attachment for Jefferson. As for Jackson, Parton remarked that, notwithstanding the good he had done, elevating him to power "was a mistake on the part of the people of the United States. The good which he effected has not continued, while the evil which he began remains, has grown more formidable . . . with regard to the corruptions and inefficiency of the government." In Parton's judgment, Jackson was a fighting man and "little more."

Subsequent biographers uniformly paid high tribute to the worth of Parton's works, which were based on sound research. Better lives of these subjects have been written since his day by students with more material at their disposal, but for a long time the popular conception of these departed figures was shaped by Parton's volumes.

The era of the Civil War contributed a number of biographical and autobiographical volumes of the leading figures of these years. That the reading public consumed a vast quantity of such material was attested to by the fact that one publishing house alone made over one

[1] M. E. Flower, *James Parton: The Father of Modern Biography* (Durham, 1951), 205.

million dollars from the publication of Civil War books.[2] Grant's *Memoirs,* the most important of this type of publication, and the reminiscences of his contemporaries John Sherman and James G. Blaine helped readers to understand something of the political history of the postwar decades. Grant's *Memoirs* (2 vols., New York, 1886) were written for the most part by Adam Badeau; Sherman's *Recollections* (New York, 1895) might well have benefited from such ghost writing. For a better understanding of many of the events of this period Edward L. Pierce wrote a *Memoir and Letters of Charles Sumner* (4 vols., 1877–93). This vast amorphous collection was the source of later studies of Sumner. The man who was acclaimed by abolitionists as their martyred hero was commemorated in Oswald Garrison Villard's *John Brown* (Boston, 1910). The author's inheritance of the antislavery tradition made him a sympathetic student of the abolitionist who had been alternately execrated and ecstatically praised.

Eighteenth-century figures still attracted the biographer, who frequently embalmed his subject in a monumental work running to two or three volumes of the conventional "life and times" pattern. Generally designed to indicate how much the subject of the biography had influenced the times, these works usually failed to show how the milieu had affected their hero. It was common, too, for a biographer to "write down" the colleagues of his subject in order to present the favored figure more advantageously. In these biographies there was rarely any attempt, artistically, to recreate the personality. We get no understanding of the inner man; whatever character analysis was attempted proved too often immature. The volumes that these biographers wrote have much of value to the historian, but as contributions to the art of biography they are negligible.

One of the more useful of these works, though incomplete, was William C. Rives' *Life and Times of James Madison* (3 vols., Boston, 1859–68). It was of the school of Marshall's earlier multivolumed *Washington,* in which the "life" seemed to be overwhelmed by the "times." Another of the same genre was *The Life and Public Services of Samuel Adams* (3 vols., Boston, 1865), by William V. Wells. Adams' efforts in behalf of the Revolution were given adequate recognition, particularly his contributions to the technique of revolution in the Committees of Correspondence. William W. Henry glowingly commemorated another

[2] R. U. Johnson, *Remembered Yesterdays* (Boston, 1923), 190.

Revolutionary figure, *Patrick Henry: Life, Correspondence, and Speeches* (3 vols., New York, 1891), although as biography Moses Coit Tyler's shorter work was to be preferred.

More skilled in its construction, and better written than these books, was *The Life of Albert Gallatin,* by Henry Adams. The biography was in one volume while the papers of the Secretary of the Treasury filled three additional volumes. Although Adams included much of the "times" in his narrative, his artistic sense enabled him to keep in the foreground the character of Gallatin, whose career and personality strongly attracted the biographer. Thomas Paine, a more rabid Republican than Gallatin, finally secured his just deserts at the hands of Moncure D. Conway, in 1892. Paine had been largely ignored or execrated because of the nineteenth-century reaction against his religious and social heterodoxy. "The filthy little atheist," so contemned by Theodore Roosevelt, was rehabilitated by Conway as the man who fired with a religious fervor the revolutionary zeal of Americans.

Figures of lesser prominence were also memorialized in careful biographies. Among the more valuable of these works was Charles J. Stillé's *Life and Times of John Dickinson* (Philadelphia, 1891), which reminded a forgetful people of Dickinson's writings (especially the *Pennsylvania Farmer*) in behalf of rebellious America in the 1760's. Two other useful studies of this Revolutionary generation were by Kate M. Rowland: *The Life of George Mason* (2 vols., New York, 1892) and the *Life of Charles Carroll of Carrollton* (2 vols., New York, 1898). Mason's work in drawing up the Virginia Bill of Rights, the model for later documents, was strongly emphasized; in the Carroll biography the Roman Catholic signer of the Declaration was presented as a warm and tolerant human being.

Biographical writing in America toward the close of the nineteenth century was well represented by the series edited by John T. Morse, *American Statesmen* (39 vols.). It was Morley's English "Men of Letters" which suggested a like work on American statesmen. Morse himself wrote five of the biographies, including those of John Adams and John Quincy Adams. Sometimes editorial plans went astray; Carl Schurz, for example, angered Morse by turning in two volumes instead of one on Henry Clay, but the editor learned to like Schurz's work, and his judgment was vindicated by the approbation that favored it. Morse had difficulty in getting Charles Francis Adams to do the biography of his father, minister to England, but the son finally agreed, and the volume was very well received. In fact the series in general was both a scholarly and a commercial success.[3]

A favorite with biographers for many years has been Franklin. Several authors in the twentieth century have done very well with him: William C. Bruce in *Benjamin Franklin, Self-Revealed* (2 vols., New York, 1917), Bernard Faÿ in *Franklin, The Apostle of Modern Times* (Boston, 1929), and Carl Van Doren in *Benjamin Franklin* (New York, 1938). A skillful arrangement of Franklin's writings made Bruce's work something of a continuation of the autobiography, but Bruce did not forego the function of a critical biographer. Faÿ's volume was a clever dissection of Franklin's intellectual growth and showed him evolving from provincialism to a cosmopolitanism that had no superior in the eighteenth century. Van Doren's work rescued Franklin from biographers who saw in him mainly the personification of bourgeois virtues of prudence and thrift, and portrayed him in the full richness of his engaging personality and magnificent versatility.

Franklin was a bridge between America and France; Lafayette was a bond between France and the New World. Lafayette found his most learned biographer in Louis R. Gottschalk, who brought to his study long familiarity with the eighteenth century. Four volumes have been published, carrying the story to 1789. Gottschalk has challenged many traditions about the Franco-American hero and altered many interpretations of his career, explaining, for example, that he went to America not out of idealism (which came later), but from dissatisfaction with conditions at home, a desire for glory, and hatred for England. The first three volumes, said Gottschalk, told of the making of a liberal; the fourth emphasized the influence of Washington and Jefferson on Lafayette, and through him, upon France.

A product of mature scholarship and ripe understanding was John S. Bassett's *Life of Andrew Jackson* (2 vols., New York, 1911). Bassett's familiarity with the history of the period gave to this work an authenticity that more lightly freighted biographies lacked. He used a great mass of Jackson's papers (later edited by himself and J. Franklin Jameson) that had not been seen by earlier biographers and from this source shed new light on his public and private career. Much more interesting-

[3] J. T. Morse, "Incidents Connected with the American Statesmen Series," Mass. Hist. Soc. *Proceedings,* Vol. LXIV (1932), 370–88.

ly written, with a fine sense of dramatic values, was Marquis James' study of Jackson.

Jackson's combative spirit vented itself against many opponents, and high on his list of disliked people was Calhoun. A number of scholars, including Dodd, long ago suggested that Calhoun's evolution from nationalist to sectionalist was gradual and that he was generally moderate compared with the more extreme Southern fire-eaters. Charles M. Wiltse's *John C. Calhoun* (3 vols., 1944–51) was a vigorous portrayal of the man who, more than any one else, dominated the thinking of the South for a whole generation. He threw his weight consistently to the side of Union, said Wiltse; his real intent was "to consolidate a pressure bloc whose aim was to secure concessions from the stronger interest." He sought "security for his class above all other considerations."

The great rival of Calhoun, Henry Clay, had to wait a long time for a biographer more learned and better balanced than Schurz. Then two works came out in the same year, 1937, Bernard Mayo's *Henry Clay: Spokesman of the New West,* and Glyndon Van Deusen's *The Life of Henry Clay*. Mayo's well-written volume, the first in a proposed trilogy, carried the story to the War of 1812, emphasizing the nationalism of Clay. The Kentuckian had an almost irresistible appeal; "neither in public nor in private," said Bancroft, "did he know how to be dull." Van Deusen's study, a complete biography in one volume, was a thorough piece of research. Clay came not from a poverty-stricken background, as legend had it, but from wealth. In his earlier years in politics he was a spokesman for the West, but he soon transformed himself into a nationalist. His presidential ambitions affected his whole political career to so great an extent, indeed, that he became a liability rather than an asset to his party after 1840.

Van Deusen's immersion in the materials of nineteenth-century political history enabled him to give a convincing portrayal of the noted political boss, *Thurlow Weed, Wizard of the Lobby* (Boston, 1947), whose role in New York and national affairs was of the first importance. Van Deusen has also completed a biography of the colorful editor Horace Greeley. Thus, in his three characters—Greeley, the newspaper man, Weed the operator behind the scenes, and Clay, the politician in the open—the biographer has presented three of the powerful forces in American politics—public opinion, the unpublicized wire-puller, and the highly publicized political personality.

With the firmer establishment of biography as a literary form, authors more consciously shaped their narratives to dramatize the lives, as well as analyzing the causes and nature of their development. Selected incidents in the lives of individuals were chosen as indices of growth or decay, and the biographer sought to penetrate the innermost recesses of his subject's soul. Though often these psychological expeditions meant groping in darkness, sometimes they were successful. Where materials were plentiful and the talent at hand adequate to use them, contributions of the first importance to biography were made. Such have been Beveridge's *Marshall* and *Lincoln,* Sandburg's *Lincoln,* Nevins' *Cleveland* and *Hamilton Fish,* Freeman's *Lee* and *Washington,* Malone's *Jefferson,* and Brant's *Madison.*

The most popular American subject has been Lincoln, his elusive personality exercising a continuing attraction for the biographer. The conflicting legends that grew up about him even before his death made the task of the biographer a difficult one indeed. The law partner of Lincoln, William H. Herndon, early began collecting material on his friend's life. In collaboration with Jesse W. Weik, in 1889, he brought out *Abraham Lincoln: The True Story of a Great Life* (3 vols.). Herndon had said that Lincoln's fame would not suffer from the truth, and therefore he would tell an unvarnished story, much of which had unfolded itself before his own eyes. Herndon gave color and vitality to the Lincoln portrait when it was in danger of being retouched beyond recognition. The material on Lincoln as a lawyer and a husband was an original contribution of value, but that portion of Herndon's biography on Lincoln as president was of minor importance. The relations between Lincoln and Herndon were made clear in a biography of the latter by David Donald.

While Herndon was gathering material on the life of Lincoln, others were also engaged in the same task. Two former secretaries of the President, John G. Nicolay and John Hay, who had lived in the White House, wrote their tribute from the fullness of their love for Lincoln. Hay had once told Herndon that Lincoln was the greatest character since Christ, and thus we may readily understand the adoration of the biographer. Hay had kept a diary which in sprightly, clever language told many of the secrets of the war years. The work of the two secretaries, which came out in 1890, was called *Abraham Lincoln, a History* (10 vols.). Hay told Charles Francis Adams that he and Nicolay had not "set down a single fact from our personal recollection, nor in the course of those ten volumes did we quote one word of which we had not a written memorandum made at the time."[4] The work was of especial value for its record of the impact of the war on the White House and its revelation of many events behind the scenes in the capital. While the history was enriched by the aid of Robert Todd Lincoln, who allowed the authors to use his father's papers, the son's editing of the manuscript marred the liveliness of the writing and "prettified" the portrait of his forebears.

Lord Charnwood's biography of Lincoln, in 1917, was a revelation to American scholars, for it made intelligible his growth and his awareness of the Civil War as a supreme test for democracy. A work of keen insight was Nathaniel W. Stephenson's *Lincoln* (Indianapolis, 1922). Stephenson had already published a masterly essay on Lincoln in the *Cambridge History of American Literature,* which analyzed the development of his mind and literary style. The biography emphasized particularly the mental growth of Lincoln in the later years of his life, and opened new paths for the analytical biographer. In the thirty years after Stephenson's volume appeared, numerous specialized studies of Lincoln were undertaken, based in part on hitherto sealed papers and revised estimates of his contemporaries, which made necessary a different interpretation of that great figure. Benjamin P. Thomas, taking advantage of the researches made by an army of investigators and adding his own deep knowledge of the original materials, published an excellent one-volume life of Lincoln, in 1952.

Lincoln might have had his greatest biographer in Beveridge had the author lived to complete his task. Unfortunately the Lincoln biography was left unfinished, but we have at least a part of this work in addition to the finished achievement of his *John Marshall.*

ALBERT J. BEVERIDGE

Although the name of Albert J. Beveridge stands high in the history of American political life, it is probable that his reputation as a biographer is of greater significance. Even during the exciting days while he was helping to create the Progressive party, Beveridge had begun serious

[4] Tyler Dennett, *John Hay: From Poetry to Politics* (New York, 1933), 137. The *Lincoln* had appeared serially in the *Century Magazine,* for which the authors were paid $50,000; book royalties were extra.

work on his biography of Marshall, and he was fearful that politics would distract him from it. "The one real ambition of my life—the writing of a Life of Chief Justice Marshall," he said, would be "completely defeated."[5] In originally planning the *Marshall,* Beveridge thought of a one-volume work, modeled after F. S. Oliver's treatment of Alexander Hamilton. His conception of it gradually developed to dimensions that no hurried treatment could satisfy. Eventually the original idea of a short biography began to appear ludicrously inadequate, and Beveridge soon found himself allotting two volumes to the period before Marshall's Supreme Court service. Another two volumes would be needed for a history and analysis of the great decisions.

In 1917 the first volumes appeared, and two years later the remainder of the Marshall was published. The counsel of leading students of American history—Channing, Jameson, W. C. Ford, Beard, and Dodd, as well as Justice Holmes—had helped Beveridge in his research. Thus, when the volumes were issued, they bore the stamp of authoritative scholarship, and the work was hailed as among the great biographies in the language. The range of learning was wide and deep and the style had unusual vigor. Viscount Haldane wrote appreciatively to Beveridge: "How he [Marshall] developed that Constitution into what was essential for the growth of a very great nation, you have made appear before us. In your hands, the task of Marshall, as well as his solution, grows as a living growth."[6] One serious blemish marred the work—Beveridge's anti-Jeffersonian bias. Belonging to the Federalist school, he championed a strong central government, and he disliked Jefferson personally. Although critical readers of his manuscript tried to dissuade Beveridge from so harsh a treatment of Jefferson, he was adamant. Some time later, however, he admitted that if he were to rewrite the *Marshall,* he would be less certain in his criticisms of Jefferson.

Beveridge believed that Marshall's national thinking stemmed from his service in the Revolutionary Army, and that it was further strengthened by his term in the Virginia legislature. In a discussion of the debate on the Federal Constitution. Beveridge pointed out that Marshall in these arguments stated the elements of most of his "immortal Nationalist opinions." The first volume, although it contained a chapter of unnecessary length on the "Life of the People: Community Isolation," was writ-

[5] C. G. Bowers, *Beveridge and the Progressive Era* (Boston, 1932), 449.
[6] *Ibid.*, 560.

ten with more spirit and interest than the others. It was very dramatic and, in his pages on the constitutional debate in Virginia, Beveridge made an important contribution to historical literature as well as to biography. The biographer noted the obvious relationship between the thought of Hamilton and Marshall: "Upon Hamilton's constitutional doctrine John Marshall was to place the seal of finality." The chapters on Marshall's part in the X Y Z affair revealed with great clarity how his experiences abroad fortified his American nationalism.

When writing of Marshall's decisions, Beveridge's emphasis was as much upon their quality as acts of statesmanship as it was upon their character as judicial verdicts; "they were nothing less than state papers and of the first rank." In order to understand the opinions in relation to contemporary events, the biographer found it necessary to include much history. The final volume, 1815–35, was subtitled "The Building of the Nation"; in writing of the effects of the Dartmouth College decision, Beveridge spoke of its stimulus to the creation of corporations and the alignment of powerful business interests on the side of nationalism. The opponents of Marshall's nationalism—Spencer Roane, of Virginia, for example—were treated with scant respect. In several instances the biographer noted the similarity between the nationalist views of Marshall and Lincoln, and in the decision of *Cohens* v. *Va.* the Chief Justice blazed "the way for Abraham Lincoln." In describing Marshall's character, appearance, and intellect, Beveridge wrote that "we must imagine a person very much like Abraham Lincoln." Thus the choice of the author's next subject seemed inevitable—the later exponent of nationalism.

With great energy Beveridge turned to the *Lincoln,* and very shortly he made disconcerting discoveries—that people were unwilling to give him access to papers, and that there was a mythical and a real Lincoln. Writing to Channing, he said, after a few months' research: "It is already clear that the Lincoln of youth, early and middle manhood showed few signs of the Lincoln of the second inaugural."[7] The more he dug into the material for the *Lincoln,* the greater did his problems become. He was soon convinced that no thoroughgoing biography had yet been written, and it was clear that the *Lincoln* would be far more difficult than the *Marshall.*

At first Beveridge had intended to pass lightly over the years before

[7] *Ibid.,* 565.

Lincoln entered politics; then he found he had to lay a firmer foundation for the later years than existing biographies could give him. Channing, who was fearful lest Beveridge might not reach the period of Lincoln's later political life, urged him on. "Lincoln needs someone schooled in affairs and the wiles of politicians to penetrate under his mask and under their masks and tell the truth," he wrote, adding, "You are the man to do it."[8]

In the vast amount of research that went into the biography, Beveridge learned things about his subject that made him sorry he had undertaken it. He had not the spirit that loved "debunking," but facing the facts as he found them, he could only conclude that Lincoln's legislative career in Illinois was shifty and opportunistic. To his friend Worthington C. Ford, Beveridge expressed his disappointment: "I wish to the Lord he could have gone straight forward about something or other. Of all uncertain, halting and hesitating conduct, his takes the prize."[9] When he finally came to write the biography, Beveridge said that Lincoln possessed in earlier years "the characteristics of the national politician, a type of which he was to become, excepting only Jefferson, the supreme example."

In the search for the real Lincoln, Beveridge rehabilitated Douglas, who was the object of much defamation by Lincoln worshipers. "It becomes clearer and clearer to me," said Beveridge to Channing, "that the literary Lincolnites had almost a hijacker conspiracy against Douglas—and against any other man of power who for any cause happened to run counter to their hero; and especially is this true of Douglas."[10] The more he studied the material, the firmer grew Beveridge's conviction that Douglas was a great man. Most of the teachings of his youth on abolitionism and the South were "bunk," concluded Beveridge, and were born out of political propaganda. But it was a sorrowful task for Beveridge to write the pages that tore to shreds the fabricated history learned in childhood. Steadily he plodded through legislative journals, newspapers, manuscripts, judicial decisions, and other material, until a Lincoln hitherto unknown gradually emerged. When the first two volumes were nearly ready for publication, Beveridge died. In 1928 *Abraham Lincoln, 1809–1858* appeared, under the editorial supervision of Worthington C. Ford.

[8] *Ibid.*, 567. [9] *Ibid.*, 569, January 28, 1925.
[10] *Ibid.*, 571, May 21, 1925.

With infinite care Beveridge had picked his way through the tangled trail of Lincolniana, making his two volumes longer than they needed to be because of his anxiety to present all the conflicting evidence. The biographer, however, had worked a clearing in the half-light, and reluctantly arrived at his conclusions. "With that strange mingling of caution, secretiveness and craft, which so confounded his opponents and puzzled his supporters in after years," said Beveridge, referring to the Lincoln of 1828–30, the latter "kept to himself his changed or changing conviction and his purposes." After all his research, Beveridge thought that perhaps no one ever understood Lincoln, "or ever will understand him." At least two decades had passed "before Lincoln showed much, if any, concern about slavery. Never the apostle of a cause, he was to become the perfect interpreter of public thought and feeling and so the instrument of events." The same idea Beveridge expressed again in speaking of Lincoln as one who, "by instinct as well as mind . . . understood and responded to the sinuosities, twists and contradictions through which a democracy expresses itself."

Herndon, Lincoln's younger law partner, was an abolitionist, and this fact, said Beveridge, "is of the greatest possible moment in the development of Lincoln's opinions, and of the origin of memorable language spoken by him." As for Lincoln himself, few people in the North were more familiar with Southern thought than he, "nor did any Northern man who was opposed to slavery on principle have a more comprehending sympathy with the Southern people in their racial situation."

In tracing the genealogy of Lincoln's ideas, Beveridge noted that in the address at Springfield, 1854, were "all the ideas, or the germs of them, that Lincoln expressed thereafter and up to the time he wrote the Emancipation Proclamation." Thus Beveridge traced the slow, halting development of Lincoln's mind up through the memorable debates with Douglas in 1858. This part of the work had been planned to end with Lincoln's inauguration, 1861; only with the sudden cessation of the biography was it fully revealed to the world of scholarship how great a loss was caused by Beveridge's death. The Lincoln of the war years would probably have been a noble monument in the hands of Beveridge, who had looked forward anxiously to the re-creation of that glorious figure.

The Lincoln portrait has been painted by many hands—the romantic, the realist, the impressionist. Readers, it seemed, could never get enough of their folk hero. Nicolay and Hay's serial in the *Century Magazine* in the 1880's had been very successful; Ida Tarbell's articles in *McClure's* in the 1890's added 100,000 new readers within three months. In time her work appeared in book form, and for the rest of her life she remained an ardent student of Lincoln. Miss Tarbell uncovered new facts about his early life; it was she who first noted, for example, the significance of his frontier environment in shaping his character. She was, said Thomas, "the pioneer scientific investigator whose work foretold the revelation of Lincoln as he really was."[11]

Professional historians were slow to turn their attention to Lincoln, believing possibly that the field had been exhausted. James G. Randall, of the University of Illinois, disabused fellow academicians of this notion, reminding them of large unworked areas in the Lincoln story, particularly the period of his presidency. Randall himself published three volumes on *Lincoln the President* (1945–52), carrying the story through the climactic year, 1863. Randall showed that Lincoln was not the crude rail splitter and country lawyer of cherished legend, but a man with a much broader culture than that of most neighbors and a successful lawyer retained by big business. Famous episodes in Lincoln's life—such as the Ann Rutledge romance—were reinterpreted or even rejected on the basis of insufficient evidence. Mary Todd Lincoln was handled much more sympathetically than by earlier biographers.

The historian spoke of a generation blundering into Civil War; and he was rather harsh in his treatment of antislavery elements. In Randall's narrative of the war years, it was pointed out that among Lincoln's sorest trials were those caused by the Northern radicals. These marplots demanded, and were given, the scalp of McClellan, whose generalship was estimated at a higher value by Randall than by other students of the Civil War. In this work the international aspects of the war were given extended treatment, especially the close ties between Lincoln and English liberals. Basic to the victory of the North was the continuance of England's neutrality. That this hands-off policy prevailed was due largely to Lincoln's skill in cultivating support among British workingmen and Whig champions of American democracy.

Randall's work, important though it is as an instructive example of historical revision, was less a biography than a series of episodes with

[11] B. P. Thomas, *Portrait for Posterity: Lincoln and his Biographers* (New Brunswick, 1947), 201.

which Lincoln was connected. In it the professor treated the episodes as problems to be solved by the seminar method of historical research. It belonged to the school of Edward Channing, and was a far cry from an artistic re-creation of a life filled with human weaknesses and moral grandeur.

Carl Sandburg attempted that re-creation in a prose-epic of six volumes (1926–39), two for the prairie years and four for the war years. The vast work reflected the color and vitality of the biographer; "the folklore Lincoln, the maker of stories, the stalking and elusive Lincoln," said Sandburg, "is a challenge for any artist." Out of what seems an amorphous mass of material, there gradually emerged the picture of Lincoln among his own people who understood him best. Sandburg was interested in Lincoln as he lived and moved among his contemporaries; always the biographer kept his sights on the image of Lincoln as it was reflected in the heart of the people. (See for example in *The War Years,* III, chap. 56, "Lincoln's Laughter—and His Religion," and chap. 57, "The Man Had Become the Issue.") And in the triumphant chapter "A Tree Is Best Measured When It's Down," Sandburg showed how the glory of Lincoln was acclaimed at home and throughout the world.

Sandburg's biography was easy to criticize for its obvious slips, and it irritated the academician by its apparent slipshod procedure. But no one has recreated the contemporary Illinois scene or the Civil War White House with greater verisimilitude. Sandburg wrote not for the specialist but for Mr. Everyman, and through the magic of his artistry he placed the twentieth-century reader in the setting of Lincoln's world, letting him enjoy his laughter or taste the bitterness of the President's agony.

Figures from the colonial past have attracted comparatively few biographers in recent years. Three of the best studies were Kenneth B. Murdock's *Increase Mather, the Foremost Puritan* (Cambridge, 1925), Samuel H. Brockunier's *The Irrepressible Democrat, Roger Williams* (New York, 1940), and Perry Miller's *Jonathan Edwards* (New York, 1949). In a stimulating reinterpretation Murdock freed Mather from many of the aspersions aimed at him by unfriendly critics and showed him to be one of the progressive intellects of his generation. Brockunier's book was designed to explain the drive toward democracy in the seventeenth century in the person of Roger Williams, and the economic and social forces which hampered the growth of libertarianism. Miller's book was less a biography than a study in the evolution of a mind. His deep knowledge of New England culture enabled him to place Edwards more surely in proper relationship to his age, and in this revaluation the personality of the great preacher seems less oppressive. Edwards was more than a theologian, said Miller; "he was one of America's five or six major artists who happened to work with ideas instead of with poems or novels." A well-written and dependable life of Edwards was written by Ola Winslow (1940).

A character of different breed was depicted in Arthur Pound's and Richard E. Day's *Johnson of the Mohawks: A Biography of Sir William Johnson* (New York, 1930). Johnson had a remarkable career in New York in strengthening the links of the British Empire in the eighteenth century, and the romance of his life with the Indians lent itself to a lightness of touch rarely adopted by biographers of colonial personalities. Esther Forbes, in her study of *Paul Revere and the World He Lived In* (Boston, 1942), made her central character a believable personality, on and off his horse. Skilled craftsman in metals and ardent worker in the cause of independence, Revere and his dramatic story were celebrated in a swiftly moving prose which caught the swirl and passion of the Revolutionary era.

Outstanding personalities of that period, notably Jefferson, have never wanted for biographers. Gilbert Chinard, a leading student of Franco-American intellectual relations, was thoroughly familiar with the manuscript materials on Jefferson, and from these and the printed sources (many of which he has himself edited) he wrote an enthusiastic study of *Thomas Jefferson, the Apostle of Americanism* (Boston, 1929). Jefferson was the American who, in European eyes, best typified his country's ideals. Chinard also wrote a study of *Honest John Adams* (Boston, 1933), which, as befitted the subject, was a more restrained bit of writing than the *Jefferson*. Bringing to the center of the stage this man whose contributions to American life have been inadequately appreciated was a valuable service to history as well as to the name of Adams. Catharine Drinker Bowen's *John Adams and the American Revolution* (Boston, 1950) was a vivid reconstruction of his earlier life, though the liberties taken by the author in inventing dialogue and imputing unverified thoughts to her cast of characters awaken doubts as to the validity of this technique. In Miss Bowen's skillful hands (she steeped herself in colonial history) there was no serious distortion of persons and events, but the professional historian remains skeptical of the wisdom of this procedure.[12]

The great emphasis in our own generation on propaganda as an instrument of social indoctrination naturally influenced a reconsideration of personalities and events in the Revolutionary era. Philip Davidson covered the whole subject in his *Propaganda and the American Revolution 1763–1783* (Chapel Hill, 1941). Davidson examined more thoroughly than previous writers the machinery of propaganda, especially in the schools and newspapers. The individual particularly worth studying in this connection was, of course, Sam Adams. Biographers have drawn heavily upon psychology and investigations of crowd behavior to explain why Adams became a Revolutionist and how he influenced people; an excellent example of such a work was John C. Miller's *Sam Adams, Pioneer in Propaganda* (Boston, 1936).

Next to Lincoln, Jefferson seems to hold the greatest attraction for biographers. The vast bulk of materials he left for posterity (now being edited on a lavish scale by Julian P. Boyd), the intriguing shadings of his character, and the significance of his ideas for a world oppressed by totalitarianism have all combined to invigorate studies of the great Virginian. The most comprehensive biography, making critical use of the new material that has been uncovered and presenting Jefferson in all the richness of his astonishing versatility, is Dumas Malone's work. Two volumes have already appeared which carry the narrative to 1792.

Traditional estimates of Jefferson were challenged by Malone: Thus, "to describe him as an agrarian is to employ an insufficient term and to rob him of part of his universality." Again: "The chief effect of Jefferson's stay in France upon his political ideas was to confirm him in the ones he held before he went there." Jefferson, indeed, was not as pro-French as hitherto imagined, he was really pro-American. Malone found, in the course of his study, that Washington's stature was enhanced, while Hamilton's was diminished. The latter, said the biographer, "lusted for personal as well as national power." Jefferson was "far more disposed to battle for principles and policies than for his own interests." To those who were inclined to scoff at Jefferson as an impractical theorist, Malone retorted that he was "a statesman who effected a distinctive combination of idealism with common sense."

[12] See Miss Bowen's *The Writing of Biography* (Boston, 1950) for an interesting exposition of her methods.

Jefferson's successor in the presidency, James Madison, long overshadowed by his more famous contemporary, has been brought forward by recent biographers to occupy a more prominent position among the front rank of the nation's illustrious men. Adrienne Koch, by the very title of her work *Jefferson and Madison: The Great Collaboration* (New York, 1950), suggested that Madison was not, as conventionally believed, the junior partner in initiating and carrying out policies, but rather a co-worker on equal terms. Irving Brant's large-scale biography (of which three volumes have been published, taking the narrative to 1800) is particularly insistent in stressing this interpretation. "Among all the men who shaped the present government of the United States of America," said Brant, "the one who did the most is known the least." He granted that Madison's achievements at the Constitutional Convention were adequately recognized, but other, later periods of his career, he argued, have been misunderstood. Brant's work, when it moves on to cover Madison's career as secretary of state and president, will offer a different interpretation of these years than is to be found in the classic volumes of Henry Adams.

A chief figure on the Federalist side, John Jay, long neglected by students, was restored to the position of eminence granted him by his own contemporaries in an excellent biography (1935) by Frank Monaghan. Jay was a very distinguished contributor to the welfare of the early Republic, and in the public mind he was associated with Washington and Hamilton as one of the outstanding men in the Federalist party.

It was Jay's misfortune to be associated with a treaty which was disliked, thus attaching to himself a clouded reputation in history. Americans ordinarily have not been sufficiently appreciative of the services to their country of their diplomats (except Franklin) or their public servants whose concern was international relations. Samuel Flagg Bemis has done more than anyone else to correct this shortsightedness through his many volumes in diplomatic history and his editing of the series on American secretaries of state. One of his best works was *John Quincy Adams and the Foundations of American Foreign Policy* (New York, 1949). It was not so much a biography of Adams as it was a study of his diplomatic achievements. "More than any other man of his time," said Bemis, "he was privileged to gather together, formulate and practice the fundamentals of American foreign policy—self-determination, independence, noncolonization, nonintervention, nonentanglement in

European politics, Freedom of the Seas, freedom of commerce—and to set them deep in the soil of the Western Hemisphere."

It might be that Bemis, influenced as he was by his own critical attitude to much of American foreign policy in recent years, overemphasized Adams' isolationism. Leaving that aside, there could be no doubt about the mastery of the subject revealed in this volume, nor could there be dissent from the estimate that Adams "grasped the essentials of American policy and the position of the United States in the world more surely than any other man of his time."

Though in his earlier years Adams was an ardent believer in "Manifest Destiny" (the phrase came later), he lived to become one of the strongest opponents of expansionism, especially if he suspected it was for more slave territory. While Adams was indicting the slave power, a vast area in the Southwest, Texas, won her independence from Mexico and then sought admission to the Union. Two of the noted figures in this period of Texas history, Houston and Austin, were fortunate in their biographers. The romantic figure of Sam Houston was presented in a racily written narrative, *The Raven* (Indianapolis, 1929), by Marquis James. The character of Houston was shown developing under the stress and strain of Tennessee politics and frontier conflict until he became one of the dominant personalities of his generation. In its entirety James' work was beautifully formed. Houston's defeated rival for the presidency of the new Republic of Texas was Austin, the builder of the American colony in the Southwest. It was Austin's statesmanship which made possible the establishment and continuance of the new community. Eugene C. Barker, the leading student of this area, wrote a scholarly biography of *Stephen F. Austin, Founder of Texas, 1793–1836* (Dallas, 1925).

Houston, unlike many other Southern leaders, was opposed to secession. The growth of the secessionist spirit in the mind and heart of a versatile Virginian was clearly pictured in *Edmund Ruffin* (New York, 1932), by Avery Craven. A distinguished reformer, interested particularly in better agricultural methods, Ruffin's character was representative of the increasing number of individuals who were clamoring for Southern independence. Another reformer of a different stripe, a militant abolitionist and champion of social and intellectual progress, was brilliantly portrayed in Henry Steele Commager's *Theodore Parker* (Boston, 1936). No American was more aware of the spirit of his time than was Parker as he blasted away at obscurantism and conservatism.

Claude M. Fuess wrote several careful biographies of nineteenth-century statesmen. His *Life of Caleb Cushing* (2 vols., New York, 1923) helped make clearer the role of this "scholar statesman" in domestic and foreign affairs. Cushing was an unpopular but courageous man whose diplomatic counsel to the government was of high value. Fuess was also the author of a scholarly and very readable biography of *Daniel Webster* (2 vols., Boston, 1930). The biographer then turned his attention to *Carl Schurz, Reformer* (New York, 1932), who was close in spirit to the New England critics of American life in the period of the Civil War and Reconstruction. The evolution of the young German radical into a mature man fighting in behalf of liberal principles was sketched with sympathy and an understanding of the historical background.

The place of many political leaders has been reassessed in numerous biographies in recent years, notably in a series edited by Allan Nevins. An outstanding work was that by Henry F. Pringle, *Theodore Roosevelt* (New York, 1931). Pringle stripped Roosevelt of much of the glamour with which he had been invested by uncritical biographers. Roosevelt's contemporaries loomed up much larger than they appeared when the blustering President held the center of the stage. A phase of the Roosevelt story inadequately handled by Pringle was filled in by George E. Mowry, *Theodore Roosevelt and the Progressive Movement* (Madison, 1946). Mowry made the interesting point that Roosevelt's "paternalistic philosophy of government was not agrarian but urban in its appeal. He was supported in the West not because of his New Nationalism but in spite of it." In Pringle's *Life and Times of William Howard Taft* (2 vols., New York, 1939), Roosevelt's successor was revealed to be an abler individual than the idolaters of "Teddy" made him out to be. With less noise than Roosevelt, he sought to control big business and monopoly.

A distinguished colleague of Roosevelt and Taft (they were known to one another as the "three musketeers") was given his rightful due in *Elihu Root* (2 vols., New York, 1938) by Philip C. Jessup. The writer made clear the importance of Root's tenure in the offices of secretary of war and secretary of state, though some readers thought Jessup too reticent in treating his career as a corporation lawyer. The familiar characterization of Root as a "cold and ruthless" man was said to be a myth invented by hostile critics. Another political figure, high in the councils of Theodore Roosevelt's administration, John Hay, was properly appraised in a volume (1933) by Tyler Dennett. Dennett showed the significant part played by Hay in shaping foreign policy at the turn of the century, and he credited him with achievements which had hitherto been attributed to Roosevelt. In David S. Muzzey's thorough and unbiased biography of James G. Blaine (New York, 1934) the idol of an earlier generation strutted before the reader once more, but the tarnish that his reputation suffered in life will not wear off in death.

The two great leaders of the Democratic party in the twentieth century, Woodrow Wilson and Franklin D. Roosevelt, have sat for many portraits. The most comprehensive, though not the most critical, study of Wilson was Ray Stannard Baker's large work (8 vols., 1927–39); the author was probably too close to Wilson to write with complete freedom. Later students were not thus inhibited; Arthur S. Link, to name one, was able freely to reinterpret Wilson's emergence into New Jersey politics and his nomination in 1912. Link's biography, when completed (as yet only one volume has been published), should make an important contribution to the literature on Wilson. A leading spokesman of the middle class in twentieth-century America told his own story in William Allen White's *Autobiography,* while a more comprehensive narrative was presented by Walter Johnson in *William Allen White's America* (New York, 1947).

Certain personalities, notably Jefferson and Lincoln, have stimulated research and publication on so vast a scale as to suggest the creation of an industry. To them must be added the name of Franklin D. Roosevelt. As yet many of the publications which deal with him and his administration are so partisan in tone that one might suppose he was running for a fifth term. The best of the work already published on this remarkable era is, however, sufficiently sound to guarantee it long life. Outstanding is Robert E. Sherwood's *Roosevelt and Hopkins* (New York, 1948), for it is skillfully constructed and written with the dramatic power to be expected of a leading playwright. The large-scale dimensions of the Roosevelt story are indicated in the plans of Frank Freidel. The first of several projected volumes has been published,

Franklin D. Roosevelt: The Apprenticeship (Boston, 1952). Freidel's work reveals careful workmanship, and it is not the fault of the author if the story of an apprenticeship is not as interesting as that of a period when an art has been mastered.

ALLAN NEVINS

Allan Nevins is one of the most productive historians and biographers in the United States. By editing the diaries of John Quincy Adams, Philip Hone, and President Polk, he has made available to a large audience publications that were out of print or otherwise difficult to secure. Alone, or in collaboration with others, he has edited other documents, including the lengthy diary of George Templeton Strong (4 vols.), a New Yorker of the nineteenth century. Nevins has written an informative volume on the American states during the Revolution, but his more concentrated attention has been given to the Civil War period and later. His four volumes on the years leading up to the war have outmoded Rhodes' treatment of this era. He wrote a life of Frémont which attempted to hold the balance between the excessive praise and detraction of earlier biographers. Nevins included as much of the account of the period of expansion as was relevant to the career of the pathfinder. The biographer's use of unpublished sources enabled him to shed new light on the careers of his subjects and also to place a number of events in a broader setting. For example, in his *Grover Cleveland: A Study in Courage* (New York, 1932), we are given a new understanding of the President's relationship to the Pullman strike and also his part in the Venezuela affair.

The theme of Cleveland's courage was constantly kept before the reader, who was reminded that the President's greatness lay "in typical rather than unusual qualities. He had no endowments that thousands of men do not have. He possessed honesty, courage, firmness, independence, and common sense. But he possessed them in a degree that others did not." Cleveland will live in history, said Nevins, "as a strong man, a man of character." In a period of low morality in business and public affairs, Cleveland's rugged honesty and firm attachment to principles invigorated the American people: "His breach with Tammany caught the public imagination as nothing else could. The groping moral forces that were slowly gathering strength below the surface, and were ready to break forth in a powerful movement, demanded a moral hero; and the spectacle of the stolid, stubborn Cleveland smiting Tammany without thought of the consequences appealed to it."

In his *Abram S. Hewitt, with Some Account of Peter Cooper* (New York, 1935), Nevins again showed how, by a judicious use of private papers, familiar events might be placed in new perspective. Among the episodes which were reinterpreted in this volume was the election of 1876.

Hamilton Fish, Grant's secretary of state and one of the outstanding figures in the period after the Civil War, stood fully revealed in one of Nevins' finest biographies. Making skillful use of Fish's lengthy diary, which was kept during the eight years that the Secretary held office, Nevins was able to clarify many events of Grant's administration hitherto incompletely known. It was the great task of Fish to prevent Grant from being embroiled in foreign complications over Cuba and Santo Domingo and to restrain Charles Sumner from wrecking the diplomatic negotiations between the United States and Great Britain. In the second administration Fish moved among a gang of intriguers who had the President almost completely under their control. Although more than once the Secretary sought release from office, he was luckily not permitted to resign: "Again and again he saved the government from misfortune, once or twice even from disaster." Hamilton Fish redeemed the reputation of public servants which in these years had sunk to a very low level.

In undertaking the biography of *John D. Rockefeller, The Heroic Age of American Enterprise* (New York, 1940), Nevins understood he would be inviting controversy.[13] The printed material, he said, was controversial, and almost none of it unbiased. The author believed his own work impartial and free from preconceptions, though he did proclaim a bias in favor of free-enterprise economy. Nevins made clear that many of those who indicted Rockefeller for alleged misdeeds, were themselves guided by less than altruistic motives. The great monopolist himself, however, conceded, long after, that the methods of big business

[13] See the exchange between Nevins and C. M. Destler, *American Historical Review,* Vol. L, No. 3 (April, 1945), 676–89, and Destler's article, "*Wealth against Commonwealth,* 1894 and 1944," *American Historical Review,* Vol. L, No. 3 (April, 1945), 49–72. See also Destler, "The Opposition of American Businessmen to Social Control During the 'Gilded Age,'" *Mississippi Valley Historical Review* (March, 1953).

of the 1870's and 1880's would not have been condoned fifty years later. This study substantiates Nevins' assertion that American "industrial history since the Civil War can hardly be understood without a clear grasp . . . of Rockefeller's work." While the chapters on business activity were important, the sections on philanthropy were of equal significance; Rockefeller was unquestionably "a bold innovator in both industry and philanthropy." His own guiding principle—"a man should make all he can and give all he can"—explained his way of life.

In each of his biographies Allan Nevins was interested not only in the development of his subject's personality and career; the evolution of the individual was depicted against a broad canvas of contemporary history. He believed that the subject of a biography should be fully related to his times, which meant more than a few brief allusions to his background. Despite his own remark that insistence on one-volume biographies means the end of full-bodied works, his own single-volume studies covered his subjects thoroughly. The ideal he set for biographers in general he has himself met—a combination of scholarship, interpretive power, and literary charm.[14]

In the intellectual climate of the Progressive Era, historians and biographers condemned big business indiscriminately. With the passing of time although distance has not necessarily lent enchantment to the actions of great captains of industry, their achievements have been appraised less emotionally. Against the background of their day, their "baronies" seem less feudal, their "robberies" less criminal. The modern student is indeed ready to acknowledge the real contribution they made to the development of America.

Some of the best of the investigations of business enterprise have been published in the Harvard *Studies* in business history. The authors were less concerned with familiar tales of iniquity associated with their subjects than with their contribution to the growth of American capitalism. Denunciation gave way to explanation, and in the process much light was shed on the accumulation of capital, investment, and the relationship, good as well as bad, of men of wealth to the community. Kenneth W. Porter's *John Jacob Astor* (2 vols., Cambridge, 1931) was of great value to the student of the West as well as to the economic historian. Porter also published a study, under the same auspices, of *The*

[14] Allan Nevins, *The Gateway to History* (New York, 1938), 328–40.

Jacksons and the Lees: Two Generations of Massachusetts Merchants 1765–1844 (2 vols., 1937). This work, together with W. T. Baxter's *The House of Hancock* (1945), covered a large segment of the economic history of Massachusetts through more than a century. In the neighboring colony of Rhode Island, a famous mercantile family will be studied in a large scale work by James B. Hedges. *The Browns of Providence Plantations: Colonial Years* (Cambridge, 1952), the first of three volumes, supplies the rich details of a remarkable family whose contributions to American business and learning were distinctive. The famous Civil War banker, Jay Cooke, was the subject of Henrietta M. Larson's able study (1936). The international affiliations of American commerce and banking, especially the closeness of Anglo-American economic relations, was the theme of Ralph W. Hidy's *The House of Baring in American Trade and Finance* (1949).

The above studies dealt with merchants and bankers and stressed the role of the entrepreneur in American economy; industrialists and masters of technology have not yet, generally, been portrayed in distinguished biographies. Burton J. Hendrick's *Life of Andrew Carnegie* (2 vols., New York, 1932) was excellent on the development of the steel industry, although in its sympathy for Carnegie it gave a distorted version of the Homestead strike of 1892. The biographer shed new light on Carnegie's interesting role in international politics. The growth of the Middle West into a great farming and industrial region was intimately bound up with the career of *Cyrus Hall McCormick* (2 vols., New York, 1930, 1935), the subject of one of the best business biographies yet written. This work, by William T. Hutchinson, was also of interest to the student of politics, for McCormick was an important factor among the Douglas Democrats.[15]

DOUGLAS SOUTHALL FREEMAN

In 1934, Douglas Southall Freeman brought out the first two volumes of his long-awaited biography of Robert E. Lee, and the final two volumes came soon after. Many years of devotion to his task lay behind the biographer, who said that he was "privileged to live, as it were, for

[15] E. N. Saveth, "What Historians Teach About Business," *Fortune,* Vol. XLV, No. 4 (April, 1952), 118ff.; K. W. Porter, "Trends in American Business Biography," *Journal of Economic and Business History,* Vol. IV, No. 4 (August, 1932), 583–610.

more than a decade in the company of a great gentleman. . . . What he seemed, he was—a wholly human gentleman, the essential elements of whose positive character were two and only two, simplicity and spirituality." Freeman unearthed a vast fund of material dealing with Lee's strategy, and he adopted the unusual device of allowing the reader no more knowledge than Lee possessed at the time of any particular battle or campaign.

The first volume took Lee through his schooling at West Point, on through his brilliant services in the Mexican War, and then to his soul-searching days in 1861, when he threw in his lot with his beloved state; "His mind was for the Union; his instinct was for his State, Virginia." He felt sure where his duty lay, and after the tragic years of war had passed, he still maintained that "if it all were to be done over again, I should act in precisely the same manner." Freeman dwelled on the unfolding of Lee's personality and emphasized particularly the value of his training in Mexico. "Twenty months of service in Mexico had been ended when Lee saw the castle and the towers of Vera Cruz fade from view, never again to be seen by him. They were probably the twenty most useful months of his training as a soldier. Their effect on him can be seen during nearly the whole of the War between the States. The lessons he learned on the road to Mexico City he applied in much of his strategy. Warnings he read in that campaign he never forgot."

The second volume took Lee through the battle of Chancellorsville, which "was undoubtedly the most remarkable victory he ever achieved." But Stonewall Jackson's death threw an ominous shadow across his path, and one gets the impression that Lee was engaged in a hopeless cause. Especially was this so after Gettysburg, the description of which is a literary masterpiece. The third volume carried on the narrative to the winter of 1864, with Grant still holding on and pressing hard on Lee's diminishing forces. But the men who served under Lee never faltered in their intense devotion to him: "He came in their minds not only to represent their cause, but to incarnate it and to idealize it. Proud as was the name of the Army of Virginia, they almost ceased to say that they belonged to that host and spoke of themselves as serving in Lee's army. And by that more personal name, with all the tribute to Lee that it implied, they usually styled the army in familiar conversation till it had become only the glamorous memory of their waning years."

The fourth volume was the climax of this moving biography. In the chapter, "The Ninth of April," Freeman described the surrender and the reaction of Lee's men to the news: "Some blasphemed and some babbled, but all who could do so crowded to say farewell to Lee. Catching hold of his hands, they looked up at him and cried the more. They touched his uniform or his bridle rein, if they could not grasp his hand, and if they could not reach him, they smoothed Traveller's flank or patted his neck. And in a confused roar, half-sob, half-acclamation, they voiced their love for him, their faith in him, their goodbye to him as their commander." The chapter, "The Sword of Robert E. Lee," was a recapitulation of the General's military exploits and an excellent analysis of the factors that made for his success as a soldier.

After the war Lee's acceptance of the presidency of Washington College (later Washington and Lee) at a low salary was a stimulus to the men of the South to adjust themselves to altered conditions. He kept counseling them that in time injustices would be remedied, and his correspondence had a note of optimism that was heartening to the discouraged. "More than any other American, General Lee kept the tragedy of the war from being a continuing national calamity." One is ready to believe that the most heroic years of Lee's life were the five that remained to him after the war. His social vision at this time marked him as one with unusual foresight who merited the veneration with which he was followed in peace as well as in war. It is hard to believe that we shall ever need another biography of Lee, for Freeman's work has no superior in the whole range of American biographical literature.

So deeply was Freeman immersed in study of the Civil War that his vast knowledge of the Confederate side of the struggle overflowed into three more volumes, *Lee's Lieutenants: A Study in Command* (New York, 1942–44). The massive work was an analysis of the command of the Army of Northern Virginia. As in the biography of Lee, great stress was placed on the disaster for the South which lay in Stonewall Jackson's death. Another adverse factor for the South was the marked attrition in the officers' corps in 1864; in the first month of Grant's assault, 37 per cent of the Confederate general officers were lost. After the summer of 1864, Southern commanders were largely a new group and not so able as their predecessors.

Freeman emphasized the importance of the West Point tradition in building the strength of the Confederate Army; "the Army of Northern Virginia could not have been organized or commanded successfully without West Point." The contributions of two Southern military schools—the Virginia Military Institute and the Carolina Military Academy—were likewise accorded high praise for welding Confederate soldiers into an effective fighting force. The laurels of some Southern leaders looked somewhat worn under Freeman's critical exposure, but Lee and Jackson emerged still the great figures of the lost cause.

Freeman next turned his superb powers as a biographer to the study of Washington, whose personality was still veiled despite investigations by countless students; the mystery was a challenge to the artist in Freeman. Long ago Hawthorne had ridiculed biographers of the first President: "Did anybody ever see Washington nude? It is inconceivable. He had no nakedness, but I imagine he was born with his clothes on and his hair powdered, and made a stately bow on his first appearance in the world."

Rupert Hughes, in a three-volume work (it stopped at 1781), had tried before Freeman to answer Hawthorne's gibe at biographers. His intention, said Hughes, was "to restore an old masterpiece by mopping off the daubs and accretions and letting the original colors shine forth in their variety and brilliance, shadow and radiance." Unlike many earlier biographers, he wished to be scrupulously fair in dealing with Washington's opponents, who had often been vilified by the General's panegyrists. Historians were familiar with much of the material presented by Hughes, but to the average reader it came as something of a shock to learn of Washington's temperamental outbursts and of his hearty dislike of many of his fellow Americans. In his desire to humanize Washington, Hughes on occasion romanticized history, thus rousing the ire of critical scholars.[16]

Freeman's large-scale biography of Washington went far beyond all previous works in the thoroughness of its research and in the amplitude of its canvas. Indeed, if there is any serious criticism to be made of it, it is that much is included with which Washington did not have close association. The first two volumes (1948) brought Washington only to the age of twenty-seven. His early career was told against a detailed portrayal of the Virginia society in which he matured. (Freeman's description is the best yet made of that society.) The young Washington was a "vital and emotional" youth, intensely ambitious; "the patriot

[16] See N. W. Stephenson, "The Romantics and George Washington," *American Historical Review,* Vol. XXXIX, No. 2 (January, 1934), 274–83.

emerged slowly." He had, at this stage in life, "no compelling faith in God." As for other characteristics, they were fixed early in his life—an orderly mind, no humor, no ease in public speech. The training he had received in these formative years, said Freeman, was a useful preparation for later events.

The third, fourth, and fifth volumes (the last published in 1952) narrated the undramatic years of 1759–73, and then the tempo was speeded up with the oncoming Revolution. In the years of peace Washington did what other large landholders were doing; he acquired new holdings in the West. During this period of his life, while certain of his characteristics remained unchanged, such as his adherence to "principles," in other respects he was subtly altered. He was now more religious than in earlier days; his character was less complex, and he was clearer in his sense of values; his judgment had matured. Washington was "neither an American Parsifal nor a biological 'sport.' What he was he made himself by will, by effort, by discipline, by ambition, and by perseverance. For the long and dangerous journeys of his incredible life, he had the needful strength and direction because he walked that 'straight line.'"

The planter and the patriot had become the leader of the Revolution. Freeman's unrivaled skill in military history carried the narrative along at a rapid rate. With French recognition of American independence the suffocation of unending conflict yielded to the relaxing hope of early victory. That success eventually came was in large measure due to French aid, a fact emphasized by the subtitle of volume five: "Victory with the Help of France." While Washington was immensely grateful for French assistance, he was anxious lest it exalt France's power too much and make manifest the secondary role of the United States in the partnership. The end of battle came at Yorktown, and the eloquence of Freeman reaches its height in describing the climax of surrender.

The technique that Freeman used in his *Lee* (in the sections on war) was repeated in the *Washington;* the biographer limited himself to the knowledge possessed by the commander at the moment of decision. Clearly this device recreated the hesitancy which hampered action and added suspense to a tale that seemed new-told. Therein lies the secret of Freeman's art—what seemed a trite and threadbare tale through uninspired retellings lives again in the freshness of its first wonder.[17]

A type of biography insufficiently exploited is that of the family, either in a single generation or in a sequence of several generations. There are families whose influence in American life should be recorded. Everyone will instantly think of the Adams family, and no one contemplating a biography of its members should be deterred by James Truslow Adams' brief sketch. C. Hartley Grattan's *The Jameses: A Family of Minds* (New York, 1932), Hendrick's *The Lees of Virginia* (Boston, 1935), Louise H. Tharp's *Peabody Sisters of Salem* (Boston, 1950), and Ferris Greenslet's *The Lowells and Their Seven Worlds* (Boston, 1946), were examples of interesting studies illustrating the place of significant family groups in American civilization.

The most important work in the field of biography as a whole is the *Dictionary of American Biography* (20 vols., New York, 1928–36). Scholars long desired a counterpart of Great Britain's *Dictionary of National Biography,* but not until the publication of the *DAB* was this wish realized. Under the editorial direction of Allen Johnson and later of Dumas Malone, many hundreds of contributors wrote the thousands of biographies of the greater and lesser men and women who have shared variously in the making of American civilization.[18] Athletes, Indian chiefs, statesmen, scientists, writers, businessmen, reformers, soldiers, scholars, *et. al.,* found a place in these volumes. Many names half-forgotten or almost wholly lost were rescued, and the reader may now discover easily the facts that were often difficult to unearth. The best of these sketches were well written (Carl Becker's "Benjamin Franklin," for example), and, having made use of the latest findings of scholarship, they were the most authoritative interpretations of eminent lives available. No work of such monumental proportions can escape serious criticism. A number of names were omitted which might better have been included, and some of the sketches seem to have been done by individuals who were unfamiliar with their subjects. More space should have been allotted to labor leaders and to social dissenters generally. The *Dictionary's* virtues made it far and away the best in America, and it compares

[17] W. B. Hendrickson, "A Review of Reviews of Douglas S. Freeman's *Young Washington," The Library Quarterly,* Vol. XXI, No. 3 (July, 1951), summarized favorable and unfavorable comments on the first two volumes.

[18] There were 13,633 biographies written by 2,243 contributors in twenty volumes; a supplementary volume was issued in 1944.

favorably with its European prototypes. It is one of the best products of co-operative scholarship ever published in the United States.[19]

Biography has come a long way from colonial eulogies of contemporary worthies, through the heavy tomes of the "life and times" writers and the later lightly cynical school of Lytton Strachey, to the studies influenced by psychoanalysis. Self-conscious "debunkers" made their brief appearance, to be followed by authors who have seen the whole man in all the complexity of human nature.

With the perfecting of biography as an art, writers have learned to picture men not so much as predestined masters of their fate (which the known end of their story seems to suggest), but rather as men wrestling with uncertainty. The victories that seem inevitable, because we know the struggles' outcome, are shown often to have hung by a thread, while the failures which history has submerged are invested with all the heartbreak of success narrowly lost. Like the French historian following Bergson's injunction, *s'installer dans le mouvement,* the biographer has learned to relive the life of his subject. He has recaptured his strength and his weakness, his faltering ascent to greatness or stumbling to disaster—in short, through intuition as well as research he has made men live again.

[19] On biography as a whole, see E. H. O'Neill, *A History of American Biography: 1800–1935* (Philadelphia, 1935). The titles discussed in this chapter are representative of American biographical writing; many good ones, unfortunately, had to be left out.

XIV

Contemporary Trends

DESPITE the intense activity in historical circles in the generation after 1880, vast areas of American history remained untouched. Research, even in political history (which had engrossed most of the energies of historians) was of the *extensive* variety, covering the story in the flat, neglectful of its unplumbed depths. As for economic, social, and intellectual history, extended surveys were being made of portions of the large field—but the pioneers had only plotted out the ground.

Economic History

Among the most successful of the pioneering accomplishments were the volumes issued under the auspices of the Carnegie Institution of Washington. They covered industry, agriculture, and transportation, and while they were not for the general reader, historians have benefited greatly from their accumulation of facts and from their bibliographies. Emory R. Johnson and his collaborators were responsible for the *History of Domestic and Foreign Commerce of the United States* (2 vols., 1915). The first volume contained the data on commerce to 1789, although the section on internal commerce ran on to a later date. In the second volume was to be found a treatment of American fisheries, as well as a discussion of government aid and commercial policy. The *History of Manufactures in the United States,* prepared by Victor S. Clark, was in two volumes, divided at 1860. An enormous amount of research went into this publication, which assembled its materials topically. The second volume contained interpretive chapters and summary conclusions which added greatly to the value of the whole work. The *History of Transportation in the United States before 1860,* compiled by Balthasar H. Meyer, Caroline E. MacGill, and others (1917), laid a satisfactory foundation for study of this key factor in American development.

Since the Carnegie series appeared, many students have made important contributions to the literature of transportation, notably Robert G. Albion, in *Square Riggers on Schedule* (Princeton, 1938) and *The Rise of New York Port* (New York, 1939). Recently the whole field of economic history in the first half of the nineteenth century was covered in a stimulating volume by George R. Taylor, *The Transportation Revolution 1815–1860* (New York, 1951). Taylor's work (which omits agriculture, a topic reserved for separate study) is the fourth volume in the co-operative *Economic History of the United States,* whose contributors have made readily available to nonspecialists the results of a wide-ranging scholarship.

The *History of Labour in the United States,* though supplemented and modified at many points, is still the standard work in its field. It was written by a group of scholars, trained for the most part by John R. Commons at the University of Wisconsin. Commons was engaged for many years in securing more liberal labor conditions, not only in Wisconsin but elsewhere in the United States. The two volumes published in 1918 carried the narrative to the 1890's; the two published in 1935 concluded with the inauguration of the New Deal.

The basis of the first two volumes had been laid in the publication of the *Documentary History of American Industrial Society,* edited by Commons (10 vols., 1910), but several years elapsed before the comprehensive narrative on American labor appeared. The story of labor before the Civil War was not so well done as the later period; more abundant materials and greater intensity of research expended upon them accounted for this unevenness. In large measure the treatment of labor in the colonial period in the Commons' work was supplanted by Abbot E. Smith's *Colonists in Bondage* (Chapel Hill, 1947), and Richard B. Morris' *Government and Labor in Early America* (New York, 1946). Smith's volume was especially useful on the recruitment of workers in Britain, Morris' on the laws that conditioned the status of free and bound labor.

The third volume of the Commons' history contained a good section on "Working Conditions," by Don D. Lescohier, and a contribution of great value on "Labor Legislation," by Elizabeth Brandeis. The fourth volume, by Selig Perlman and Philip Taft, picked up the story of organized labor's development since the late 1890's. Commons, in his editorial introduction, pointed to the differences between the two periods covered by the earlier and later volumes. In the former, he said, "We dealt with a period of employer capitalism, where the employer and the wage-earner were rather closely connected in the same localities. But this [latter] is a period when the owners of industry are absentee stock and bond holders." The long tale of conflict between capital and labor justified the conclusion that "American labor history has been principally a fighting history."

A vast amount of material was brought together in these volumes, though it was not always well integrated. The point of view consistently maintained was the editor's—an emphasis on American experimentalism in the adjustment to new conditions, with a distinct aversion to doctrinaire positions. American labor, so ran the argument, should get what it can when it can and not wait for its improvement upon the creation of some Utopia.

The whole literature of economics in the United States was surveyed in a comprehensive study by Joseph Dorfman, *The Economic Mind in American Civilization* (3 vols., New York, 1946–49). Many familiar, as well as little-known, names were assigned their proper place in the long roll of figures who made their contributions to economics in the United States. So exhaustive was Dorfman's work it may be believed that whatever further studies are made in the field will be additions to, or corrections of, portions of his volumes, but no large-scale substitute treatment will be required for many years to come.

A History of American Life

By the time the last of the volumes of the *American Nation* had come from the press, the series had acquired, for younger students, a slightly old-fashioned look. The newer generation, believing that politics had been overemphasized in historical writing, proclaimed their purpose to record the cultural history of the American people, which had been ignored by previous historians. In the remarks of critical scholars there was implicit the conviction that social history was the real guardian of the values of the past, as well as a guide to future social progress, whereas political and military history seemed to celebrate man's idolatry of false gods—war and the state. There was, however, less novelty in these self-conscious proclamations than was supposed.

The importance of including more of a people's activities than politics and war in a historical narrative had been granted long since. A vigorous proponent of the "new history" as a record of the culture of a people, was Edward Eggleston, who had already attained fame as the author of *The Hoosier Schoolmaster*. Having long been interested in historical fiction, he very easily made the transition to studying and writing history for its own sake. He planned a series of volumes to constitute a history of American life—the sources of its ideas and habits, and the course of their development. "It will be a work," he said, "designed to answer the questions 'How?' and 'Whence?' and 'Why?'" Unfortunately Eggleston lived to finish only two volumes, *The Beginners of a Nation* (1896) and *The Transit of Civilization* (1901), which covered less than half of the seventeenth century. Because his work was incomplete, his volumes are not as well known as they should be. They were informative and were better written than most books on American history. Eggleston, opposed as he was to "drum and trumpet" history, had a strong influence on the younger generation of scholars, who saw in his work an excellent example of social history written with charm and coherence.[1]

It remained however for *A History of American Life* (1928–43), under the editorship of Dixon R. Fox and Arthur M. Schlesinger, to swing over wholly to the position that politics might be almost entirely neglected in a narrative. A series of twelve volumes was projected (a thirteenth was added later); illustrations and bibliographies were important features of this publication. Herbert I. Priestley wrote *The Coming of the White Man 1492–1848,* making special reference to the French and Spanish settlements, noting particularly the existence of a rich Spanish culture long before the English colonies were established. Included in the last two chapters were the Dutch and Swedes, the

[1] See Eggleston's presidential address before the American Historical Association, "The New History," American Historical Association *Annual Report* for the year 1900, Vol. I (1901), 35–47: Charles Hirschfeld, "Edward Eggleston: Pioneer in Social History," in *Historiography and Urbanization: Essays in American History in Honor of W. Stull Holt* (ed. by E. F. Goldman, Baltimore, 1941), 189–210; W. P. Randel, *Edward Eggleston* (New York, 1946), especially Chap. XVI.

former receiving a sensible estimate of their legacy to posterity. Thomas J. Wertenbaker, in the next volume, wrote on *The First Americans,* which covered the seventeenth century to 1690, at which point James Truslow Adams continued the social history of the colonies to 1760 in *Provincial Society*. Evarts B. Greene, who had spent many years studying the years of Revolution, wrote *The Revolutionary Generation 1763–1790*. The succeeding period through the Civil War was covered in three volumes: John A. Krout and Dixon R. Fox, *The Completion of Independence 1790–1830;* Carl Russell Fish, *The Rise of the Common Man;* and Arthur C. Cole, *The Irrepressible Conflict.* The next volumes, by Allan Nevins on *The Emergence of Modern America* and Arthur M. Schlesinger on *The Rise of the City 1878–1898,* covered the period of economic and social reconstruction; Ida Tarbell's *The Nationalizing of Business 1878–1898* dealt specifically with economic development. Harold U. Faulkner's *The Quest for Social Justice* was filled with the successes and failures of the liberal movement (1898–1914) and the abandonment of *laissez faire,* while Preston W. Slosson's *The Great Crusade and After 1914–1928* continued the narrative to the time of publication. The war and postwar years with their exhilaration and their disillusionment were the theme of this volume, which contained many of the facts but which was weak in interpretation. Dixon Wecter's *The Age of the Great Depression 1929–1941* was a supplement to the original.

The defect of Slosson's volume was indeed the weakness of most of the books in *A History of American Life*—a lack of comment on what the facts mean; too often the work has the appearance of a catalogue. Because the historian may not be sure what the facts mean, he is not therefore absolved from some attempt at interpretation. Although it would have been possible to write each one of these volumes with a different set of facts, the ones selected do give a picture of what was happening in American society. The proper scope of social history is a matter filled with controversial elements, as is the problem of relative emphasis on the materials involved.[2]

Comprehensive treatments of American culture, such as those represented by the volumes in the Fox-Schlesinger series, must depend in large measure upon specialized studies—in literature, philosophy, the

[2] W. E. Lingelbach (ed.), *Approaches to American Social History* (New York, 1937), a good discussion of the *History of American Life* series.

arts and sciences, law, education, religion, the press, and immigration. Students of literature have been comparatively successful in relating their subject to the general history of society. Consciously or unconsciously they have been animated by the same spirit that moved Moses Coit Tyler to probe American civilization through her literature. Tyler broadened the scope of literature to cover far more than belles-lettres, and he was aware of the need to place literature in its proper social setting. It remained, however, for Parrington to interrelate literary expression more closely, with concurrent political and economic ideas.

VERNON L. PARRINGTON

In 1927 two volumes of a proposed three-volume work on *Main Currents in American Thought* were published by Vernon Louis Parrington, professor of English in the University of Washington. While he was in the midst of his third volume, in 1929, Parrington died. Despite the fact that most of the final portion was left only in sketch form, his publishers paid him the tribute of presenting it to the public.

It was Parrington's wish to relate the literature of a people to its whole civilization; to do so meant the selection of material on other than belletristic grounds. Through the influence of Taine's *Histoire de la Littérature* and the work of a close friend and colleague, J. Allen Smith, who wrote on the economic basis of politics, Parrington was stimulated to a re-examination of American literature.[3] He "envisaged American literature as American thought; . . . economic forces imprint their mark upon political, social, and religious institutions; literature expresses the result in its thought content." Parrington's youth in Kansas was clouded by experiences that forced many of his generation to become Populists, and dictated his own interpretation of American life and letters. Memories of low prices for crops and mortgaged farms left lifelong scars. Corn was used for fuel, he remembered, "and if while we sat around such a fire, watching the year's crop go up the chimney, the talk sometimes became bitter . . . who will wonder?"

Parrington, making no pretense to objectivity, indicated that his point of view was "liberal rather than conservative, Jeffersonian rather than Federalistic." Through the personalities of Roger Williams, Franklin, and Jefferson, he traced the line of liberalism in colonial America.

[3] See Parrington's introduction to Smith's *The Growth and Decadence of Constitutional Government* (New York, 1930).

"The first transported to the new world the plentiful liberalism of a great movement and a great century"; Franklin "gathered up the sum of native liberalisms that had emerged spontaneously from a decentralized society"; Jefferson "strengthened these native liberalisms with borrowings from the late seventeenth-century natural-rights school and from French romantic theory engrafting them upon the vigorous American stock." Against these individuals whose liberalism lay near to Parrington's heart, he placed "the complementary figures of John Cotton, Jonathan Edwards, and Alexander Hamilton, men whose grandiose dreams envisaged different ends for America and who followed different paths."

The early part of the first volume, *The Colonial Mind 1620–1800,* discussed the New England theocracy and Roger Williams' rebellion against it: "He lived and dreamed in a future he was not to see, impatient to bring to men a heaven they were unready for." The twilight of the Puritan oligarchy came before 1720; thence through the middle of the century was "the creative springtime of democratic America—plebeian years that sowed what after times were to reap. . . . The psychology of democratic individualism" that was fashioned in these years (partly because of numerous small landholdings and also as an effect of the frontier) was, said Parrington, the "determining influence" in shaping "the creative outlines of our history." Jonathan Edwards did not belong in that tradition; "the greatest mind of New England had become an anachronism in a world that bred Benjamin Franklin."

The awakening of the American mind came in the Revolutionary era: "The liberalism that before had been vaguely instructive quickly became eager and militant, [and] out of this primary revolution were to come other revolutions, social and economic, made possible by the new republican freedom." In Parrington's judgment, "the most important consequence of the Revolution was the striking down of this mounting aristocratic spirit that was making rapid headway with the increase of wealth." The passing of the Loyalists left the middle class "free to create a civilization after its own ideals." It did so through the agency of the centralized state, which began to check "the long movement of decentralization . . . the most revolutionary changes in three hundred years of American experience." Parrington's material on the Revolution owed a good deal to the works of Arthur M. Schlesinger, Claude H. Van Tyne, and particularly to Tyler's *Literary History of the American Revolution*. In fact, throughout his work Parrington was heavily indebted to contemporary historians whose critical scholarship, he believed, had much to offer students of literature.

The Federalists, under Hamilton's leadership, were victorious over the agrarian democracy. But shortly, because of the influence of French Revolutionary ideas, opposition "to the aristocratic arrogance of Federalism, and disgust at its coercive measures," mounted quickly. The organizer and director of that discontent was Jefferson who, "far more completely than any other of his generation . . . embodied the idealism of the great revolution."

The Hartford Wits and the group represented by Philip Freneau were examined mainly in the light of their political affiliations. Parrington's own liberal sympathies helped determine the judgment that Freneau, Joel Barlow, and Hugh Henry Brackenridge represented the "best intelligence then being devoted to literature in America." Although "the new liberalism was in the saddle" with the Republican victory of 1800, it had a precarious seat because the forces of capitalism and industrialism "were already at work preparing a different pattern of life for America . . . wholly unlike that of the simpler agrarianism with its domestic economy, which Jefferson represents. A new romanticism of the middle class was eventually to shoulder aside the aspirations of gentleman and farmer alike, and refashion America after its own ideal."

The theme of Parrington's second volume, *The Romantic Revolution in America 1800–1860,* was the growth of an acquisitive society whose way of life, he thought, had less to commend it than did the ideals of the colonial farmer. The philosophy of this middle-class society, expressed by Adam Smith, came into conflict with French Revolutionary equalitarianism, which had found a ready response in America in the Mississippi Valley at the close of the eighteenth century. In the South was developed "the conception of a Greek democracy" with slave labor, which rejected "alike French equalitarianism and English individualism." Because it took no account of the aspirations of the middle class, the latter destroyed the dream of the South, and "with the overthrow of the aristocratic principle in its final refuge the ground was cleared of the last vestiges of the eighteenth century."

The absence of a treatment on the South in the first volume was somewhat compensated for in the second. The seed centers of Southern culture were Virginia and South Carolina; from the former came the intellectual offspring Kentucky and Tennessee, from the latter, Alabama and Mississippi. The intellectual leaders of these respective groups were Jefferson and Calhoun—the latter rejected equalitarian idealism and substituted for it economic realism. Through opposing representative figures like the agrarian democrat John Taylor, and John Marshall, Parrington traced a chart of the Virginia mind "with its liberalisms and conservatisms running at cross purposes." By the late 1820's Southern leadership had passed from Virginia to the more aggressive South Carolina. High praise was lavished upon William Gilmore Simms; he was, said Parrington, "the most richly endowed of any son" South Carolina "ever gave birth to . . . by far the most virile and interesting figure of the Old South."

In the mind of the Middle East, New York and Philadelphia, there was more diversity of thought than in the intellectual centers of New England or the South. A friendliness, not so marked in his estimate of Irving, was apparent in Parrington's appraisal of Cooper: "The more intimately one comes to know him, the more one comes to respect his honest, manly nature that loved justice and decency more than popularity." New York's world of literature was greatly indebted to New England, wrote Parrington, who set up against Irving, Paulding, and Cooper the contributions to idealism made by Bryant, Greeley, and Melville.

The New England renaissance of these years, whose stimulus to American life was of unusual strength, was, in Parrington's view, "the last flowering of a tree that was dying at the roots; . . . it was the last and in certain respects the most brilliant of the several attempts to domesticate in America the romantic thought of revolutionary Europe; and with its passing, civilization in this western world fell into the hands of another breed of men to fashion as they saw fit."

In Emerson and Webster, Parrington found the "diverse New England tendencies that derived from the Puritan and the Yankee; the idealistic and the practical . . . the intellectual revolutionary . . . and the soberly conservative." Webster "was a great man, built on a great pattern, who never achieved a great life." Along with Emerson, Thoreau and Theodore Parker best typified the ferment in the mind and heart of New England. A sense of kinship quickened the language of Parrington when he wrote of them; Emerson was "a free soul . . . the flowering of two centuries of spiritual aspiration—Roger Williams and

Jonathan Edwards come to more perfect fruition. . . . In Thoreau the eighteenth-century philosophy of individualism . . . came to fullest expression in New England." Parker was an unsparing critic of his contemporaries, and he was "one of the greatest, if not the last, of the excellent line of Puritan preachers."

The Civil War, said Parrington, hurried the nation "forward along the path of an unquestioning and uncritical consolidation, that was to throw the coercive powers of a centralizing state into the hands of the new industrialism"; this revolution engulfed "the older romantic America, its dignified literary ideals as well as its democratic political theory." But from the vague romanticism of these years was born at length "a spirit of realistic criticism, seeking to evaluate the worth of this new America" and to evolve, if possible, new ways of life. The expressions of this critical spirit were to be the theme of a third volume.

Parrington intended to trace the decline of "romantic optimism" after 1860, which resulted from three forces: "The stratifying of economics under the pressure of centralization; the rise of a mechanistic science, and the emergence of a spirit of skepticism which . . . is resulting in the questioning of the ideal of democracy as it has been commonly held hitherto, and the spread of a spirit of pessimism." America's intellectual history, thought Parrington, fell into the three broad phases of Calvinistic pessimism, romantic optimism, and mechanistic pessimism.

Although much of his material on this last period had a deep gloom, Parrington never failed to strike the courageous note that was a tocsin to a drooping liberalism. No longer were the theologians, political philosophers, industrial masters, or bankers "the spokesmen of this vibrant life of a continent, but the intellectuals, the dreamers, the critics, the historians, the men of letters, in short; and to them one may turn hopefully for a revelation of American life." To the end, Parrington held out Jeffersonian democracy as a hopeful ideal.

There was thrilling writing in these volumes that called a wayward America back from the drab reality of a business civilization to the day-dream of an agrarian democracy. Parrington never escaped the influence of that arch foe of industrialism, William Morris. "In lovely prose," the American said, Morris "laid bare the evils of industrialism. . . . It was a message that stirred me to the quick and convinced me . . . that the business man's society, symbolized by the cash register and existing solely for profit, must be destroyed to make way for another and better ideal."

In Parrington's history there were serious omissions of whole fields of activity without which an observer cannot really understand the main currents of American thought, and there were also mistakes in judgment. For example, he was too harsh to the Puritans, whose virtues he neglected while emphasizing their limitations. He exaggerated French ideological influences in American politics. Historians complained that Parrington did not know enough history, while students of literature often disagreed with his estimates of literary figures. And yet, after everything unfavorable was said, there remained an important body of achievement. Many students of American society have used it as a point of departure for further research, and the stimulating quality of its fruitful generalizations will continue to inspire additional study. This study may bear fruit of a kind different from that fancied by Parrington but, whether in agreement or in disagreement with his main theses, no student of America should forego the joy of reading him.[4]

The Cambridge History of American Literature (4 vols., New York, 1917–21), modeled on the English publication, specifically stated that its intention was to make "a survey of the life of the American people as expressed in their writings rather than a history of belles-lettres alone." Travels, oratory, memoirs, philosophy, newspapers, and histories (the last well summarized by John Spencer Bassett) were all included as departments of literature. The final volume included chapters on economists, scholars, book publishing, non-English writing done in America, and a lengthy bibliography covering the whole work. The fact that these volumes, edited by professors of literature—William P. Trent, John Erskine, Stuart P. Sherman, and Carl Van Doren—have been widely used by historians is one illustration of the process by which scholars have been erasing boundary lines of departmentalized knowledge.

A later generation, believing the *Cambridge History of American Literature* outmoded, produced the *Literary History of the United States* (3 vols., New York, 1948), edited by Robert E. Spiller and others. Scholars, said the editors, "can no longer be content to write for scholars; they must make their knowledge meaningful and applicable to humanity."

[4] W. T. Utter, "Vernon Louis Parrington," *Jernegan Essays,* 394–408; E. F. Goldman, *Rendezvous with Destiny* (New York, 1952), 37–38, 106 and note.

In obedience to this principle the many contributors wrote simply and directly, avoiding the professional language of the ivory tower. The third volume was a remarkably comprehensive bibliography, possibly the most important contribution of the entire enterprise.

Interpretations of the American spirit have been made with rare charm and literary brilliance by Lewis Mumford in the *Golden Day* (New York, 1926) and Van Wyck Brooks in his series of books beginning with the *Flowering of New England* (Boston, 1936). Mumford's was an enthusiastic study of the literary renaissance before the Civil War, a period treated more fully in Brooks' volume. The studies of Brooks, comprising a history of letters in the United States since 1800, have been severely criticized for their impressionistic, anecdotal quality and their alleged failure to probe deeply into the structure of American literature. No doubt much of this criticism is justified, but it should not be forgotten that a vast audience, hitherto unreached, has been led by the charm of Brooks' style to learn something of American literary achievement. For the student who sought more solid fare, F. O. Mathiessen's *American Renaissance: Art and Expression in the Age of Emerson and Whitman* (New York, 1941) was one of the ablest studies ever made in cultural history. A successful effort to integrate the history of art with social development was made by Oliver W. Larkin's *Art and Life in America* (New York, 1949).

New England, in its cultural as well as political history, has received more attention than any other section of the country. The Middle West, however, has also had its literary historians who have celebrated her contribution to the national culture. William H. Venable in his *Beginnings of Literary Culture in the Ohio Valley* (Cincinnati, 1891) included miscellaneous matter of use to later writers. Ralph L. Rusk went over similar ground, but with much deeper knowledge and greater inclusiveness, in *The Literature of the Middle Western Frontier* (2 vols., New York, 1925). Rusk's work was rather formal, lacking the unifying interpretation found in Dorothy A. Dondore's *The Prairie and the Making of Middle America* (Cedar Rapids, 1926), or in Lucy L. Hazard's *The Frontier in American Literature* (New York, 1927), though the latter applied the Turner thesis too rigidly. Constance Rourke's studies, especially *American Humor* (New York, 1931) and *The Roots of American Culture* (New York, 1942), were splendid portrayals of the relation between the social setting and the evolution of distinct culture expressions. Henry L. Mencken's *The American Language* (1936 and supplements) is invaluable for students of culture in the United States. Two related works added greatly to an understanding of the evolution of a distinctive society on this side of the Atlantic—*A Dictionary of American English on Historical Principles,* edited by Sir William Craigie and James R. Hurlbert (Chicago, 1938–44), and *A Dictionary of Americanisms on Historical Principles,* edited by Mitford M. Mathews (Chicago, 1951).

In a democratic culture the role of mass media of communications was early recognized to be of prime significance. Isaiah Thomas, himself a colorful figure in the newspaper world of the Revolutionary era, wrote a *History of Printing in America* (2 vols., Worcester, 1810) which is still a standard authority for the earlier period. The most learned student of American publishing, especially in its formative years, is Lawrence C. Wroth, whose *The Colonial Printer* (Portland, 1938) was one of his many contributions to the history of the fourth estate. The most satisfactory treatment of the whole story of the newspaper in America was Frank L. Mott's *American Journalism: A History of Newspapers in the United States* (New York, 1941). As his narrative was restricted to one volume, it was impossible to treat with adequate coverage the two and one-half centuries of newspaper history in the United States. Mott gave himself broader scope in his *History of American Magazines* (1930–38), whose three volumes carried the narrative to 1885. Possibly nowhere else could one get so readily a picture of the changes in popular literary taste in this country.

A deep insight into American culture may be gained from studies of several books which have had a mass appeal—the New England primer, whose history was written by Paul L. Ford (New York, 1897); the McGuffey readers, whose historians were Harvey C. Minnich (New York, 1936) and R. D. Mosier, *Making the American Mind: Social and Moral Ideas in the McGuffey Readers* (New York, 1941); and the dime novel, whose place in the native scene was assessed in a delightful volume by Edmund Pearson, *Dime Novels* (Boston, 1929). The millions of copies of Noah Webster's books were of great importance in molding a common culture, and their creator received the attention of two biographers within a single year—Harry R. Warfel, *Noah Webster* (New York, 1936), and Ervin Shoemaker, *Noah Webster* (New York, 1936). Publishing in America still awaits a thorough study, but until it appears there is much to be learned from Hellmut Lehmann-Haupt's *The Book in America: A History of the Making, the Selling, and the Collecting of Books in the United States* (New York, 1939).

The history of American education, on both lower and higher levels, has not been satisfactorily surveyed, though historians of particular schools, Morison on Harvard, Bruce on Virginia, Curti and Carstensen on Wisconsin, and Cheyney on Pennsylvania, have set a high standard. The story of women's education in the United States was written by Thomas Woody, one of the most learned students of educational history in America. A splendid study of the interrelations between education and American society was made by Merle Curti in *The Social Ideas of American Educators* (New York, 1935).

For a long time education in all its branches was largely controlled by the clergy, but no complete study of their influence in American history has been written. In view of the overwhelming importance of religion in American civilization, it is surprising that so little of a satisfactory nature has been done to relate it to the main stream of life in the United States. The *American Church History* series, edited by Philip Schaff and others, has long been in use. It was published in thirteen volumes (1893–1901) of which the first, Henry K. Carroll's *The Religious Forces of the United States,* covers all religions. Two of the best volumes in the series were Williston Walker's on the Congregational church and Edward T. Corwin's on the Dutch Reformed church. More recent studies have been made by William W. Sweet, but these are not always dependable. More volumes are needed like Alice M. Baldwin's *The New England Clergy and the American Revolution* (Durham, 1928) and Edward F. Humphrey's *Nationalism and Religion in America 1774–1789* (Boston, 1924). A more general work of much value was that by Auguste Jorns, *The Quakers as Pioneers in Social Work* (New York, 1931). The impact of an urban America upon religion was the fundamental theme of C. H. Hopkins' *The Rise of the Social Gospel in American Protestantism 1865–1915* (New Haven, 1940) and A. I. Abell's *The Urban Impact on American Protestantism 1865–1900* (Cambridge, 1943). The always troublesome problem of the relation between church and state was the topic of A. P. Stokes' *Church and State in the United States* (3 vols., New York, 1950). Its narrative and extensive collection of documents made it the most important treatment of the subject.

The whole history of American culture has been intimately bound up with the subject of immigration. This was a field of study long neglected by students of history, although chroniclers of various immigrant stocks had left many narratives which tended to exaggerate the role of their forebears in American life. Eventually a school of critical scholars arose who found it possible to treat impartially all immigrant groups, their own included.

The best work in the field has been done for Scandinavian migrants and for early Irish migration in Oscar Handlin's *Boston's Immigrants 1790–1865* (Cambridge, 1941) and W. F. Adams' *Ireland and Irish Emigration . . . from 1815 to the Famine* (New Haven, 1932). Theodore C. Blegen's two volumes on Norwegian emigrants and their adaptation to American life are among the best that we have. The Old World background has been studied for an understanding of the circumstances that lay behind the migration, while the interplay between the transplanted Scandinavians and those who stayed at home was often made clear. With this approach the future student will be able to work out the interconnection between American and European economic and cultural developments, thus attaining more nearly to a true history of the modern Western world.

Short surveys of immigration have been written by Carl Wittke, *We Who Built America* (New York, 1939) and Handlin, *The Uprooted* (Boston, 1951). The latter is particularly interested in the adaptation of the immigrant to American life, which he found exacted far more from the newcomer than is generally supposed. Wittke has written extensively on immigration and the contributions of newcomers to America. His special competence is in German emigration, one of his best works being *Refugees of Revolution* (Philadelphia, 1952), a study of the forty-eighters in America. This group, said Wittke, "were the cultural leaven and the spiritual yeast for the whole German element," and they "influenced materially the political and social history of America during one of its most critical periods."

The ablest historian of the whole field of migration was Marcus L. Hansen, whose early death was a tragic loss to scholarship. His three volumes, *The Atlantic Migration 1607–1860* (Cambridge, 1940), his essays on *The Immigrant in American History* (Cambridge, 1940), and *The Mingling of the Canadian and American Peoples* (New Haven, 1940, finished by J. B. Brebner) revealed his full mastery of the materials, especially for the nineteenth century. All writers on immigration have profited from Hansen's insights and from the stimulating quality of his suggestions. Students were too long under the spell of the Anglo-Saxon school of historians, who divided immigrants into worthy and unworthy groups, the latter coming from Ireland, southern and eastern Europe. The influence of this particular bias has been harmful and long lasting, as Edward N. Saveth showed in *American Historians and European Immigrants 1875–1925* (New York, 1948).

Whatever the conflicting claims made by various stocks to their share in building a national culture, there could be no dispute over responsibility for American legal customs. They are basically English, although the common law of England has undergone mutations in the American environment. This subject has long lain in too much obscurity because of the inaccessible nature of the materials, many of which are still in manuscript. For some time a vigorous effort has been under way to lay the foundations for a satisfactory history of American law. Earlier publications of useful materials were *Two Centuries Growth of American Law* (New York, 1901) and *Select Essays in Anglo-American Legal History* (3 vols., Boston, 1907). Some of the best work in the field has been done by Richard B. Morris, author of *Studies in the History of American Law* (New York, 1930), and Julius Göbel, who has written extensively on legal institutions in the United States. A number of volumes have been written on the courts and the legal profession. Carl B. Swisher's *Roger B. Taney* (New York, 1935) re-established the just fame of that controversial figure. Outstanding among works on lawyers and the law were those by Charles Warren, whose *History of the American Bar* (Cambridge, 1911) and *The Supreme Court in United States History* (Boston, 1923) revealed great erudition.

Too often a series of biographies strung together has done duty for the history of science in America. Francis D. Packard's *History of Medicine in the United States* (2 vols., New York, 1931) was better than most studies in this field, but the writings of Richard H. Shryock pointed the way to a more satisfactory understanding of the place of medicine in society. There is no satisfactory history of science in America, but there are studies of individual fields. The work of I. B. Cohen in colonial science and the survey by Dirk Struik, *Yankee Science in the Making* (Boston, 1948), indicated the manner in which this special area of intellectual life may be interrelated with the general history of American society. The impact of Darwinism on the American mind has been studied in a volume edited by Stow Persons, *Evolutionary Thought in America* (New Haven, 1950).

It is this type of investigation which is badly needed, for not until more studies have been made of the impact of European scientific ideas in America can a comprehensive history of science in the United States be written. The history of philosophy has been more satisfactorily treated than has science. That special aspect of American thought, transcendentalism, had able students in Octavius B. Frothingham and Harold C. Goddard; Ralph Barton Perry's biography of William James was necessarily concerned with the development of philosophy in America. Herbert W. Schneider is one of the most learned students of American thought, and his long devotion to this subject eventually resulted in the writing of his comprehensive work, *The History of American Philosophy* (New York, 1946).

Many subjects of fundamental importance to the historian of American culture were treated in the monographs comprising *Recent Social Trends in the United States,* whose more valuable materials and conclusions were brought together in a summary study bearing the same title (1934). But this type of publication, useful as it is, seemed to belong to a kind of narrative that was being outmoded by the works of historians who were attempting to probe deep beneath the surface of events.

Recently historians have been analyzing in close detail the inner structure of American society, patterns of class arrangements, and political leadership. Some noteworthy studies have been made of these themes in the colonial era, including Leonard W. Labaree's *Conservatism in Early American History* (New York, 1948) and Charles S. Sydnor's *Gentlemen Freeholders: Political Practices in Washington's Virginia* (Chapel Hill, 1952). The anatomy of the ruling group was exposed by these writers, who were at pains to note that in Northern as well as Southern colonies the mass of people were generally deferential to a traditional governing class. Oscar Zeichner's *Connecticut's Years of Controversy 1750–1776* (Chapel Hill, 1949) revealed the conflict between conservatives and radicals which occurred in many of the colonies in the Revolutionary era. The governments of the Continental Congress and the Confederation have been sympathetically reappraised by Edmund C. Burnett and Merrill Jensen. Dixon Ryan Fox's *The Decline of Aristocracy in the Politics of New York* (New York, 1919) illustrated the transition from the patrician society of the eighteenth century to the democracy of the nineteenth century.

That democracy found its eloquent champion in Arthur M. Schlesinger, Jr., whose *Age of Jackson* (Boston, 1945) attempted to interpret its spirit in terms of liberals versus conservatives. While he may have misinterpreted the relation between Jacksonianism and capitalism[5] and exaggerated the support of urban workingmen for the Democratic leader,[6] he did show better than any previous writer the manner in which the struggle for democracy interpenetrated all phases of American life.

One of the theses advanced by Schlesinger was that Western agrarian strength was less influential than urban factors in Jacksonian democracy. This suggestion, that the city was a more significant force in American development than hitherto imagined, was part of the general modification that historians have been making of Turner's interpretation of American history. The elder Schlesinger has been particularly active in emphasizing the role of urbanism in American life, many of his students at Harvard having written in support of his position.[7] Carl Bridenbaugh, beginning with his *Cities in the Wilderness* (New York, 1938), continued in several other studies to remind us of the importance of urban communities even in the colonial era when Americans were overwhelmingly rural. Michael Kraus' *Intercolonial Aspects of American Culture on the Eve of the Revolution* (New York, 1928) integrated various fea-

[5] Joseph Dorfman, "The Jackson Wage-Earner Thesis," *American Historical Review,* Vol. LIV, No. 2 (January, 1949), 296–306; Bray Hammond, in *Jackson versus Biddle,* G. R. Taylor (ed.) *Problems in American Civilization,* III, 54–71.

[6] William Sullivan, "Did Labor Support Andrew Jackson," *Political Science Quarterly,* Vol. LXII, No. 4 (December, 1947), 569–80; Edward Pessen, "Did Labor Support Jackson: The Boston Story," *Political Science Quarterly,* Vol. LXIV, No. 2 (June, 1949), 262–75.

[7] A. M. Schlesinger, "The City in American History," *Paths to the Present* (New York, 1949); Blake McKelvey, "American Urban History Today," *American Historical Review,* Vol. LVII, No. 4 (July, 1952), 919–29.

tures of colonial urban life with the rise of nationalism. In recent years the number of studies covering the rise of cities in all parts of the country has grown rapidly. Among the best of them is Bessie L. Pierce's *History of Chicago* (Chicago, 1937–), which, when completed, should set a high standard for comparable books.

The emergence of the United States in the twentieth century as a world power focused attention on its relations with other countries. Studies were not restricted to political contacts with other sovereign powers, but ranged over the whole field of interrelationships in economics. literature, the arts, and sciences. One of the best studies was that of Howard M. Jones, *America and French Culture 1750–1848* (Chapel Hill, 1927). An important contribution of historical research in this general area stressed not only the reception and use in the United States of ideas, capital, and products from elsewhere, but also the impact of American civilization on the rest of the world. The latter theme has been briefly sketched in Halvdan Koht's *The American Spirit in Europe* (Philadelphia, 1949).

The most significant studies have been done for the Revolutionary period, during and after which America's example had a profound effect on Europe. Bernard Faÿ's *The Revolutionary Spirit in France and America at the End of the Eighteenth Century* (New York, 1927), though not sufficiently aware of the operation of power politics, was a valuable work. Several important studies showed the interplay of the American Revolution and British politics: G. H. Guttridge, *English Whiggism and the American Revolution* (University of California *Publications in History,* XXVIII, 1928); D. M. Clark, *British Opinion and the American Revolution* (New Haven, 1930); and Leon Fraser, *English Opinion of the American Constitution and Government 1783–1798* (New York, 1915). *The Atlantic Civilization: Eighteenth Century Origins* (Ithaca, 1949), by Michael Kraus, went beyond previous studies in emphasizing the impact of America on Europe in art, science, humanitarianism, religion, economics, and politics.

In the nineteenth century the line of division in Europe between conservatives and liberals was continually sharpened by reference to American example. Conservatives anticipated the failure of the American experiment; liberals hoped for its success. A great test for democracy was our Civil War, and overseas reaction to it was the subject of Donaldson Jordan and E. J. Pratt's *Europe and the American Civil War* (Boston, 1931). Conservers of Europe's traditional culture have long been sensitive to the challenge from the United States and its unsettling effect on the mass of European people. Richard H. Heindel made this clear in *The American Impact on Great Britain 1898–1914* (Philadelphia, 1940). On the other hand, some skeptical liberals in Europe were fearful that America's industrialization was resulting in a class stratification comparable to that in the Old World. David Hecht's *Russian Radicals Look to America* (Cambridge, 1947) discussed the hopes and fears of those whose star hung in the Western sky.

American material and ideological penetration since our Revolutionary era reached areas other than Europe. In Latin America, early in the nineteenth century, combustible materials were ignited by the joint impact of American and European example. William S. Robertson included much of this story in his biography of Miranda, while Charles Griffin and Arthur P. Whitaker wrote in detail of the relationship between the United States and the struggle for independence in Latin America. Harry Bernstein's *Origins of Inter-American Interest* (Philadelphia, 1945) pointed out the nature of contacts between the United States and Latin America from the colonial period to the Monroe Doctrine.

The most detailed treatment of contacts between ourselves and others in the Western Hemisphere was found in the series on Canadian-American relations edited by James T. Shotwell. The United States has affected not only the internal development of members of the British Commonwealth, but also the relations of these members to one another and of each to the mother country. An example of influence exerted internally was the theme of Erling Hunt's *American Precedents in Australian Federation* (New York, 1930), while J. B. Brebner's *North Atlantic Triangle* (New Haven, 1945) stressed the interlocking interests of Britain, Canada, and the United States. Knowledge of the relationship between America and other communities is still too fragmentary, particularly the impact of the United States on the imagination of other peoples; few fields for research promise richer rewards.[8]

[8] See pamphlet, R. H. Heindel (ed.), *American Influences Abroad: An Exploration* (Carnegie Endowment for International Peace, 1950).

A generation which has participated in ideological warfare (along with the more usual kind) seems under a natural compulsion to study the history of ideas. The tendency of historians is to observe how key beliefs—democracy, Puritanism, capitalism, authoritarianism—have evolved and altered society and themselves been altered in the process. Historians favoring an ideological interpretation transformed the Revolution and the Civil War into conflicts between differing civilizations, the victors in both instances apparently representing the more progressive way of life.

The bulk of studies in the history of ideas in America has been written by those who were antipathetic to conservatism. Older authors of this group had grown up in the tradition of agrarianism that nurtured Parrington; younger ones saw much of American history with New Deal eyes and heard in every favorite of an earlier day the ringing voice of Franklin D. Roosevelt. Recently conservatism has dusted off its mirror and has seen a past in which self-interested political leaders have been transmuted into wise statesmen (which many of them were), and the hard faces of some old piratical captains of industry have been retouched to seem benign.

Ralph H. Gabriel's *The Course of American Democratic Thought: An Intellectual History Since 1815* (New York, 1940) was a study of the democratic faith and its vicissitudes. His was a story of the challenges thrown at individualism, nationalism, and the idea of progress, by new economic, intellectual, and political forces. Though noting the obstacles, Gabriel was confident that through the give and take of democracy ("its normal solutions are compromises"), man can yet be "master of his destiny."

Richard Hofstadter, *Social Darwinism in American Thought 1816–1915* (Philadelphia, 1944), analyzed the pervasive influence of the great scientist's thought in this country's politics and intellectual life, pointing out that it was made use of by both conservative and progressive elements. In Hofstadter's *American Political Tradition and the Men who made it* (New York, 1948), the two lines of conservatism and liberalism were traced. While the author's inclination to progressivism was apparent, he saw the flaws in many of liberalism's idols of earlier and later days—Bryan, Theodore Roosevelt, Wilson, and Franklin D. Roosevelt. George E. Mowry observed that many of the participants in the progressive movement came from the middle class. This interpretation was in line with much contemporary writing that attributes to middle-class liberals the motive power for social change which had formerly been credited to workingmen.

The role of small groups of intellectuals in hastening great social changes in America during the past half-century has been analyzed by several historians. They have traced the flow of ideas from a small, imaginative nucleus to a large mass of people who were themselves often unaware of their intellectual godfathers. Morton White, in *Social Thought in America* (New York, 1949), credited Thorstein Veblen, John Dewey, Justice Holmes, Charles A. Beard, and James Harvey Robinson with being a composite dynamo that generated a reform energy yet unspent. Eric F. Goldman, in *Rendezvous with Destiny* (New York, 1952), a history of American reform, went beyond White's book to speak of the transformation of the political climate brought about by the nonconformists.

Henry Steele Commager's *The American Mind* (New Haven, 1950) was in the nature of a completion of Parrington's unfinished work. Commager's range of interests went beyond Parrington's, however, to cover a wide group of topics, from journalism and literature to law and architecture. Even when oppressed by awareness of disquieting tendencies to enforced conformity, he revealed a robust faith in the persistence of the best in the American achievement. The continuity of the finest strain in that tradition he found in the writings and decisions of Justice Holmes, in the ideas of architects Louis Sullivan and Frank Lloyd Wright, in the work of William James, John Dewey, Lester Ward, Parrington, and among the economists, Veblen, Richard T. Ely and John R. Commons.

Possibly Commager remained on too rarefied a level, failing to note how these dynamos of mental energy were "hooked up" with the rest of the population. Indeed this was a defect in many studies (including Parrington's) which traced a continuity of ideological change in the United States but generally neglected to note how these ideas percolated through the mass of the population.

Merle Curti's *Growth of American Thought* (New York, 1943) was a successful pioneer effort to survey the history of this country's intellectual life from its European origins to the twentieth century. Curti had well prepared himself for his large task by such studies as those he had published on American education, the peace movement, nationalism, and the influence of John Locke on political thought in the United States. Like others who have been most influential in writing American intellectual history, Curti confessedly writes with a liberal preference. Unlike others who sometimes failed to trace the connection between theory and implementation, Curti frequently was at pains to note the nearness of ivory tower to the market place.

Many of this generation's best scholars have sat, literally or figuratively, at the feet of Charles A. Beard. His skepticism, his inspired teaching, his literary skill, and his insistence on a scholar's active participation in public life endeared him to a host of people in and out of the groves of academe.

CHARLES AUSTIN BEARD

No American historian in the twentieth century had a wider influence than Charles A. Beard, with a large audience among scholars and a larger one among the general public. Beard's youthful mind was stirred to question the *status quo,* influenced as he was by Colonel James Riley Weaver, his teacher at DePauw University, and stimulated by his experiences at Oxford and his reading of John Ruskin. He in turn, during his years at Columbia, became a freshening breeze that swept away academic staleness.

In association with James Harvey Robinson, he produced textbooks of European history which immensely improved the standard of such publications. With the same collaborator, he published sources which made it possible for young students to become acquainted with the primary materials of history; he was also sole author of texts on American history and politics. Beard made at least two significant contributions of original research with his *An Economic Interpretation of the Constitution* and the *Economic Origins of Jeffersonian Democracy.* The former was something of a bombshell in historical circles, although other writers had anticipated Beard in pointing to the economic factor that played its part in the adoption of the Constitution. Beard, however, dug up forgotten records showing that holders of the government debt were especially anxious to create a strong government which would pay it off. While he later admitted that he had overstated the case, his work left a lasting impression on historiography.[9]

Beard's *Interpretation of the Constitution* became an important docu-

[9] See introduction to 1935 edition; Goldman, *Rendezvous with Destiny,* 154–55.

ment in the literature of progressivism, Western Populists hailing it as a weapon against conservatism. "The time has come," said a Wisconsin Populist, "when all of us, who are looking toward a wider national life, must realize that the Constitution, which has ever been the retreat of privilege, must be changed. When we once realize that this was a human document, written by men acting in many cases under human impulse, we shall have achieved the initial attitude necessary to change it. Professor Beard's book, scholarly and incisive, will do more than any other volume to set us right."

Beard insistently called attention to the manner in which the milieu affected the judgment of the historian, repudiating the "conception dominant among schoolmen during the latter part of the nineteenth century and the opening years of the twentieth century—the conception that it is possible to describe the past as it actually was, somewhat as the engineer describes a single machine." In selecting and ordering materials, the personal bias as well as the social and economic experience of historians play a determining part. In the very act of writing history, the historian performed an "Act of Faith." "He is thus in the position of a statesman dealing with public affairs; in writing he acts and in acting he makes choices . . . with respect to some conception of the nature of things. And the degree of his influence and immortality will depend upon the length and correctness of his forecast—upon the verdict of history yet to come. His faith is at bottom a conviction that something true can be known about the movement of history and his conviction is a subjective decision, not a purely objective discovery." While the historian must continue to use the scientific method, its limitations must be recognized, for a science of history cannot be established which will recreate the past in all its fullness. The historian's task is to define his own relationship to contemporary thought, and it is his function to read the trend of the times. Beard's conjecture was that the world was moving in the direction of collectivist democracy.[10]

In 1927 Charles and Mary Beard published *The Rise of American Civilization,* "The history of a civilization," they said, "is essentially dynamic, suggesting capacities yet unexplored and hinting of emancipation from outward necessities." Their conception of history, like Voltaire's, was that it should be a stimulant to self-criticism and an aid in

[10] Beard, "Written History as an Act of Faith," *American Historical Review,* Vol. XXXIX, No. 2 (January, 1934), 219–31.

producing a richer intellectual climate. A more important place was given to women than was customary in the works of most historians. The need for artistry in composition was emphasized with the remark that "the history of a civilization cannot be written by patching together constitutions, statutes, political speeches, newspaper items, private letters, memoirs, and diplomatic notes." The distance that Beard had traveled since the time when a strict economic determinism had appeared of overwhelming significance to him may be measured by the statement: "The heritage, economics, politics, culture, and international filiations of any civilization are so closely woven by fate into one fabric that no human eye can discern the beginnings of its warp or woof. And any economic interpretation, any political theory, any literary criticism, any aesthetic appreciation, which ignores this perplexing fact, is of necessity superficial."

The work was in two large divisions—the era of Agriculture and the era of Industry—and the authors were concerned to show the influence of these respective ways of life on the psychology of people living them. With a grasp of the literature that astonished even specialists, the Beards managed to convey most vividly the interrelationship of various phases of American civilization and its dynamic quality. In certain passages, which were perhaps overwritten, that dynamism appears too self-conscious, though admittedly the American people were hurrying forward.

The revolt of the colonies against England, the authors asserted, was an "economic, social and intellectual transformation of prime significance—the first of those modern world-shaking reconstructions in which mankind has sought to cut and fashion the tough and stubborn web of fact to fit the pattern of its dreams." The writers showed, too, a better understanding of the middle period than has been expressed by most. In the long perspective, they believed, this period will "appear as the most changeful, most creative, most spirited epoch between the founding of the colonies and the end of the nineteenth century." The Civil War, they pointed out, "was merely the culmination of the deep-running transformation that shifted the center of gravity in American society between the inauguration of Jackson and Lincoln"; and that shift resulted in the triumph of industry over agriculture. The fundamental question at issue was whether the political revolution, which was anticipated by the economic change, was to be peaceful or violent.

The programs of Northern industrialists and Southern planters indicated the line of cleavage between them. The American currency system was in bad shape by 1860, dangerous for business enterprise, but relatively beneficial to agrarians; the courts, too, had let down safeguards for property rights. These were the weaknesses that business enterprise was to remedy as a result of the war. As for slavery, in the mistaken view of Mr. and Mrs. Beard, abolition "was a minor element in bringing on the irrepressible conflict" and of far less importance than economics.

Thus the authors reached the period of the Civil War, which they termed the Second American Revolution. The program of the planter aristocracy in 1860 demanded the surrender of the Northern and Western majority "to the minority stockholders under the Constitution. It offered nothing to capitalism but capitulation. . . . Finally—and this was its revolutionary phase—it called upon the farmers and mechanics who had formed the bulk of Jacksonian Democracy in the North to acknowledge the absolute sovereignty of the planting interest. Besides driving a wedge into the nation the conditions laid down by the planters also split the Democratic party itself into two factions."

The results of the war were shown to be of far-reaching significance; a new power—the industrialists—was placed in the government, great changes were made in the relationship of classes, in the acquisition and distribution of wealth, in industrial development, and in the Constitution as well, in order to safeguard these changes. "Viewed in the large, the supreme outcome of the civil strife was the destruction of the planting aristocracy which, with the aid of northern farmers and mechanics, had practically ruled the United States for a generation. A corollary to that result was the undisputed triumph of a new combination of power; northern capitalists and free farmers who emerged from the conflict richer and more numerous than ever. It was these . . . facts . . . that made the Civil War a social revolution." Four billion dollars' worth of property (slaves) was destroyed without compensation—"the most stupendous act of sequestration in the history of Anglo-Saxon jurisprudence."

The remaining treatment of American history followed lines more familiar to the general student. Even the section on the middle period, although it had especial freshness, did not offer a great deal that was new to those already acquainted with the older work of Thomas H. Benton and the more recent publications of Channing and Dodd. The presentation of the material, however, here as elsewhere in the Beards' history, was masterly. The authors might err in minimizing the place of abolition in bringing on the war; they might overestimate the economic factor as a cause of the war with Spain, missing the full significance of the weight of public opinion manufactured by the newspapers;[11] but even with its defects, *The Rise of American Civilization* is likely to stand for some time as one of the most brilliant interpretations offered by historical scholarship. That this work has been referred to as an essay on American history scarcely lessens its value; almost any kind of treatment of an interpretive character will have that quality. Perhaps the special student will ask for more facts and less interpretation; the general reader likes his history written in the grand manner.

The Rise of American Civilization was followed by *America in Midpassage* (1939) which carried the narrative through "the golden glow" of the 1920's to 1939. It was a good survey of those years; the biting quality of chapters on the panic and aftermath of 1929 was in Beard's best vein, but it lacked the interpretive power of the earlier publication. Beard's dislike of the course of much in American foreign policy was manifest. What he objected to particularly was the alleged use "of the power of the United States to force any scheme of politics or economy on other peoples. . . . Foreign policy," it was held, "could easily be made the instrument to stifle domestic wrongs under a blanket of militarist chauvinism, perhaps disguised by the high sounding title of world peace." The interpretation of Roosevelt's foreign policy was generally hostile, for the government was represented as deliberately wishing to intervene in the European crisis, 1938–39.

The first half of *America in Midpassage* was a study of politics and business; the second half was concerned with labor organization and the various manifestations of culture in the United States. While the authors were skeptical or even scornful of certain phases of New Deal politics, they had nothing but praise for the Federal Art Project; for the first time Americans were made aware "of the extent and nature of their esthetic resources." Though Roosevelt came off poorly in various writings by Beard, in this work the concluding estimate was generous: "In his numerous discourses [he] discussed the basic human and economic problems of American society with a courage and range displayed by no

[11] See J. E. Wisan, *The Cuban Crisis as Reflected in the New York Press 1895–1898* (New York, 1934).

predecessor in his office; . . . he thrust their challenges into spheres hitherto indifferent or hostile; . . . he set in swift circulation, through the use of the radio, ideas once confined to groups more or less esoteric; . . . and in doing this he carried on the tradition of humanistic democracy which from colonial times had been a powerful dynamic in the whole movement of American civilization and culture—economic, political, literary, scientific, and artistic."

Toward the end of *America in Mid-passage* the Beards spoke of the intensification of the love for democracy in the United States, producing "a tumult of praise for the idea and its institutional embodiments." In a subsequent work, *The American Spirit* (1942), the whole complex of ideas which expressed themselves in American civilization was analyzed at considerable length. The meaning which was given to the word civilization itself and the transformations it had experienced since the end of the eighteenth century were the theme of the volume. It represented, said the authors, an "effort to grasp . . . the intellectual and moral qualities that Americans have deemed necessary to civilization in the United States." The Beards, stressing the unique character of American civilization, colored their study with a faint antiforeign view, which became more marked in their *Basic History of the United States*.

The wide-ranging mind of Charles A. Beard grasped the significance of Lord Acton's precept: "Study problems, not periods." In Collingwood's language, "Scissors-and-paste historians study periods; they collect all the extant testimony about a certain limited group of events, and hope in vain that something will come of it. Scientific historians study problems; they ask questions, and if they are good historians they ask questions which they see their way to answering." Beard was forever asking questions, and, following in the train of European scholars (notably Croce) who were more than a generation in advance of Americans in this matter, he and Carl Becker asked fellow historians to consider the meaning of their research and their writing. Beard reminded them that in every era contestants had used the writing of history to capture the human mind. Catholics and Protestants had done so, and Voltaire had made history "a dynamic force for the French Revolution." At a later time, "under the guise of romanticism, history had served the reaction." Every history, it was maintained, was "a selection of facts made by some person or persons and is ordered or organized under the influence of some scheme of reference, interest or emphasis—

avowed or unavowed—in the thought of the author or the authors." As Collingwood expressed it, "history is nothing but the re-enactment of past thought in the historian's mind." Modern historians, said Beard, "working in the scientific spirit, seeking emancipation from the tyranny of old assumptions" should legitimately use their discipline to illuminate "all divisions of contemporary thought and all formulations of public policy." Historical writing, he believed, was to be an instrument for the advancement of social reform.

More than anyone else, Beard stimulated scholars to recognize frankly the functional nature of historical knowledge and to make them aware of what they were doing. "Just what intellectual operations does the historian perform in studying and writing history?" he asked. "For what reason . . . are particular aspects of history chosen for emphasis and other aspects excluded?"

The "relativist" school of historical writing came under attack from various quarters. One criticism was that history would be made vulnerable to the activities of pressure groups who would dictate interpretations historians would have to employ.[12] The accent on "presentism" by the "relativist school," it was said, tended to distort the significance of earlier periods of history. As Robert L. Schuyler observed, the "presentist" will "omit or play down those past events and developments that do not seem to him to account for the present, no matter how important they may have seemed to men at the time, and conversely, he will throw his spotlight on those that do appear to him to explain the present, no matter how unimportant they may have seemed at the time." Genuine historical-mindedness evaluates institutions in the light of the needs they serve, and not in relation to a later set of conditions. Out of "presentism" may come a type of partisan history whose real intent is not so much to discover the truth about the past as it is to reveal the historian's emotions toward it.[13]

However much "presentism" may be deplored, it is a fact that historians have, consciously or unconsciously, generally been guided by it, though not always in an obvious manner. Even historians, such as Channing and McLaughlin, who are thought of as "objective," free of the

[12] C. M. Destler, "Some Observations on Contemporary Historical Theory," *American Historical Review,* Vol. LV, No. 3 (April, 1950), 503–29.

[13] R. L. Schuyler, "Man's Greatest Illusion," American Philosophical Society *Proceedings,* Vol. XCII, No. 1 (1948). 46–51.

compulsion to see the past by the light of their own day, were clearly conscious of the effect of their own cultural experience in dictating their view of American history. In a vigorous defense of the "relativists" Merle Curti maintained that historians of that persuasion were no less likely to be "objective" and accurate in their narratives than their critics. Howard K. Beale, indeed, argued that "writers with a determined philosophy of life of which they are fully conscious and which they make clear to the reader stand a better chance of approaching 'objectivity' than did the older writers who, if they used 'scientific tools,' thought themselves completely 'objective.' "[14]

Clearly most historians of our time are under no illusions that they are free of preconceptions in their approach to the past. They know the fallacy of Ranke's assumption, that there exists an uncommitted "present" to which alone the key to the past is committed. Yet Ranke's ideal is still a lamp to light the dark beyond, for implicit in its methods of research was the demand that we measure the men of the past by their achievement in creating institutions that fitted the needs of their own time. "The realties of the past," said William A. Dunning, "will never be scientifically apprehended so long as the student of history stands contemplating in a stupor of admiration the reversals of ancient beliefs effected in our own age. Contempt for those who lacked our light is the worst of equipments for understanding their deeds."

Conclusion

In the seventeenth century, among a people with intense conviction of direct relationship to God, history was a testament of deeds done for the Lord's service. When the nation became proudly conscious of its unique place in the system of world governments and of its growing strength, history became a record of deeds done for (or against) the country's good. In their narratives, political historians were usually swayed by their party convictions, so that their works may be generally divided into two schools, Jeffersonian or Hamiltonian.

In the middle of the nineteenth century, historical writing on both

[14] Curti, "The Democratic Theme in American Historical Literature," *Mississippi Valley Historical Review*, Vol. XXXIX, No. 1 (June, 1952), 3–28; Beale, in *Theory and Practice in Historical Study*, 91.

sides of the Atlantic was dominated by the "romantic" school. With the spread of German academic influence, however, preference fell to scholarship of the "scientific," "objective" variety, which seemed to eschew interpretation in the belief that the reader would draw his own conclusions on the basis of the facts laid before him. Since modern science demanded organization, historical scholars claimed scientific standing and joined together in professional organizations, founding journals and the like for the accumulation and dissemination of data on which scientific generalizations were to rest. The artist was a lost individual in a group of collective artisans who became entombed in their own labyrinth. Most Americans who had studied abroad brought home with them an idolatry of foreign scholarship. Important as was the contribution to teaching and writing made by the European-trained men of the 1870's and 1880's, they depreciated earlier American scholarship, thus obscuring its genuine value.

It should be remembered that the early historian had to depend mainly on his own ingenuity in gathering materials, and the quality of his achievement was heavily dependent upon his personal resources. When the circle of students of history grew larger, a historian might levy upon his fellows for aid to scholarship, but on the whole his remained a pioneer effort. With the accumulation of wealth came the opportunity to gather libraries of great value; only a Bancroft, or Parkman, or Prescott had at his command materials that are accessible today to the humblest student. The early tradition of individual enterprise in history was paralleled by an equally early tradition of public support, as the grants of Massachusetts to Hubbard and of New Hampshire to Belknap indicate. The greater resources of the national government in the early nineteenth century were drawn upon in aiding Sparks and Peter Force, while in our own time philanthropic foundations and governmental agencies have eased the path of scholars.

The historian's emphasis on political democracy was broadened to include social and industrial democracy, and the wider vistas thus opened to him enlarged the scope of his research—and also multiplied his problems. It had been comparatively easy to keep a narrative of political and military history moving briskly in a chronological sequence. It was not so easy to make a dramatic story of manners, customs, ideas, and the like, which are the materials of social history. This work usually lacked not only drama but also interpretation. The historian was generally content to limit himself to description, crowding as much data together as his conscience and publisher allowed. Interpretation was condescendingly left to the "philosophic" historian, who was credited with knowing more philosophy than history.

A surfeit of merely descriptive material may lead to intellectual indigestion and not to wisdom, and the reader has been asking for some time that the historian cease merely to photograph, that he try also to find, if possible, a significance in the events described. He is to use the tools of scientific research to evaluate his materials, but once again is urged to find, as did former historians, a meaning in the patterns he has traced. Happily, contemporary writers not only are aware of this task laid upon them—to interpret—but are conscious, too, of the need to tell their story with as much art as their talents will allow. Erudition, interpretation, artistry—these are required in the historian. Out of dusty books and faded manuscripts he recreates people instinct with life, committing follies and yet redeeming humanity by courage and wisdom.[15]

[15] In addition to the references in the previous footnotes, the following (out of many more) may also be consulted for the debate on the nature and purpose of historical writing: R. G. Collingwood, *The Idea of History* (Oxford, 1946); E. N. Anderson, "Meinecke's 'Ideengeschichte' and the Crisis in Historical Thinking," in *Medieval and Historical Essays in Honor of James Westfall Thompson;* R. V. Burks, "Benedetto Croce," in B. E. Schmitt (ed.), *Some Historians of Modern Europe* (Chicago, 1942); Carl Becker, "What is Historiography," *American Historical Review,* Vol. XLIV, No. 1 (October, 1938), 20–28; Pendleton Herring, "A Political Scientist Considers the Question," *Pennsylvania Magazine of History and Biography,* Vol. LXII, No. 2 (April, 1948), 118–36; Herman Ausubel, *Historians and Their Craft* (New York, 1950).

Index

Abell, A. I.: 358
Abernethy, T. P.: 288
Acton, Lord: 124, 372
Adam, of Bremen: 6
Adams, Abigail: 78
Adams, Brooks: 294
Adams, Charles Francis: 99, 106
Adams, Charles Francis, Jr.: 128, 165, 168, 172, 188, 206, 293, 294, 294–97, 318, 321
Adams, Charles K.: 167, 170, 171
Adams, Hannah: 77–78
Adams, Henry: 114, 154, 165, 166, 167, 168, 170, 172, 174, 177–89, 216, 232, 236, 295, 300, 309, 318
Adams, Herbert Baxter: 119, 167, 168, 169, 170, 171, 215, 260, 280, 302
Adams, James Truslow: 84, 293, 294, 296, 297–300, 343, 349
Adams, John: 60, 71, 77, 79, 87, 89, 90, 91, 92, 93, 105, 120, 132, 135, 164, 199, 245, 295, 318, 329
Adams, John Quincy: 106, 111, 122, 164, 179, 318, 331, 332, 335
Adams, Samuel: 121, 215, 235, 330
Adams, W. F.: 359
Albion, R. G.: 346
Alexander, James: 45
Allen, William: 140
Allen, W. F.: 279
Alvord, C. W.: 267–68
American Antiquarian Society: 233
American Historical Association: 4, 172, 278, 281
American Historical Review: 162, 172, 244
American Historical Society: 95
American Quarterly Review: 98, 140
American Review: 99
Ames, Fisher: 180
Ames, Nathaniel: 58, 244
Andrews, Charles M.: 17, 31, 40, 121, 173, 213, 230, 234, 242, 251, 254, 257, 260–65, 269, 298
Andros, Edmund: 30
Annual Register: 59, 61, 72, 73, 86
Aptheker, Herbert: 308
Astor, John J.: 96
Austin, S. F.: 332

Backus, Isaac: 58
Bacon, Nathaniel: 119
Badeau, Adam: 317
Bagehot, Walter: 215
Baird, Charles W.: 163
Baker, Ray S.: 334
Baldwin, Alice M.: 358
Bancroft, Aaron: 115
Bancroft, Frederick: 206, 308
Bancroft, George: 4, 68, 82, 85, 93, 95, 97, 98, 99, 100, 101, 104, 106, 108, 113, 115–27, 129, 130, 135, 137, 139, 148, 154, 157, 164, 177,

191, 198, 200, 202, 209, 224, 225, 228, 231, 242, 315, 316, 375
Bancroft, Hubert H.: 272–74
Barker, E. C.: 332
Barlow, Joel: 86, 352
Barlow, S. L. M.: 158, 159
Bartlett, J. R.: 96
Bassett, John S.: 231, 302, 319, 355
Baxter, W. T.: 338
Beale, H. K.: 374
Beard, Charles A.: 173, 174, 225, 240, 299, 312, 323, 366, 367–74
Beard, Mary R.: 312, 368, 370
Becker, Carl: 107, 175, 279, 343, 372
Beer, George L.: 215, 242, 250, 251, 257–60, 266, 268, 298
Belknap, Jeremy: 49, 57, 59, 68, 73–76, 82, 101, 103, 294
Bemis, S. F.: 277, 291, 331, 332
Bentham, Jeremy: 135
Bentley, William: 103
Benton, Thomas H.: 143–44, 370
Bergson, Henri: 344
Bernstein, Harry: 364
Beveridge, Albert J.: 321, 322–26
Beverley, Robert: 3, 39–40, 80
Bidgood, Lee: 267
Bidwell, P. W.: 289
Billington, R. A.: 292, 293
Biography: early nineteenth-century, 140–44
Bismarck, Otto von: 12, 125, 126, 193, 195, 277
Black, J. B.: 123
Blaine, J. G.: 317, 334
Bledsoe, A. T.: 302
Blegen, Theodore: 359
Bluntschli, J. K.: 169
Bolton, H. E.: 286–87, 291
Bond, B. W.: 289
Boston Athenaeum: 77
Botta, C. W.: 90, 91, 103, 104–105
Boucher, Jonathan: 245
Bourne, E. G.: 143, 230
Bowen, C. D.: 329
Bowers, C. G.: 309–10
Bowles, Samuel: 162
Boyd, J. P.: 330
Boyd, W. K.: 303, 307
Bozman, J. L.: 136
Brackenridge, H. H.: 352
Bradford, John: 47
Bradford, William: 3, 14, 17, 20–24, 27, 29, 30, 32
Bradford, William (printer): 44
Bradstreet, Anne: 300
Brandeis, Elizabeth: 347
Brant, Irving: 187, 321, 331
Brebner, J. B.: 360, 364
Brevoort, J. C.: 158
Brewster, William: 20
Brigham, C. L.: 163
Brockunier, S. H.: 328
Brodhead, J. R.: 97, 98
Broglie, V. M.: 113
Brooks, Phillips: 211
Brooks, Van Wyck: 356
Brown, Alexander: 304–305
Brown, John: 192, 197, 201
Brown, J. C.: 96, 158
Brown, W. G.: 207, 303
Bruce, P. A.: 303, 304, 358
Bruce, W. C.: 319
Bryan, W. J.: 217, 365
Bryant, W. C.: 76, 353
Bryce, James: 170, 186, 278
Buchanan, James: 313
Buck, P. H.: 313
Buck, S. J.: 290
Buckle, H. T.: 4, 165, 166, 167, 205, 243
Buel, C. C.: 162
Buley, R. C.: 289
Burgess, J. W.: 171, 191, 202–204, 251, 252, 257, 305
Burk, J. D.: 77, 80–81
Burke, Edmund: 247
Burnet, William: 54
Burnett, E. C.: 362
Burr, Aaron: 187

Byrd, William: 41–43, 51

Cabot, John: 160
Cabot, Sebastian: 160
Calhoun, J. C.: 144, 192, 320, 353
Callender, John: 48, 49–50
Canning, George: 183
Carey, Mathew: 87
Carlyle, Thomas: 122, 150
Carnegie, Andrew: 338
Carnegie Institution of Washington: 98, 171, 345
Carroll, B. R.: 94
Carroll, H. K.: 358
Carter, C. E.: 267
Casgrain, H. R.: 154
Caughey, J. W.: 292
Century Magazine: 327
Chalmers, George: 62, 68–70, 74, 85, 246
Chamberlain, Mellen: 228
Channing, Edward: 72, 88, 111, 135, 171, 175, 178, 187, 228, 229, 232–41, 242, 285, 300, 323, 324, 325, 328, 370, 373
Channing, W. E.: 99, 164, 237
Chansey, Charles: 23
Charnwood, Lord: 322
Cheyney, E. P.: 230, 358
Chinard, Gilbert: 329
Chipman, Nathaniel: 60
Chittenden, H. M.: 292
Christian Review, The: 130
Church, Benjamin: 32
Church, Thomas: 32
Clark, D. M.: 363
Clark, V. S.: 345
Clarke, M. St. Clair: 95
Clay, Henry: 184, 318, 320
Cleveland, Grover: 205, 217, 335, 336
Clinton, De Witt: 97
Cogswell, J. G.: 96, 115, 169
Cohen, I. B.: 361
Colden, Cadwallader: 43–45, 54
Cole, A. C.: 349
Coleman, J. W.: 174
Collingwood, R.: 372, 373
Columbus, Christopher: 7, 8, 10, 141, 142, 159, 160, 300
Coman, Katharine: 292
Commager, H. S.: 332, 366
Commons, J. R.: 346, 347, 366
Comte, Auguste: 4, 166, 186, 188, 295
Conway, M. D.: 318
Cooke, Jay: 338
Cooper, J. F.: 145, 353
Corey, Lewis: 173
Cornbury, Lord: 54, 250
Corwin, E. T.: 358
Cosby, William: 45
Cotton, John: 351
Coulanges, Fustel de: 169
Coulter, E. M.: 313–14
Craigie, William: 357
Crane, V. W.: 277, 291
Craven, A. O.: 311, 312, 332
Craven, W. F.: 313
Crèvecoeur, M. G. J. de (J. H. St. John): 43
Croce, Benedetto: 372
Curti, Merle: 358, 366, 367, 374
Cushing, Caleb: 333
Curtis, G. T.: 228

Darwin, Charles: 5, 166, 168, 191, 209, 212, 361
Davenport, F. G.: 261
David, Henry: 174
Davidson, Philip: 330
Davis, Jefferson: 202
Dawson, H. B.: 162
Day, R. E.: 329
De Bow's Review: 137
Dennett, Tyler: 334
De Voto, Bernard: 272, 292
Dewey, John: 366
Dexter, H. M.: 163
Díaz del Castillo, Bernal: 10

Dick, Everett: 291
Dickerson, O. M.: 265–67
Dickinson, John: 245, 318
Dilke, Charles: 242
Discovery and exploration, literature of: 158–61
Dodd, W. E.: 320, 323, 370
Donald, David: 321
Dondore, D. A.: 356
Dorfman, Joseph: 347
Douglas, S. A.: 196, 205, 223, 312, 325, 338
Douglass, William: 55–56
Doyle, J. A.: 243, 246, 248–51
Drake, S. G.: 31, 162
Draper, J. W.: 166, 167, 205
Draper, L. C.: 271, 274
Du Bois, W. E. B.: 310, 311
Dulany, Daniel: 245
Dunning, W. A.: 191, 204, 230, 232, 302, 305–307, 310, 374
Dwight, Timothy: 180

Eames, Wilberforce: 163
Eaton, Clement: 312
Ebeling, C. D.: 76, 83, 96, 103–104, 169
Eden, Richard: 11, 12
Edwards, Jonathan: 35, 354
Eggleston, Edward: 228, 348
Eliot, C. W.: 178, 209
Eliot, John: 32, 46
Eliot, John (biographer): 140
Elliot, Jonathan: 94
Ely, R. T.: 366
Emerson, R. W.: 115, 122, 353
Erskine, John: 355
Evans, Charles: 163
Everett, A. H.: 141
Everett, Edward: 91, 96, 115, 122, 169

Falconer, J. I.: 289
Faulkner, H. U.: 349
Faÿ, Bernard: 319, 363
Firth, C. H.: 208
Fish, C. R.: 349
Fish, Hamilton: 336
Fisher, S. G.: 126
Fiske, John: 119, 155, 191, 209–13, 225, 248, 252, 298
Fitch, John: 219
Fleming, W. L.: 303
Folsom, Charles: 109
Forbes, Esther: 329
Force, Peter: 95, 96, 158
Ford, P. L.: 162, 171, 220, 246, 357
Ford, W. C.: 20, 171, 323, 325
Fothergill, John: 58
Fox, C. J.: 246, 247
Fox, D. R.: 252, 348, 349, 362
Franklin, Benjamin: 88, 111, 223, 244, 256, 319, 331, 350, 351
Franklin, J. H.: 310
Fraser, Leon: 363
Freeman, D. S.: 297, 338–42
Freeman, Edward: 119, 168, 169, 191, 212, 260, 321
Frémont, J. C.: 335
Freneau, Philip: 245, 352
Frothingham, O. B.: 361
Fuess, C. M.: 333

Gabriel, R. H.: 365
Gallatin, Albert: 179, 236
Galloway, Joseph: 245
Garcilaso de la Vega: 10
Garrison, G. P.: 232, 288
Gaskell, C. M.: 170
Gates, Horatio: 71
Gates, P. W.: 290
Gayarré, C. E. A.: 138–40
Gerry, Elbridge: 89
Ghent, W. J.: 292
Gibbon, Edward: 93, 123
Gilbert, Humphrey: 12
Gilman, D. C.: 165, 168
Girard, Stephen: 223
Girardin, L. H.: 80
Gneist, R. von: 202

Göbel, Julius: 360
Goddard, H. C.: 361
Godkin, E. L.: 154, 227, 278
Gomara, F. L. de: 10, 11
Goodell, A. C.: 65
Gookin, Daniel: 32–33
Gordon, William: 59, 70–72, 73, 78, 114
Gottschalk, L. R.: 319
Grahame, James: 85, 98, 103, 105–107
Grant, U. S.: 204, 317, 336, 339
Grattan, C. H.: 343
Gray, L. C.: 311
Greeley, Horace: 320, 353
Green, J. R.: 168, 214
Greene, E. B.: 230, 231, 349
Greenslet, Ferris: 343
Griffin, Charles: 364
Guizot, F. P. G.: 122
Gurney, E. W.: 178
Guthrie, William: 82
Guttridge, G. H.: 363

Hakluyt, Richard: 8, 11–13, 15
Haldane, Viscount: 323
Hall, T. C.: 119
Hamilton, Alexander: 4, 102, 109, 132, 138, 180, 193, 198, 236, 323, 324, 330, 331, 351, 352, 374
Hamilton, J. G. de R.: 303, 307
Hancock, John: 267
Handlin, Oscar: 359
Hansen, M. A.: 359, 360
Hariot, Thomas: 12
Harper, L. A.: 265–66
Harrison, W. H.: 194
Harrisse, Henry: 11, 143, 159–61, 162
Hart, A. B.: 171, 225, 229, 230, 232
Hawks, F. L.: 94, 163
Hawthorne, Nathaniel: 341
Hay, John: 179, 183, 321, 334
Hayes, R. B.: 202, 311
Haynes, F. E.: 290
Haywood, John: 136
Hazard, Ebenezer: 59, 74, 75, 82, 83
Hazard, L. L.: 356
Hazard, Samuel: 98
Hecht, David: 364
Hedges, J. B.: 338
Heeren, A. H. L.: 116
Heindel, R. H.: 364
Hendrick, B. J.: 338, 343
Henry, Patrick: 92, 234, 244
Henry, W. W.: 317
Herndon, W. H.: 321, 326
Herrera, Antonio de: 9
Hewat, Alexander: 61, 67–68
Hicks, J. D.: 290
Hidy, R. W.: 338
Higginson, John: 29
Higginson, T. W.: 157
Hildreth, Richard: 108, 129–35, 148, 157, 164, 193, 198, 205, 219, 231, 233
Historical Magazine: 161, 162
Historical societies: 96–97
Hoar, E. R.: 204
Hodder, F. H.: 312
Hofstadter, Richard: 365
Hollis, Thomas: 61
Holmes, Abiel: 4, 58, 100–101, 103, 104, 114, 120, 199
Holmes, O. W.: 100
Holmes, Justice O. W.: 101, 323, 366
Holst, H. von: 191, 192–98, 205, 280
Hone, Philip: 335
Hopkins, C. H.: 358
Hopkinson, Francis: 245
Houston, Sam: 332
Hubbard, William: 20, 27, 30–31, 32, 45, 47, 375
Hubbart, H. C.: 289
Hughes, Rupert: 341
Humboldt, A. von: 160
Hume, David: 93
Humphrey, E. F.: 358
Hunt, Erling: 364
Hunter, L. C.: 289, 290

Huntington Library: 283
Hurlbert, J. R.: 357
Hutchinson, Anne: 25, 28, 127, 249
Hutchinson, Thomas: 3, 47, 57, 62–65, 66, 76, 77, 78, 79, 101, 121, 294
Hutchinson, W. T.: 338

Irving, Washington: 10, 141–43, 353

Jackson, Andrew: 4, 122, 124, 138, 144, 193, 194, 200, 216, 222, 224, 236, 288, 315, 316, 319, 320, 369, 370
Jackson, T. J. ("Stonewall"): 339, 340
James, Marquis: 320, 332
James, William: 361, 366
Jameson, J. F.: 27, 171, 173, 214, 319, 323
Jay, John: 109, 132, 216, 331
Jefferson, Thomas: 4, 76, 79, 80, 86, 87, 91, 92, 93, 96, 105, 117, 137, 179, 180, 181, 182, 183, 187, 193, 198, 199, 216, 219, 235, 236, 295, 309, 316, 319, 323, 325, 329, 331, 350, 352, 353, 354, 374
Jenkins, W. S.: 312
Jensen, Merrill: 271, 362
Jessup, P. C.: 333
Jogues, Isaac: 151
Johnson, Allen: 343
Johnson, Andrew: 125, 201, 207, 226, 288, 306, 313
Johnson, Edward: 27–28, 47
Johnson, E. R.: 345
Johnson, William: 329
Jones, H. M.: 363
Jones, Skelton: 80
Jordan, Donaldson: 364
Jordy, W. H.: 186
Jorns, Auguste: 358

Kapp, Friedrich: 192
Kent, James: 86
Kinnaird, Lawrence: 287
Kirkland, E. C.: 294
Kirkland, J. T.: 116
Kittredge, G. L.: 101
Knickerbocker magazine: 146
Koch, Adrienne: 331
Koht, Halvdan: 363
Kraus, Michael: 362, 363
Krout, J. A.: 349

Labaree, L. W.: 298, 361
Laboulaye, Edouard de: 170
Lafayette, Marquis de: 109, 110, 319
Lamprecht, Karl: 174, 175, 239
Larkin, O. W.: 356
Larson, H. M.: 338
Las Casas, Bartolomé de: 8–9, 211
Latané, J. H.: 303
Laughlin, J. L.: 167
Lawson, John: 41
Lea, H. C.: 166, 297
Lecky, W. E. H.: 166, 167, 243
Lee, G. C.: 303
Lee, "Light-Horse Harry": 136
Lee, R. E.: 206, 302, 338, 339, 340
Lehman-Haupt, H.: 358
Lenox, James: 96, 158
Leonard, Daniel: 245
Lescohier, D. D.: 346
Libby, O. G.: 61, 73
Libraries, first half of nineteenth century: 95–97, 104, 109
Library of Congress: 95, 96, 109
Lieber, Francis: 164
Lincoln, Abraham: 196, 197, 202, 207, 218, 223, 321, 324, 326, 327, 328, 330, 369
Lincoln, Mary T.: 327
Lincoln, R. T.: 322
Lincoln, William: 94
Lindsey, Almont: 174
Link, Arthur: 334
Locke, John: 235, 367
Lodge, H. C.: 167, 178, 180, 225, 233, 275, 278, 293
Longfellow, H. W.: 5, 88

Lossing, B. J.: 157, 248
Lowell Institute: 211
Ludewig, H. E.: 96
Lyell, Charles: 169

Mably, Abbé de: 60
Macaulay, T. B.: 99, 100, 168, 179, 224, 246, 297
McCall, Hugh: 136
McClure, A. K.: 162
McClure's Magazine: 327
McCormick, C. H.: 338
McCrady, Edward: 305
MacDonald, William: 230
McDuffie, George: 143
MacGill, C. E.: 346
McKean, Thomas: 89, 90, 93
McKinley, William: 224, 226
McLaughlin, A. C.: 230, 231, 373
McMaster, J. B.: 5, 172, 191, 193, 218–25, 226, 227, 240, 278, 287, 293, 309
Madison, James: 86, 91, 92, 96, 105, 179, 181, 182, 187, 216, 249
Magazine of American History: 162
Magazines, historical writing in early American: 58–59
Mahan, A. T.: 191, 293
Maine, Henry: 168
Malone, Dumas: 321, 330, 343
Marcy, W. L.: 117
Margry, M. Pierre: 151, 155, 159
Marion, Francis: 88
Marshall, Humphrey: 137
Marshall, John: 76, 84–86, 110, 111, 142, 317, 323, 331, 353
Marshall, T. M.: 287
Martin, B. N.: 205
Martin, F. X.: 138
Martyr, Peter: 8, 11
Marx, Karl: 134, 135, 173, 186
Mason, John: 32
Massachusetts Historical Society: 59, 75
Mather, Cotton: 3, 14, 20, 33–37, 45, 46, 47, 92, 140, 293, 294
Mather, Increase: 31–32, 45, 47, 328
Mathews, L. K.: 289
Mathews, M. M.: 357
Mathiessen, F. O.: 356
Mauduit, Jasper: 77
Mayhew, Jonathan: 61, 245
Mayo, Bernard: 320
Melville, Herman: 353
Mencken, H. L.: 357
Merk, Frederick: 293
Meyer, B. H.: 346
Michelet, Jules: 177
Mill, J. S.: 166, 295
Miller, J. C.: 330
Miller, Perry: 328, 329
Milton, G. F.: 312
Minnich, H. C.: 357
Minot, George: 76–77
Mississippi Valley Historical Review: 288
Monaghan, Frank: 331
Monroe, James: 182, 200, 221
Monthly Anthology, The: 85, 92, 140
Morison, S. E.: 9, 31, 36, 37, 294, 300–301, 358
Morley, John: 318
Morris, R. B.: 346, 360
Morris, William: 354
Morse, Jedidiah: 59, 81, 82–84, 90, 103
Morse, J. T.: 318
Morton, Nathaniel: 29–30, 32, 45, 47
Morton, Thomas: 21, 28, 295
Mosier, R. D.: 357
Motley, J. L.: 4, 100, 113, 164, 177, 191
Mott, F. L.: 357
Moultrie, William: 136
Mowry, G. E.: 333, 365
Muenster, Sebastian: 11
Mumford, Lewis: 356
Murdock, K. B.: 294, 328
Murphy, H. C.: 159
Muzzey, D. S.: 334

Myers, Gustavus: 173

Nation, The: 206, 227, 278, 302
Navarrete, M. Fernández de: 141, 142
Neal, Daniel: 45, 47
Neumann, Karl: 170
Nevill, Samuel: 58
Nevins, Allan: 313, 321, 333, 335–37, 349
New England Historical and Genealogical Register: 162
New England Quarterly: 294
New York Mirror: 140
Nichols, R. F.: 312
Nicolay, J. G.: 321, 327
Niles, Hezekiah: 90, 94
Norse Voyages: 5–7
North American Review: 91, 92, 99, 101, 106, 108, 109, 116, 117

Oberholtzer, E. P.: 174, 226–27
Oldmixon, John: 39, 40, 41
Oliver, F. S.: 323
Osgood, H. L.: 106, 173, 211, 215, 234, 242, 251–57, 258, 260, 261, 269, 298
Otis, James: 78, 92, 118, 234
Oviedo y Valdes, G. F. de: 9–10, 11
Owen, Robert: 135
Owsley, F. L.: 308

Packard, F. D.: 360
Paine, Thomas: 318
Palfrey, J. G.: 108, 127–29, 242, 249
Paltsits, V. H.: 171
Parish, Elijah: 84
Parker, Theodore: 134, 147, 166, 333, 353, 354
Parkman, Francis: 113, 114, 145–56, 159, 164, 172, 177, 191, 267, 276, 297, 375
Parrington, V. L.: 350–55, 366
Parton, James: 316
Paulding, J. K.: 353
Paxson, F. L.: 292
Pearson, Edmund: 357
Penhallow, Samuel: 32
Penn, William: 66
Pennsylvania Magazine of History and Biography: 162
Perkins, Dexter: 293
Perlman, Selig: 347
Perry, R. B.: 361
Perry, W. S.: 163
Persons, Stow: 361
Peter, Hugh: 119
Phillips, U. B.: 216, 303, 307–308
Phips, William: 46
Pierce, B. L.: 363
Pierce, E. L.: 206, 317
Pierce, Franklin: 201
Pintard, John: 49
Pitkin, Timothy: 4, 101–103, 114
Political Science Quarterly: 172, 252
Polk, J. K.: 124, 194, 335
Pontiac: 147–49
Poole, W. F.: 65
Porter, K. W.: 337
Pound, Arthur: 329
Pratt, E. J.: 364
Pratt, J. W.: 293
Prescott, W. H.: 4, 96, 98, 100, 113, 123, 164, 177, 297, 310, 375
Priestley, H. I.: 348
Prince, Thomas: 3, 20, 47–49, 51, 54, 66, 73, 100, 199
Pringle, H. F.: 333
Proud, Robert: 62, 66–67
Purchas, Samuel: 13

Quincy, Josiah: 107

Raleigh, Sir Walter: 12, 118
Ramsay, David: 59, 68, 71, 72–73, 78, 103, 114
Ramusio, G. B.: 11, 12
Ramsdell, C. W.: 307
Randall, J. G.: 313, 327
Randolph, John: 144, 179

Randolph, T. J.: 92, 93
Ranke, L. von: 4, 124, 169, 202, 252, 374
Reinor, John: 23
Renan, Ernest: 160 ,177
Revere, Paul: 5, 329
Rhodes, J. F.: 164, 168, 174, 190, 201, 204–209, 211, 313, 335
Rich, Obadiah: 96, 141
Rives, W. C.: 317
Roane, Spencer: 324
Robbins, R. M.: 292
Robertson, William: 93
Robertson, W. S.: 364
Robinson, J. H.: 175, 223, 366, 367
Rockefeller, J. D.: 336, 337
Roosevelt, Franklin D.: 334, 365, 371
Roosevelt, Theodore: 154, 225, 248, 275–78, 280, 293, 318, 333, 334, 365
Root, Elihu: 333, 334
Rourke, Constance: 356
Rowland, K. M.: 318
Rowlandson, Mary: 33
Rush, Benjamin: 59, 90
Rusk, R. L.: 356
Ruskin, John: 367
Russel, R. R.: 312

Sabin, Joseph: 162
Sabine, Lorenzo: 163
Saloutos, Theodore: 290
Sandburg, Carl: 321, 328
Sanderson, John: 112, 140
Sandys, Sir Edwin: 52
Sargent, Nathan: 315
Schaff, Philip: 358
Schlesinger, A. M.: 107, 174, 348, 349, 351, 362
Schlesinger, A. M., Jr.: 362
Schlüter, Herman: 173
Schneider, H. W.: 361
Schouler, James: 187, 198–202, 204, 213, 227
Schurz, Carl: 162, 318
Schuyler, R. L.: 213, 257, 373
Scott, Sir Walter: 139, 145
Scribner's Sons, Charles: 203
Seeley, John: 242
Seelye, J. H.: 251
Seligman, E. R. A.: 173, 257
Sewall, Samuel: 315
Seward, W. H.: 313
Shannon, Fred: 290–91
Shays, Daniel: 77, 78, 125, 131, 219
Shea, J. G.: 114, 158, 162, 163
Sherman, John: 317
Sherman, S. P.: 355
Sherwood, R. E.: 334
Shippee, L. B.: 208
Shipton, C. K.: 294
Shirley, William: 256
Shoemaker, Ervin: 357
Shotwell, J. T.: 364
Shryock, R. H.: 360
Shugg, R. W.: 311
Simms, W. G.: 88, 136, 353
Simons, A. M.: 173
Slosson, P. W.: 349
Smith, A. E.: 346
Smith, Adam: 55
Smith, H. N.: 290
Smith, J. A.: 174, 350
Smith, John: 14, 15–17, 18, 39, 51, 80, 305
Smith, Juliana: 101
Smith, Samuel: 54–55
Smith, S. H.: 60
Smith, William: 52–54, 60
Southern Historians, early nineteenth-century: 136–37
Southern Historical Society: 302
Southern History Association: 302
Southern Literary Messenger: 137
Southern Quarterly Review: 137, 302
Spanish histories of America: 7–11
Sparks, Jared: 4, 13, 93, 94, 95, 96, 98, 99, 105, 106, 108–14, 123, 127, 140, 141, 142, 147, 164, 316

Spencer, Herbert: 5, 166, 168, 191, 209
Spiller, R. E.: 355
Sprague, W. B.: 163
Steiner, B. C.: 303
Stephenson, N. W.: 322
Stevens, Abel: 163
Stevens, B. F.: 171
Stevens, Henry: 96
Stevens, Thaddeus: 217, 306, 310
Stiles, Ezra: 30, 57, 58, 64, 100, 101, 103
Stillé, C. J.: 318
Stilwell, L. D.: 289
Stith, William: 3, 51–52
Stokes, A. P.: 358
Stone, F. D.: 225
Strachey, Lytton: 344
Struik, Dirk: 361
Stubbs, William: 168
Sullivan, Louis: 366
Sumner, Charles: 206, 310, 336
Sweet, W. W.: 358
Swift, Lindsay: 178
Sybel, H. von: 192
Sydnor, C. S.: 313, 361

Tacitus: 89, 93
Taft, Philip: 347
Taft, H. W.: 333
Taine, H. A.: 177, 350
Tappan, H. P.: 165
Tarbell, Ida: 327, 349
Taylor, G. R.: 346
Taylor, H. O.: 167
Taylor, John: 353
Thacher, Thomas: 29
Tharp, L. H.: 343
Thomas, B. P.: 322, 327
Thomas, Isaiah: 357
Thompson, Holland: 307
Thoreau, H. D.: 353, 354
Thorndike, Augustus: 169
Thorpe, F. N.: 157, 303
Thwaites, R. G.: 171, 274–75, 280
Thucydides: 93
Ticknor, George: 92, 94, 96, 115, 169
Tilden, S. J.: 202, 311
Tocqueville, A. de: 75, 144, 166, 200
Torrey, H. W.: 178
Trent, W. P.: 355
Trescot, W. H.: 114, 161
Trevelyan, G. O.: 243, 246–48
Trumbull, Benjamin: 61, 81–82, 101
Trumbull, John: 245
Tucker, George: 137–38, 271
Tudor, William: 91
Turner, F. J.: 171, 172, 214, 216, 217, 225, 230, 237, 267, 277, 278–86, 287, 288, 293, 307, 362
Tyler, John: 315
Tyler, M. C.: 162, 166, 243–46, 318, 350, 351

Uncle Tom's Cabin: 239
Universities, improvement of teaching in: 113, 115–16, 164–71

Vail, Robert: 163
Van Buren, Martin: 117
Van Der Kemp, Francis: 97
Van Deusen, G. G.: 320
Van Deusen, J. G.: 312
Van Doren, Carl: 319, 355
Van Tyne, C. H.: 231, 240, 351
Veblen, Thorstein: 173, 366
Venable, W. H.: 356
Villard, O. G.: 317
Voltaire: 61, 372

Wade, J. A.: 217
Walker, Williston: 358
Ward, Artemus: 111
Ward, Lester: 366
Warfel, H. R.: 357
Warren, Charles: 360
Warren, James: 78
Warren, Joseph: 235
Warren, M. O.: 76, 78–80, 89

Washington, Bushrod: 84, 109
Washington, George: 71, 72, 84, 85, 86, 87, 88, 102, 109, 110, 111, 112, 115, 132, 135, 142, 198, 210, 224, 248, 249, 319, 330, 331, 341
Waterhouse, Benjamin: 92
Wayne, Anthony: 277
Weaver, J. R.: 367
Webb, W. P.: 291
Webster, Daniel: 223, 224, 238, 239, 353
Webster, Noah: 59, 219, 357
Wecter, Dixon: 349
Weeden, W. B.: 293
Weik, J. W.: 321
Weinberg, A. K.: 293
Weems, M. L.: 86–88, 112, 141
Wells, W. V.: 317
Wendell, Barrett: 36
Wertenbaker, T. J.: 304, 349
Whitaker, A. P.: 277, 291, 364
White, A. D.: 165, 166, 167, 170
White, Morton: 366
White, W. A.: 334
Whitman, Walt: 187
Whittier, J. G.: 88
Wiley, B. I.: 313
Wilkinson, James: 90
Williams, Roger: 21, 25, 36, 118, 264, 329, 350, 351, 353
Williamson, Hugh: 136
Wilson, Woodrow: 303, 334, 365
Wiltse, C. M.: 320
Winslow, Edward: 17–18, 45
Winslow, Ola: 329
Winsor, Justin: 4, 159, 162, 171, 227–29, 267, 280
Winther, O. O.: 292
Winthrop, John: 14, 24–27, 28, 30, 32, 249
Wirt, William: 92
Wisconsin Historical Society: 274
Wise, H. A.: 315
Wise, John: 244
Wittke, Carl: 359
Wood, Fernando: 223
Wood, William: 18–20, 45
Woodson, C. G.: 310
Woodward, C. V.: 311, 314
Woody, Thomas: 358
Wright, B. F.: 248, 285
Wright, F. L.: 366
Wroth, L. C.: 357

Xérez, Francisco de: 10

Youmans, E. L.: 168

Zeichner, Oscar: 362
Zenger, J. P.: 45

UNIVERSITY OF OKLAHOMA PRESS
NORMAN

The Author

A professor of history in City College of New York, MICHAEL KRAUS received his Ph.D. degree from Columbia University in 1928, and since then he has become one of America's best-known historiographers. His *A History of American History* has been the standard work in American historiography for many years. In this new book Mr. Kraus has incorporated all of the material in the earlier volume besides the additional research of almost two decades.